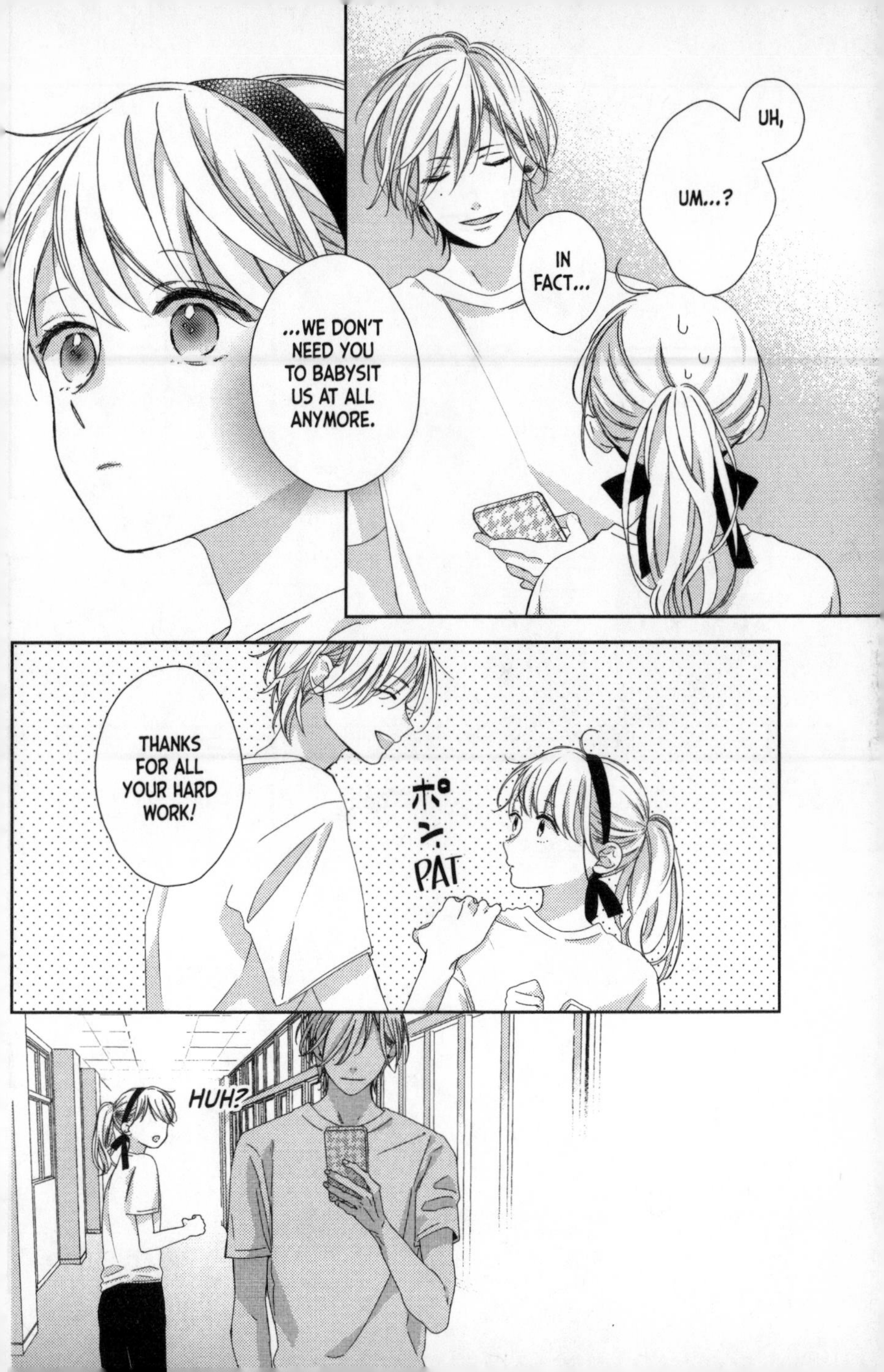
UH,
UM...?
IN FACT...
...WE DON'T NEED YOU TO BABYSIT US AT ALL ANYMORE.
THANKS FOR ALL YOUR HARD WORK!
ポン
PAT
HUH?

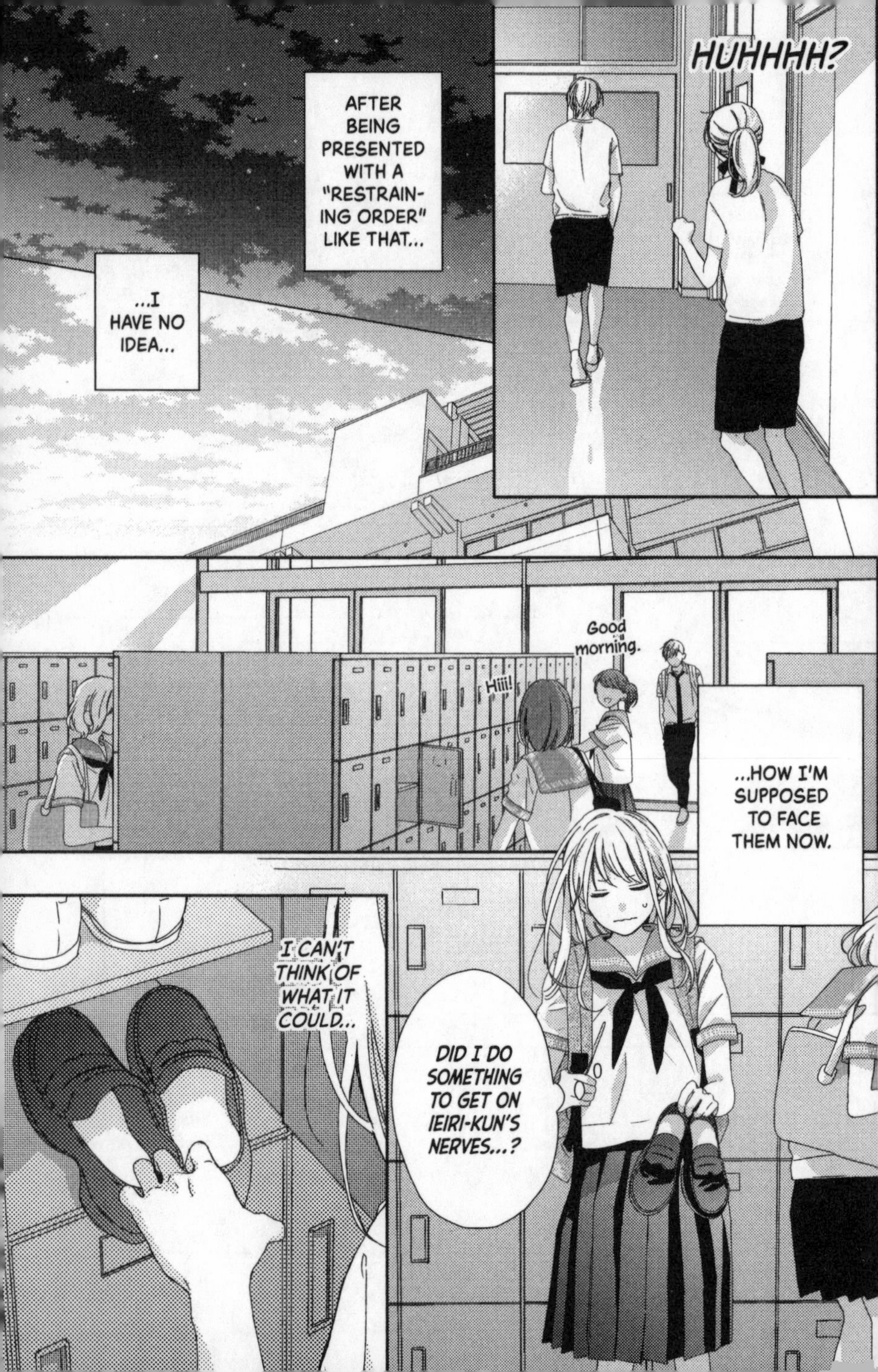
HUHHHH?
AFTER BEING PRESENTED WITH A "RESTRAIN-ING ORDER" LIKE THAT...
...I HAVE NO IDEA...
Good morning.
Hiii!
...HOW I'M SUPPOSED TO FACE THEM NOW.
DID I DO SOMETHING TO GET ON IEIRI-KUN'S NERVES...?
I CAN'T THINK OF WHAT IT COULD...

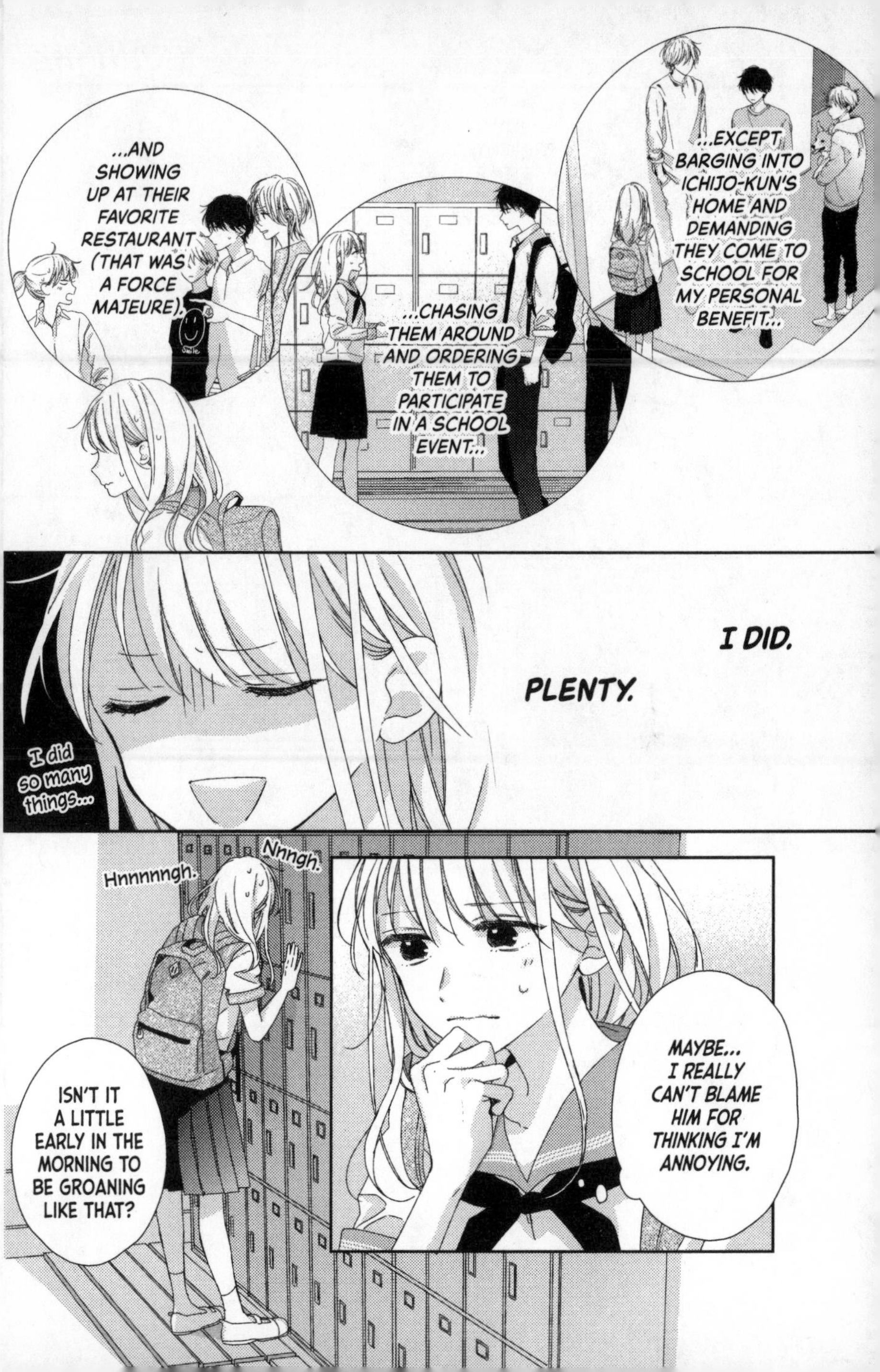
...EXCEPT BARGING INTO ICHIJO-KUN'S HOME AND DEMANDING THEY COME TO SCHOOL FOR MY PERSONAL BENEFIT...
...CHASING THEM AROUND AND ORDERING THEM TO PARTICIPATE IN A SCHOOL EVENT...
...AND SHOWING UP AT THEIR FAVORITE RESTAURANT (THAT WAS A FORCE MAJEURE).
I DID.
PLENTY.
I did so many things...
MAYBE... I REALLY CAN'T BLAME HIM FOR THINKING I'M ANNOYING.
Nnngh.
Hnnnnngh.
ISN'T IT A LITTLE EARLY IN THE MORNING TO BE GROANING LIKE THAT?

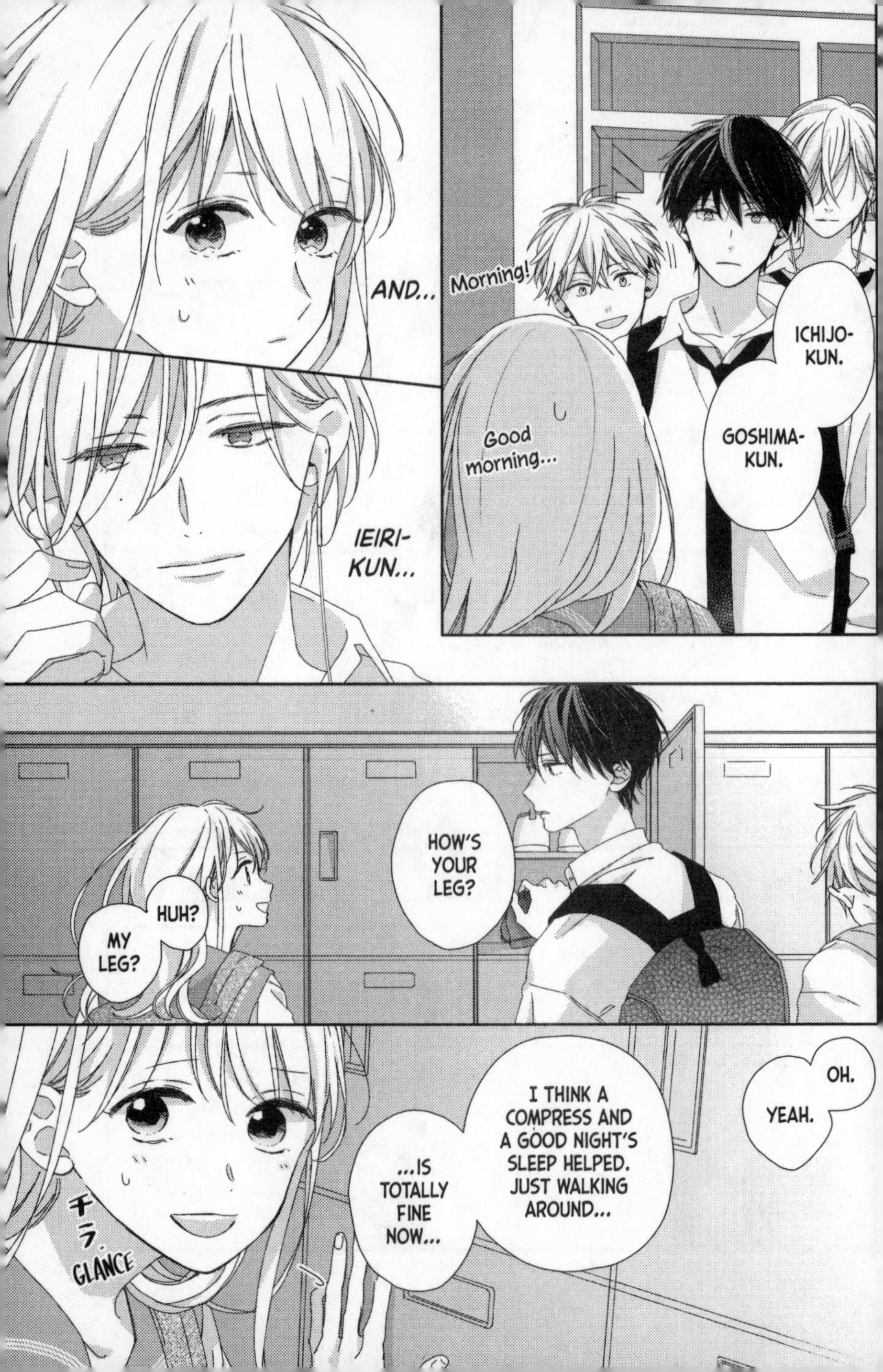
Morning!
Good morning...
ICHIJO-KUN.
GOSHIMA-KUN.
AND...
IEIRI-KUN...
HOW'S YOUR LEG?
HUH?
MY LEG?
OH.
YEAH.
I THINK A COMPRESS AND A GOOD NIGHT'S SLEEP HELPED. JUST WALKING AROUND...
...IS TOTALLY FINE NOW...
チラ
GLANCE

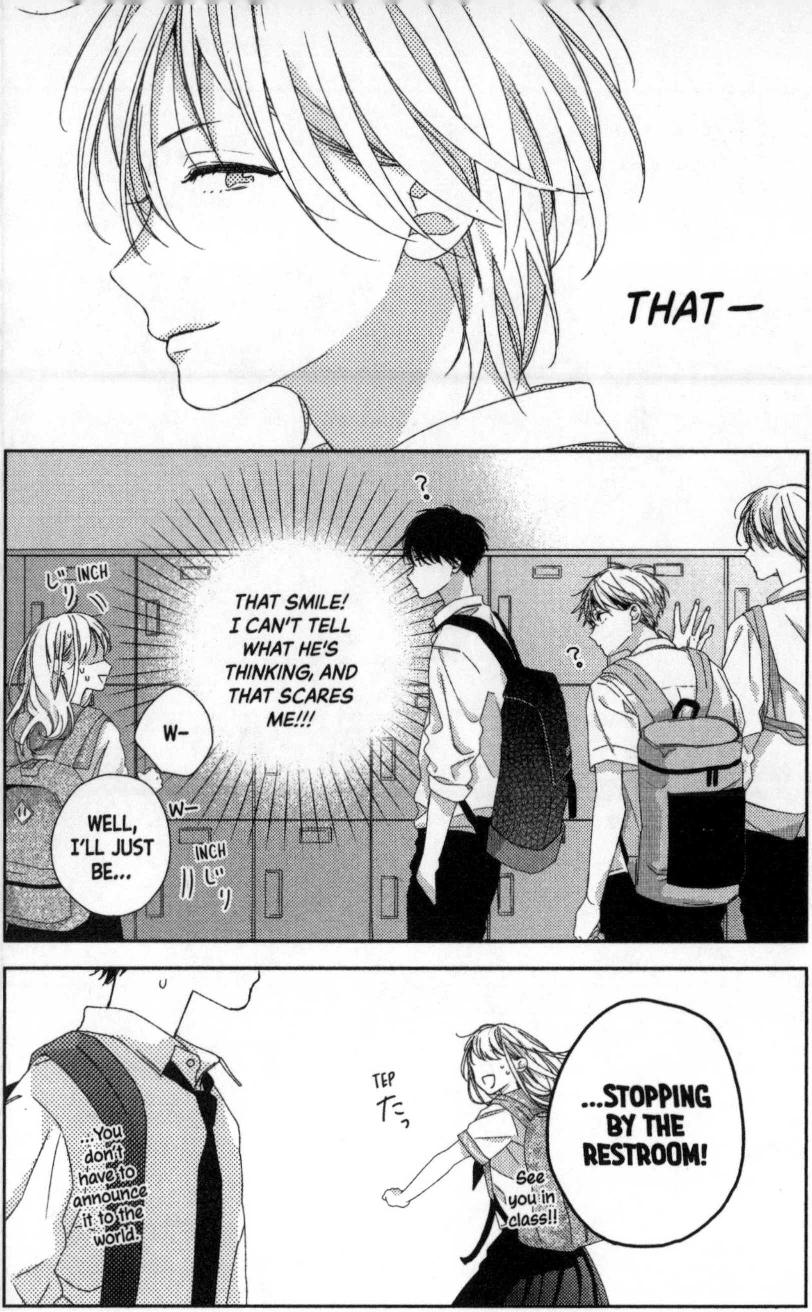
THAT—
THAT SMILE! I CAN'T TELL WHAT HE'S THINKING, AND THAT SCARES ME!!!
INCH
W—
W—
INCH
WELL, I'LL JUST BE...
...STOPPING BY THE RESTROOM!
See you in class!!
TEP
...You don't have to announce it to the world.

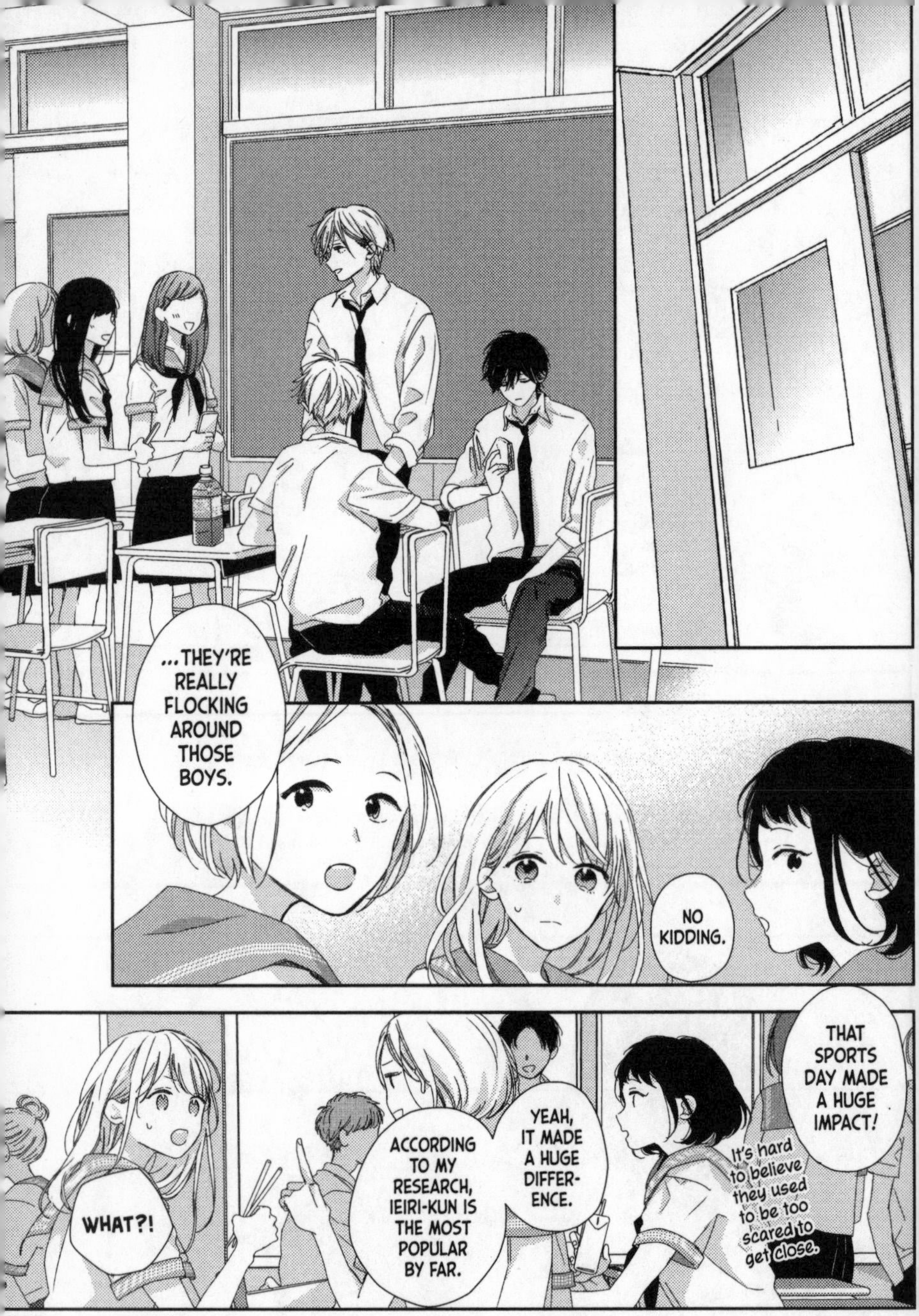
...THEY'RE REALLY FLOCKING AROUND THOSE BOYS.
NO KIDDING.
THAT SPORTS DAY MADE A HUGE IMPACT!
It's hard to believe they used to be too scared to get close.
YEAH, IT MADE A HUGE DIFFER-ENCE.
ACCORDING TO MY RESEARCH, IEIRI-KUN IS THE MOST POPULAR BY FAR.
WHAT?!

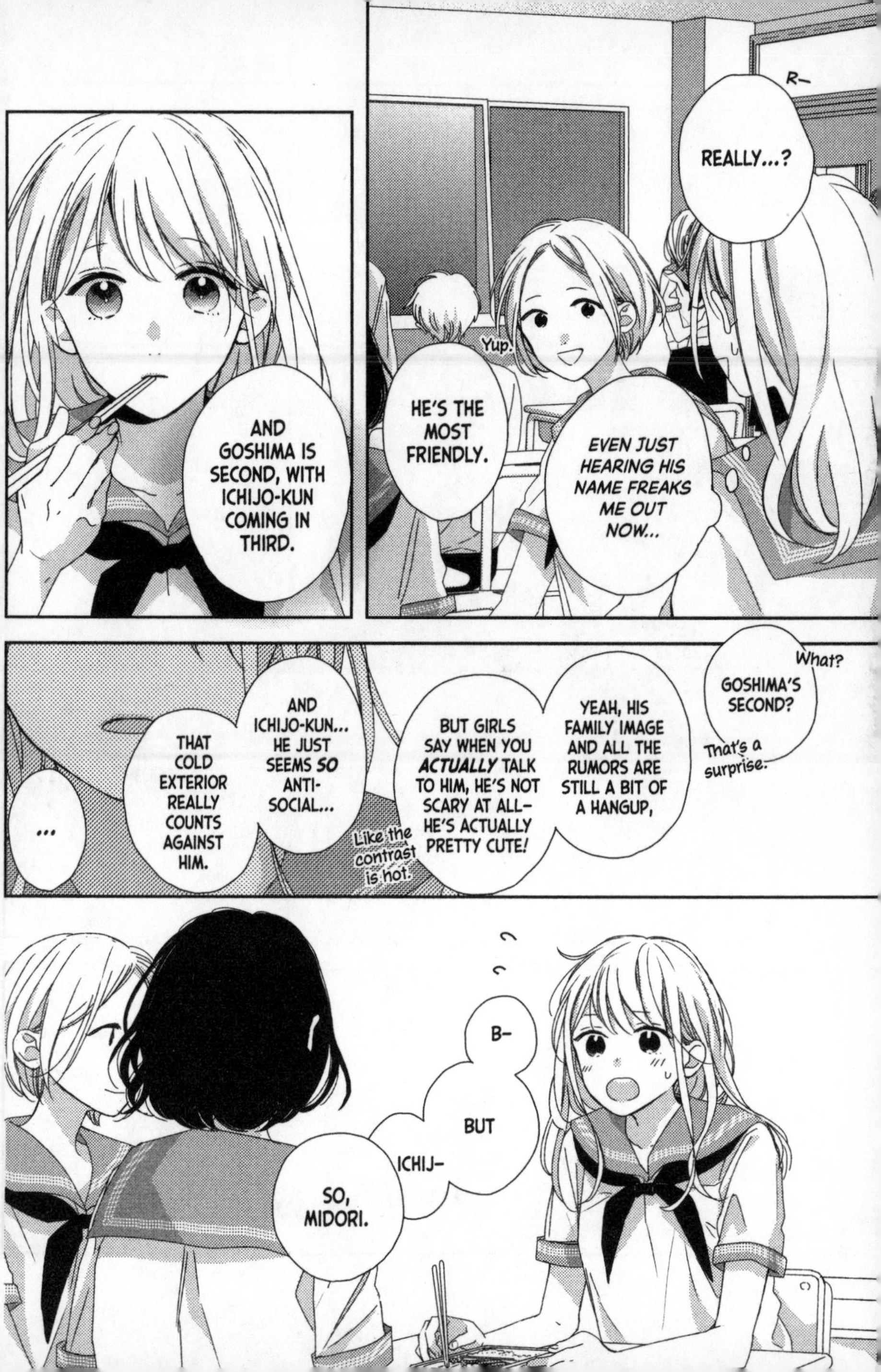
R–
REALLY...?
EVEN JUST HEARING HIS NAME FREAKS ME OUT NOW...
Yup.
HE'S THE MOST FRIENDLY.
AND GOSHIMA IS SECOND, WITH ICHIJO-KUN COMING IN THIRD.
What?
GOSHIMA'S SECOND?
That's a surprise.
YEAH, HIS FAMILY IMAGE AND ALL THE RUMORS ARE STILL A BIT OF A HANGUP,
BUT GIRLS SAY WHEN YOU ACTUALLY TALK TO HIM, HE'S NOT SCARY AT ALL– HE'S ACTUALLY PRETTY CUTE!
Like the contrast is hot.
AND ICHIJO-KUN... HE JUST SEEMS SO ANTI-SOCIAL...
THAT COLD EXTERIOR REALLY COUNTS AGAINST HIM.
...
B–
BUT
ICHIJ–
SO, MIDORI.

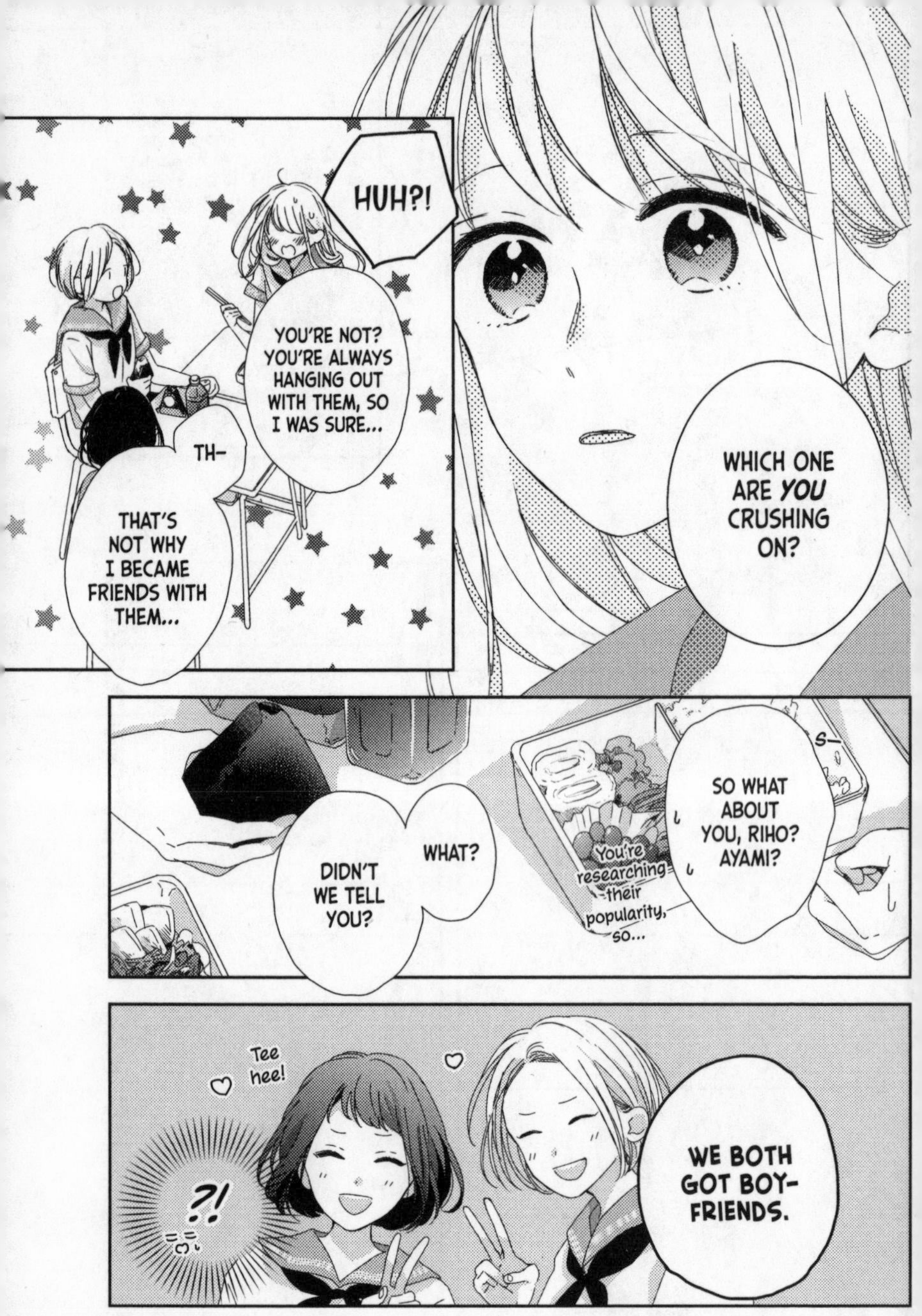
WHICH ONE ARE YOU CRUSHING ON?
HUH?!
YOU'RE NOT? YOU'RE ALWAYS HANGING OUT WITH THEM, SO I WAS SURE...
TH-
THAT'S NOT WHY I BECAME FRIENDS WITH THEM...
S-
SO WHAT ABOUT YOU, RIHO? AYAMI?
You're researching their popularity, so...
WHAT?
DIDN'T WE TELL YOU?
WE BOTH GOT BOY-FRIENDS.
Tee hee!
?!

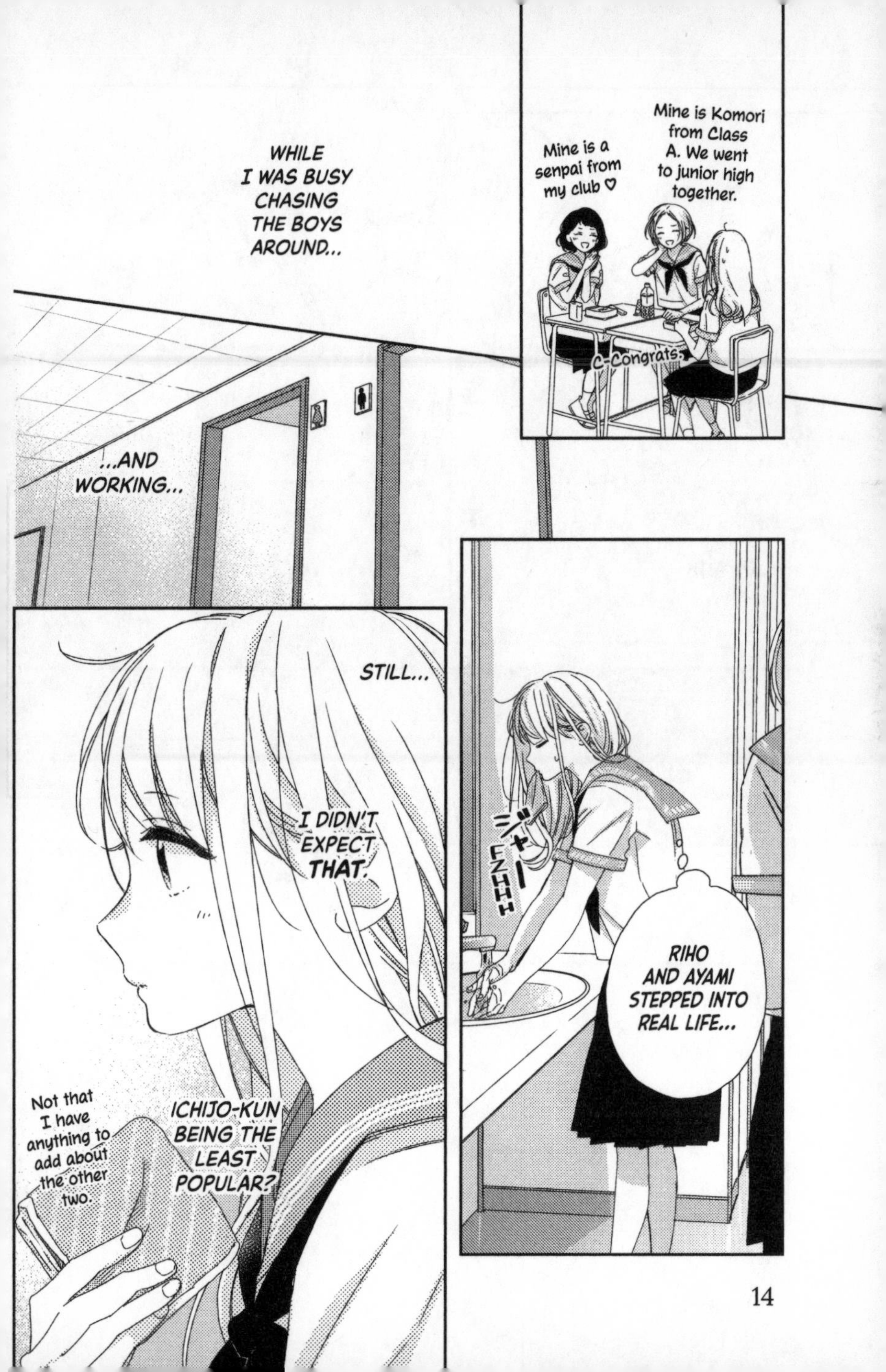
Mine is Komori from Class A. We went to junior high together.
Mine is a senpai from my club ♡
C-Congrats.
WHILE I WAS BUSY CHASING THE BOYS AROUND...
...AND WORKING...
FZHHH
RIHO AND AYAMI STEPPED INTO REAL LIFE...
STILL...
I DIDN'T EXPECT THAT.
ICHIJO-KUN BEING THE LEAST POPULAR?
Not that I have anything to add about the other two.

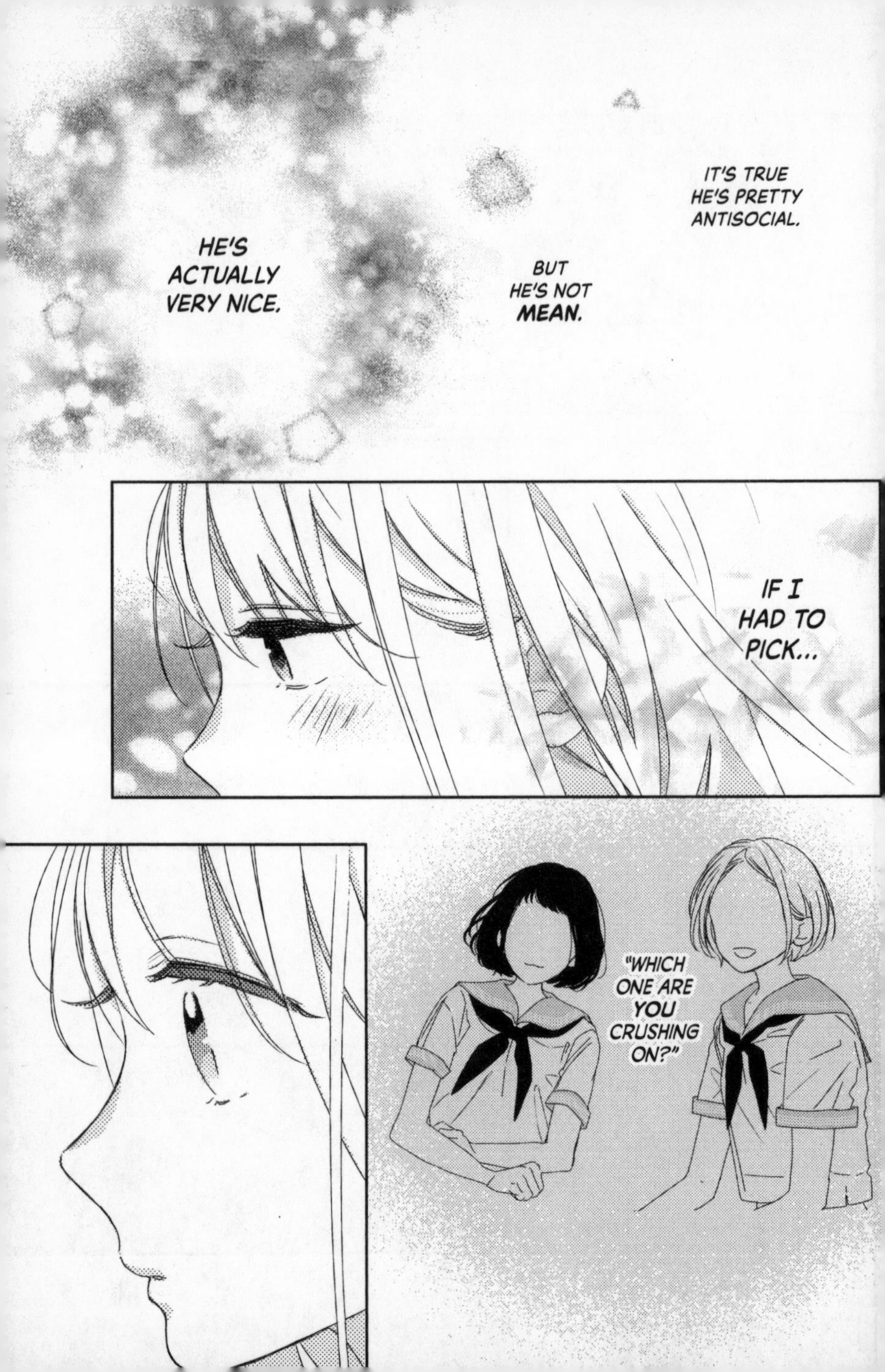
IT'S TRUE HE'S PRETTY ANTISOCIAL.
BUT HE'S NOT MEAN.
HE'S ACTUALLY VERY NICE.
IF I HAD TO PICK...
"WHICH ONE ARE YOU CRUSHING ON?"

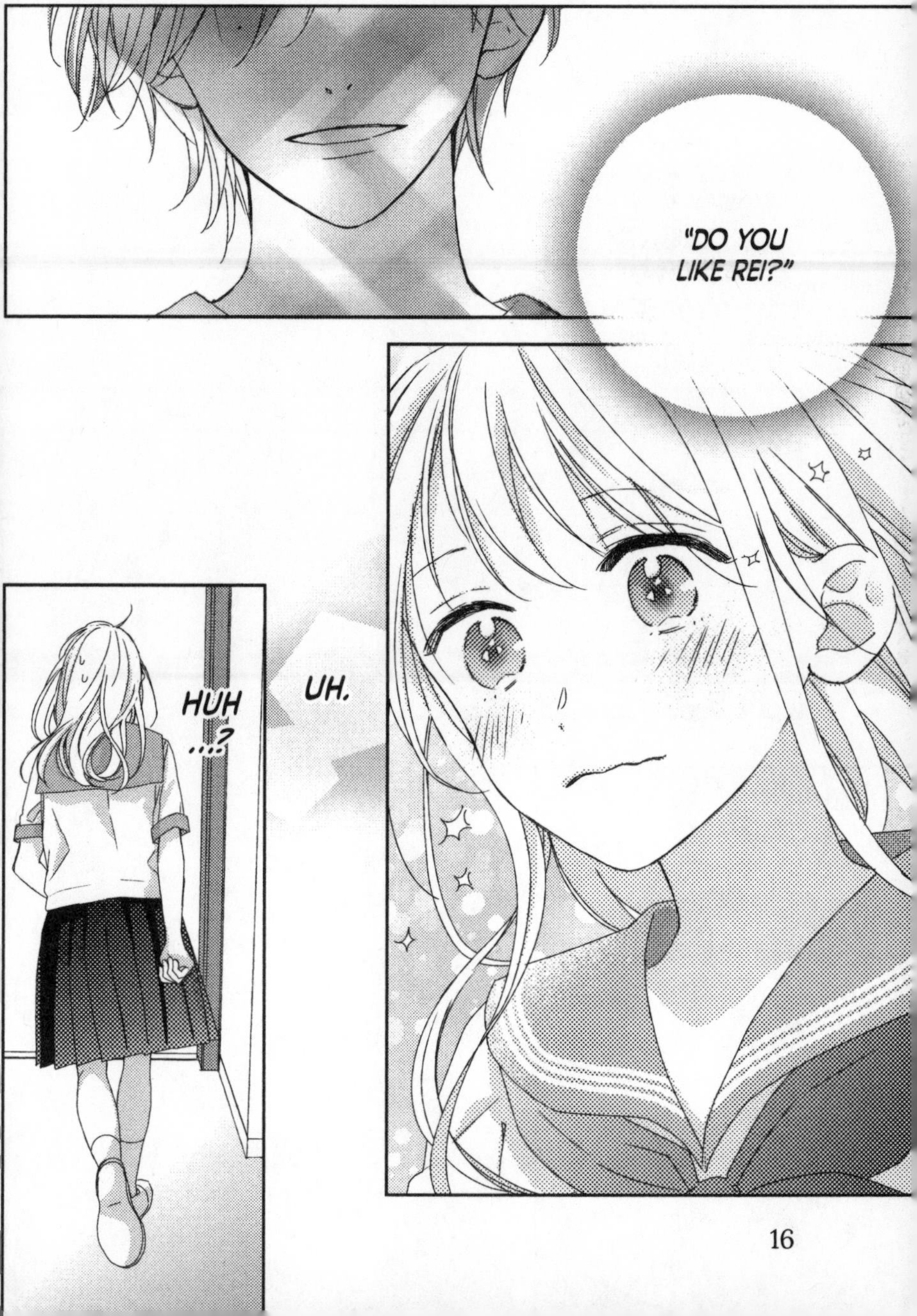
"DO YOU LIKE REI?"
UH.
HUH ...?

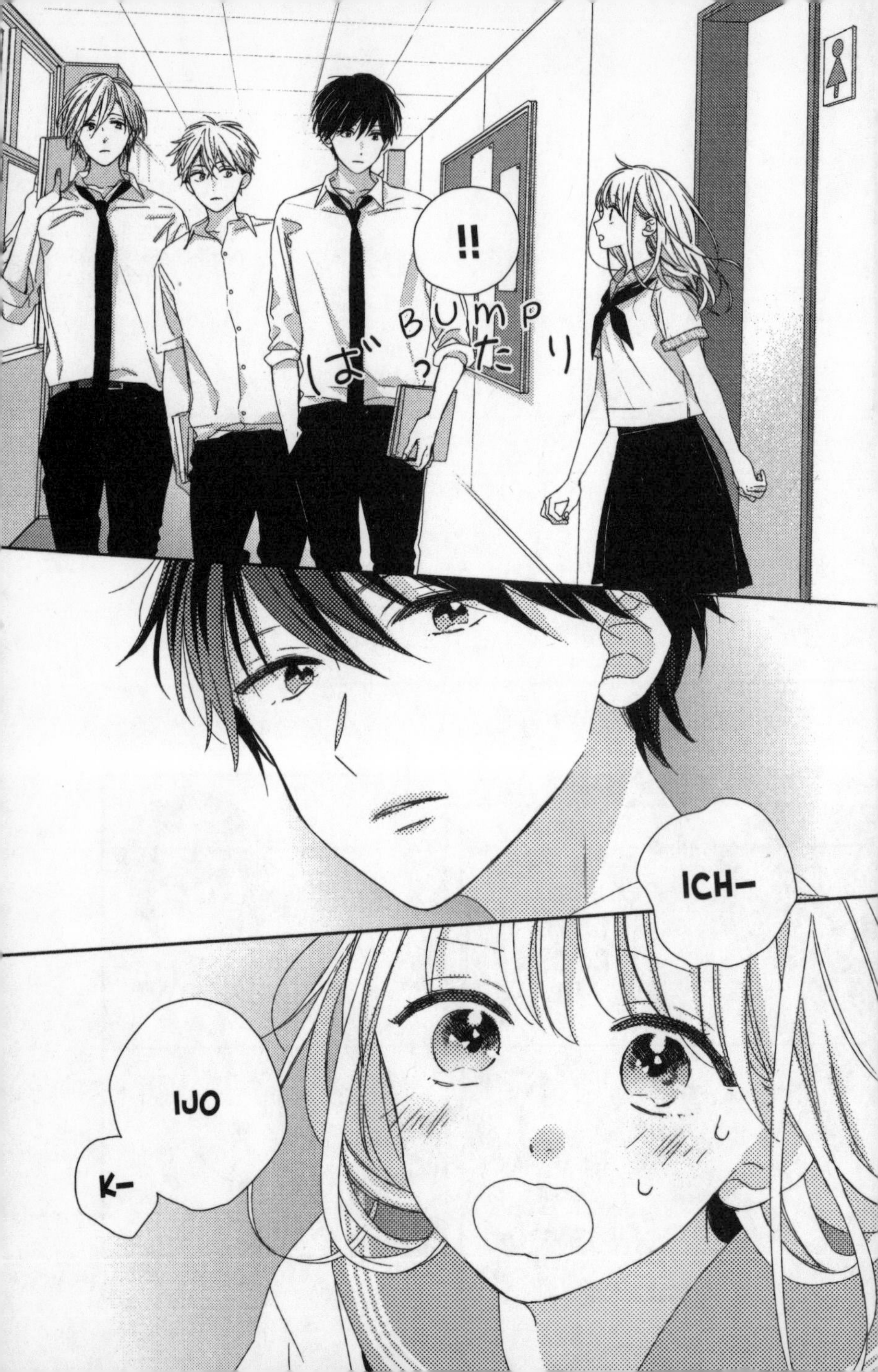
!!
ばったり
BUMP
ICH-
IJO
K-

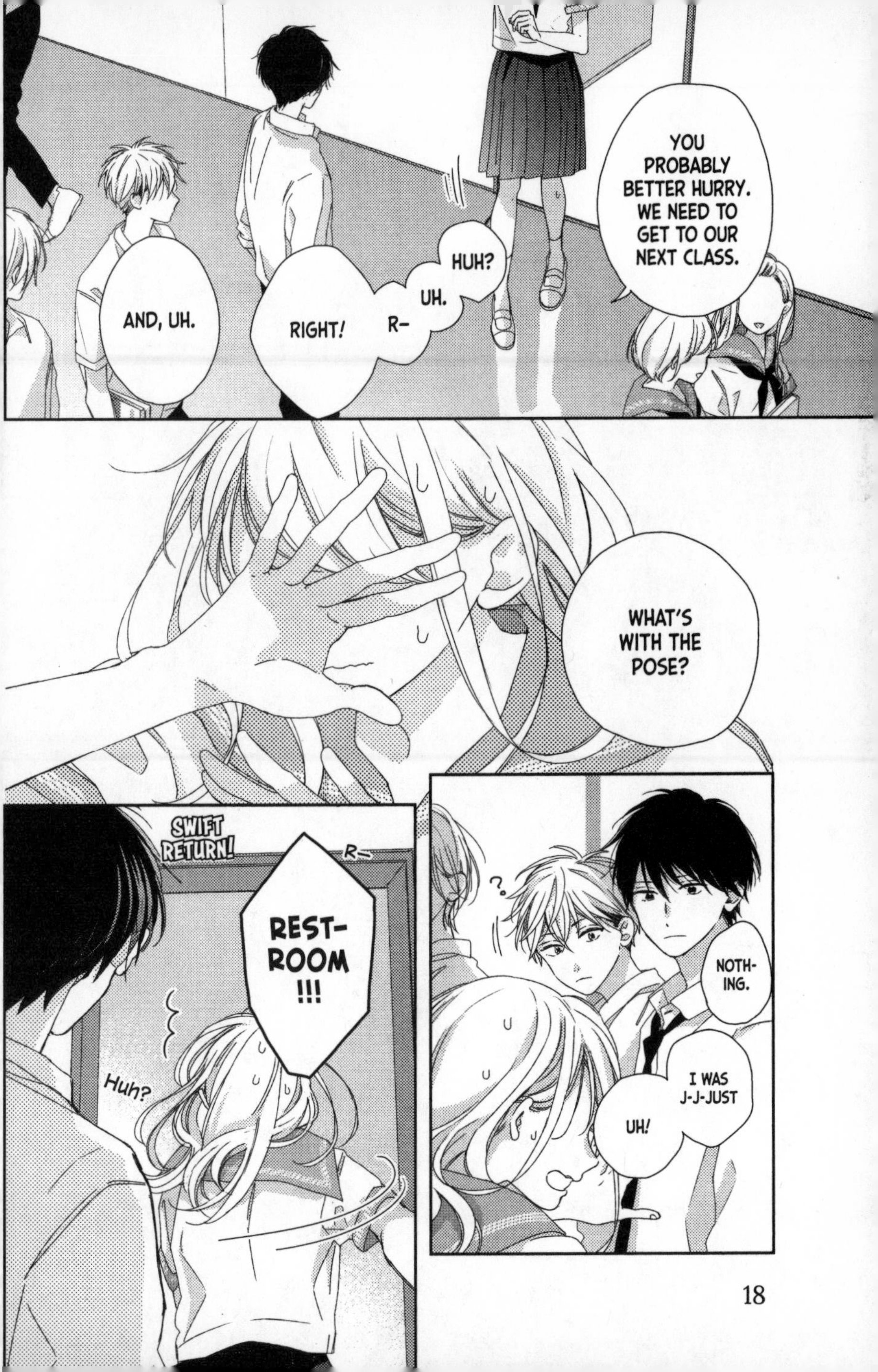
YOU PROBABLY BETTER HURRY. WE NEED TO GET TO OUR NEXT CLASS.
HUH?
UH.
R–
RIGHT!
AND, UH.
WHAT'S WITH THE POSE?
NOTH-ING.
I WAS J-J-JUST
UH!
R–
SWIFT RETURN!
REST-ROOM!!!
Huh?

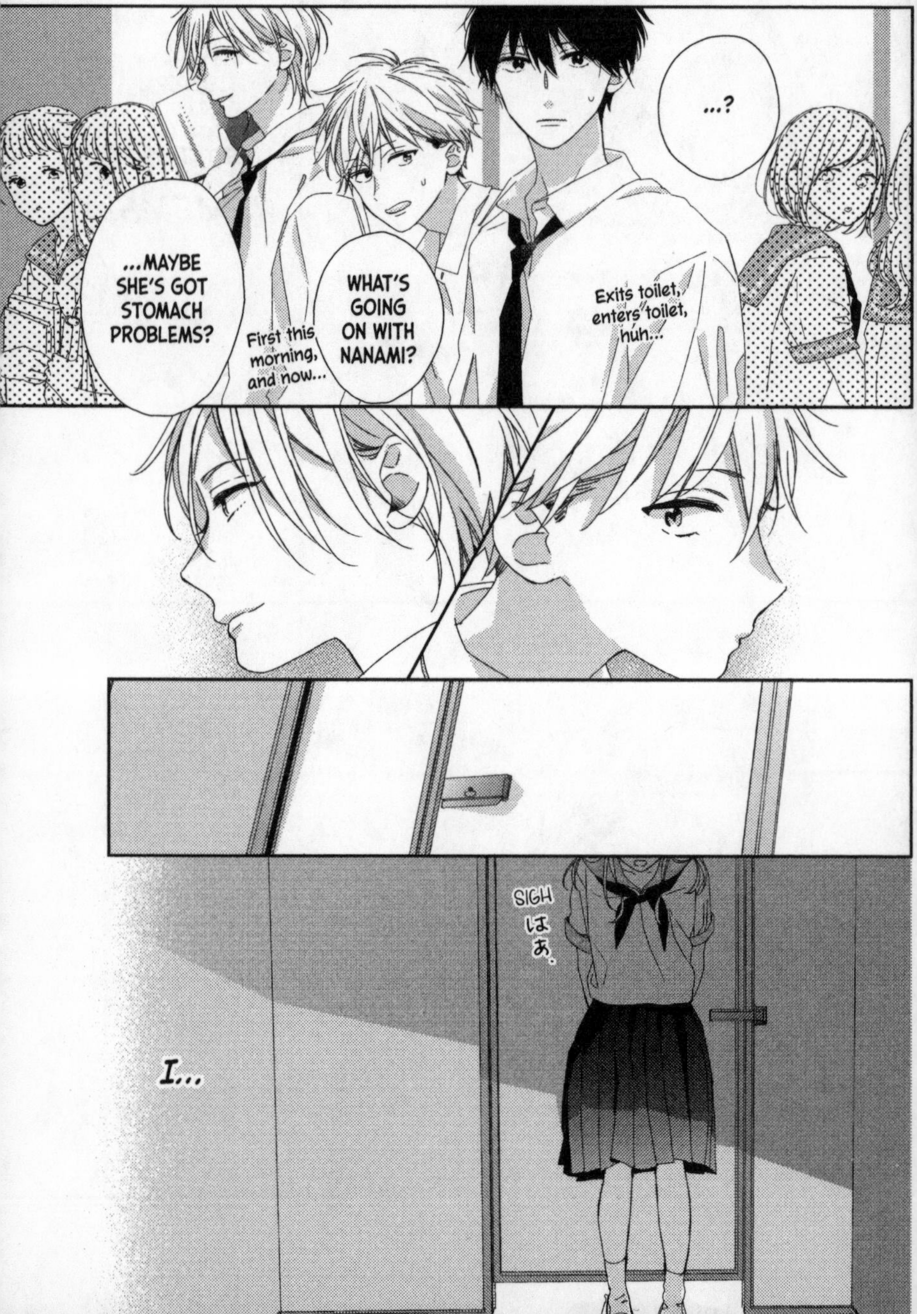
...?
Exits toilet, enters toilet, huh...
WHAT'S GOING ON WITH NANAMI?
First this morning, and now...
...MAYBE SHE'S GOT STOMACH PROBLEMS?
SIGH はあ.
I...

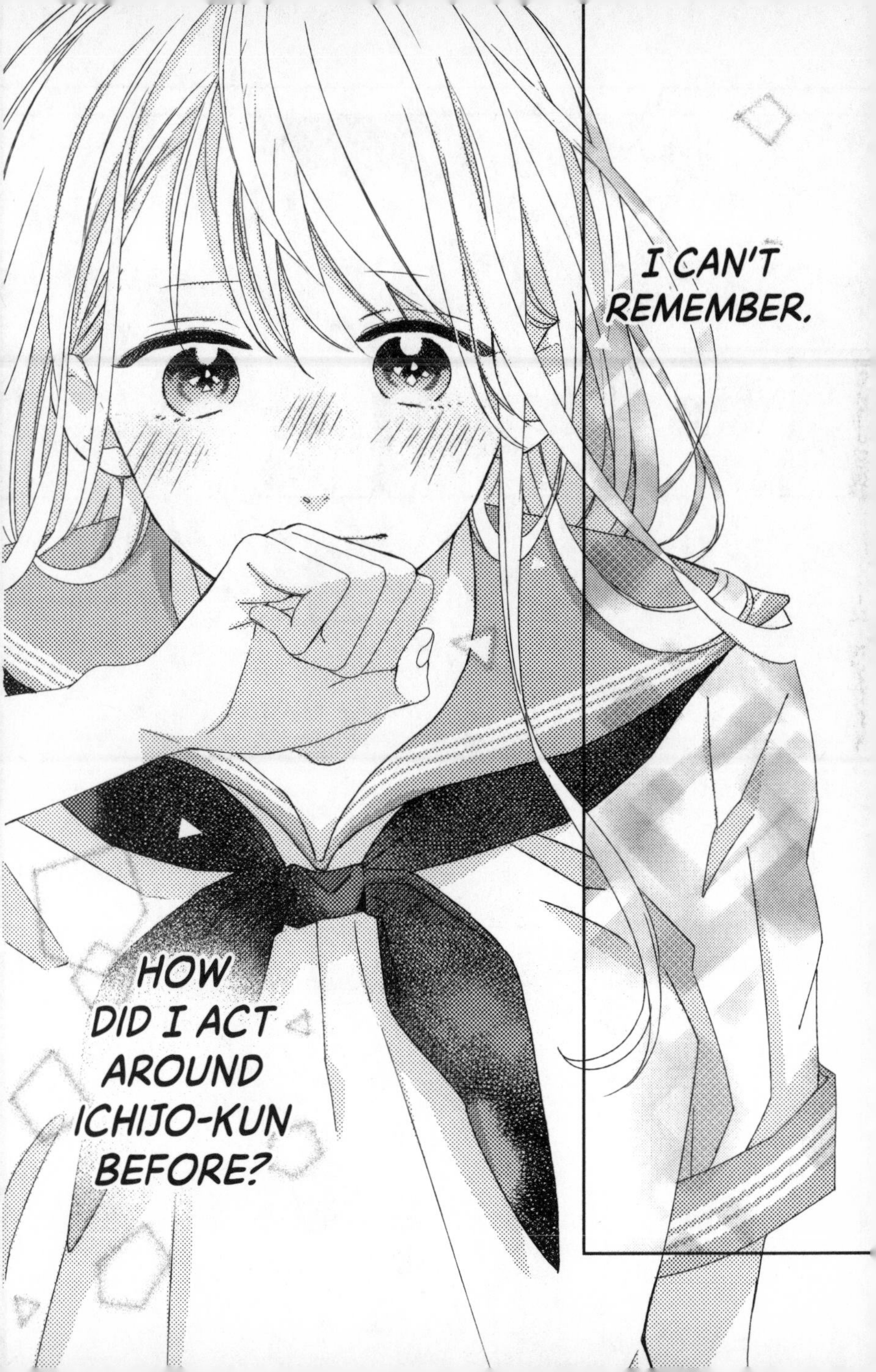
I CAN'T REMEMBER.
HOW DID I ACT AROUND ICHIJO-KUN BEFORE?

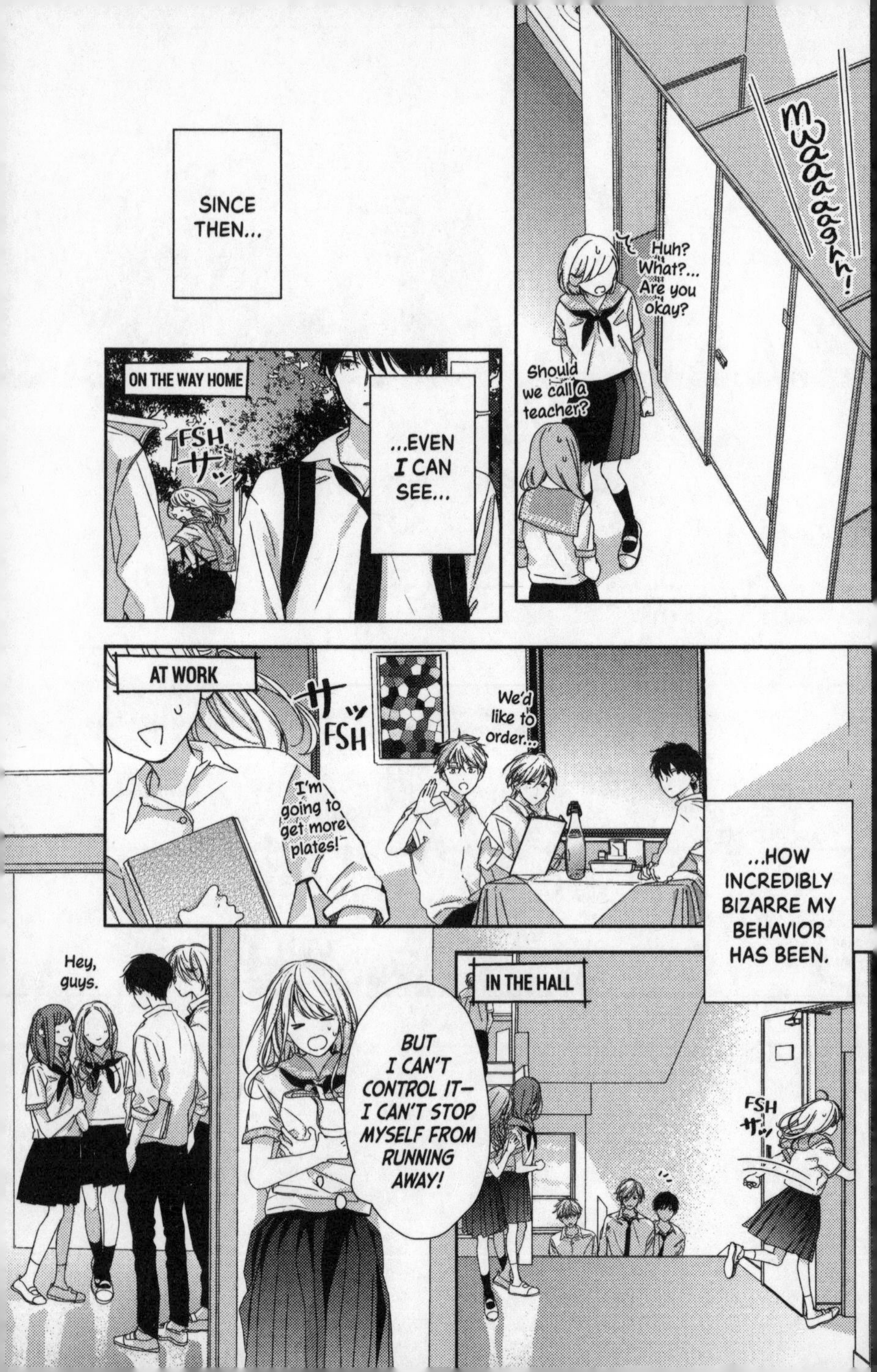
Mwaaaagrh!
Huh? What?... Are you okay?
Should we call a teacher?
SINCE THEN...
ON THE WAY HOME
FSH
...EVEN I CAN SEE...
...HOW INCREDIBLY BIZARRE MY BEHAVIOR HAS BEEN.
We'd like to order...
FSH
AT WORK
I'm going to get more plates!
IN THE HALL
FSH
BUT I CAN'T CONTROL IT— I CAN'T STOP MYSELF FROM RUNNING AWAY!
Hey, guys.

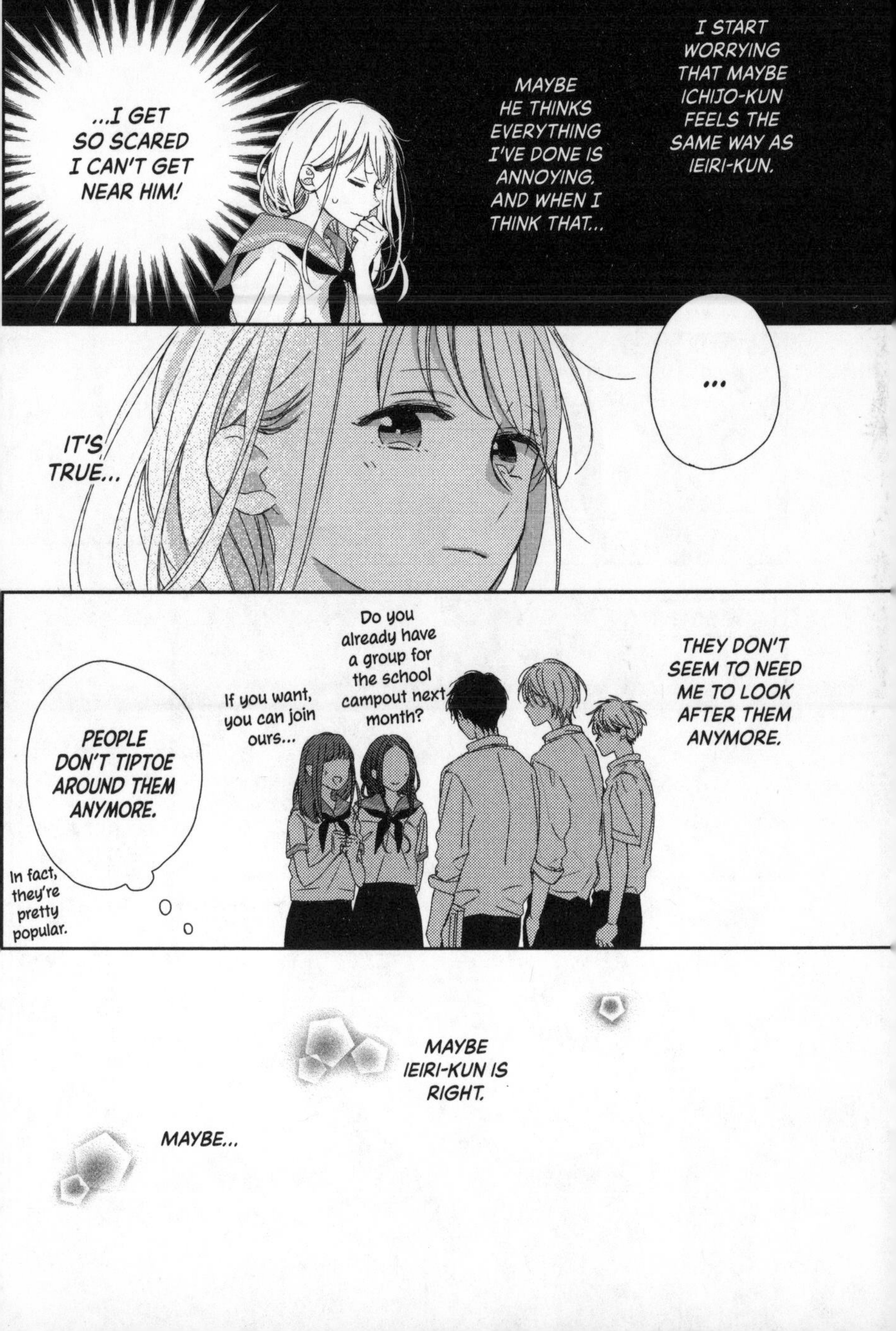
I START WORRYING THAT MAYBE ICHIJO-KUN FEELS THE SAME WAY AS IEIRI-KUN.
MAYBE HE THINKS EVERYTHING I'VE DONE IS ANNOYING. AND WHEN I THINK THAT...
...I GET SO SCARED I CAN'T GET NEAR HIM!
...
IT'S TRUE...
THEY DON'T SEEM TO NEED ME TO LOOK AFTER THEM ANYMORE.
Do you already have a group for the school campout next month?
If you want, you can join ours...
PEOPLE DON'T TIPTOE AROUND THEM ANYMORE.
In fact, they're pretty popular.
MAYBE IEIRI-KUN IS RIGHT.
MAYBE...

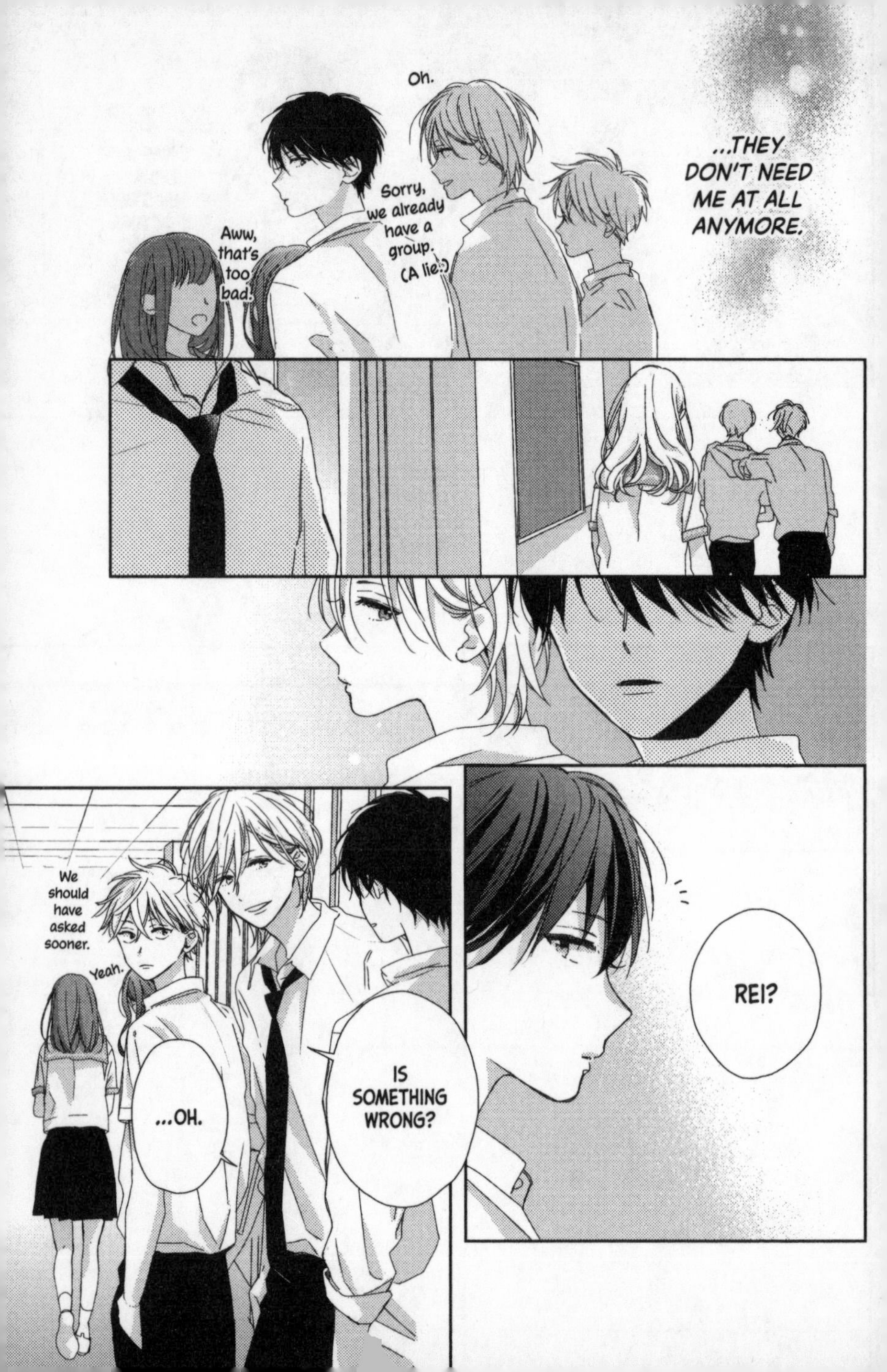
...THEY DON'T NEED ME AT ALL ANYMORE.
Oh.
Sorry, we already have a group.
(A lie.)
Aww, that's too bad.
REI?
IS SOMETHING WRONG?
...OH.
We should have asked sooner.
Yeah.

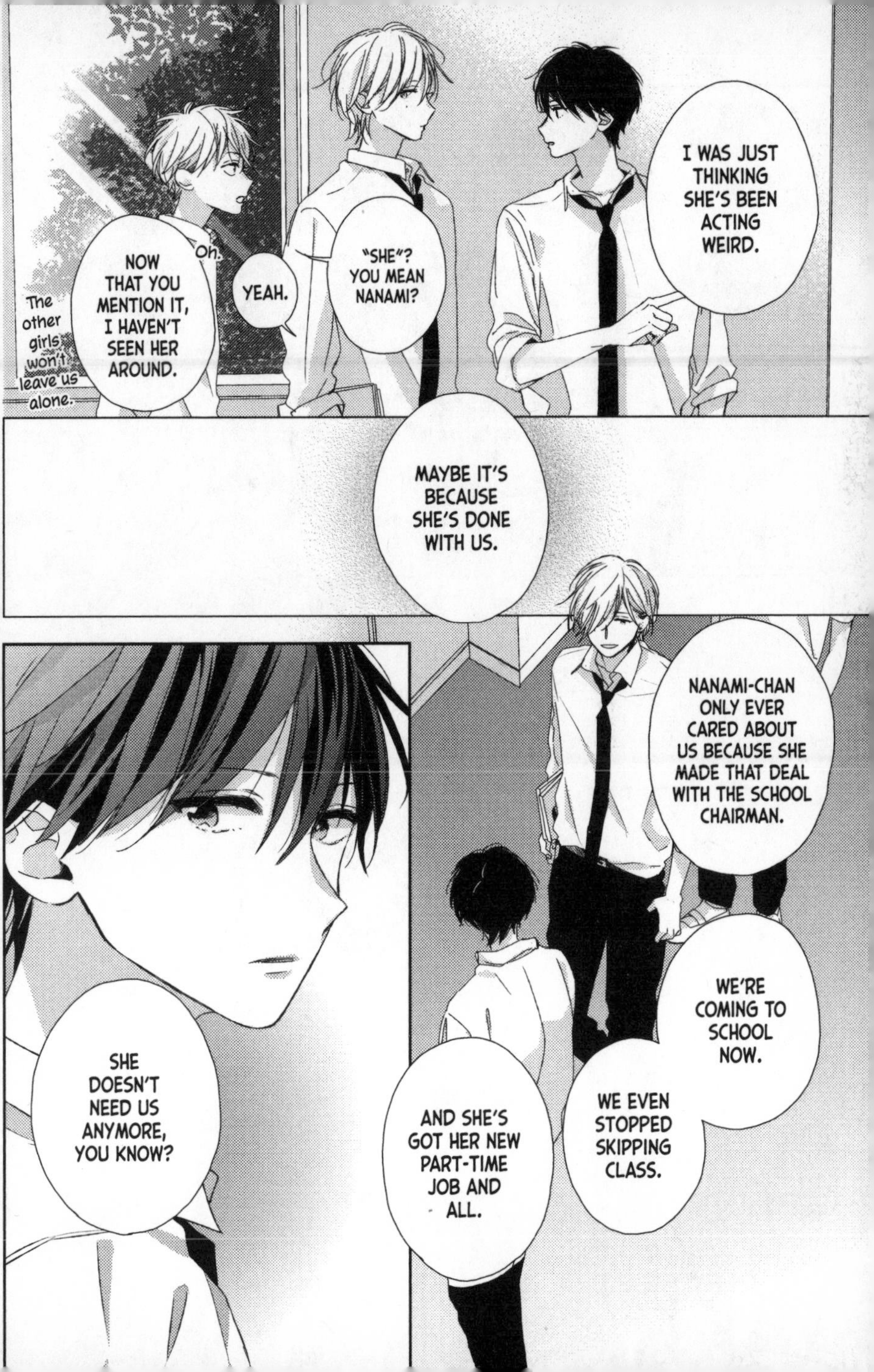
I WAS JUST THINKING SHE'S BEEN ACTING WEIRD.
"SHE"? YOU MEAN NANAMI?
YEAH.
Oh.
NOW THAT YOU MENTION IT, I HAVEN'T SEEN HER AROUND.
The other girls won't leave us alone.
MAYBE IT'S BECAUSE SHE'S DONE WITH US.
NANAMI-CHAN ONLY EVER CARED ABOUT US BECAUSE SHE MADE THAT DEAL WITH THE SCHOOL CHAIRMAN.
WE'RE COMING TO SCHOOL NOW.
WE EVEN STOPPED SKIPPING CLASS.
AND SHE'S GOT HER NEW PART-TIME JOB AND ALL.
SHE DOESN'T NEED US ANYMORE, YOU KNOW?

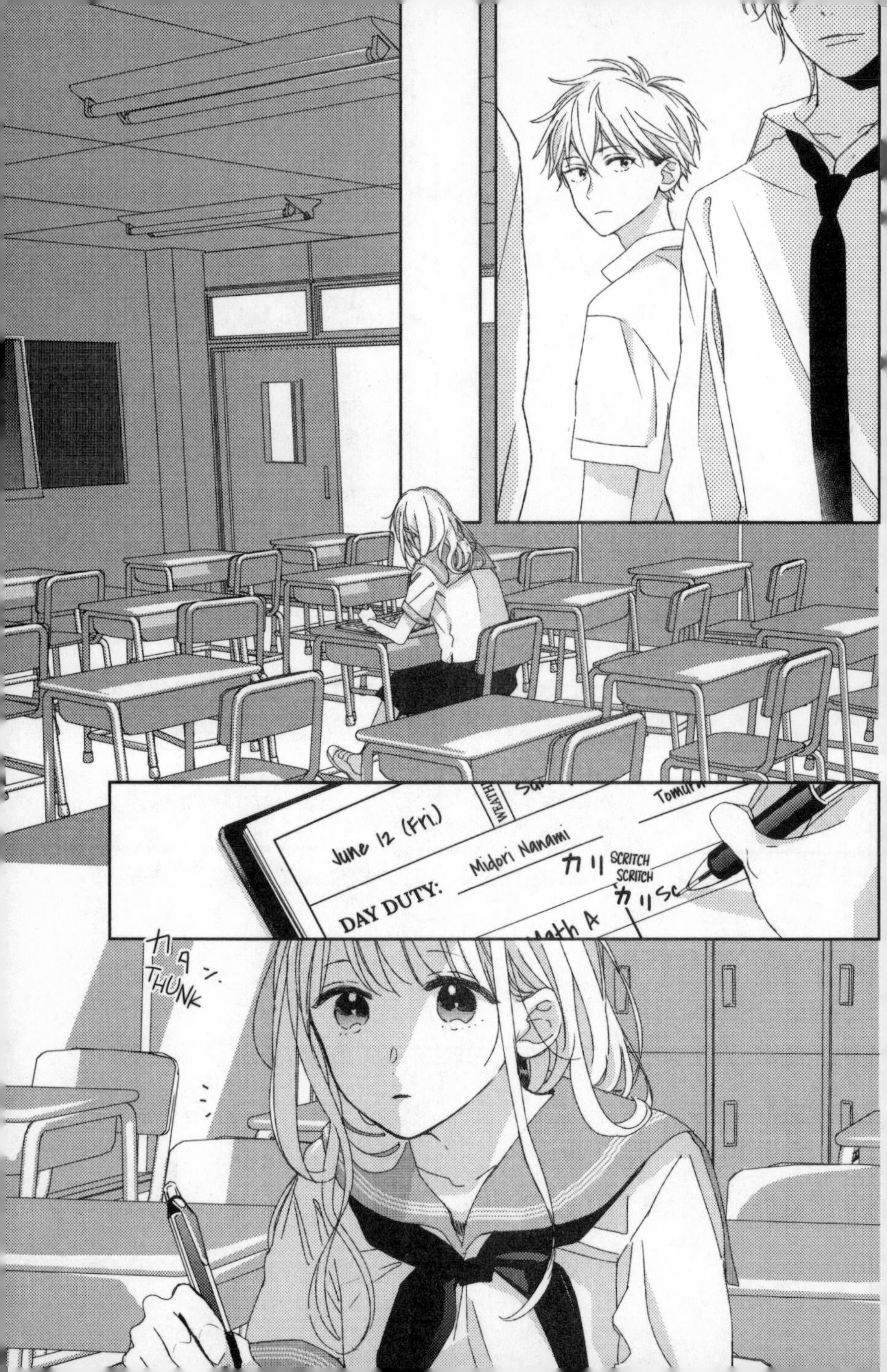

June 12 (Fri.)
Tomura
Midori Nanami
DAY DUTY:
Math A
SCRITCH SCRITCH
THUNK

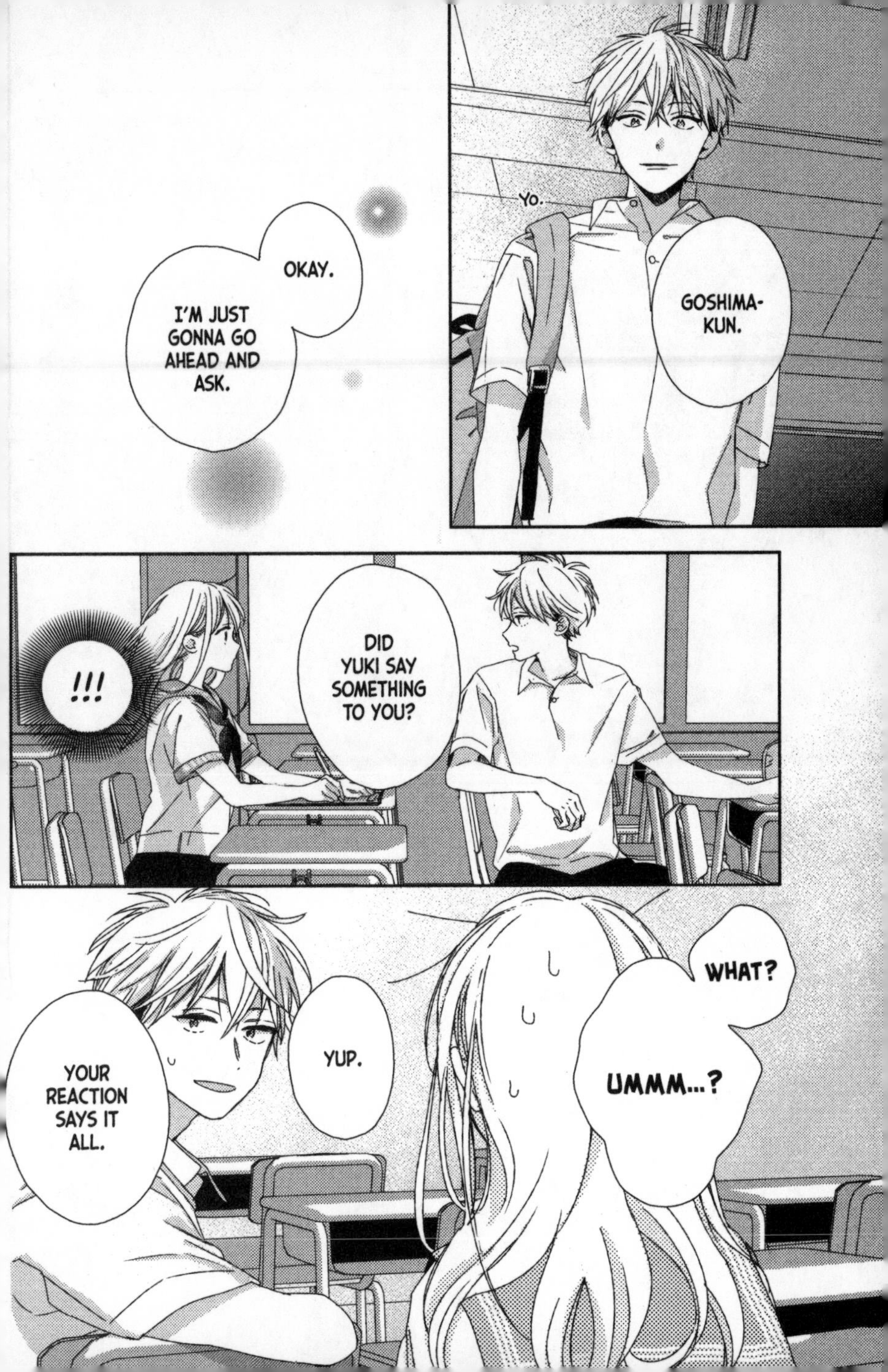
GOSHIMA-KUN.
YO.
OKAY.
I'M JUST GONNA GO AHEAD AND ASK.
DID YUKI SAY SOMETHING TO YOU?
!!!
WHAT?
UMMM...?
YUP.
YOUR REACTION SAYS IT ALL.

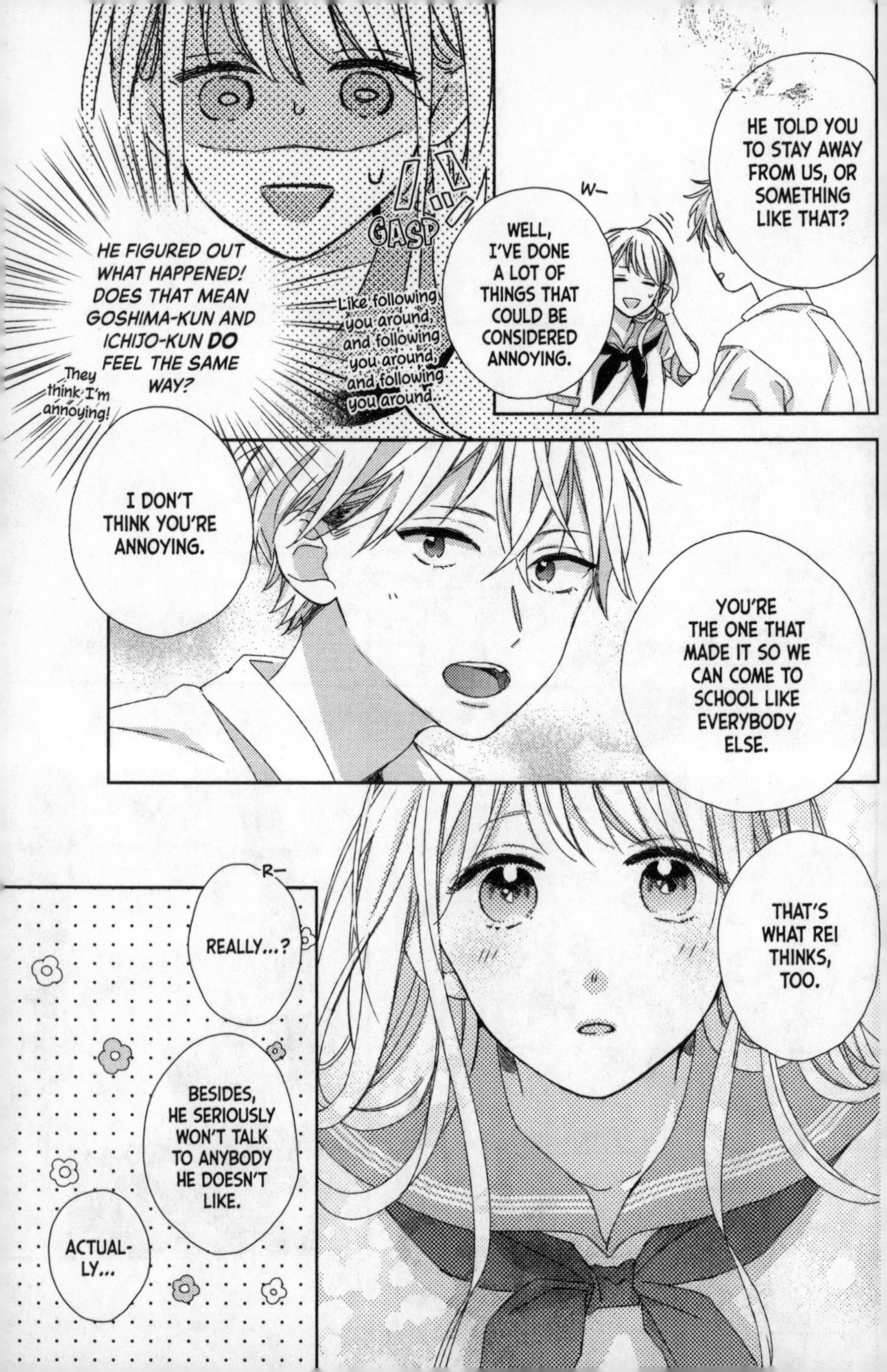
HE TOLD YOU TO STAY AWAY FROM US, OR SOMETHING LIKE THAT?
W—
WELL, I'VE DONE A LOT OF THINGS THAT COULD BE CONSIDERED ANNOYING.
GASP
HE FIGURED OUT WHAT HAPPENED! DOES THAT MEAN GOSHIMA-KUN AND ICHIJO-KUN DO FEEL THE SAME WAY?
Like following you around, and following you around, and following you around...
They think I'm annoying!
I DON'T THINK YOU'RE ANNOYING.
YOU'RE THE ONE THAT MADE IT SO WE CAN COME TO SCHOOL LIKE EVERYBODY ELSE.
THAT'S WHAT REI THINKS, TOO.
R—
REALLY...?
BESIDES, HE SERIOUSLY WON'T TALK TO ANYBODY HE DOESN'T LIKE.
ACTUAL-LY...

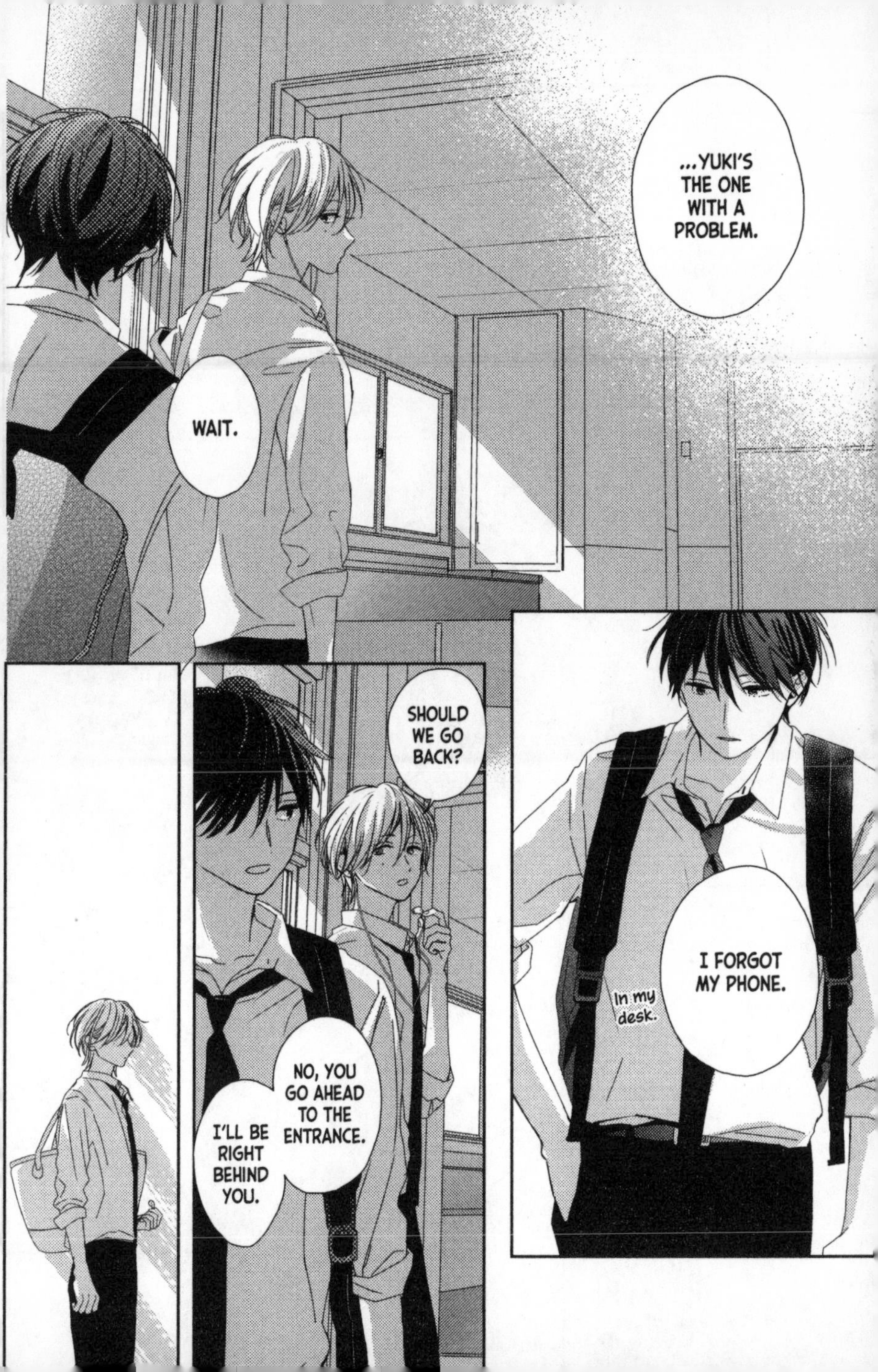
...YUKI'S THE ONE WITH A PROBLEM.
WAIT.
I FORGOT MY PHONE.
In my desk.
SHOULD WE GO BACK?
NO, YOU GO AHEAD TO THE ENTRANCE.
I'LL BE RIGHT BEHIND YOU.

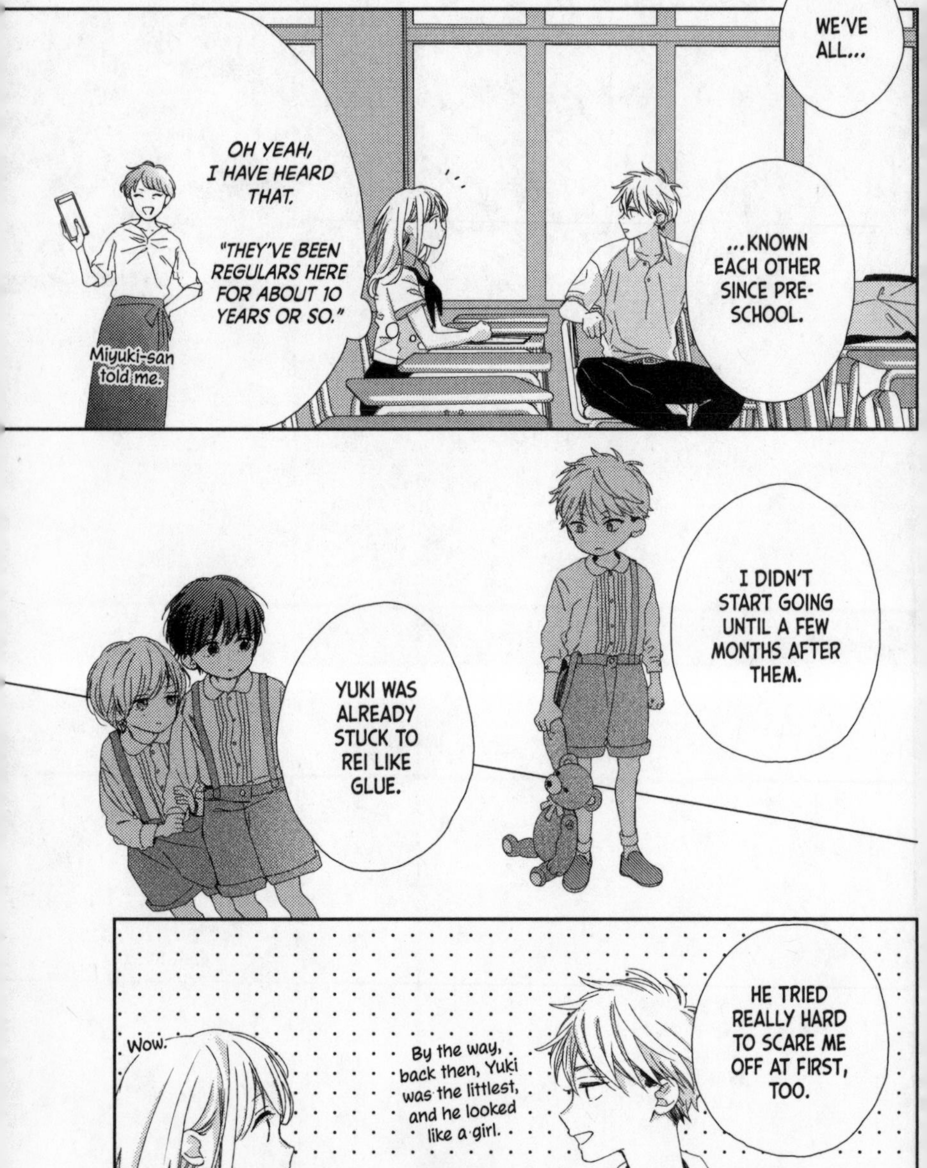
WE'VE ALL...
...KNOWN EACH OTHER SINCE PRE-SCHOOL.
OH YEAH, I HAVE HEARD THAT.
"THEY'VE BEEN REGULARS HERE FOR ABOUT 10 YEARS OR SO."
Miyuki-san told me.
I DIDN'T START GOING UNTIL A FEW MONTHS AFTER THEM.
YUKI WAS ALREADY STUCK TO REI LIKE GLUE.
HE TRIED REALLY HARD TO SCARE ME OFF AT FIRST, TOO.
By the way, back then, Yuki was the littlest, and he looked like a girl.
Wow.

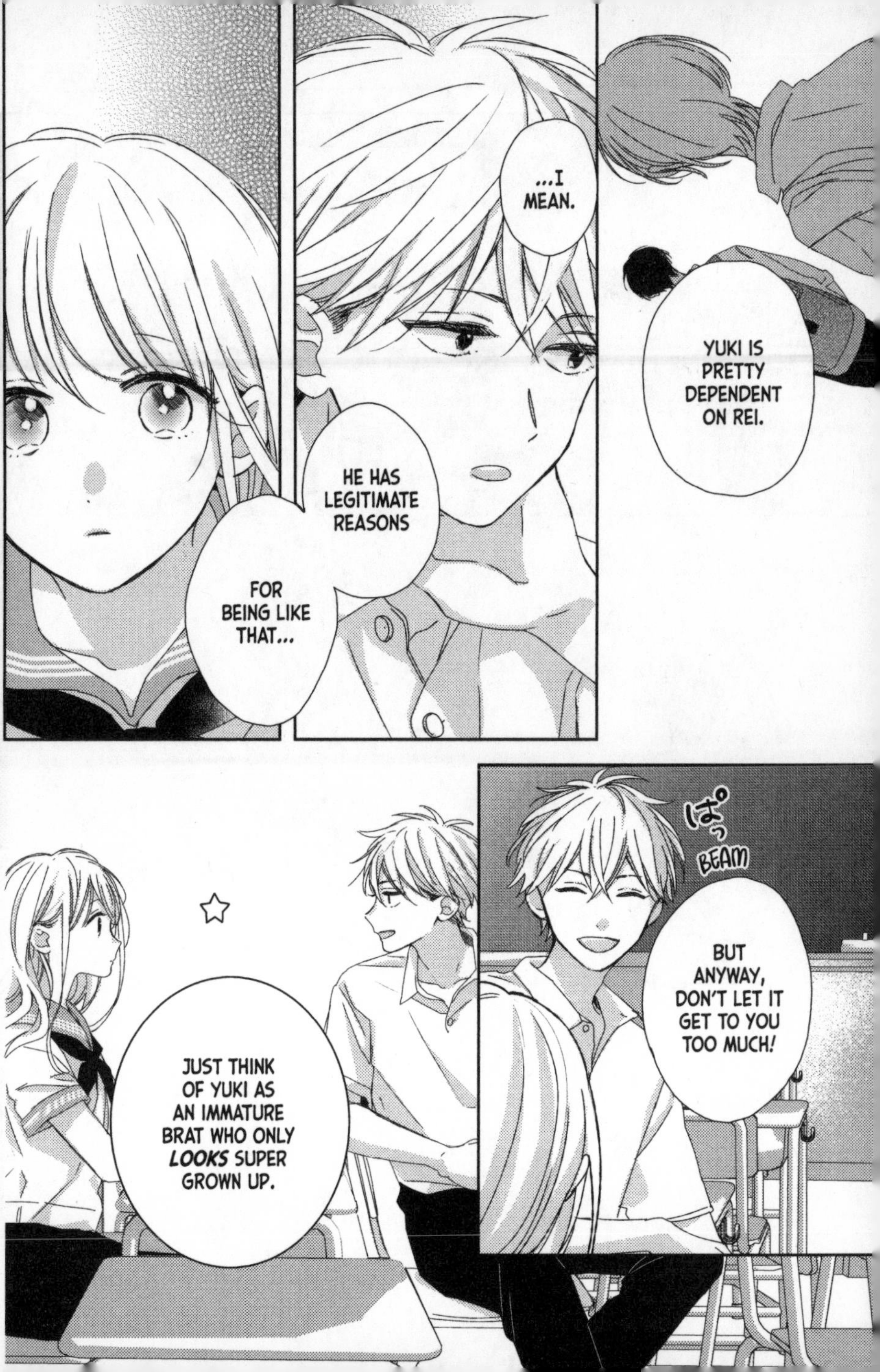
YUKI IS PRETTY DEPENDENT ON REI.
...I MEAN.
HE HAS LEGITIMATE REASONS
FOR BEING LIKE THAT...
ぱっ BEAM
BUT ANYWAY, DON'T LET IT GET TO YOU TOO MUCH!
JUST THINK OF YUKI AS AN IMMATURE BRAT WHO ONLY *LOOKS* SUPER GROWN UP.

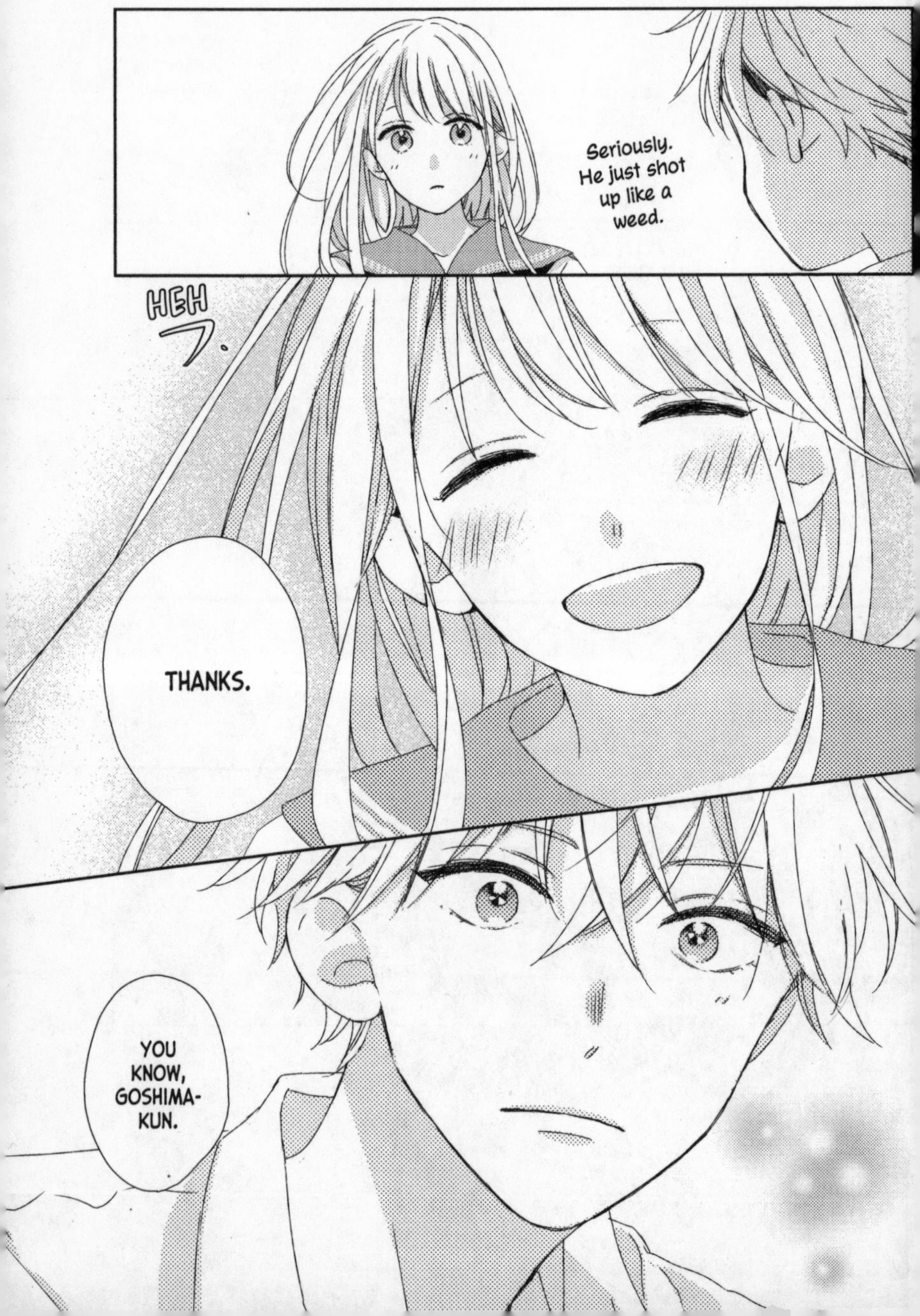
Seriously. He just shot up like a weed.
HEH
THANKS.
YOU KNOW, GOSHIMA-KUN.

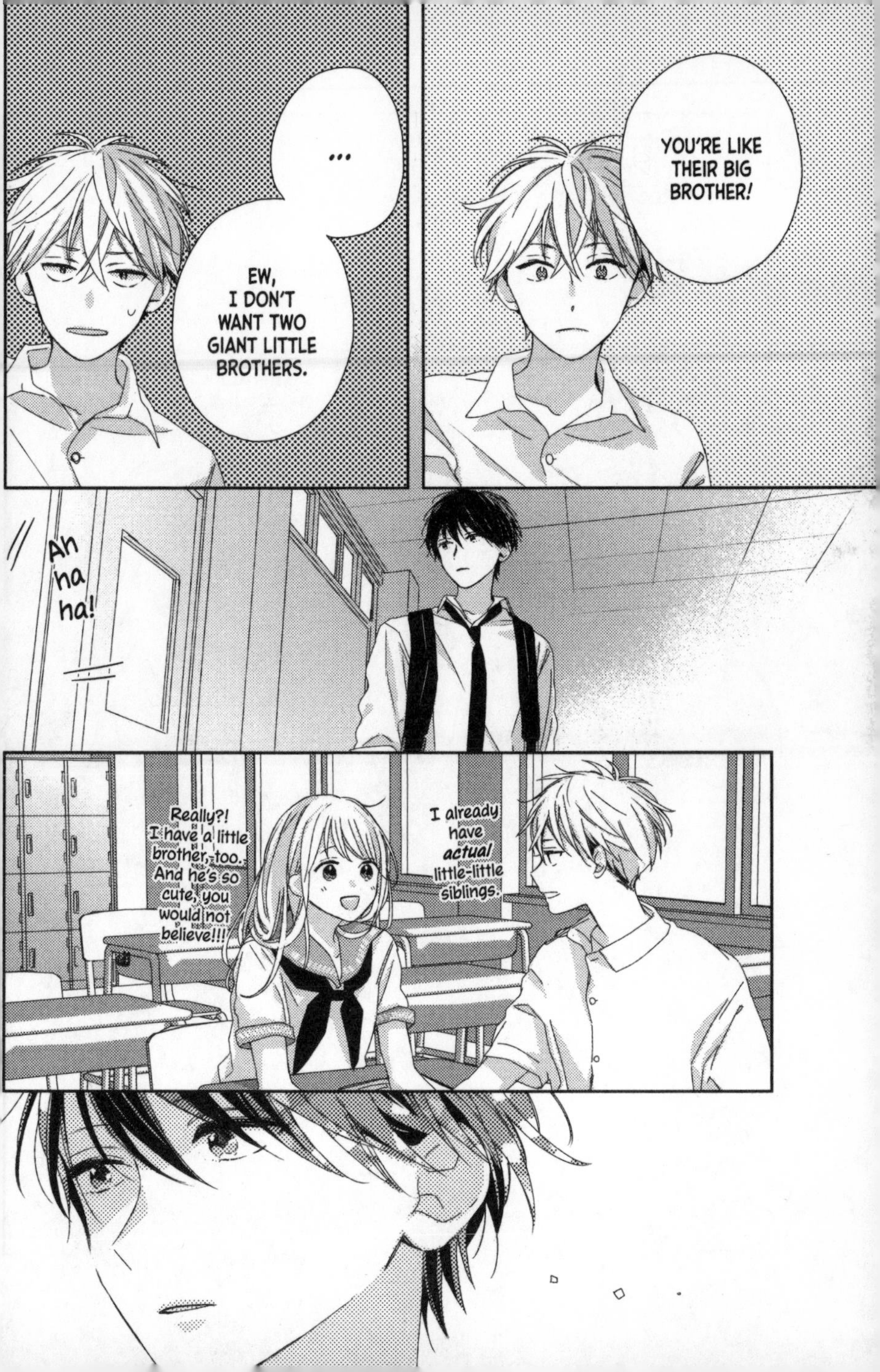
YOU'RE LIKE THEIR BIG BROTHER!
...
EW, I DON'T WANT TWO GIANT LITTLE BROTHERS.
Ah ha ha!
I already have *actual* little-little siblings.
Really?! I have a little brother, too. And he's so cute, you would not believe!!!

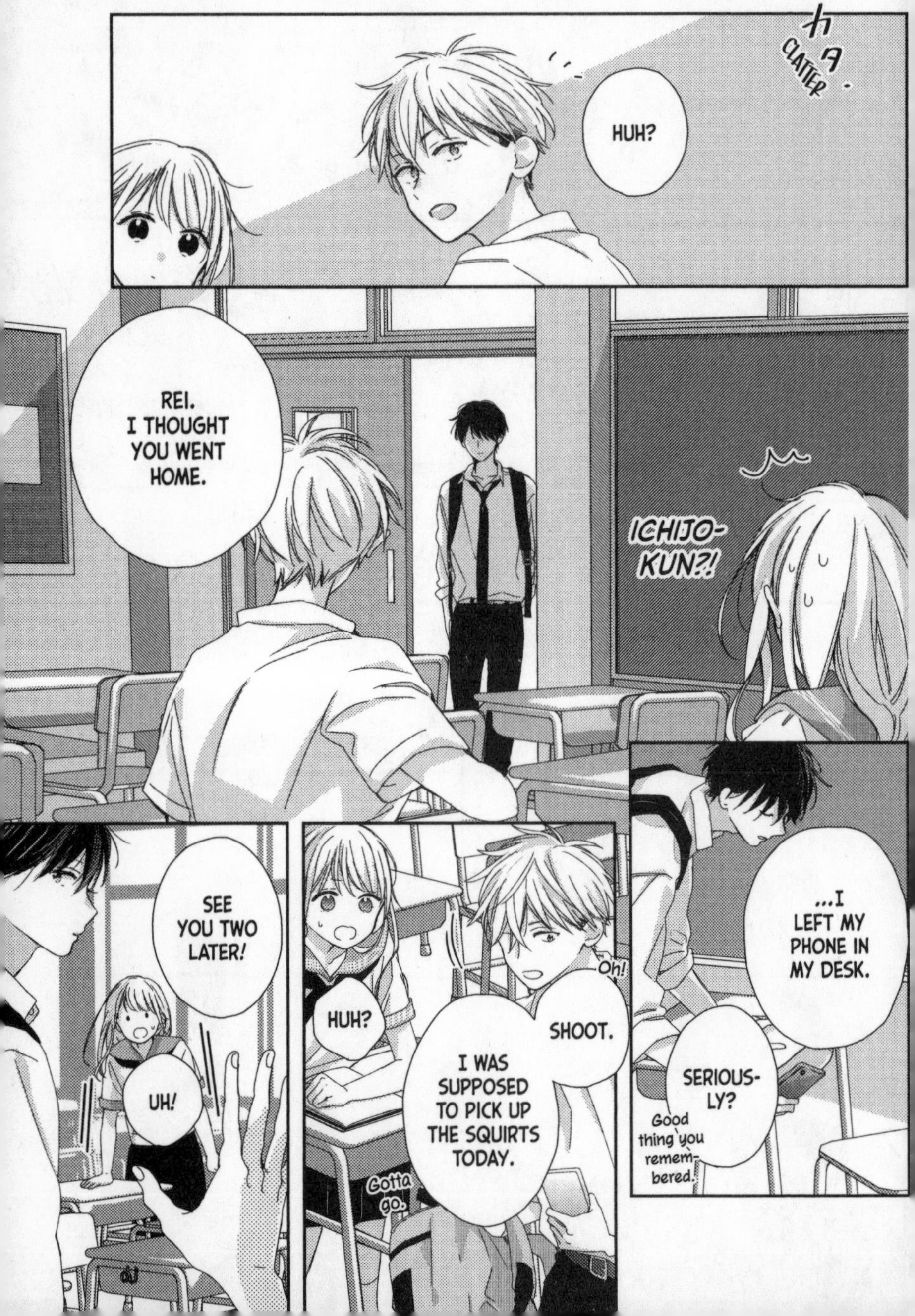
カタ
CLATTER
HUH?
ICHIJO-KUN?!
REI. I THOUGHT YOU WENT HOME.
...I LEFT MY PHONE IN MY DESK.
SERIOUS-LY?
Good thing you remem-bered.
Oh!
SHOOT.
I WAS SUPPOSED TO PICK UP THE SQUIRTS TODAY.
HUH?
Gotta go.
SEE YOU TWO LATER!
UH!

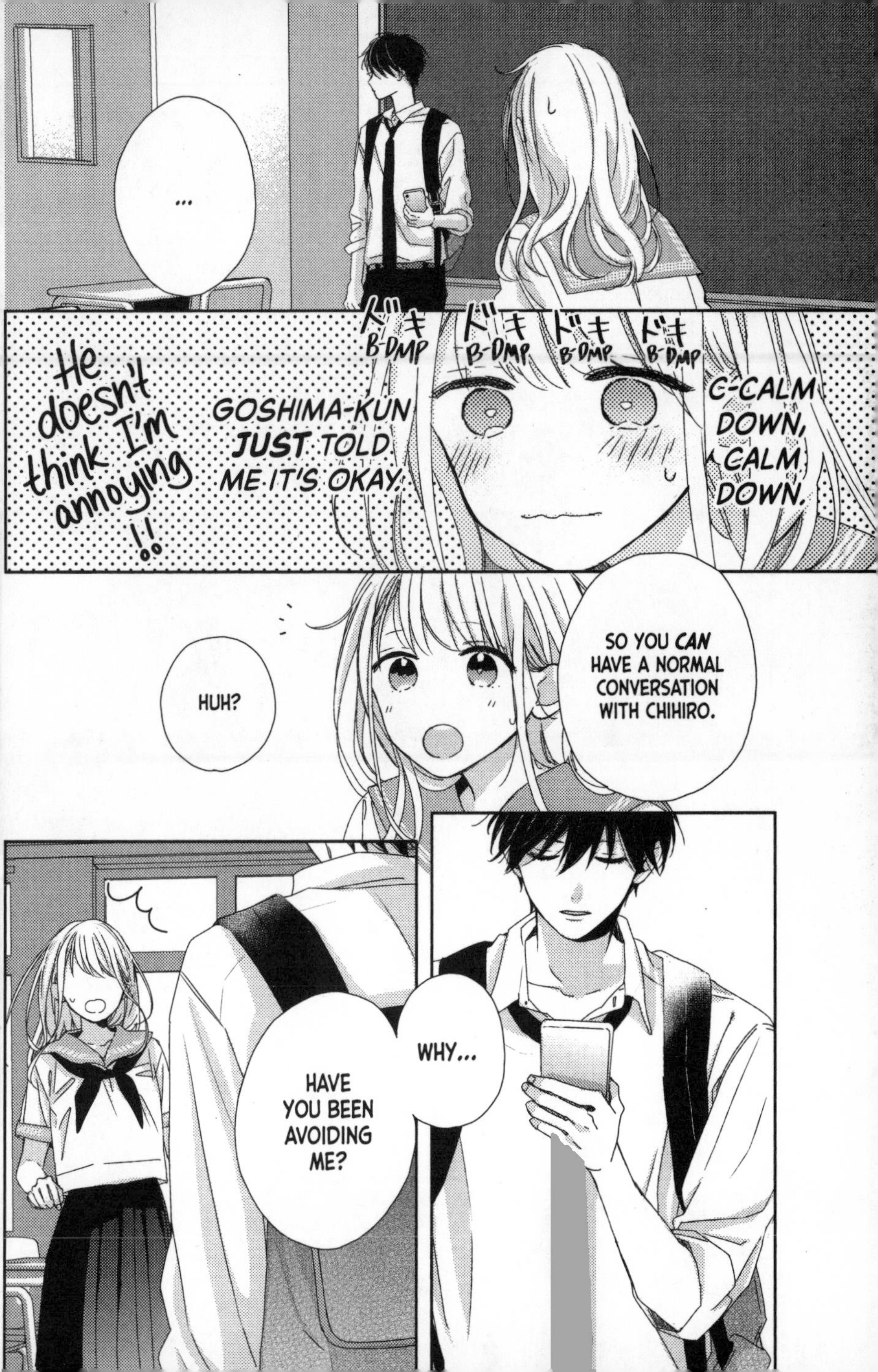
...
ドキ B-DMP
ドキ B-DMP
ドキ B-DMP
ドキ B-DMP
C-CALM DOWN, CALM DOWN.
GOSHIMA-KUN JUST TOLD ME IT'S OKAY.
He doesn't think I'm annoying!!
SO YOU CAN HAVE A NORMAL CONVERSATION WITH CHIHIRO.
HUH?
WHY...
HAVE YOU BEEN AVOIDING ME?

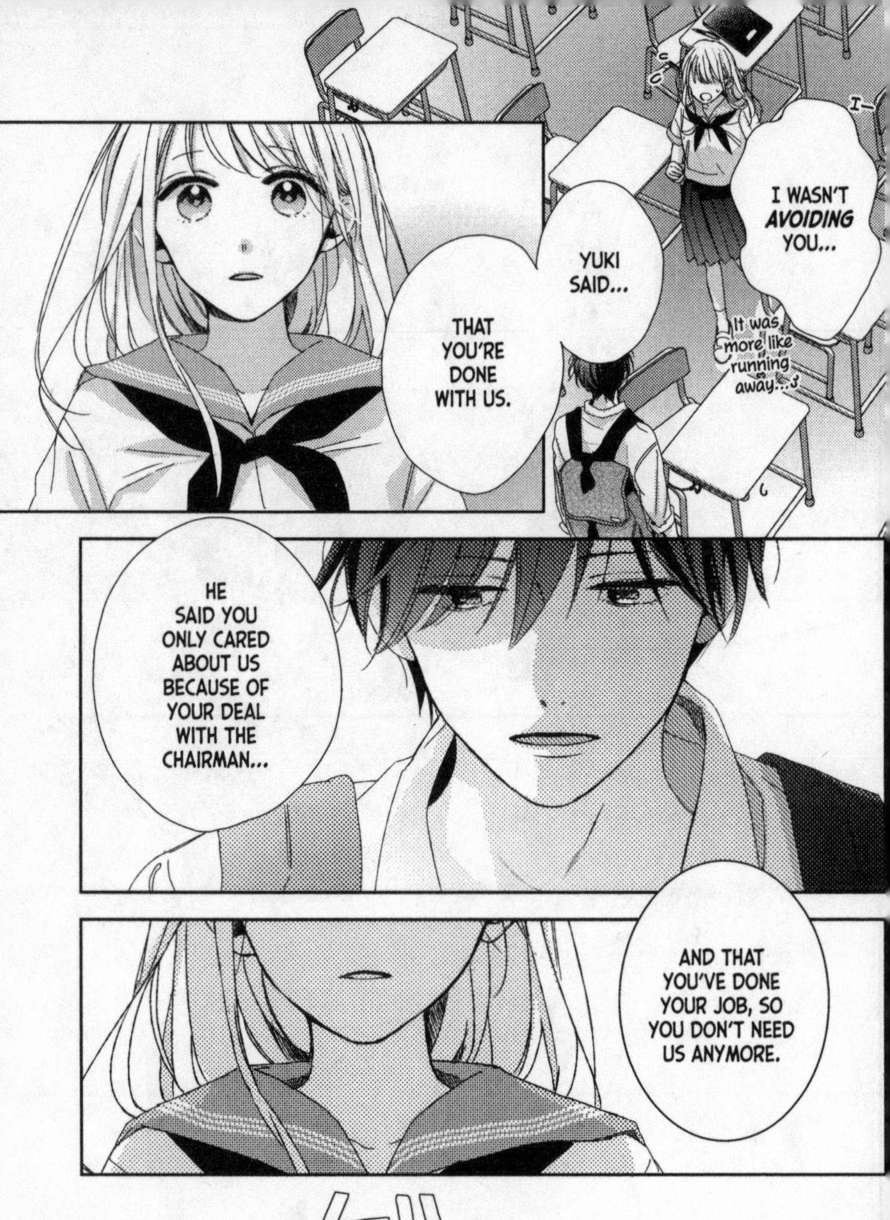
I—
I WASN'T *AVOIDING* YOU...
It was more like running away...
YUKI SAID...
THAT YOU'RE DONE WITH US.
HE SAID YOU ONLY CARED ABOUT US BECAUSE OF YOUR DEAL WITH THE CHAIRMAN...
AND THAT YOU'VE DONE YOUR JOB, SO YOU DON'T NEED US ANYMORE.
HE—
CLATTER

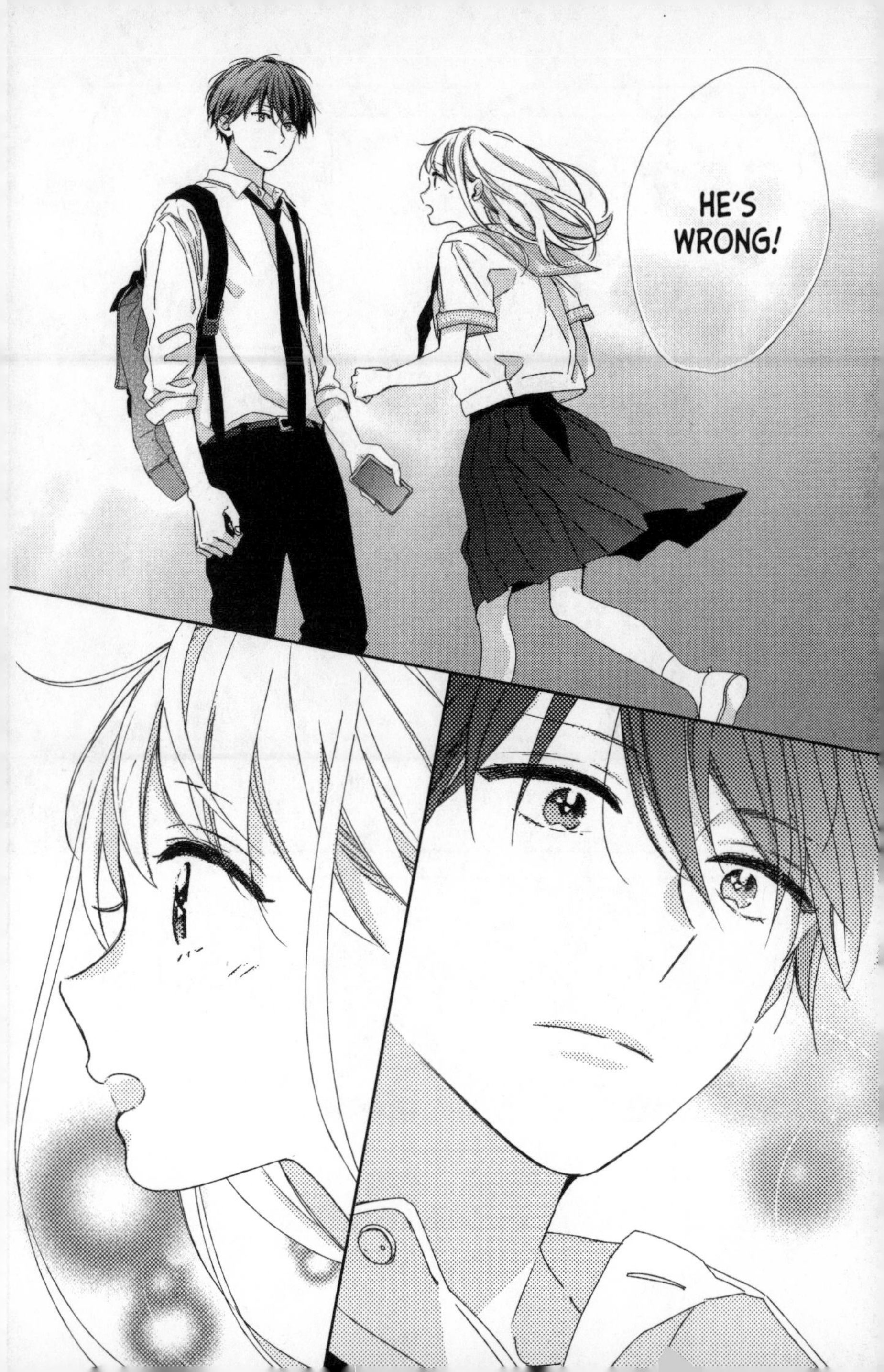
HE'S WRONG!

OF COURSE.
...THIS DID ALL START...
BECAUSE I TALKED TO THE CHAIRMAN.
IT'S NOT BECAUSE I'M THEIR BABY-SITTER.
BUT REALLY, I JUST WANTED TO ENJOY OUR LIFE AT SCHOOL TOGETHER.
IT'S NOT BECAUSE OF ANY NEED.
I WANTED TO GET TO KNOW YOU.

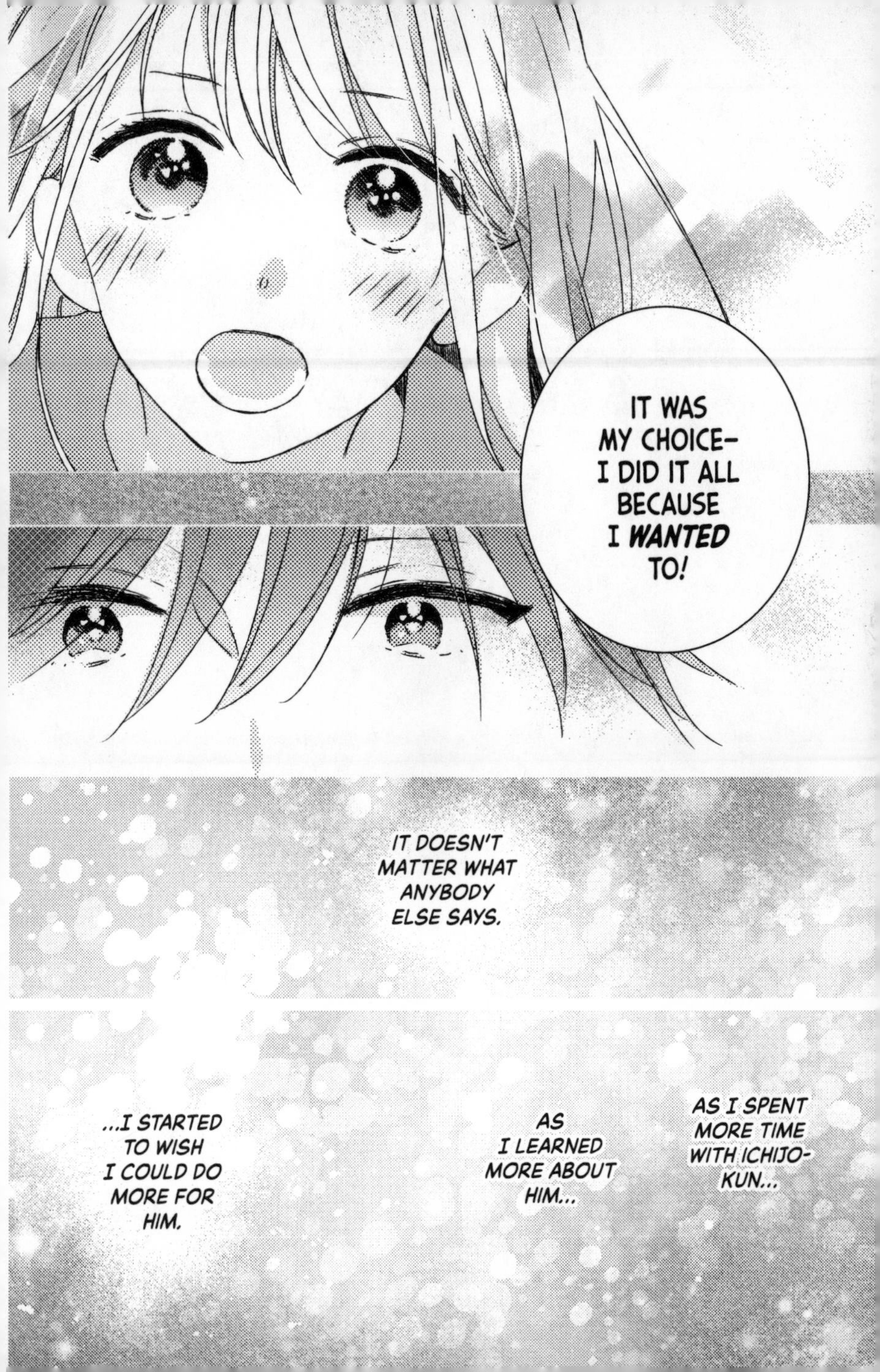
IT WAS MY CHOICE– I DID IT ALL BECAUSE I WANTED TO!
IT DOESN'T MATTER WHAT ANYBODY ELSE SAYS.
AS I SPENT MORE TIME WITH ICHIJO-KUN...
AS I LEARNED MORE ABOUT HIM...
...I STARTED TO WISH I COULD DO MORE FOR HIM.

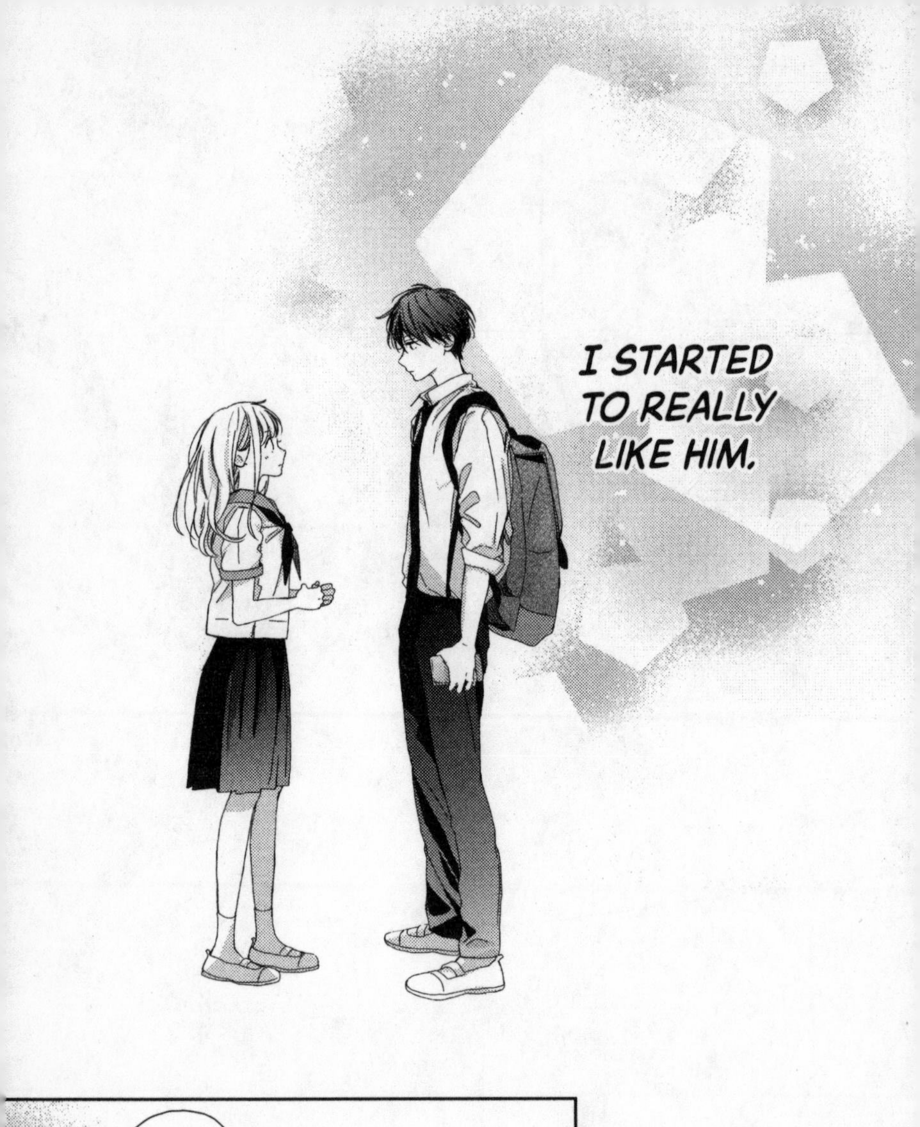
I STARTED TO REALLY LIKE HIM.

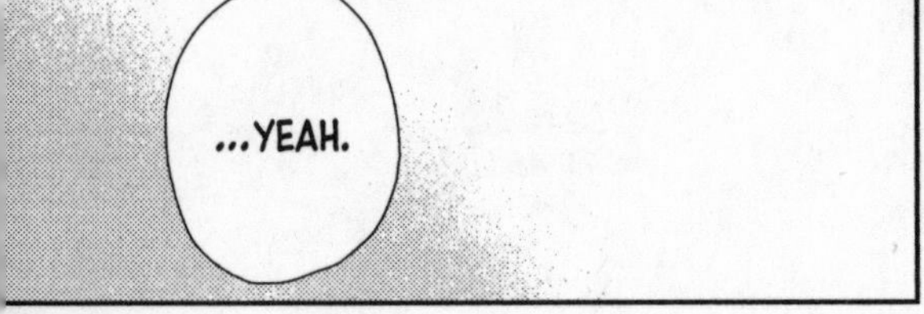
...YEAH.

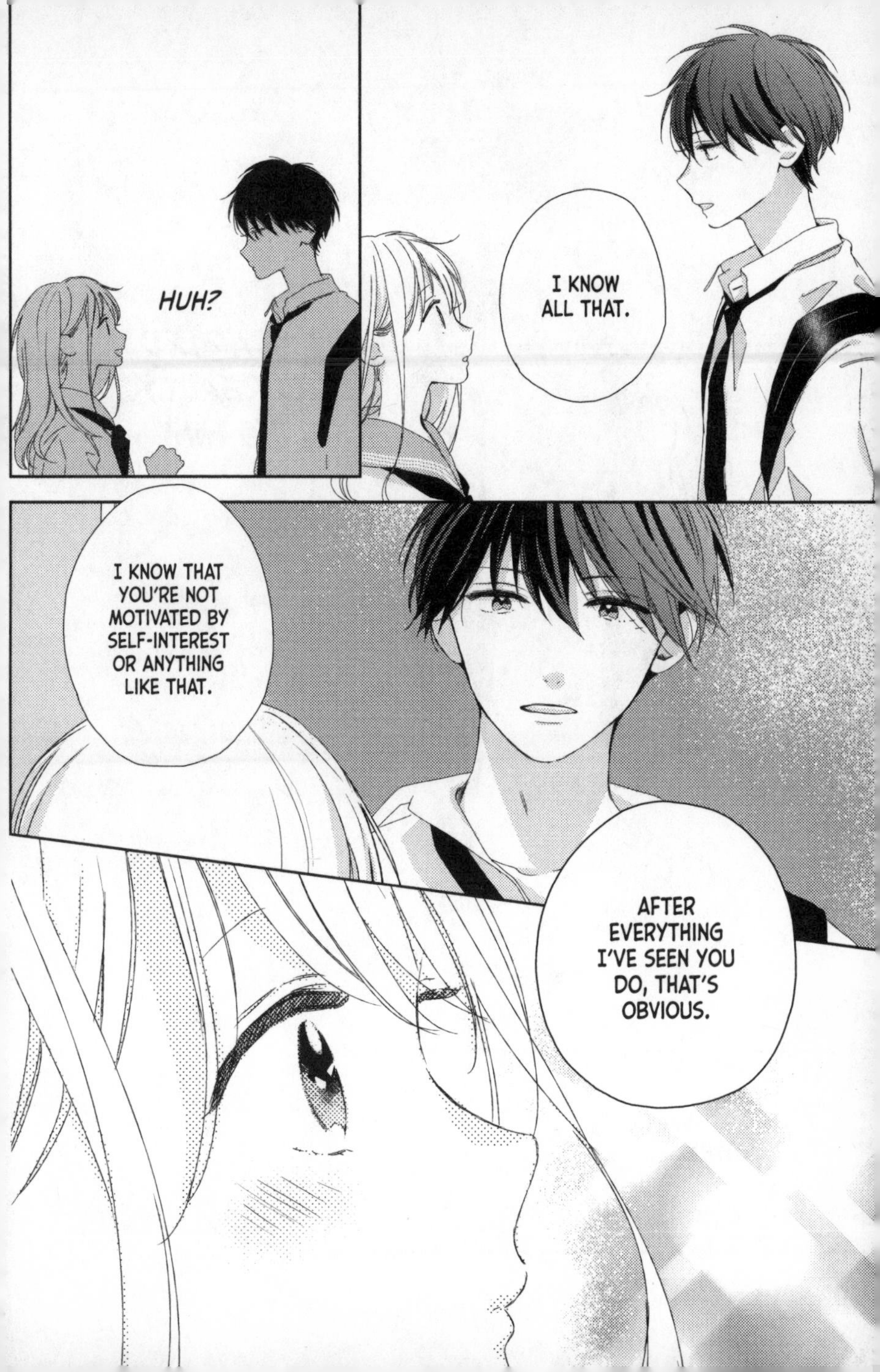
I KNOW ALL THAT.
HUH?
I KNOW THAT YOU'RE NOT MOTIVATED BY SELF-INTEREST OR ANYTHING LIKE THAT.
AFTER EVERYTHING I'VE SEEN YOU DO, THAT'S OBVIOUS.

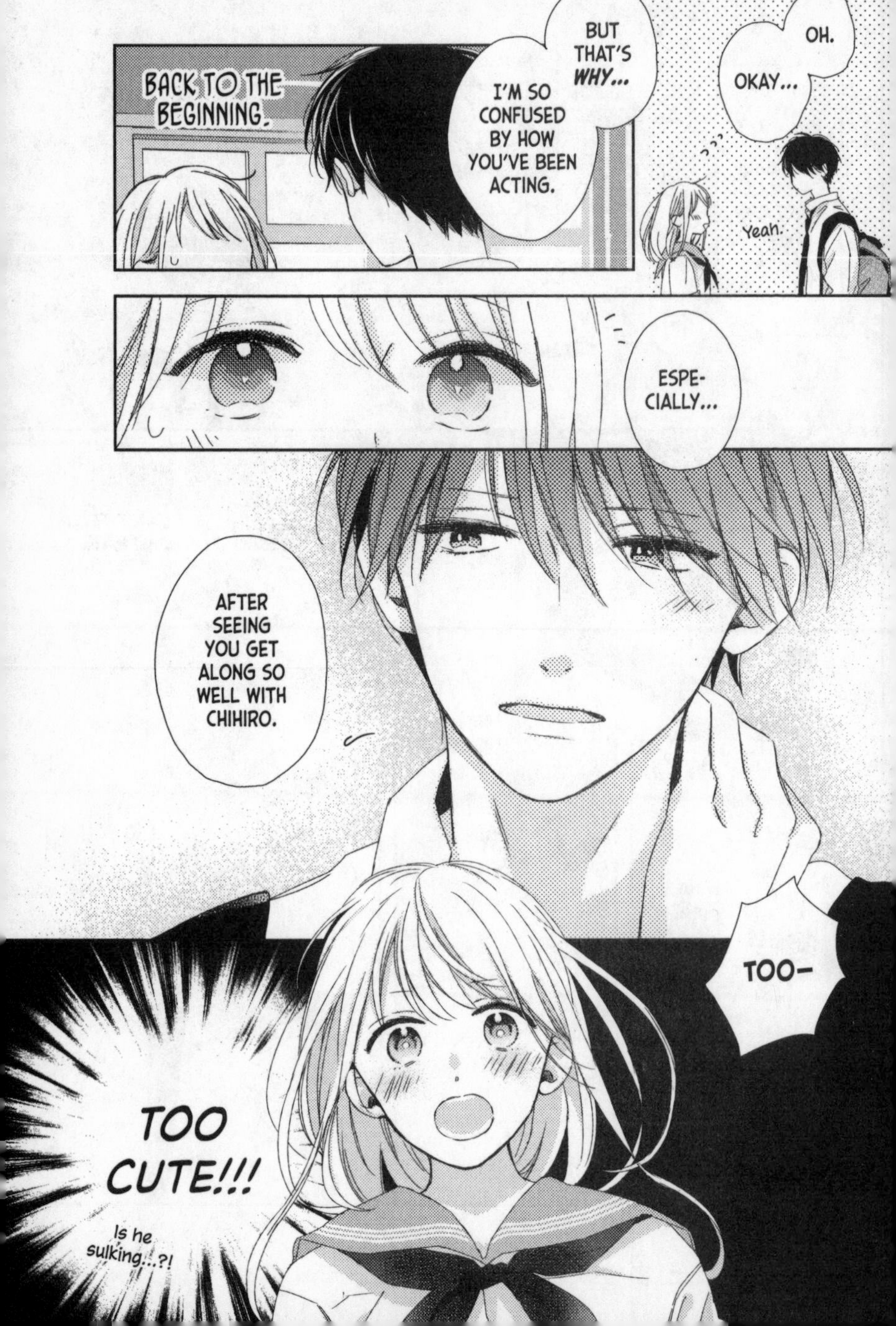
OH.
OKAY...
Yeah.
BUT THAT'S *WHY...*
I'M SO CONFUSED BY HOW YOU'VE BEEN ACTING.
BACK TO THE BEGINNING.
ESPE-CIALLY...
AFTER SEEING YOU GET ALONG SO WELL WITH CHIHIRO.
TOO-
TOO CUTE!!!
Is he sulking...?!

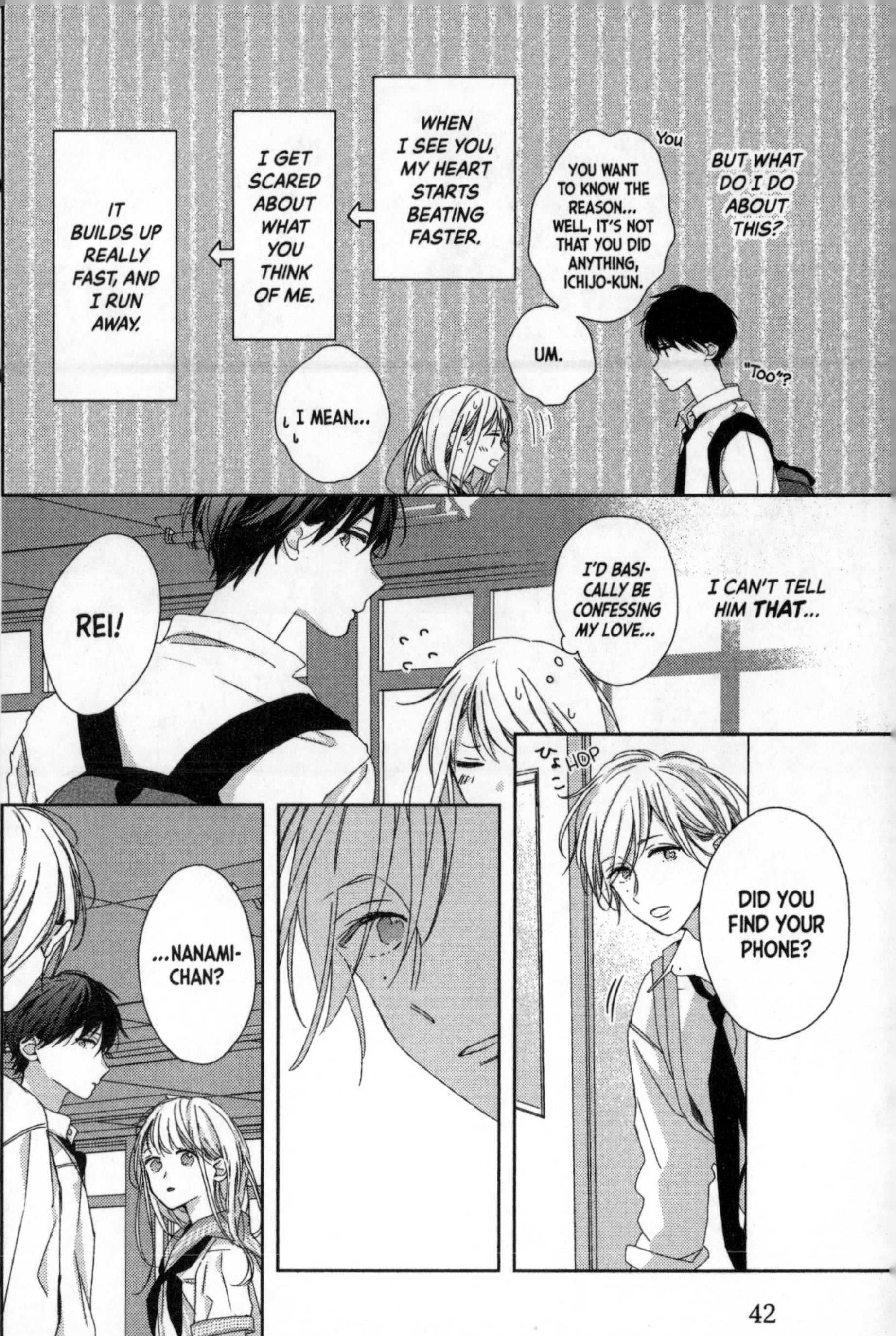
BUT WHAT DO I DO ABOUT THIS?
You
YOU WANT TO KNOW THE REASON... WELL, IT'S NOT THAT YOU DID ANYTHING, ICHIJO-KUN.
"Too"?
UM.
I MEAN...
WHEN I SEE YOU, MY HEART STARTS BEATING FASTER.
I GET SCARED ABOUT WHAT YOU THINK OF ME.
IT BUILDS UP REALLY FAST, AND I RUN AWAY.
I CAN'T TELL HIM THAT...
I'D BASICALLY BE CONFESSING MY LOVE...
REI!
HOP
DID YOU FIND YOUR PHONE?
...NANAMI-CHAN?

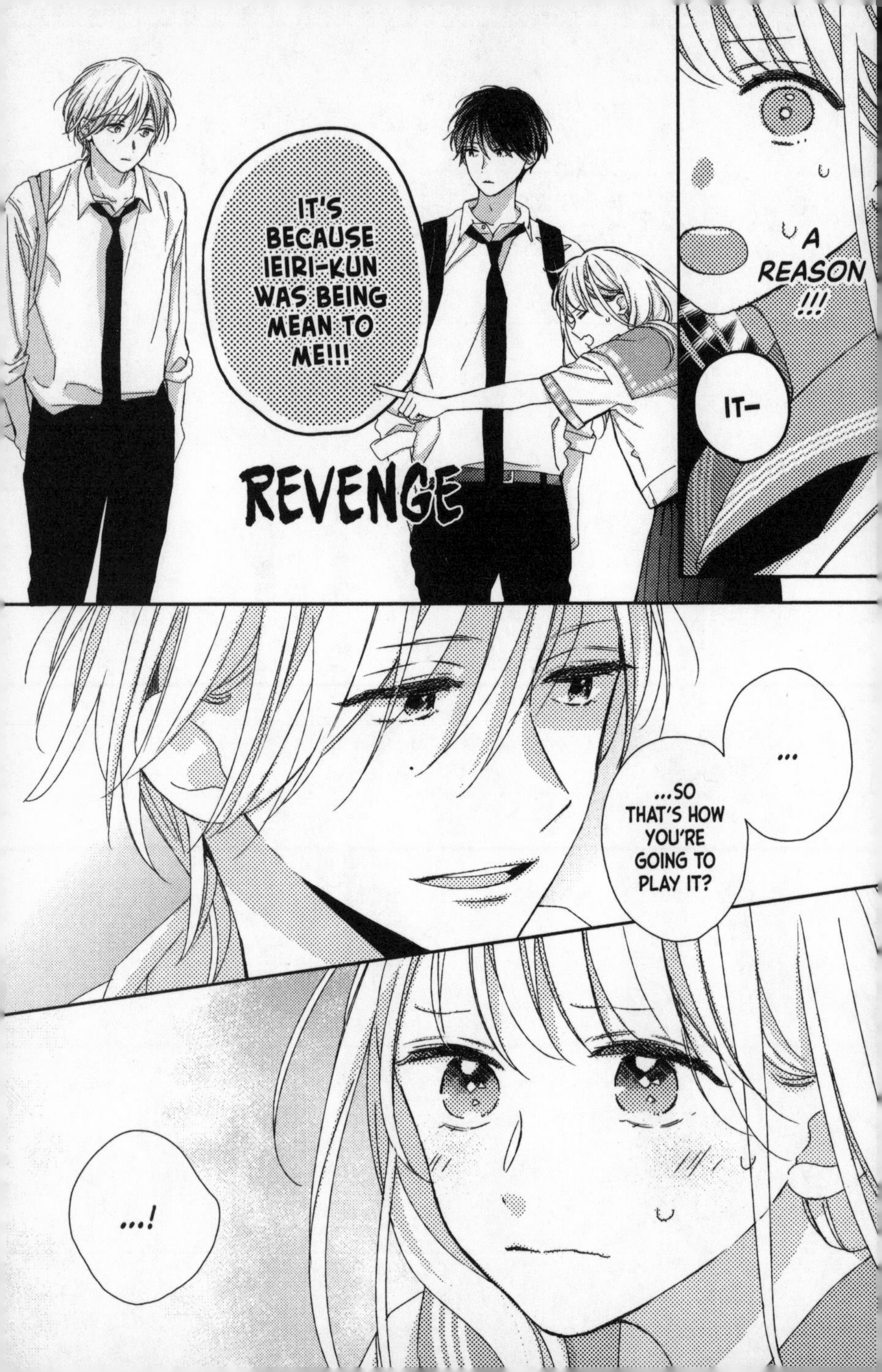
A REASON!!!
IT–
IT'S BECAUSE IEIRI-KUN WAS BEING MEAN TO ME!!!
REVENGE
...
...SO THAT'S HOW YOU'RE GOING TO PLAY IT?
...!

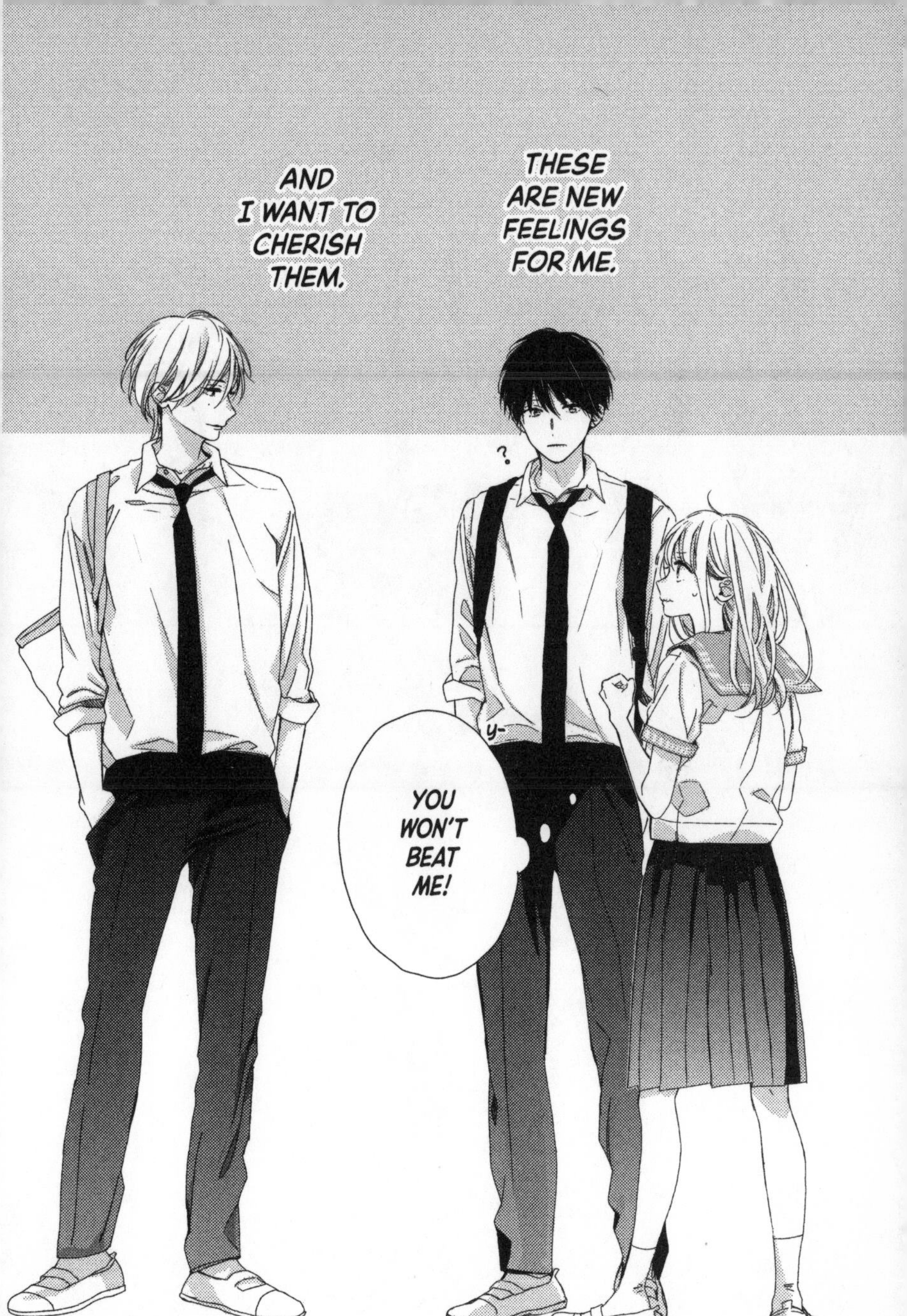
THESE ARE NEW FEELINGS FOR ME.
AND I WANT TO CHERISH THEM.
?
Y-
YOU WON'T BEAT ME!

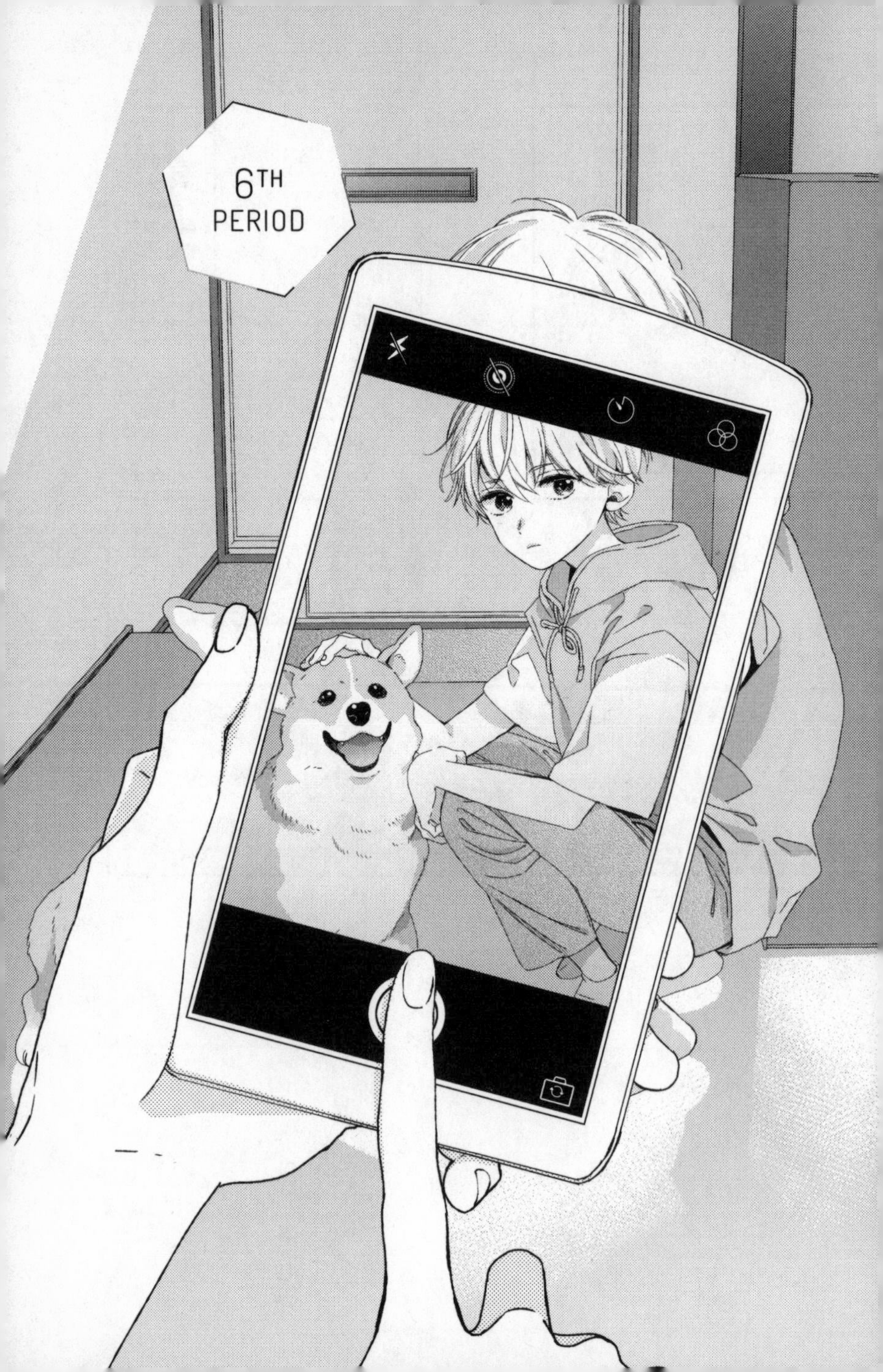
6TH
PERIOD

Oh.

I HAVE "DECLARED WAR" AGAINST IEIRI-KUN.

AND EVER SINCE...

ICHIJO-KUN.

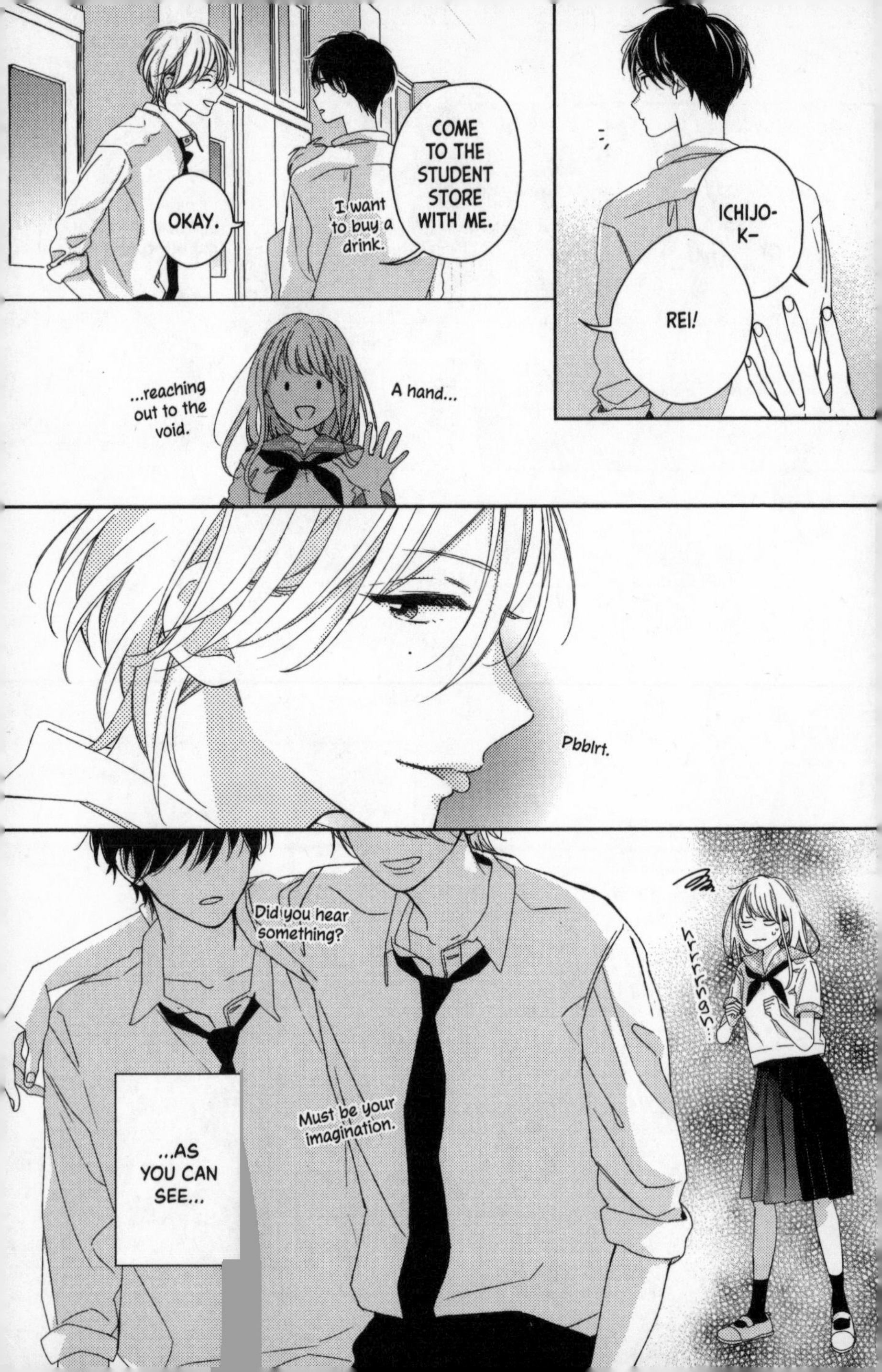

ICHIJO-K–
REI!
COME TO THE STUDENT STORE WITH ME.
I want to buy a drink.
OKAY.
A hand...
...reaching out to the void.
Pbblrt.
hrrrrngs...
Did you hear something?
Must be your imagination.
...AS YOU CAN SEE...

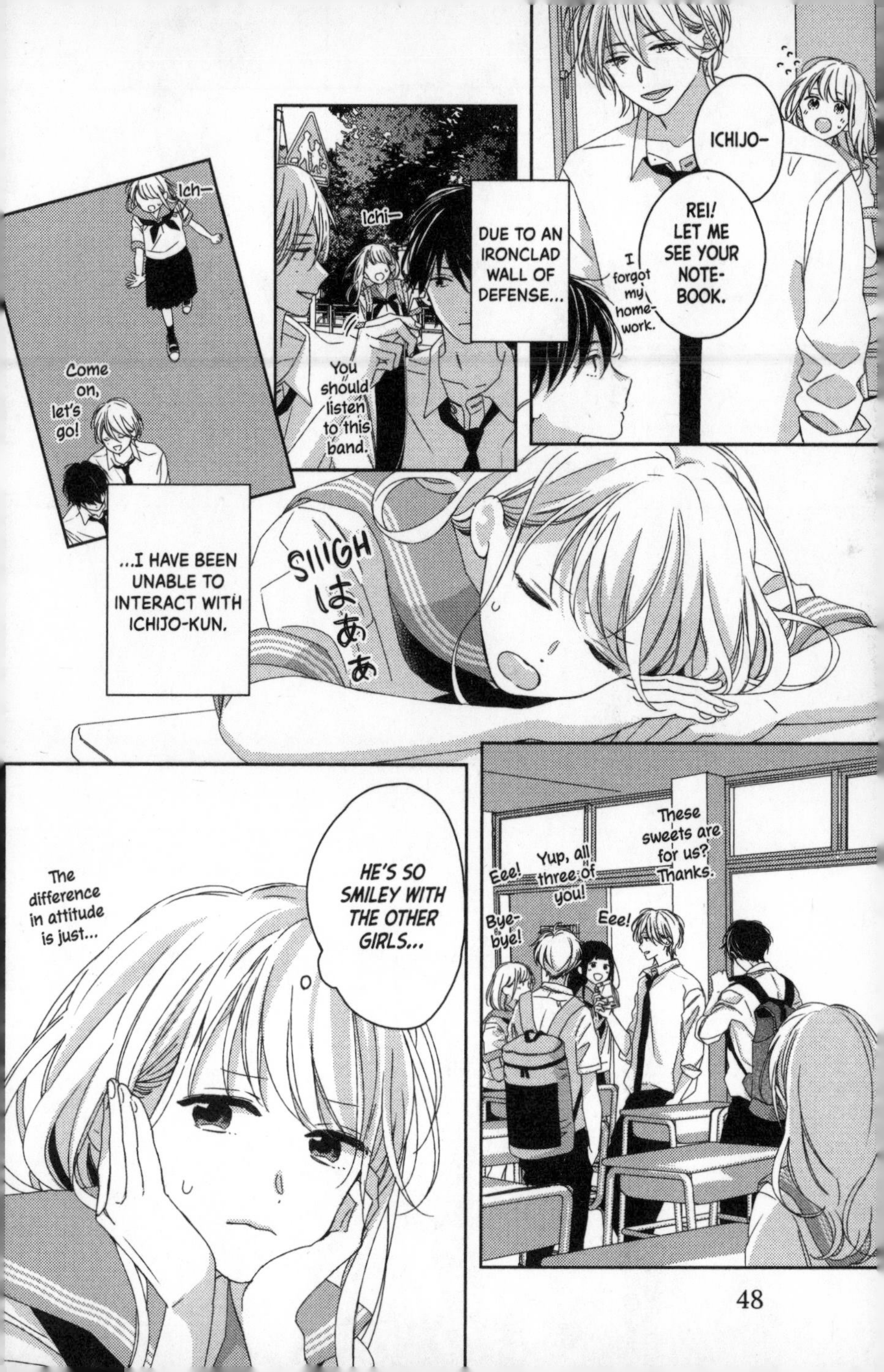

ICHIJO–
REI! LET ME SEE YOUR NOTEBOOK.
I forgot my homework.
DUE TO AN IRONCLAD WALL OF DEFENSE...
Ichi–
You should listen to this band.
Ich–
Come on, let's go!
SIIIGH
はぁぁ
...I HAVE BEEN UNABLE TO INTERACT WITH ICHIJO-KUN.
These sweets are for us? Thanks.
Yup, all three of you!
Eee!
Eee!
Bye-bye!
HE'S SO SMILEY WITH THE OTHER GIRLS...
The difference in attitude is just...

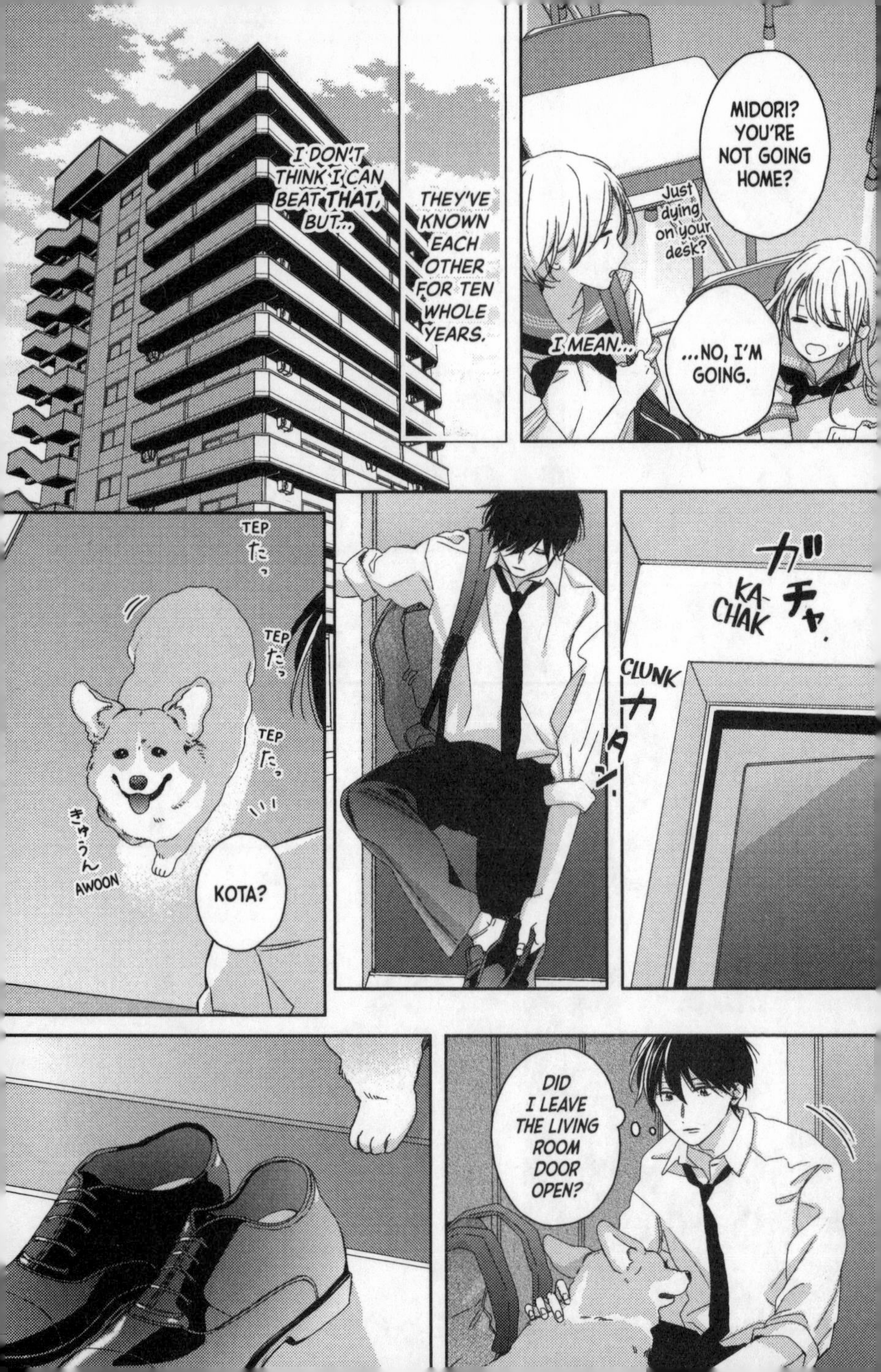
MIDORI? YOU'RE NOT GOING HOME?
Just dying on your desk?
I MEAN...
...NO, I'M GOING.
THEY'VE KNOWN EACH OTHER FOR TEN WHOLE YEARS.
I DON'T THINK I CAN BEAT THAT, BUT...
ガチャ
KA-CHAK
CLUNK
カタン
TEP
たっ
TEP
たっ
TEP
たっ
KOTA?
きゅうん
AWOON
DID I LEAVE THE LIVING ROOM DOOR OPEN?

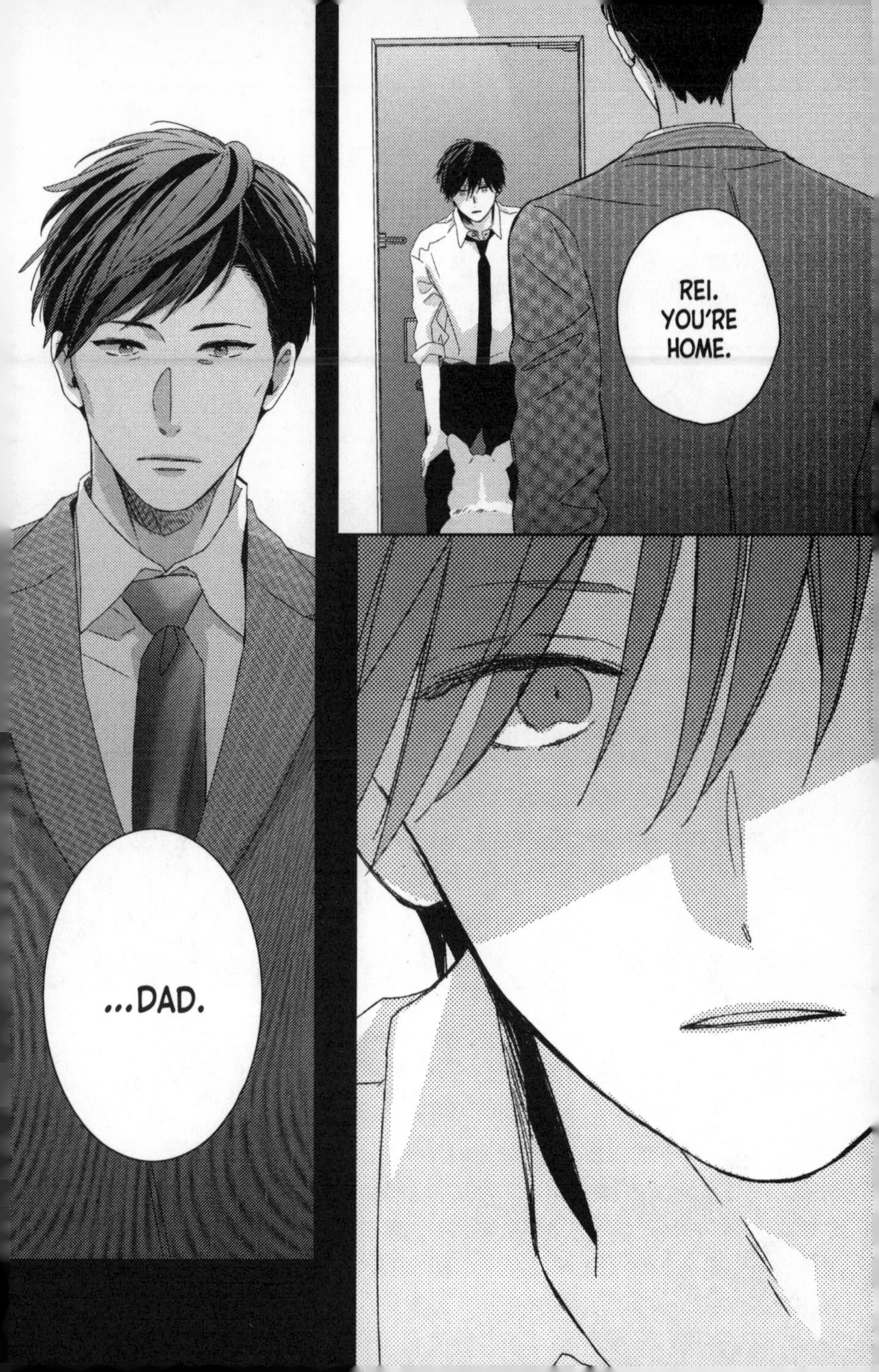
REI. YOU'RE HOME.
...DAD.

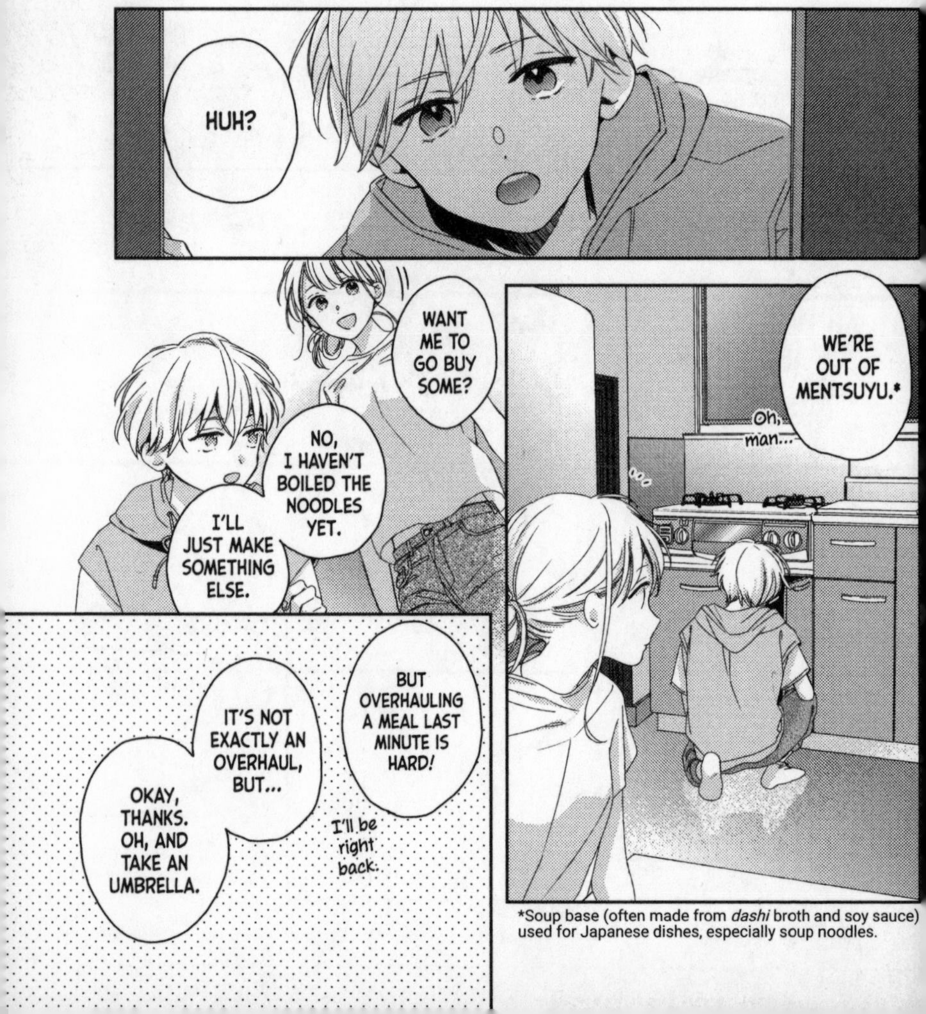
HUH?
WE'RE OUT OF MENTSUYU.*
Oh, man...
WANT ME TO GO BUY SOME?
NO, I HAVEN'T BOILED THE NOODLES YET.
I'LL JUST MAKE SOMETHING ELSE.
BUT OVERHAULING A MEAL LAST MINUTE IS HARD!
IT'S NOT EXACTLY AN OVERHAUL, BUT...
I'll be right back.
OKAY, THANKS. OH, AND TAKE AN UMBRELLA.

*Soup base (often made from *dashi* broth and soy sauce) used for Japanese dishes, especially soup noodles.

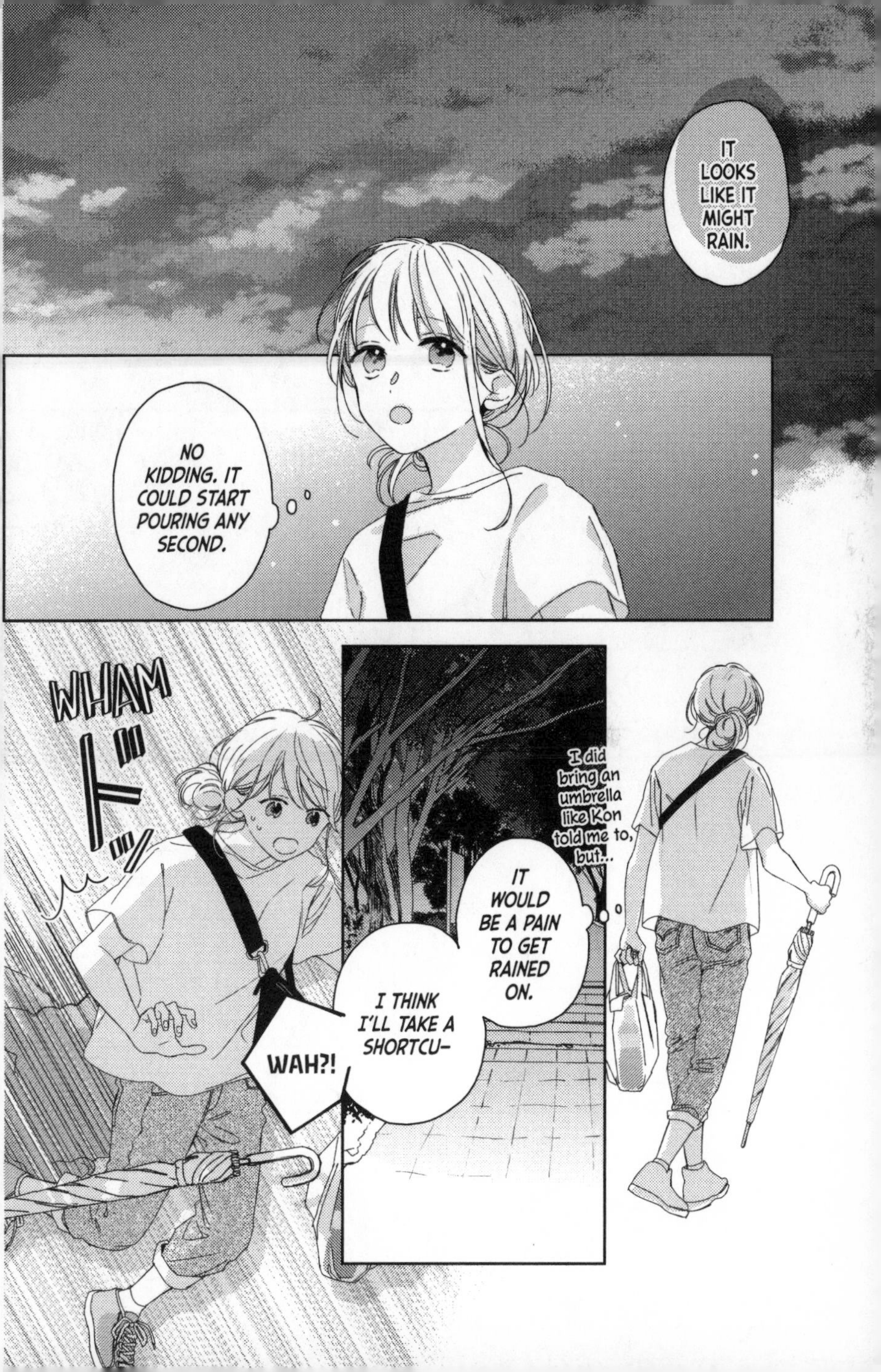
IT LOOKS LIKE IT MIGHT RAIN.
NO KIDDING. IT COULD START POURING ANY SECOND.
I did bring an umbrella like Kon told me to, but...
IT WOULD BE A PAIN TO GET RAINED ON.
I THINK I'LL TAKE A SHORTCU–
WHAM
WAH?!

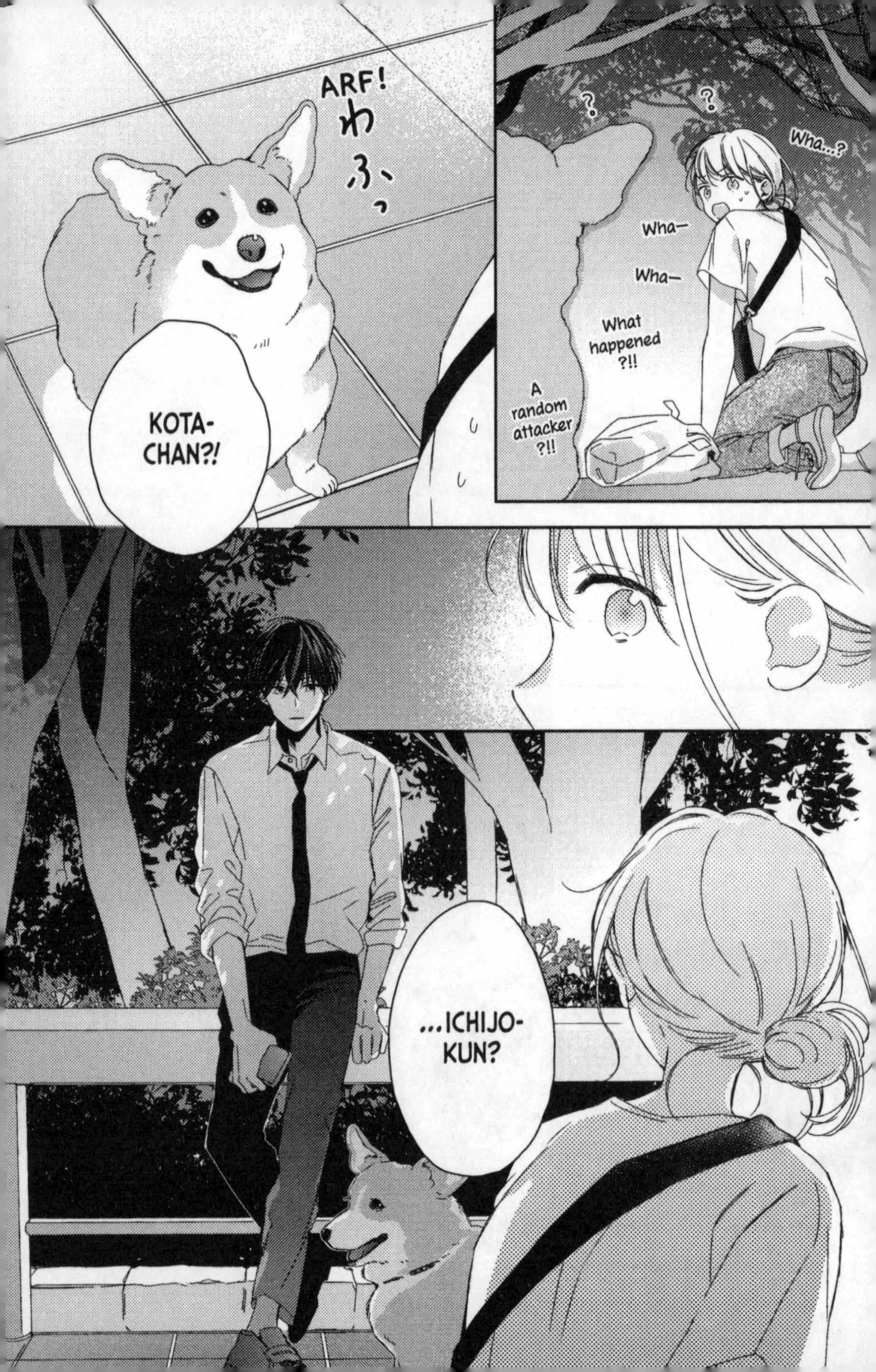
?
?
Wha...?
Wha—
Wha—
What happened ?!!
A random attacker ?!!
ARF!
わふっ
KOTA-CHAN?!
...ICHIJO-KUN?

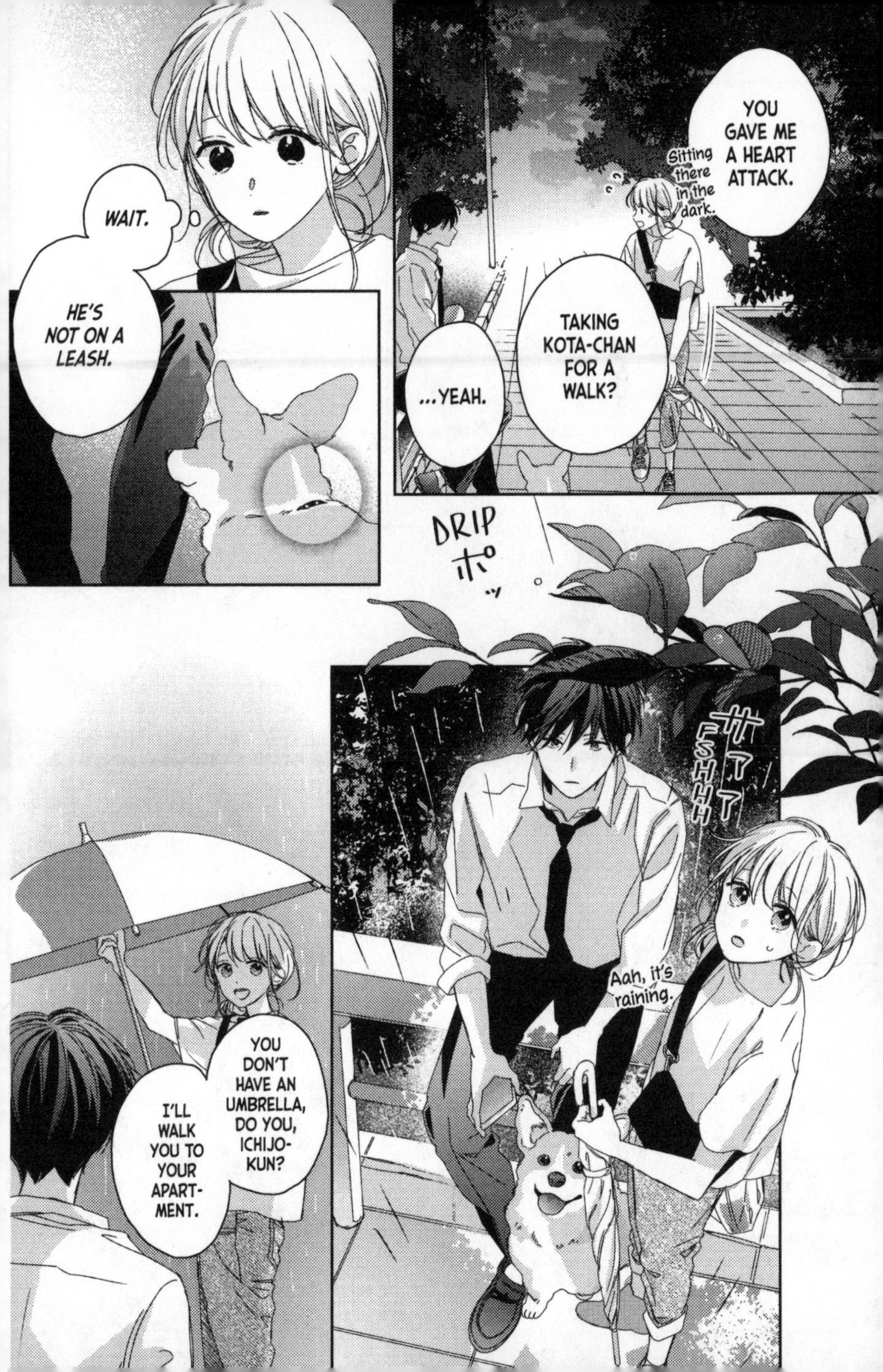
YOU GAVE ME A HEART ATTACK.
Sitting there in the dark.
TAKING KOTA-CHAN FOR A WALK?
...YEAH.
WAIT.
HE'S NOT ON A LEASH.
DRIP
ポッ
サァァ
FSHHH
Aah, it's raining.
YOU DON'T HAVE AN UMBRELLA, DO YOU, ICHIJO-KUN?
I'LL WALK YOU TO YOUR APARTMENT.

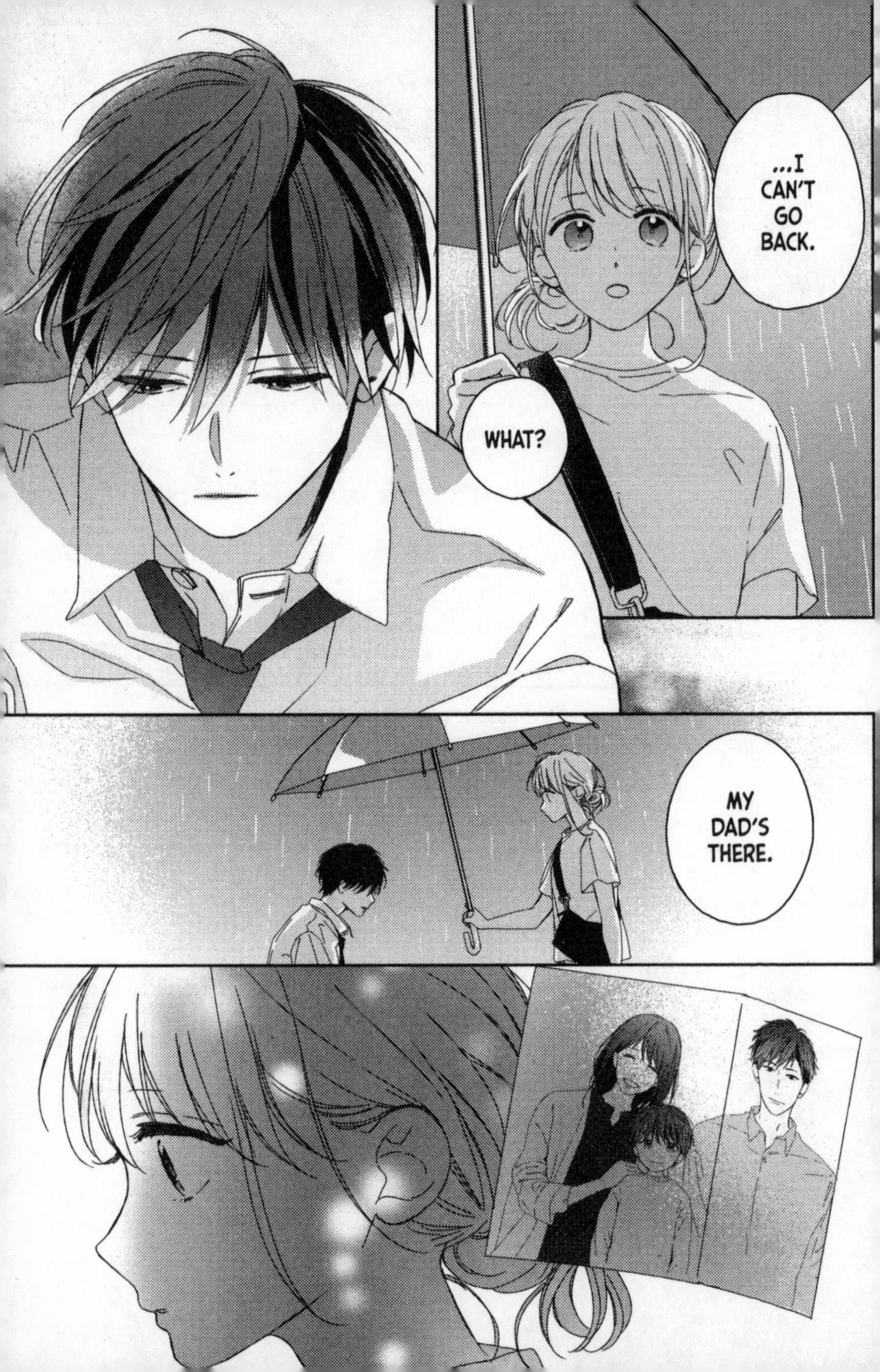
...I CAN'T GO BACK.
WHAT?
MY DAD'S THERE.

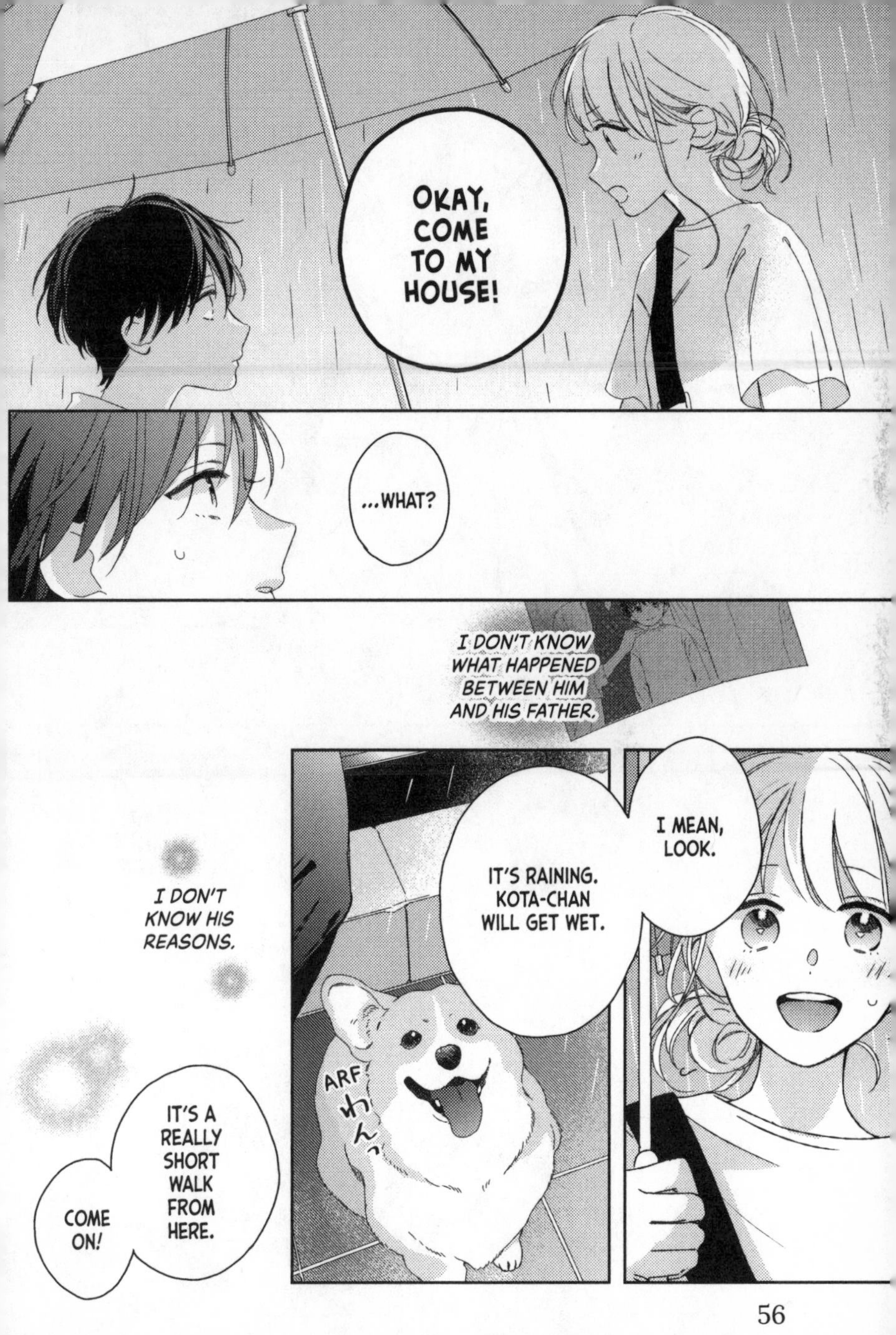
OKAY, COME TO MY HOUSE!
...WHAT?
I DON'T KNOW WHAT HAPPENED BETWEEN HIM AND HIS FATHER.
I MEAN, LOOK.
IT'S RAINING. KOTA-CHAN WILL GET WET.
ARF
わんっ
I DON'T KNOW HIS REASONS.
IT'S A REALLY SHORT WALK FROM HERE.
COME ON!

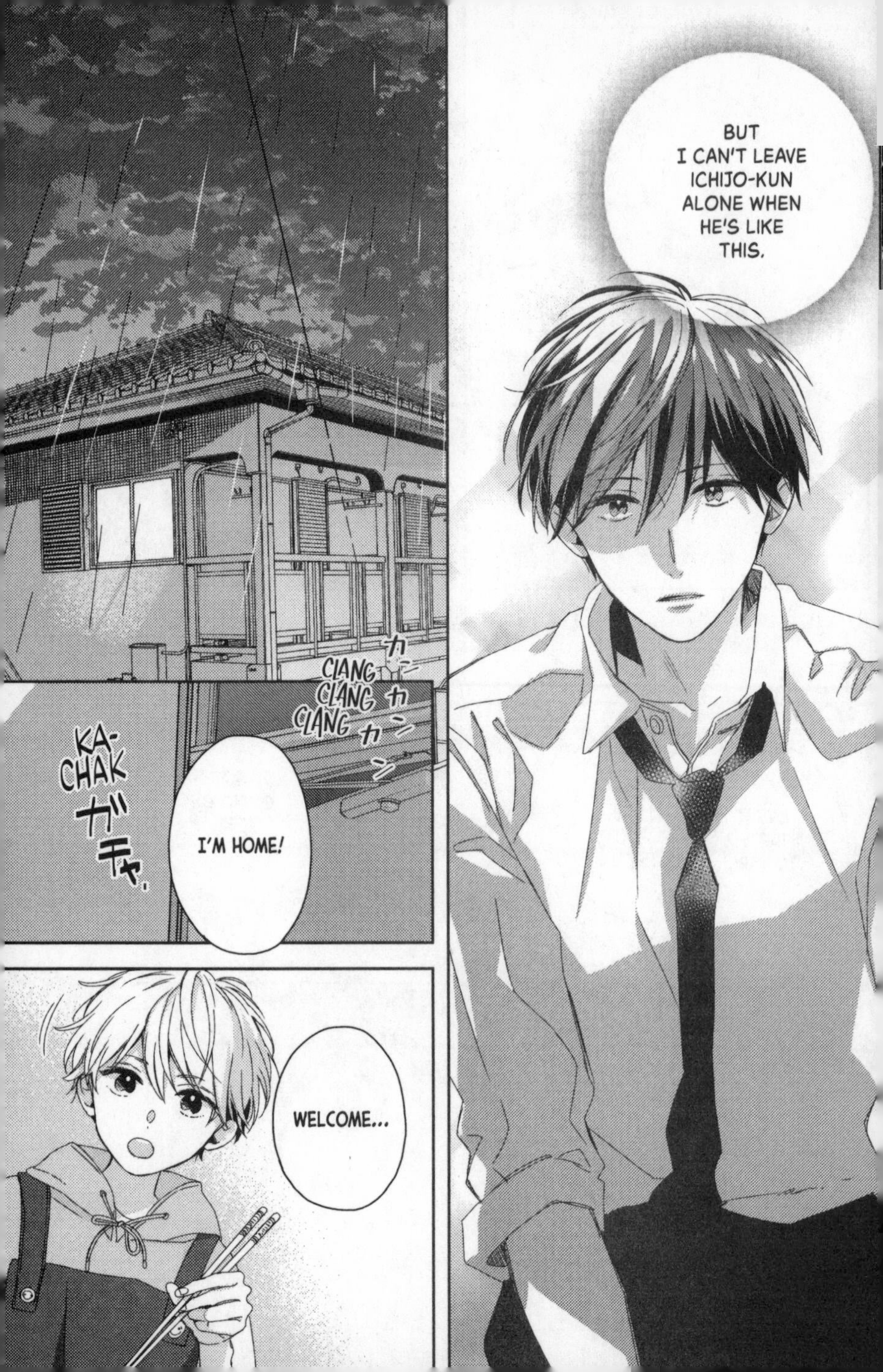
BUT I CAN'T LEAVE ICHIJO-KUN ALONE WHEN HE'S LIKE THIS.
CLANG CLANG CLANG
カンカンカン
KA-CHAK
ガチャ
I'M HOME!
WELCOME...

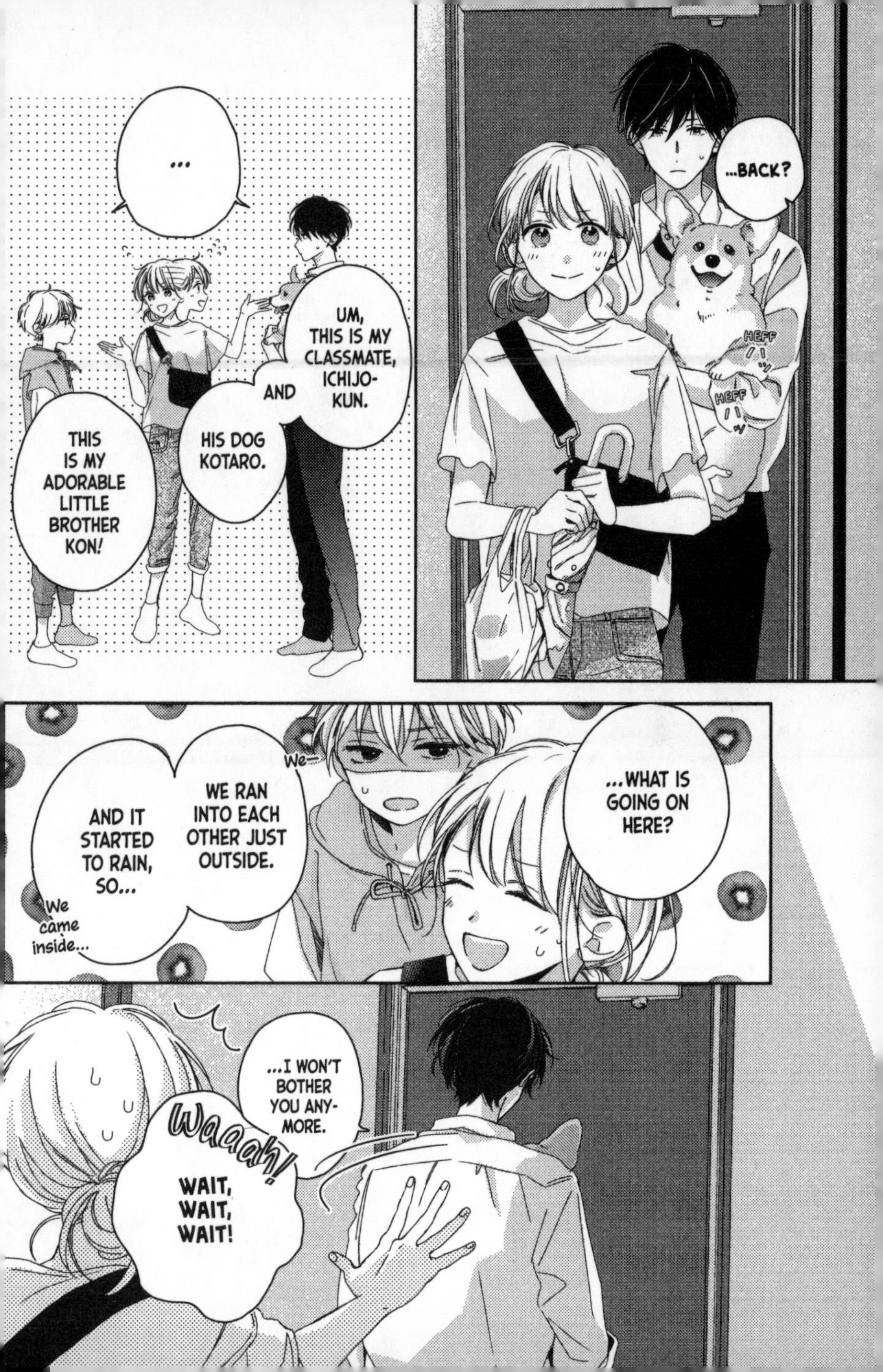
...BACK?
HEFF HEFF
...
UM, THIS IS MY CLASSMATE, ICHIJO-KUN.
AND HIS DOG KOTARO.
THIS IS MY ADORABLE LITTLE BROTHER KON!
...WHAT IS GOING ON HERE?
We—
WE RAN INTO EACH OTHER JUST OUTSIDE.
AND IT STARTED TO RAIN, SO...
We came inside...
...I WON'T BOTHER YOU ANYMORE.
Waaah!
WAIT, WAIT, WAIT!

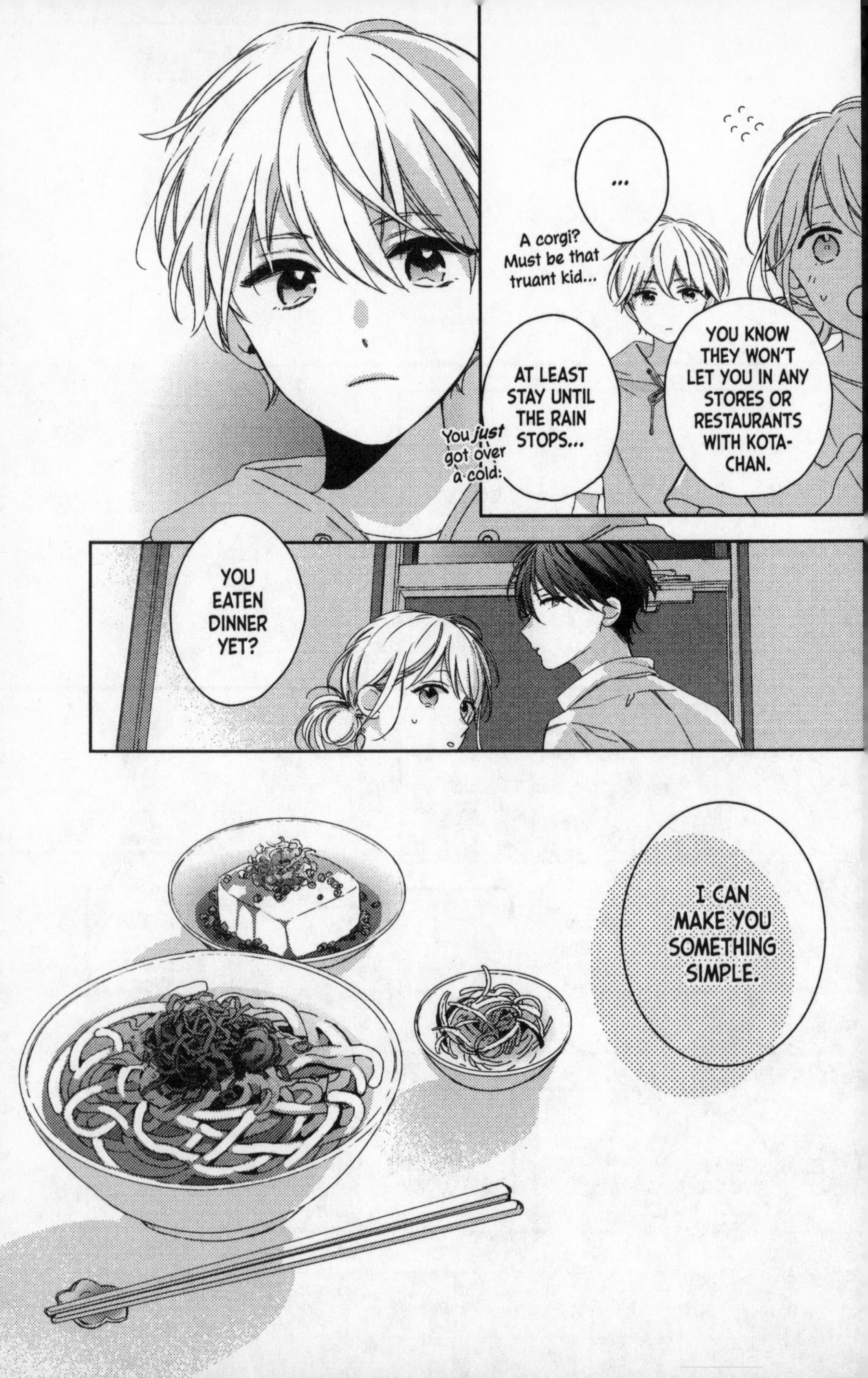
...
A corgi? Must be that truant kid...
YOU KNOW THEY WON'T LET YOU IN ANY STORES OR RESTAURANTS WITH KOTA-CHAN.
AT LEAST STAY UNTIL THE RAIN STOPS...
You *just* got over a cold.
YOU EATEN DINNER YET?
I CAN MAKE YOU SOMETHING SIMPLE.

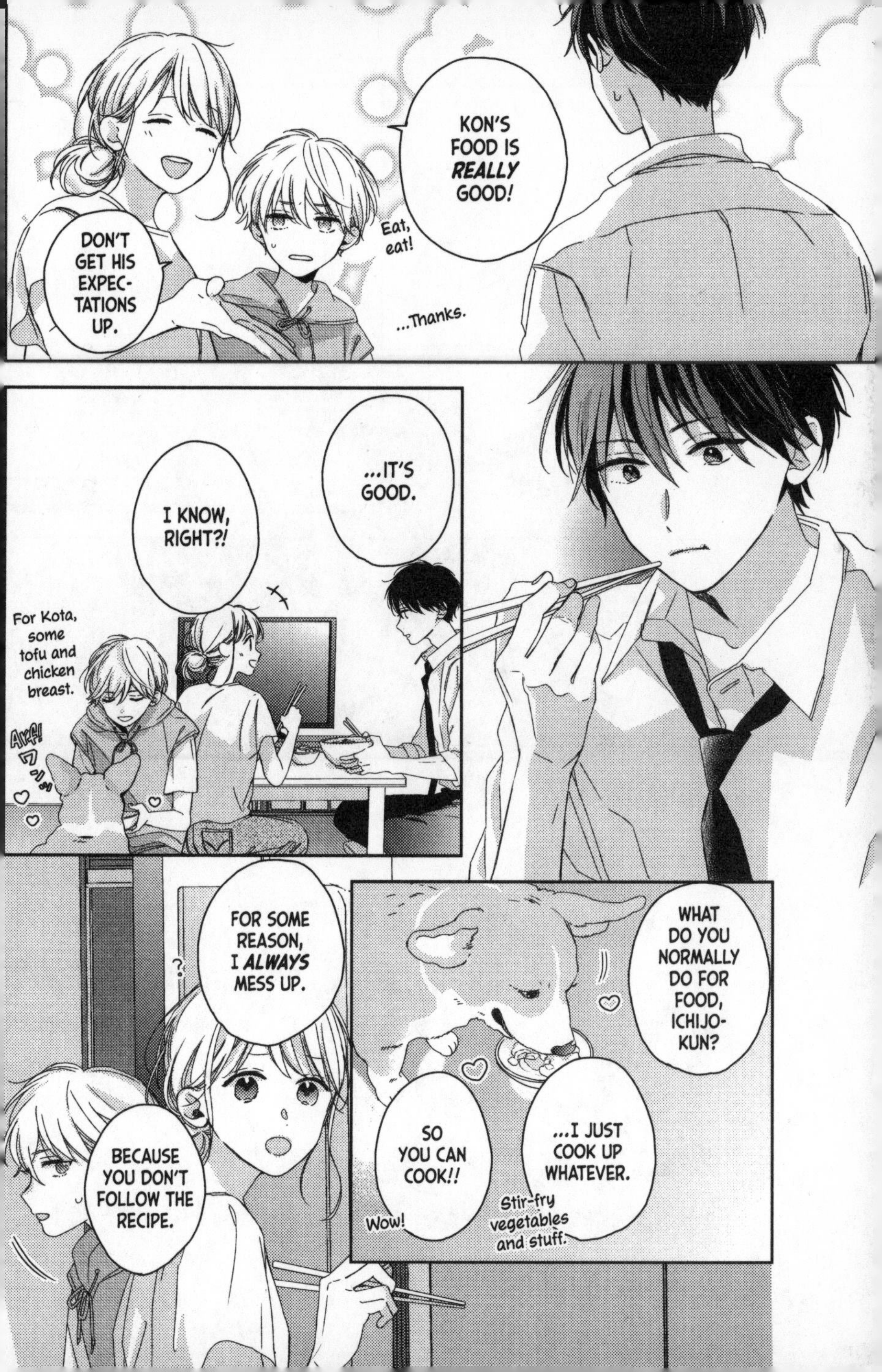
KON'S FOOD IS **REALLY** GOOD!
Eat, eat!
...Thanks.
DON'T GET HIS EXPECTATIONS UP.
...IT'S GOOD.
I KNOW, RIGHT?!
For Kota, some tofu and chicken breast.
Arf!
WHAT DO YOU NORMALLY DO FOR FOOD, ICHIJO-KUN?
...I JUST COOK UP WHATEVER.
Stir-fry vegetables and stuff.
SO YOU CAN COOK!!
Wow!
FOR SOME REASON, I **ALWAYS** MESS UP.
BECAUSE YOU DON'T FOLLOW THE RECIPE.

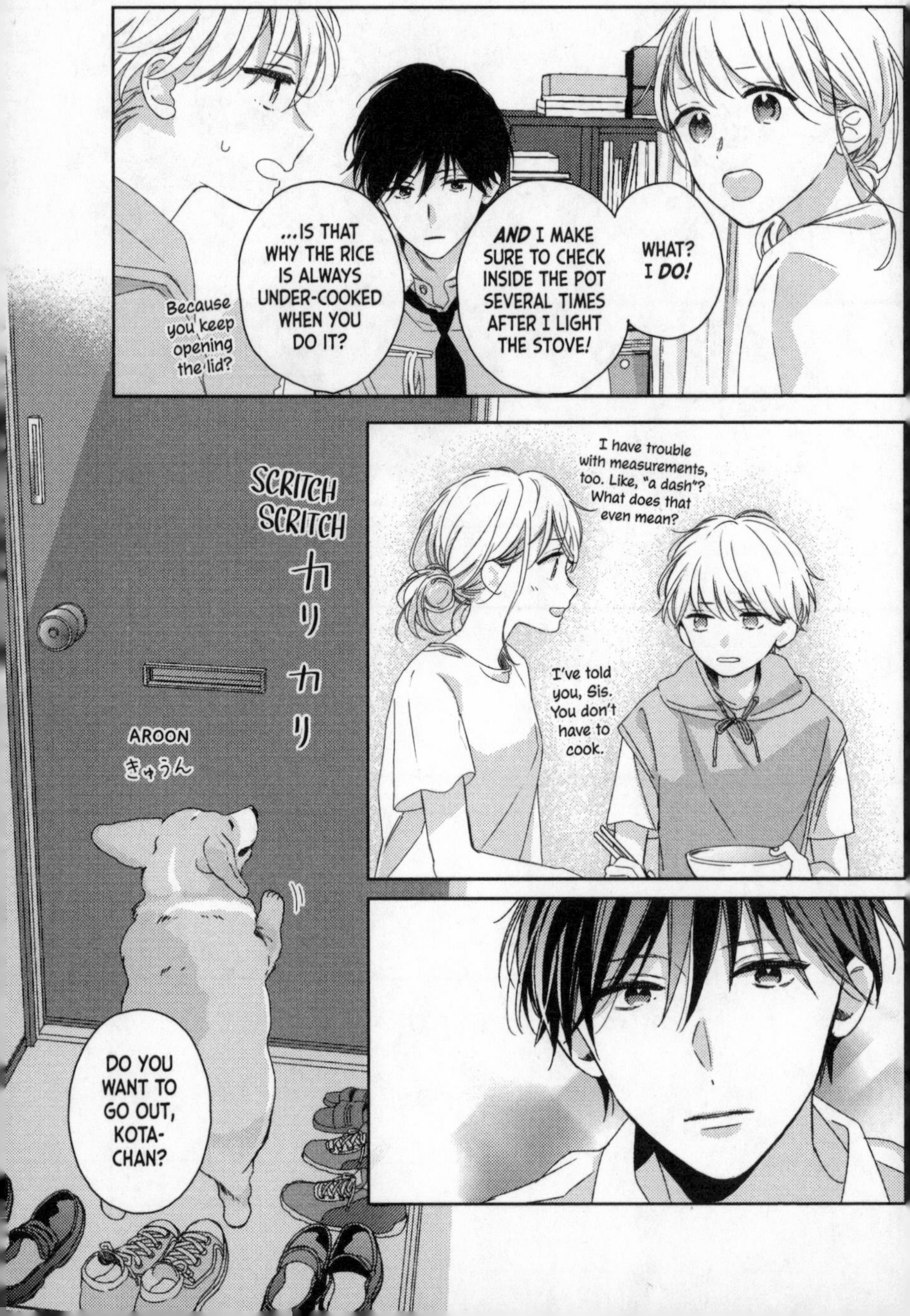
WHAT? I DO!
AND I MAKE SURE TO CHECK INSIDE THE POT SEVERAL TIMES AFTER I LIGHT THE STOVE!
...IS THAT WHY THE RICE IS ALWAYS UNDER-COOKED WHEN YOU DO IT?
Because you keep opening the lid?
I have trouble with measurements, too. Like, "a dash"? What does that even mean?
I've told you, Sis. You don't have to cook.
SCRITCH SCRITCH
カリカリ
AROON
きゅうん
DO YOU WANT TO GO OUT, KOTA-CHAN?

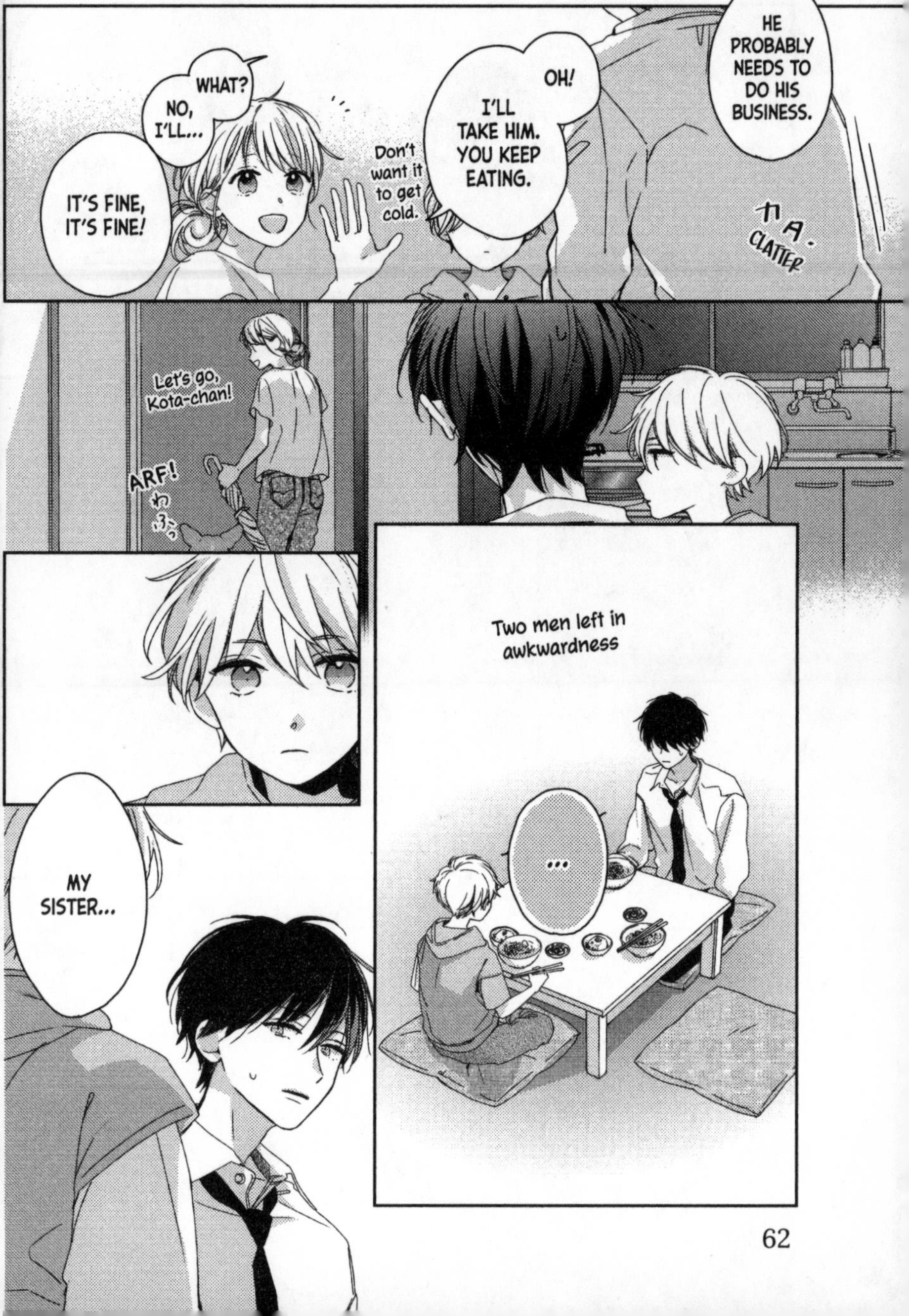
HE PROBABLY NEEDS TO DO HIS BUSINESS.
カタ
CLATTER
OH!
I'LL TAKE HIM. YOU KEEP EATING.
Don't want it to get cold.
WHAT?
NO, I'LL...
IT'S FINE, IT'S FINE!
Let's go, Kota-chan!
ARF!
わふっ
Two men left in awkwardness
...
MY SISTER...

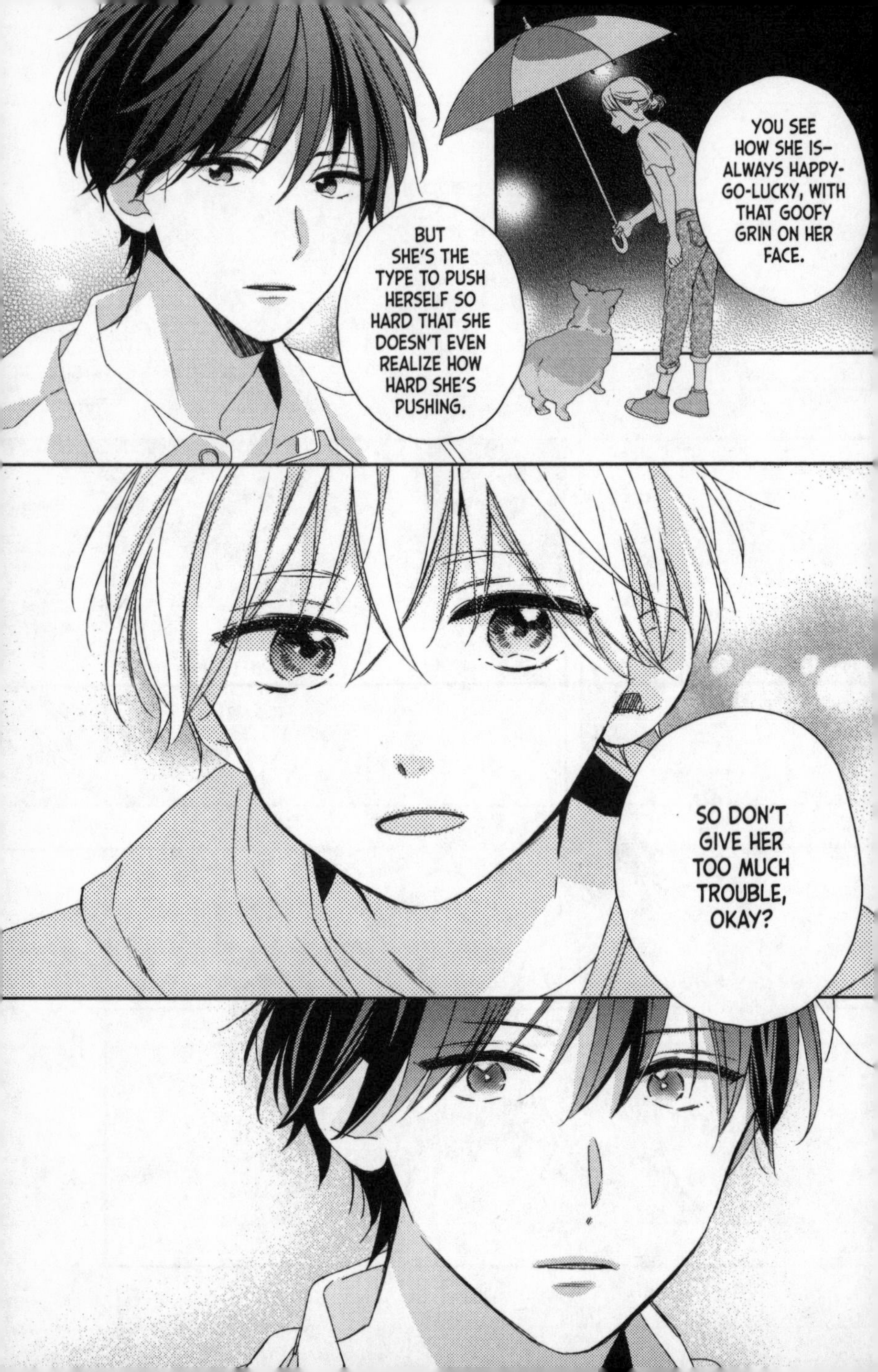
YOU SEE HOW SHE IS— ALWAYS HAPPY-GO-LUCKY, WITH THAT GOOFY GRIN ON HER FACE.
BUT SHE'S THE TYPE TO PUSH HERSELF SO HARD THAT SHE DOESN'T EVEN REALIZE HOW HARD SHE'S PUSHING.
SO DON'T GIVE HER TOO MUCH TROUBLE, OKAY?

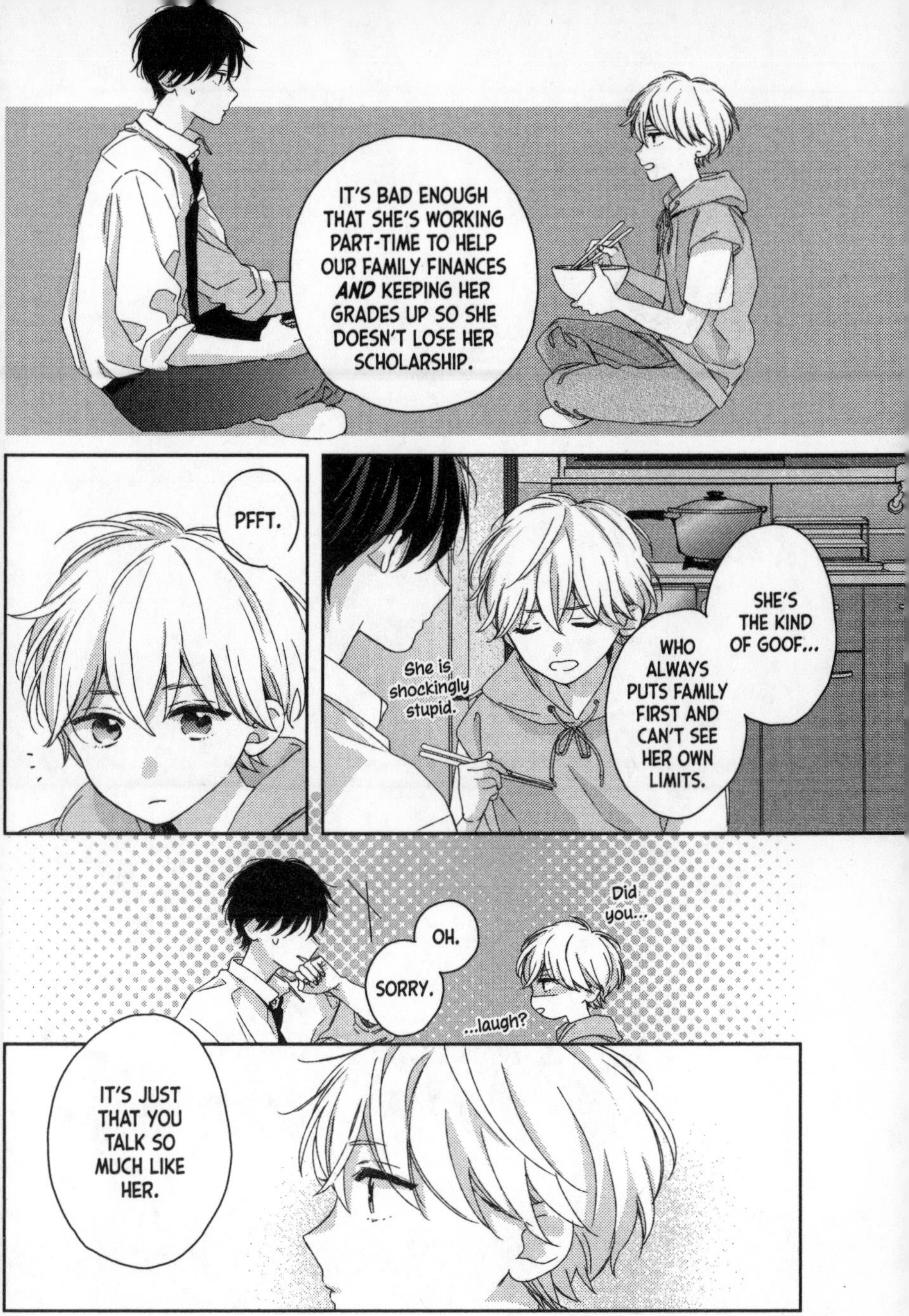
IT'S BAD ENOUGH THAT SHE'S WORKING PART-TIME TO HELP OUR FAMILY FINANCES *AND* KEEPING HER GRADES UP SO SHE DOESN'T LOSE HER SCHOLARSHIP.
SHE'S THE KIND OF GOOF...
WHO ALWAYS PUTS FAMILY FIRST AND CAN'T SEE HER OWN LIMITS.
She is shockingly stupid.
PFFT.
Did you...
OH.
SORRY.
...laugh?
IT'S JUST THAT YOU TALK SO MUCH LIKE HER.

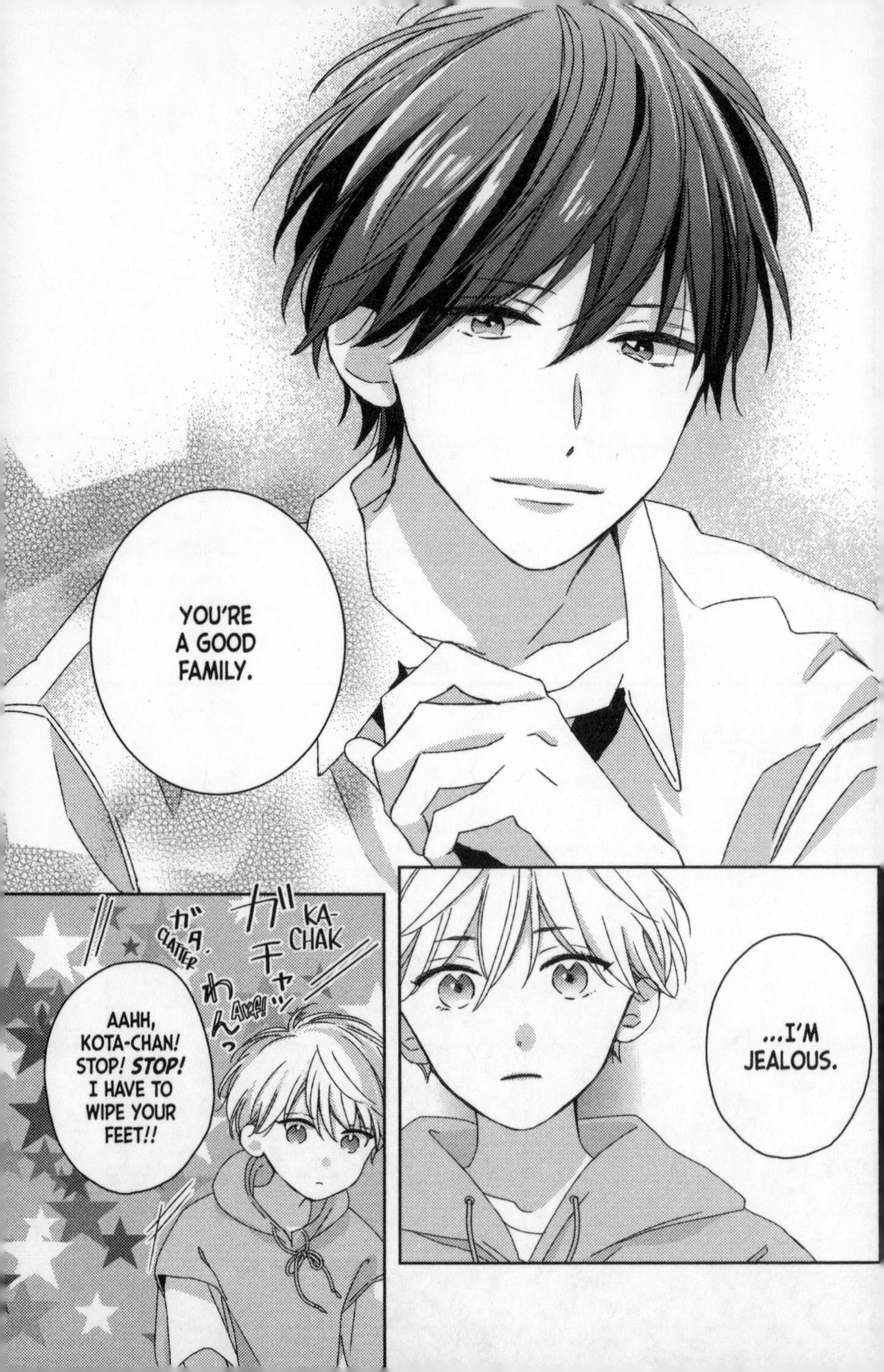
YOU'RE A GOOD FAMILY.
...I'M JEALOUS.
ガチャッ
KA-CHAK
ガタ
CLATTER
わんっ
ARF!
AAHH, KOTA-CHAN! STOP! **STOP!** I HAVE TO WIPE YOUR FEET!!

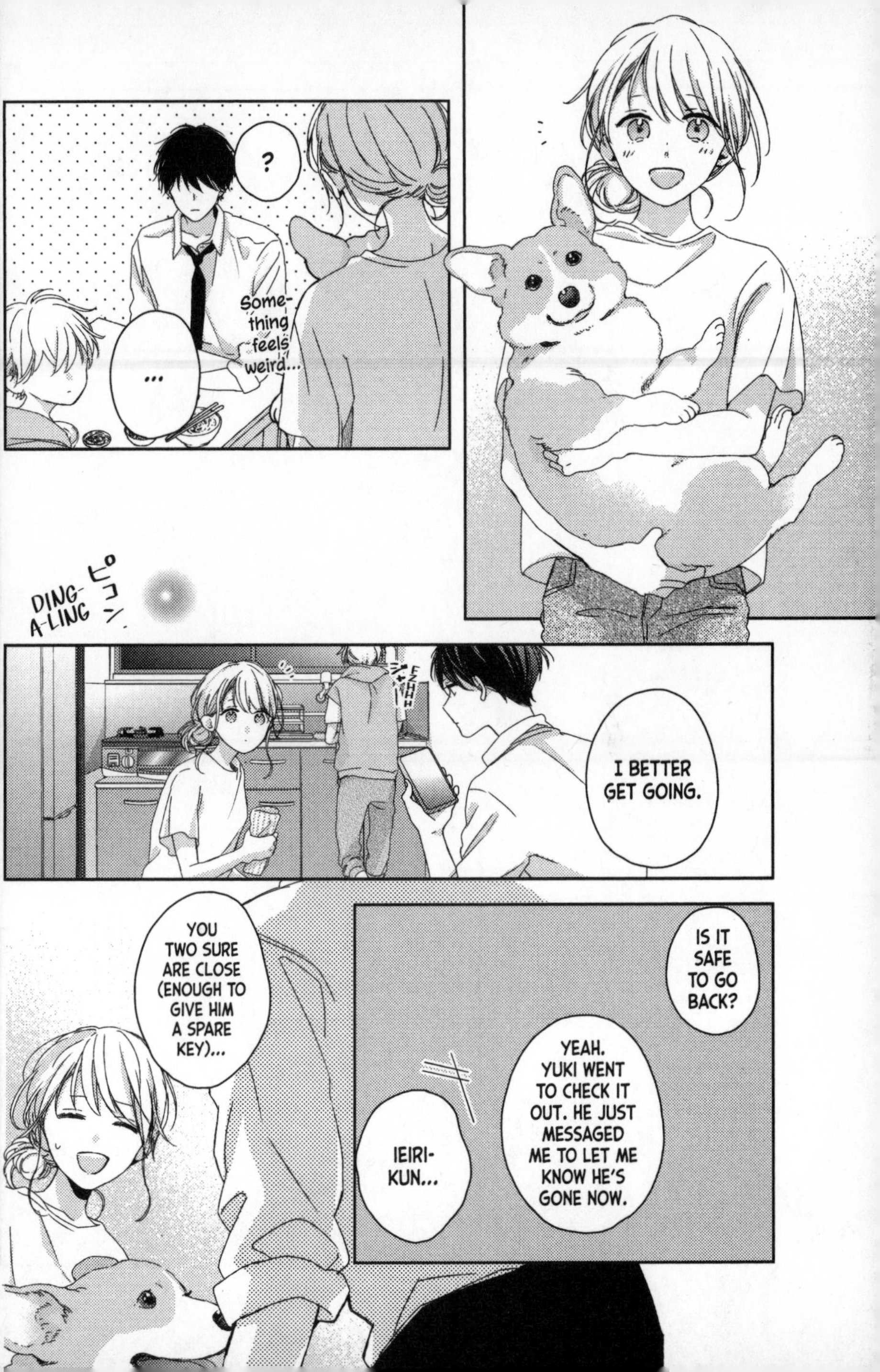
?
Something feels weird...
...
DING-A-LING ピコン
FZHHH
I BETTER GET GOING.
IS IT SAFE TO GO BACK?
YEAH. YUKI WENT TO CHECK IT OUT. HE JUST MESSAGED ME TO LET ME KNOW HE'S GONE NOW.
IEIRI-KUN...
YOU TWO SURE ARE CLOSE (ENOUGH TO GIVE HIM A SPARE KEY)...

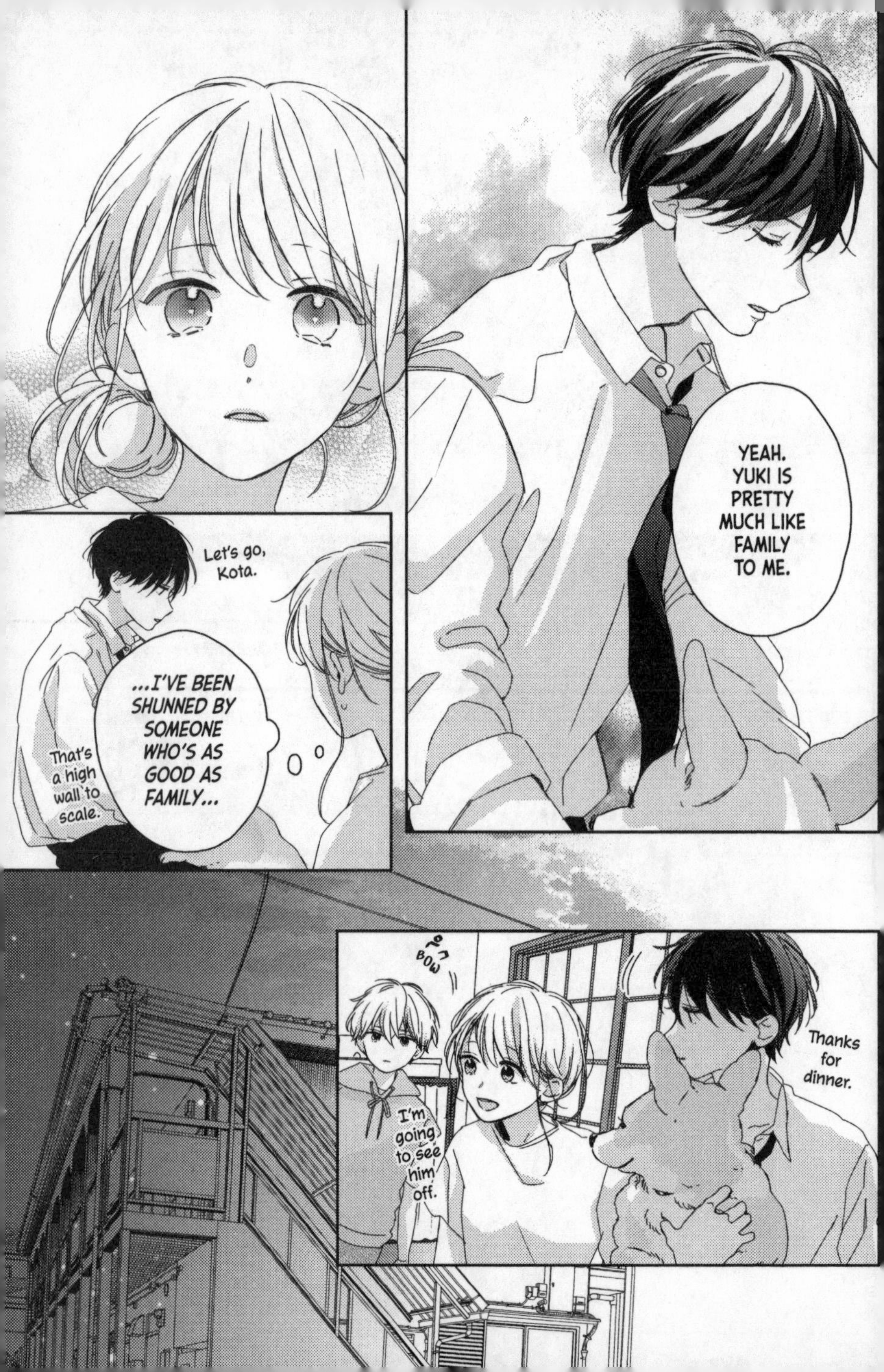
YEAH. YUKI IS PRETTY MUCH LIKE FAMILY TO ME.
Let's go, Kota.
...I'VE BEEN SHUNNED BY SOMEONE WHO'S AS GOOD AS FAMILY...
That's a high wall to scale.
Thanks for dinner.
BOW
I'm going to see him off.

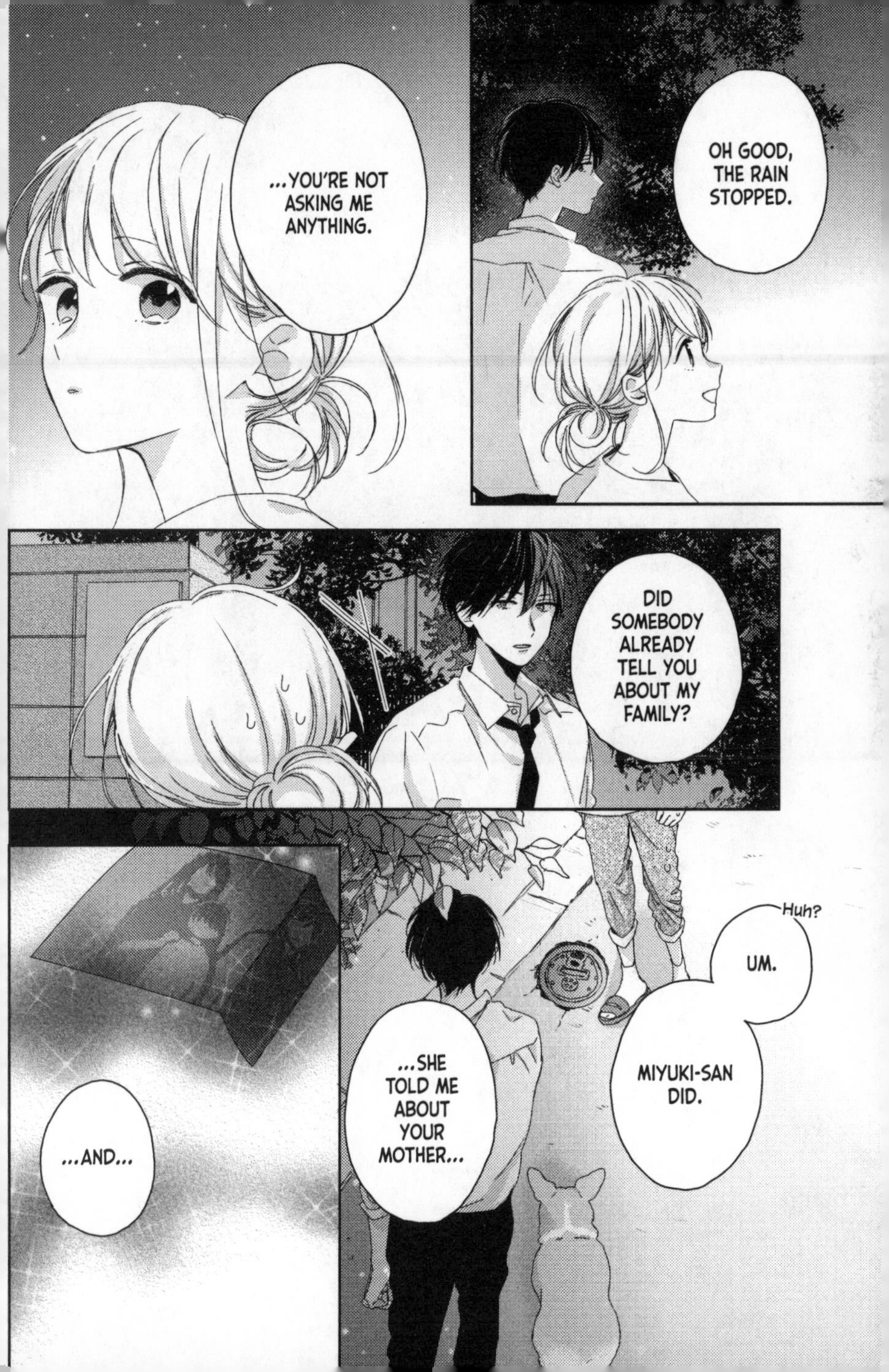
OH GOOD, THE RAIN STOPPED.
...YOU'RE NOT ASKING ME ANYTHING.
DID SOMEBODY ALREADY TELL YOU ABOUT MY FAMILY?
Huh?
UM.
MIYUKI-SAN DID.
...SHE TOLD ME ABOUT YOUR MOTHER...
...AND...

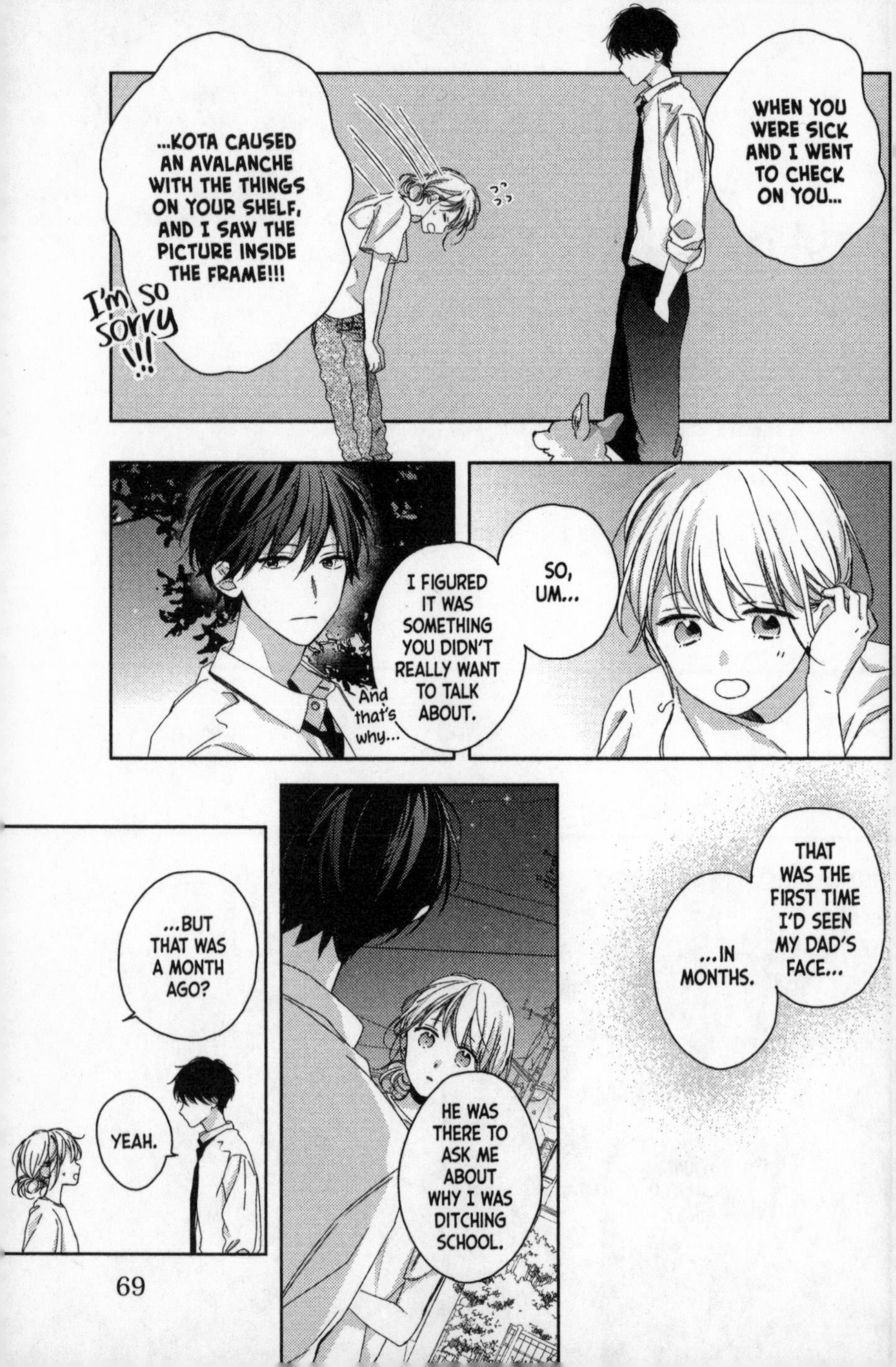
WHEN YOU WERE SICK AND I WENT TO CHECK ON YOU...
...KOTA CAUSED AN AVALANCHE WITH THE THINGS ON YOUR SHELF, AND I SAW THE PICTURE INSIDE THE FRAME!!!
I'm so sorry!!!
SO, UM...
I FIGURED IT WAS SOMETHING YOU DIDN'T REALLY WANT TO TALK ABOUT.
And that's why...
THAT WAS THE FIRST TIME I'D SEEN MY DAD'S FACE...
...IN MONTHS.
HE WAS THERE TO ASK ME ABOUT WHY I WAS DITCHING SCHOOL.
...BUT THAT WAS A MONTH AGO?
YEAH.

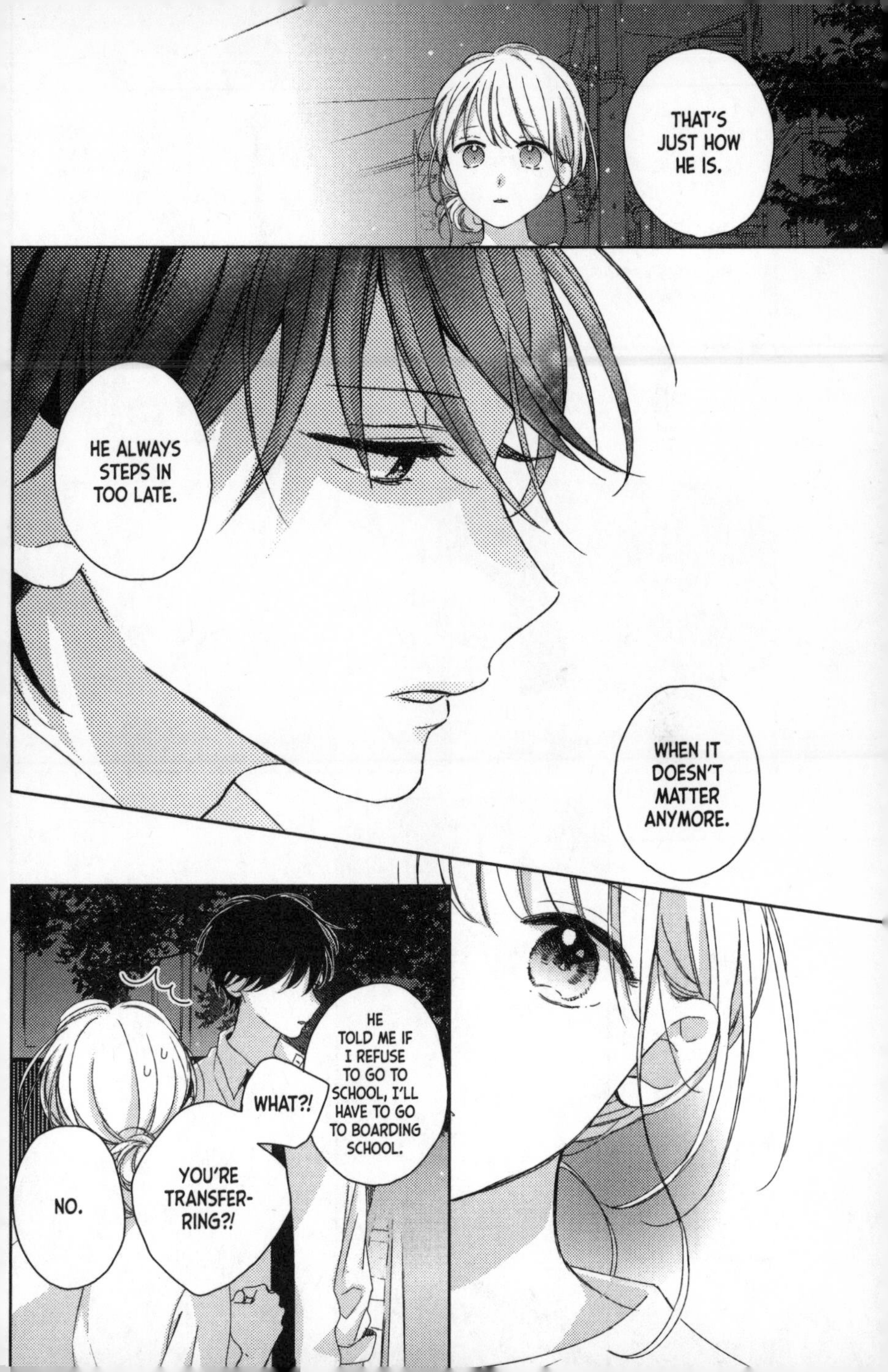
THAT'S JUST HOW HE IS.
HE ALWAYS STEPS IN TOO LATE.
WHEN IT DOESN'T MATTER ANYMORE.
HE TOLD ME IF I REFUSE TO GO TO SCHOOL, I'LL HAVE TO GO TO BOARDING SCHOOL.
WHAT?!
YOU'RE TRANSFER-RING?!
NO.

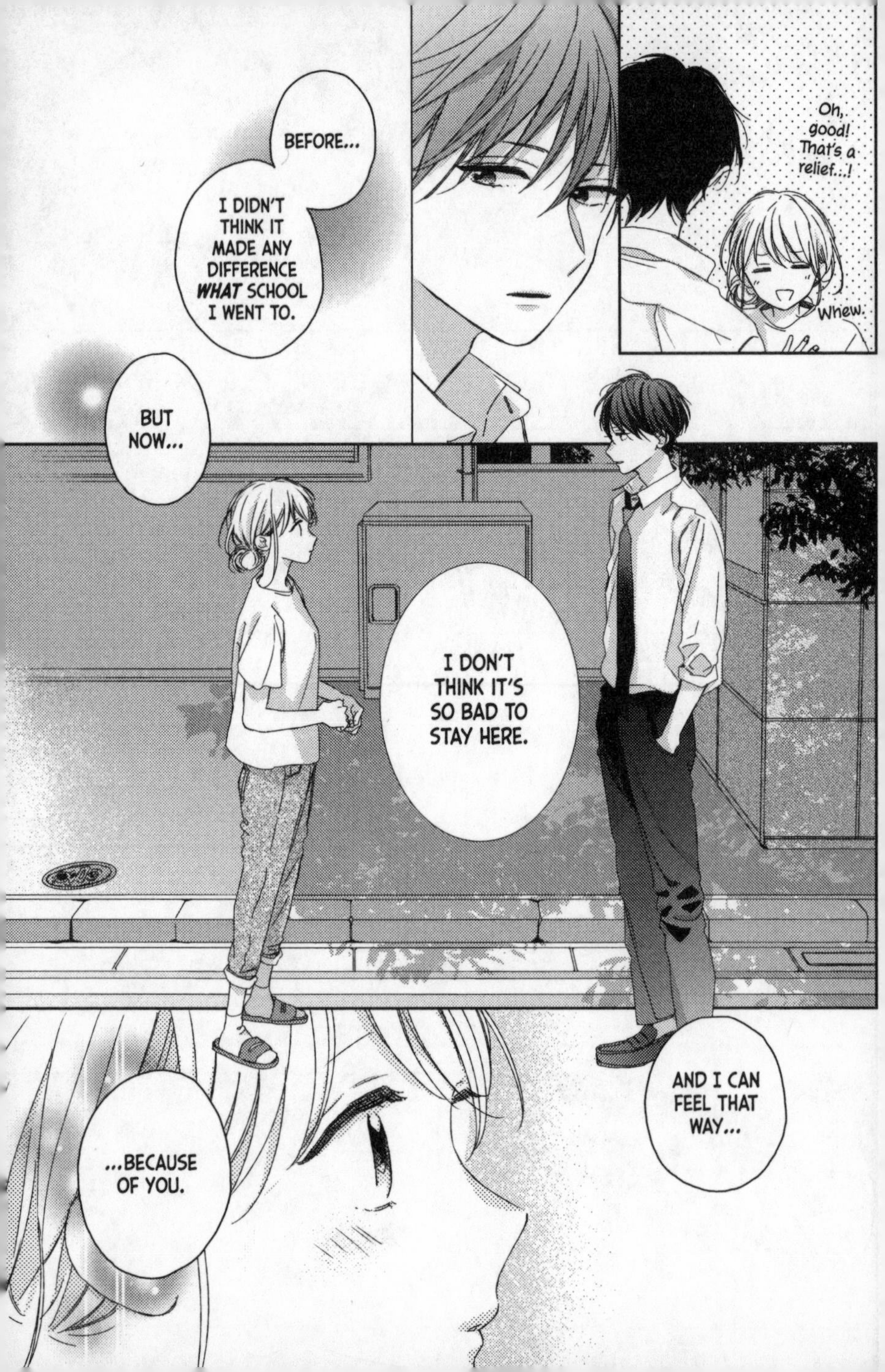
Oh, good! That's a relief...!
Whew.
BEFORE...
I DIDN'T THINK IT MADE ANY DIFFERENCE ***WHAT*** SCHOOL I WENT TO.
BUT NOW...
I DON'T THINK IT'S SO BAD TO STAY HERE.
AND I CAN FEEL THAT WAY...
...BECAUSE OF YOU.

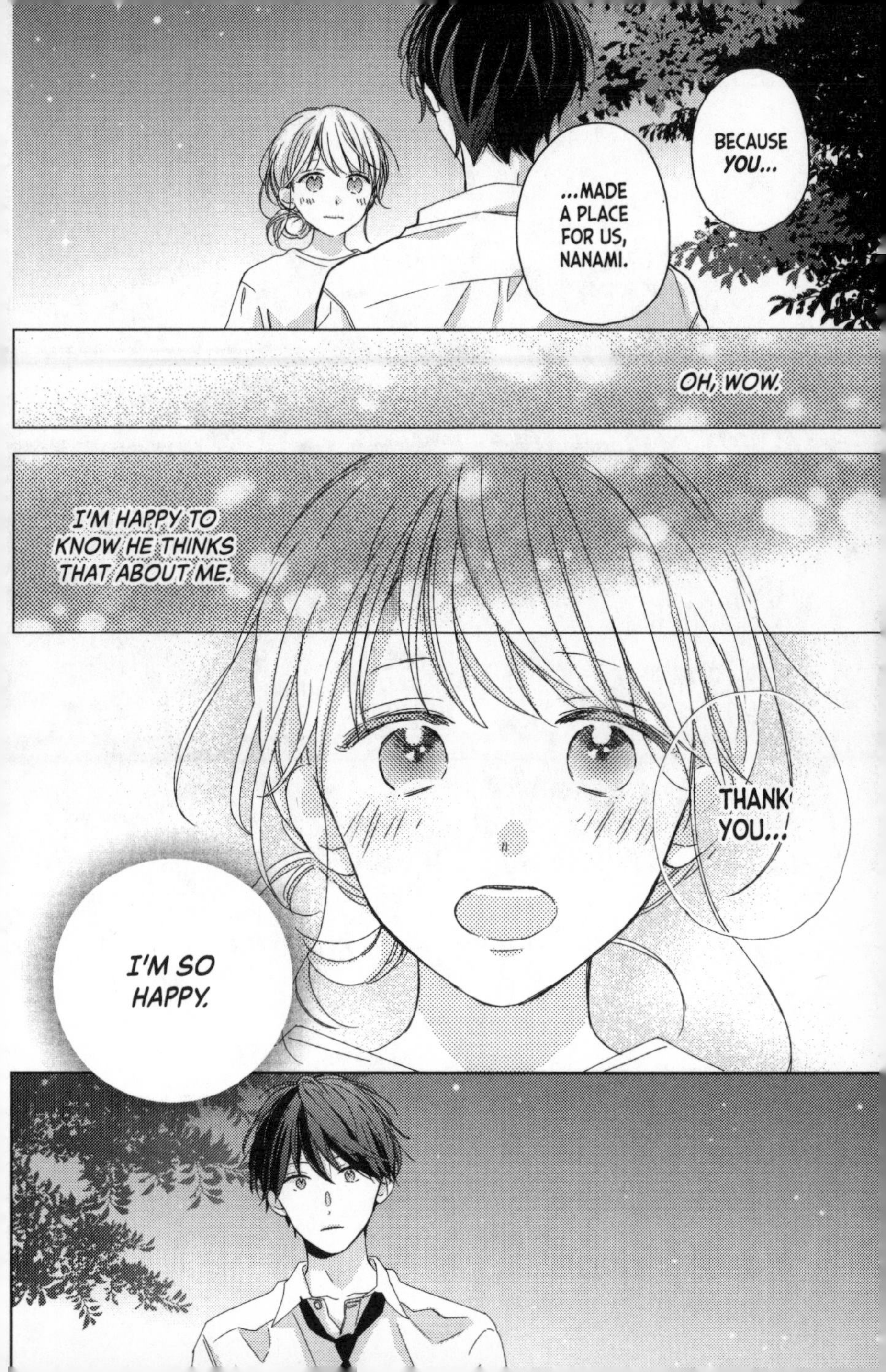
BECAUSE YOU...
...MADE A PLACE FOR US, NANAMI.
OH, WOW.
I'M HAPPY TO KNOW HE THINKS THAT ABOUT ME.
THANK YOU...!
I'M SO HAPPY.

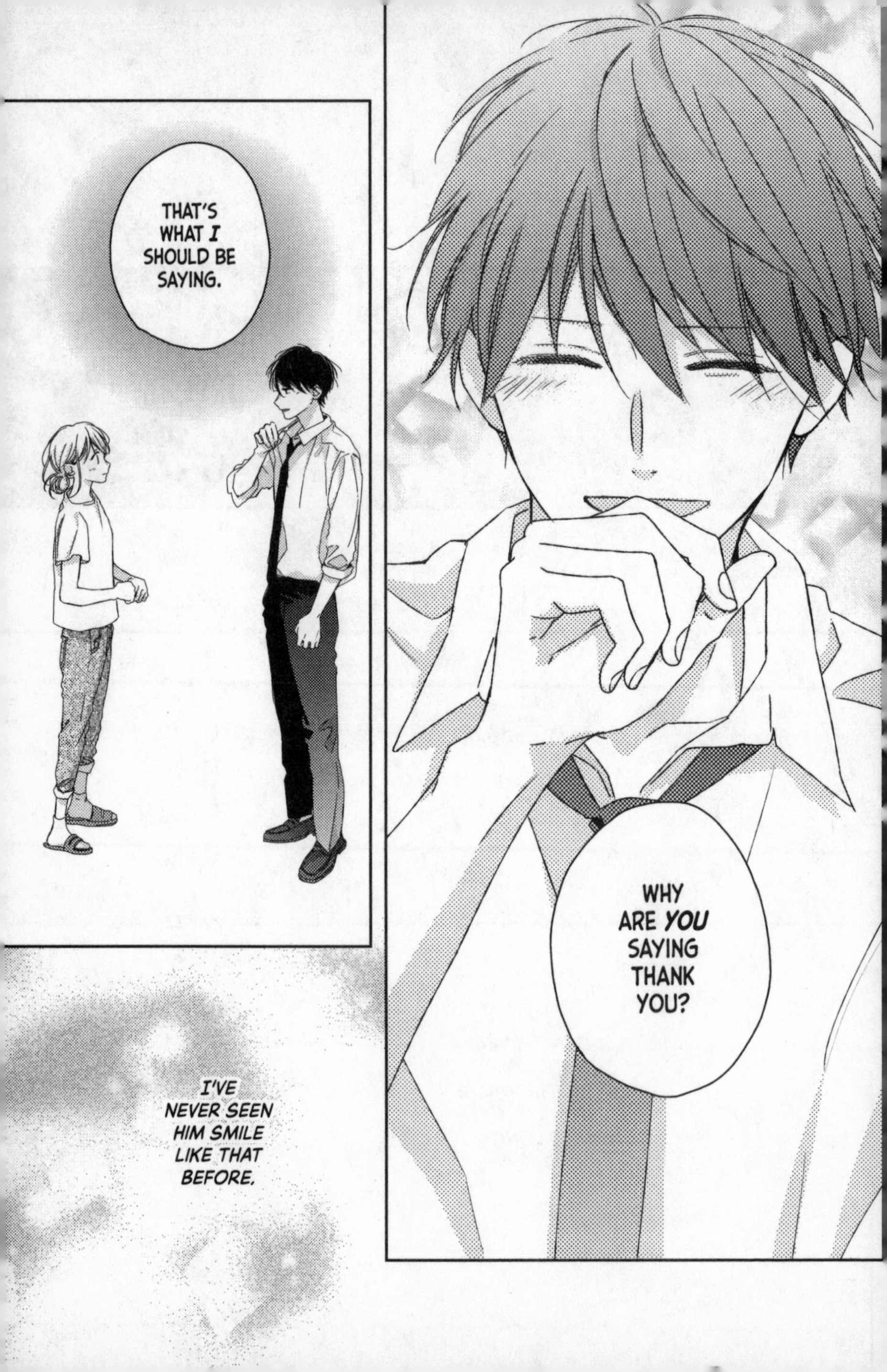
WHY ARE *YOU* SAYING THANK YOU?
THAT'S WHAT *I* SHOULD BE SAYING.
I'VE NEVER SEEN HIM SMILE LIKE THAT BEFORE.

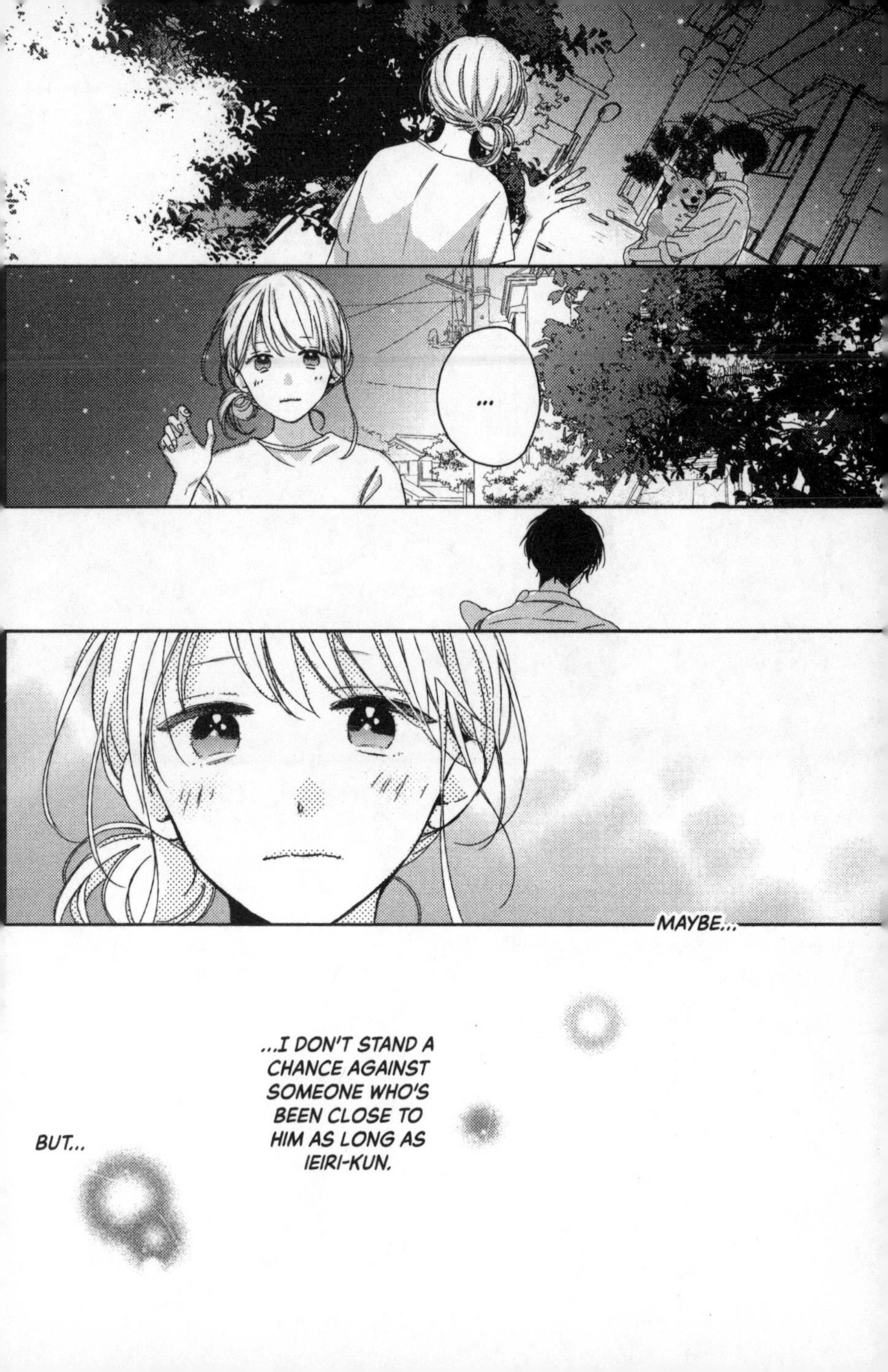
...
MAYBE...
...I DON'T STAND A CHANCE AGAINST SOMEONE WHO'S BEEN CLOSE TO HIM AS LONG AS IEIRI-KUN.
BUT...

"BECAUSE OF YOU."
I BET THERE IS SOMETHING I CAN DO FOR HIM, TOO.
ICHIJO-KUN SMILED.
I REALLY LIKE THAT.
I WANT TO SEE MORE OF THAT.
I WANT HIM TO SMILE...

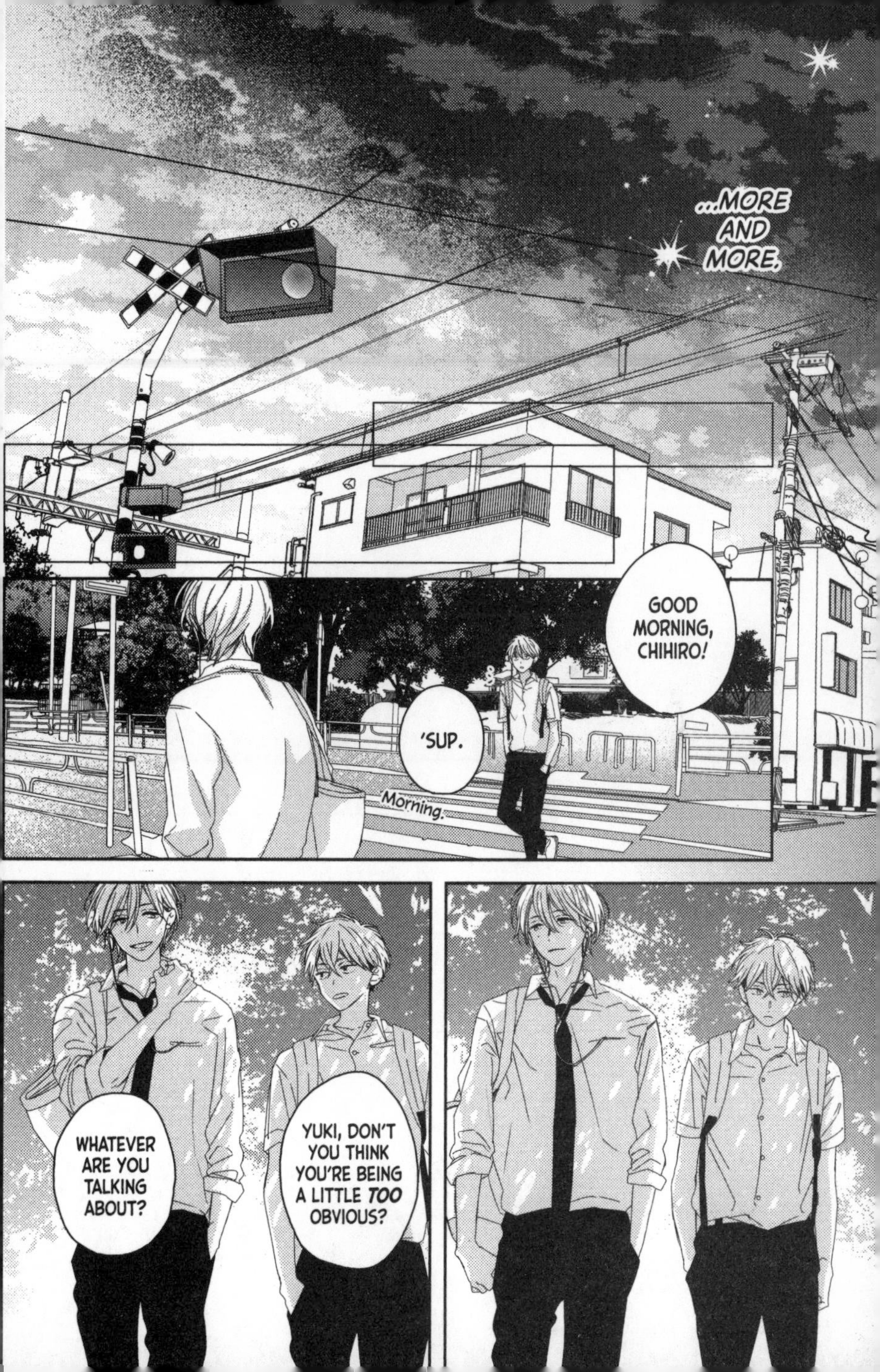
...MORE AND MORE.
GOOD MORNING, CHIHIRO!
'SUP.
Morning.
YUKI, DON'T YOU THINK YOU'RE BEING A LITTLE *TOO* OBVIOUS?
WHATEVER ARE YOU TALKING ABOUT?

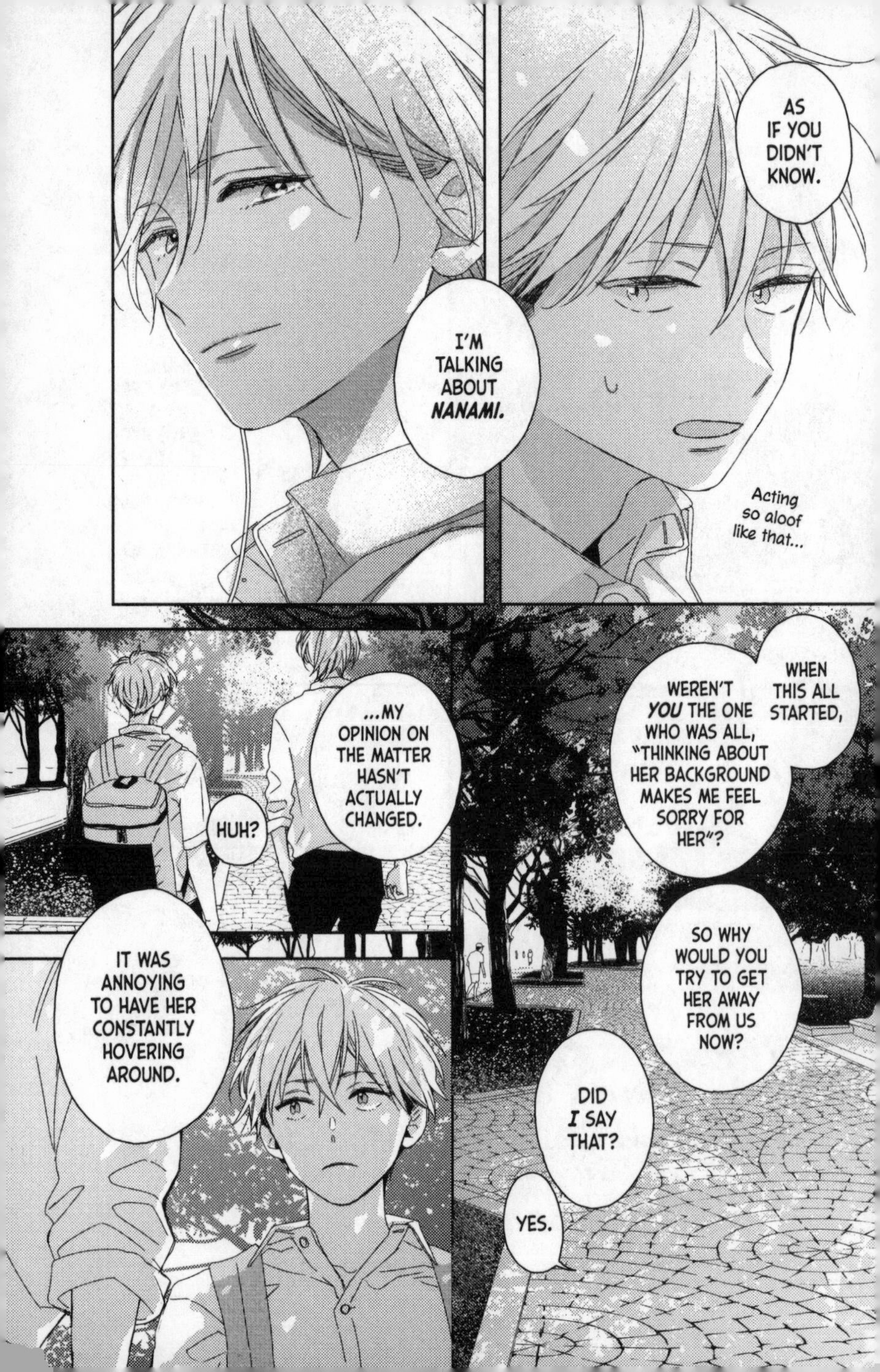
AS IF YOU DIDN'T KNOW.
Acting so aloof like that...
I'M TALKING ABOUT NANAMI.
WHEN THIS ALL STARTED,
WEREN'T YOU THE ONE WHO WAS ALL, "THINKING ABOUT HER BACKGROUND MAKES ME FEEL SORRY FOR HER"?
SO WHY WOULD YOU TRY TO GET HER AWAY FROM US NOW?
DID I SAY THAT?
YES.
...MY OPINION ON THE MATTER HASN'T ACTUALLY CHANGED.
HUH?
IT WAS ANNOYING TO HAVE HER CONSTANTLY HOVERING AROUND.

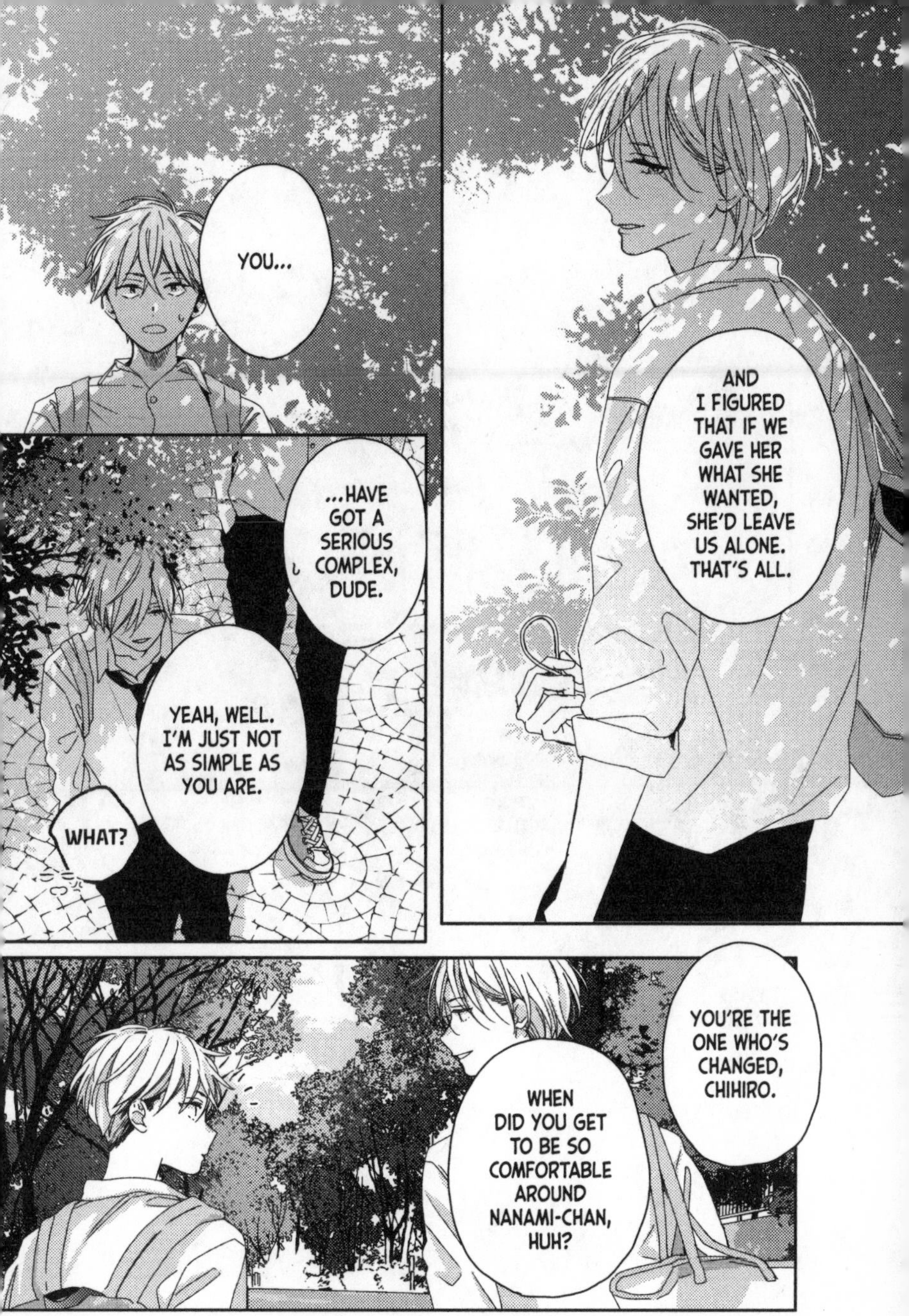
AND I FIGURED THAT IF WE GAVE HER WHAT SHE WANTED, SHE'D LEAVE US ALONE. THAT'S ALL.
YOU...
...HAVE GOT A SERIOUS COMPLEX, DUDE.
YEAH, WELL. I'M JUST NOT AS SIMPLE AS YOU ARE.
WHAT?
YOU'RE THE ONE WHO'S CHANGED, CHIHIRO.
WHEN DID YOU GET TO BE SO COMFORTABLE AROUND NANAMI-CHAN, HUH?

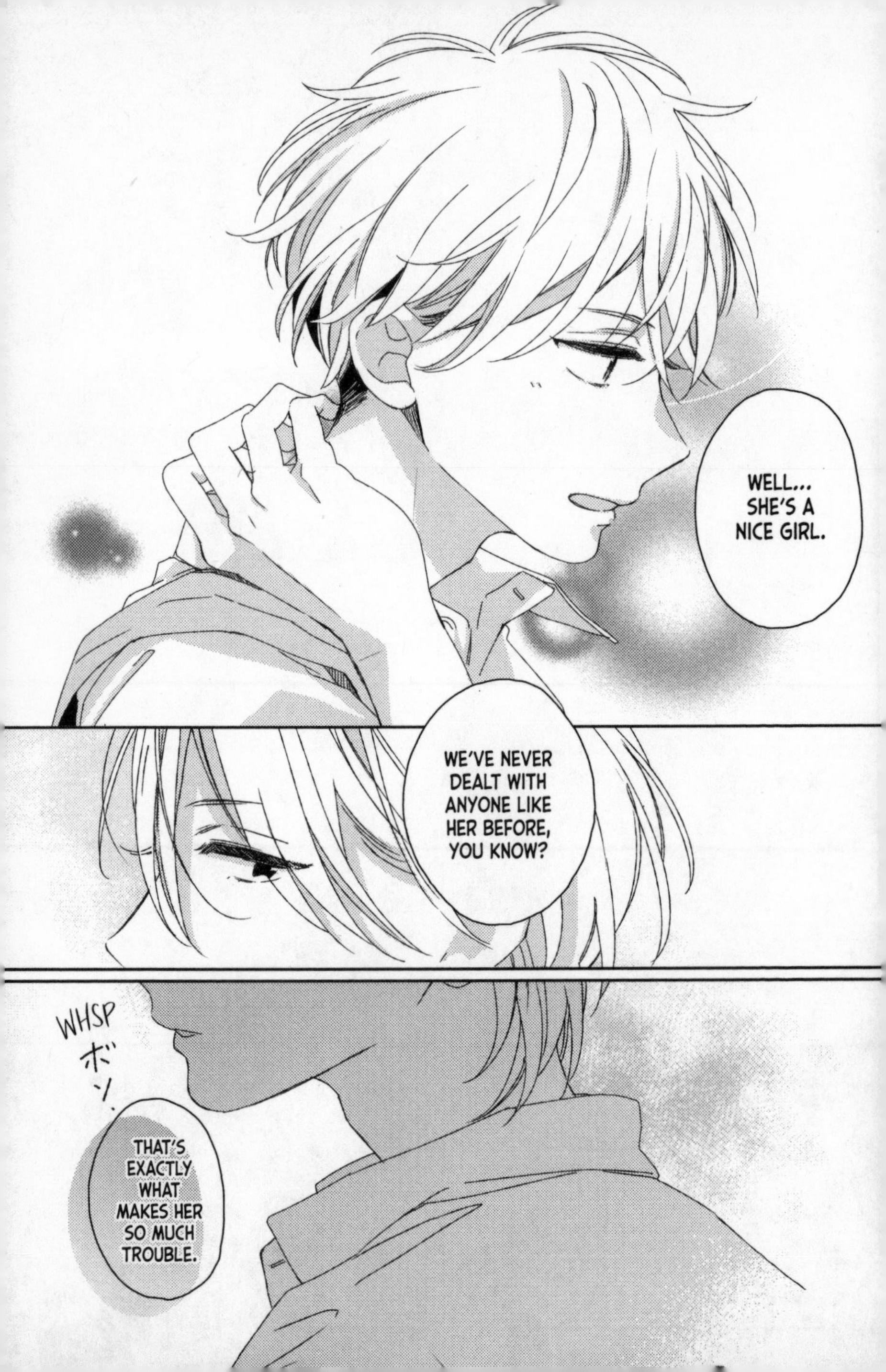
WELL... SHE'S A NICE GIRL.
WE'VE NEVER DEALT WITH ANYONE LIKE HER BEFORE, YOU KNOW?
WHSP
ボン.
THAT'S EXACTLY WHAT MAKES HER SO MUCH TROUBLE.

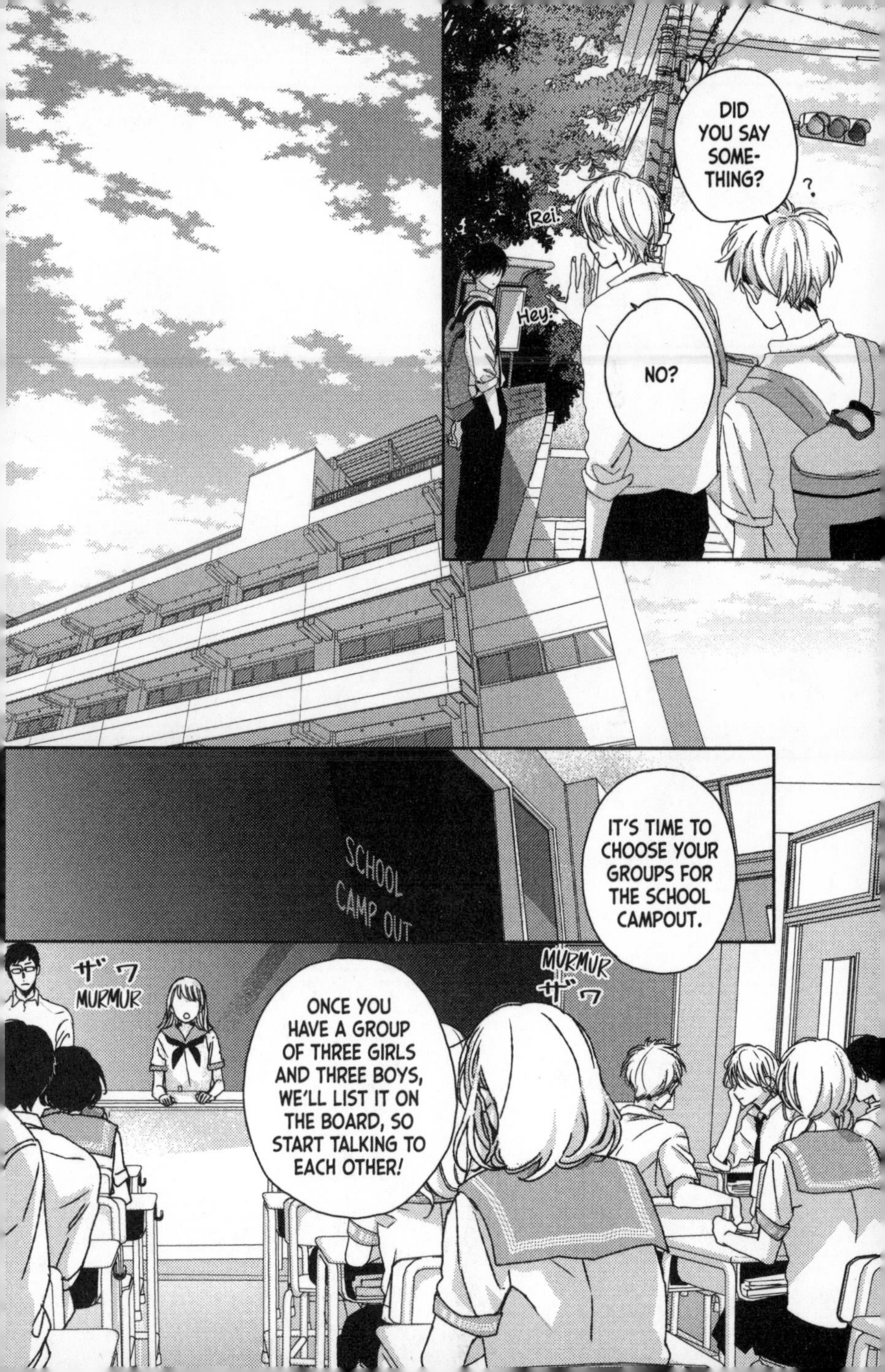
DID YOU SAY SOME-THING?
?
Rei.
Hey.
NO?
IT'S TIME TO CHOOSE YOUR GROUPS FOR THE SCHOOL CAMPOUT.
SCHOOL CAMP OUT
MURMUR ザワ
ONCE YOU HAVE A GROUP OF THREE GIRLS AND THREE BOYS, WE'LL LIST IT ON THE BOARD, SO START TALKING TO EACH OTHER!
ザワ MURMUR

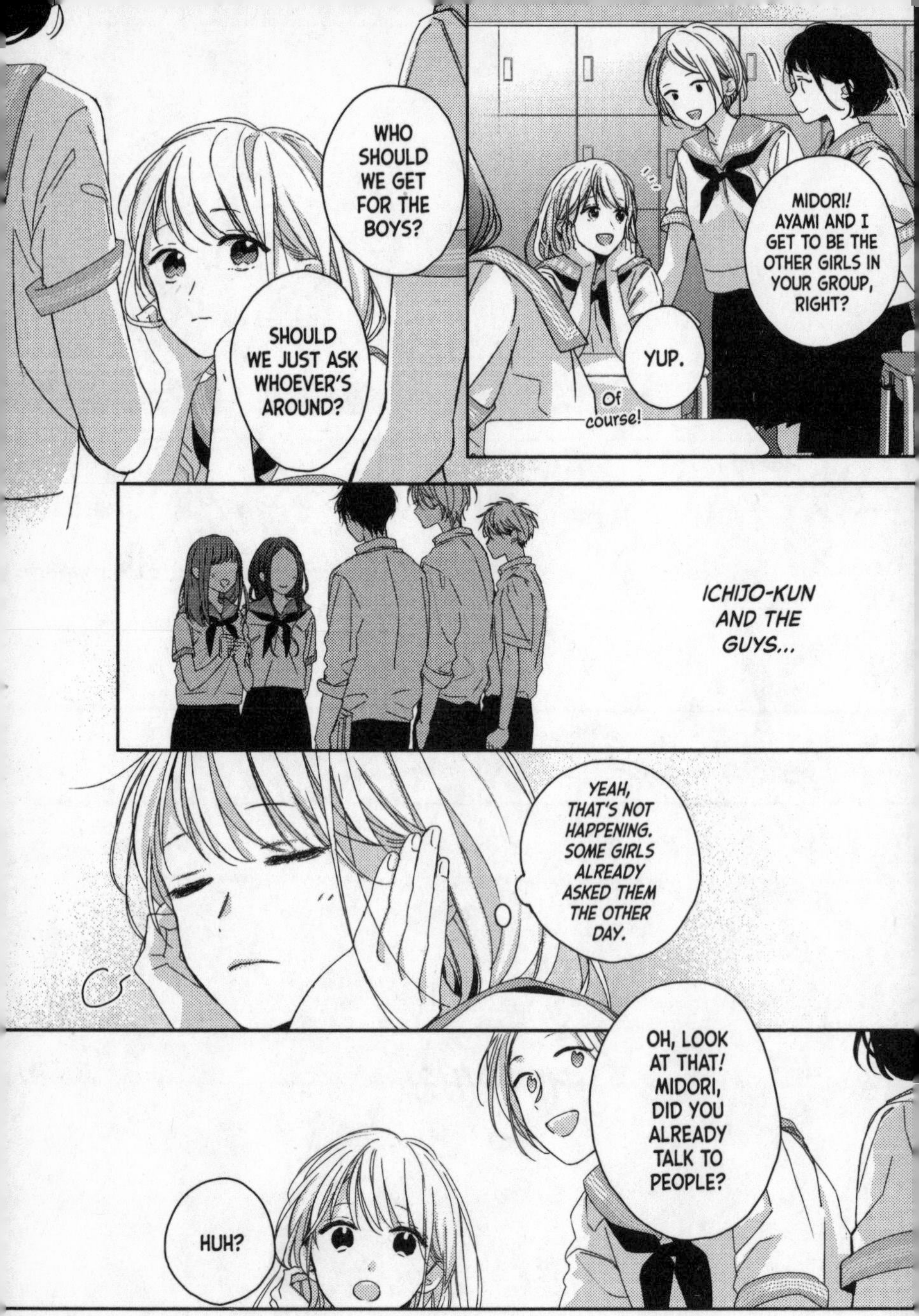
MIDORI! AYAMI AND I GET TO BE THE OTHER GIRLS IN YOUR GROUP, RIGHT?
YUP.
Of course!
WHO SHOULD WE GET FOR THE BOYS?
SHOULD WE JUST ASK WHOEVER'S AROUND?
ICHIJO-KUN AND THE GUYS...
YEAH, THAT'S NOT HAPPENING. SOME GIRLS ALREADY ASKED THEM THE OTHER DAY.
OH, LOOK AT THAT! MIDORI, DID YOU ALREADY TALK TO PEOPLE?
HUH?

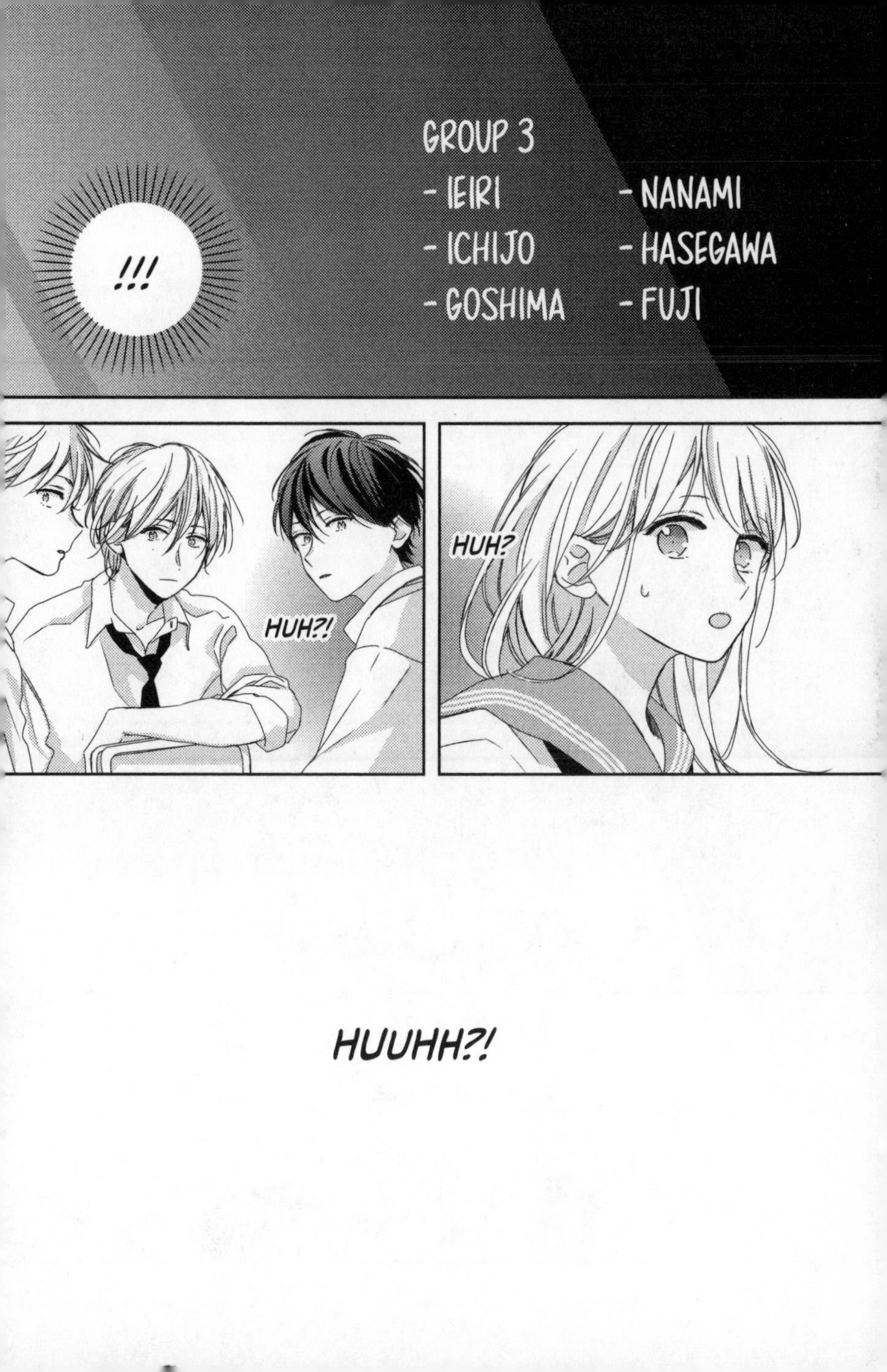
GROUP 3
- IEIRI
- ICHIJO
- GOSHIMA
- NANAMI
- HASEGAWA
- FUJI
!!!
HUH?
HUH?!
HUUHH?!

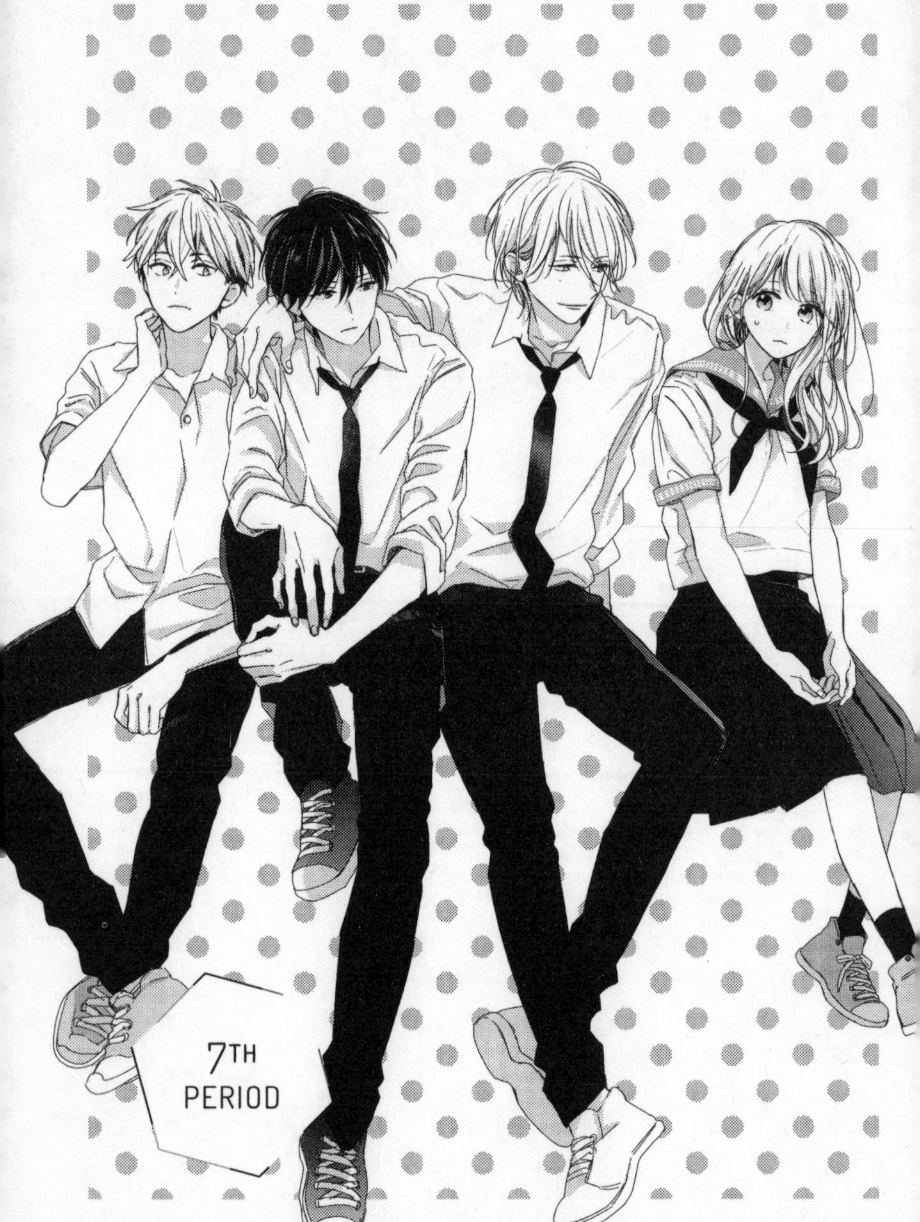
7TH
PERIOD

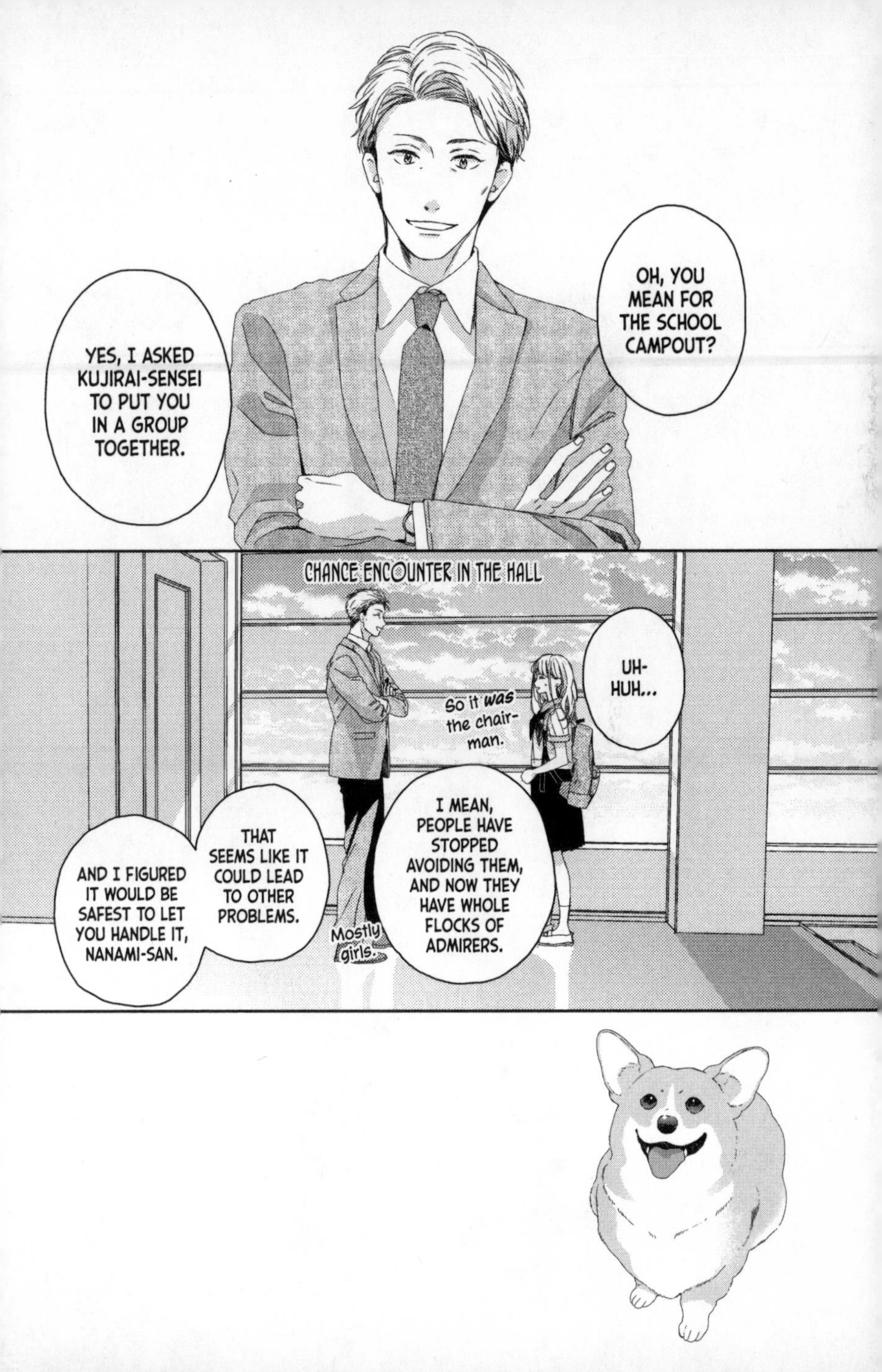
OH, YOU MEAN FOR THE SCHOOL CAMPOUT?
YES, I ASKED KUJIRAI-SENSEI TO PUT YOU IN A GROUP TOGETHER.
CHANCE ENCOUNTER IN THE HALL
UH-HUH...
So it *was* the chairman.
I MEAN, PEOPLE HAVE STOPPED AVOIDING THEM, AND NOW THEY HAVE WHOLE FLOCKS OF ADMIRERS.
Mostly girls.
THAT SEEMS LIKE IT COULD LEAD TO OTHER PROBLEMS.
AND I FIGURED IT WOULD BE SAFEST TO LET YOU HANDLE IT, NANAMI-SAN.

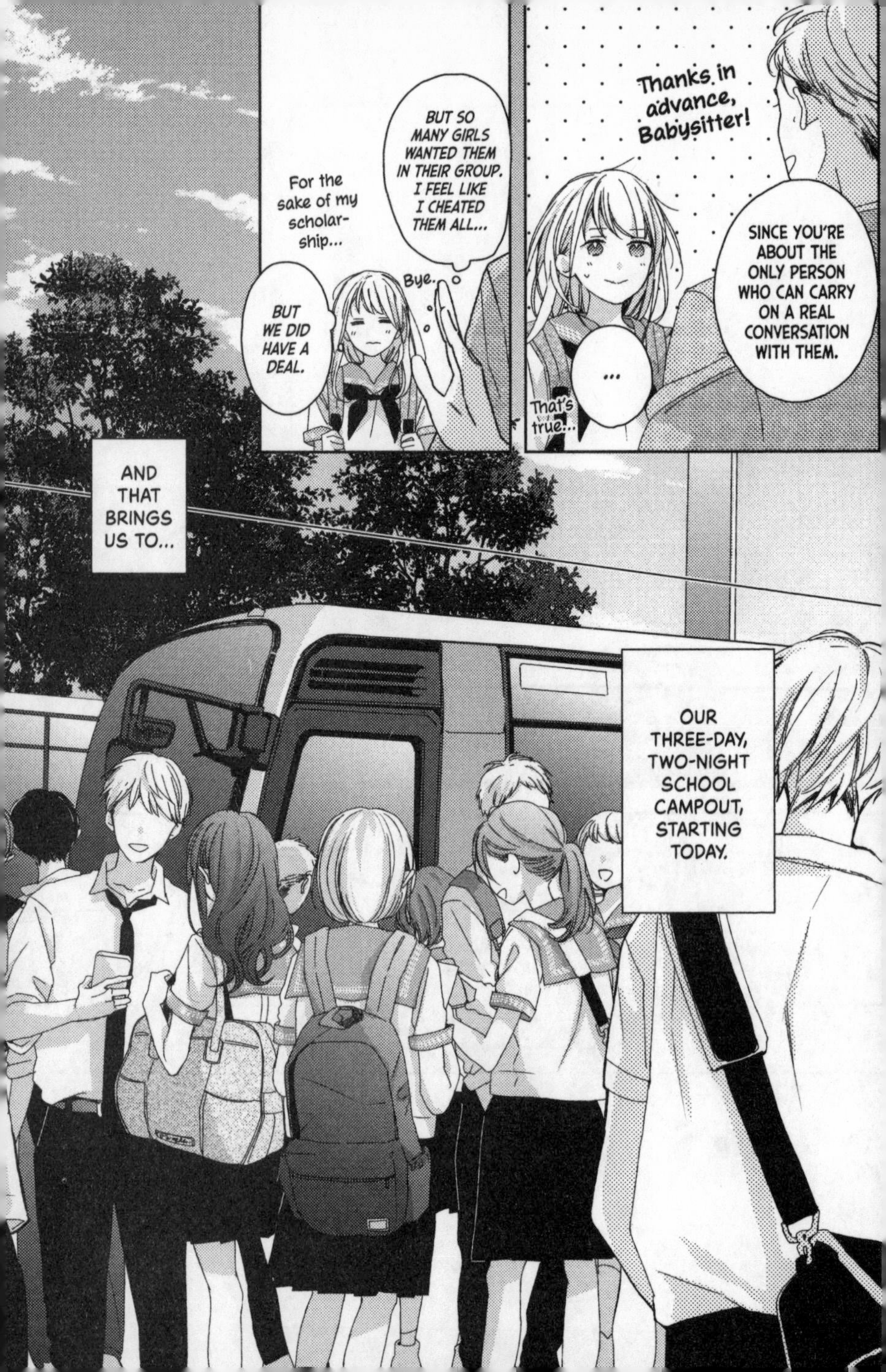
Thanks in advance, Babysitter!
SINCE YOU'RE ABOUT THE ONLY PERSON WHO CAN CARRY ON A REAL CONVERSATION WITH THEM.
...
That's true...
BUT SO MANY GIRLS WANTED THEM IN THEIR GROUP. I FEEL LIKE I CHEATED THEM ALL...
For the sake of my scholar-ship...
Bye.
BUT WE DID HAVE A DEAL.
AND THAT BRINGS US TO...
OUR THREE-DAY, TWO-NIGHT SCHOOL CAMPOUT, STARTING TODAY.

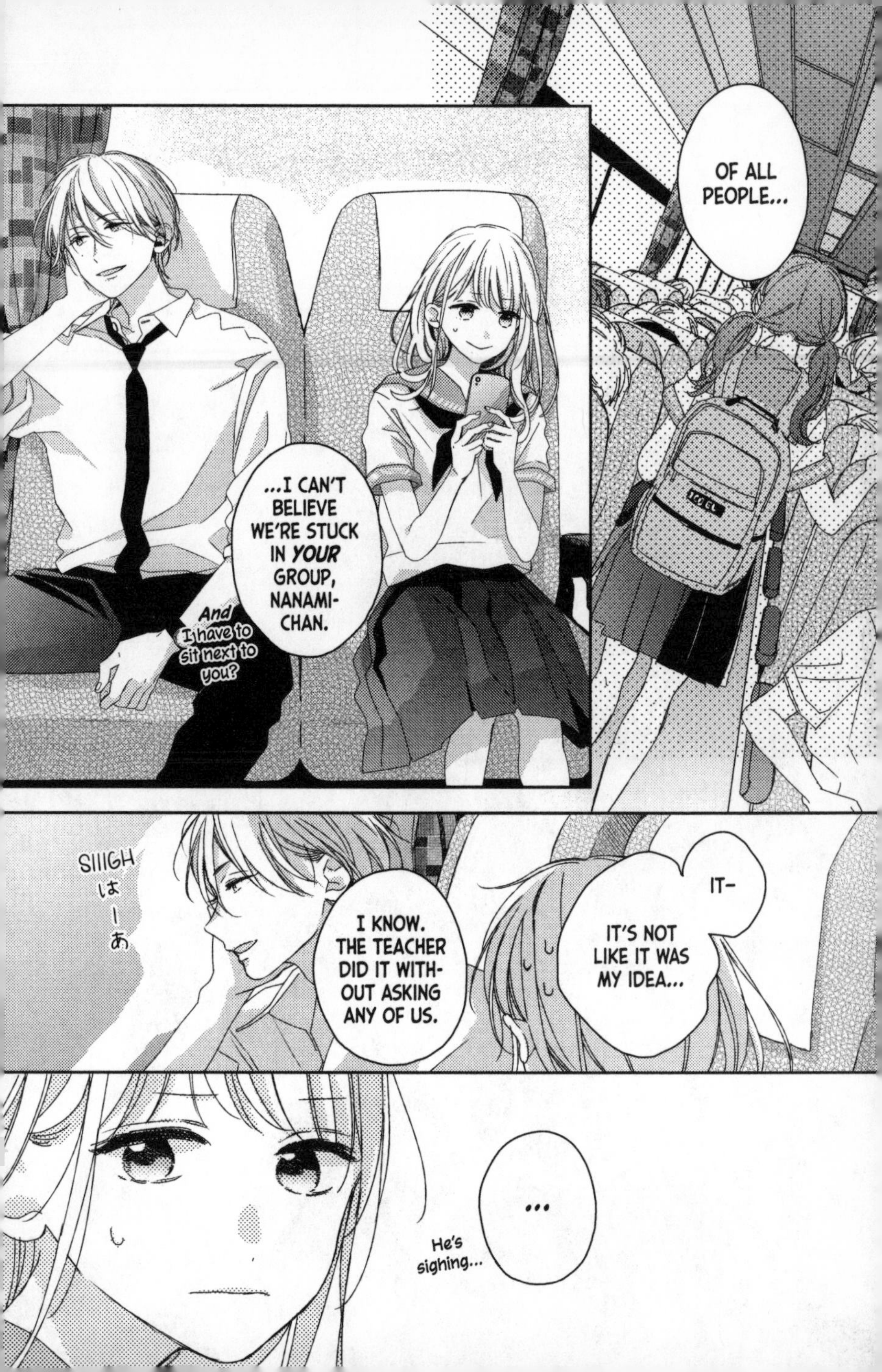
OF ALL PEOPLE...
...I CAN'T BELIEVE WE'RE STUCK IN *YOUR* GROUP, NANAMI-CHAN.
And I have to sit next to you?
IT–
IT'S NOT LIKE IT WAS MY IDEA...
I KNOW. THE TEACHER DID IT WITH-OUT ASKING ANY OF US.
SIIIGH
はーあ
...
He's sighing...

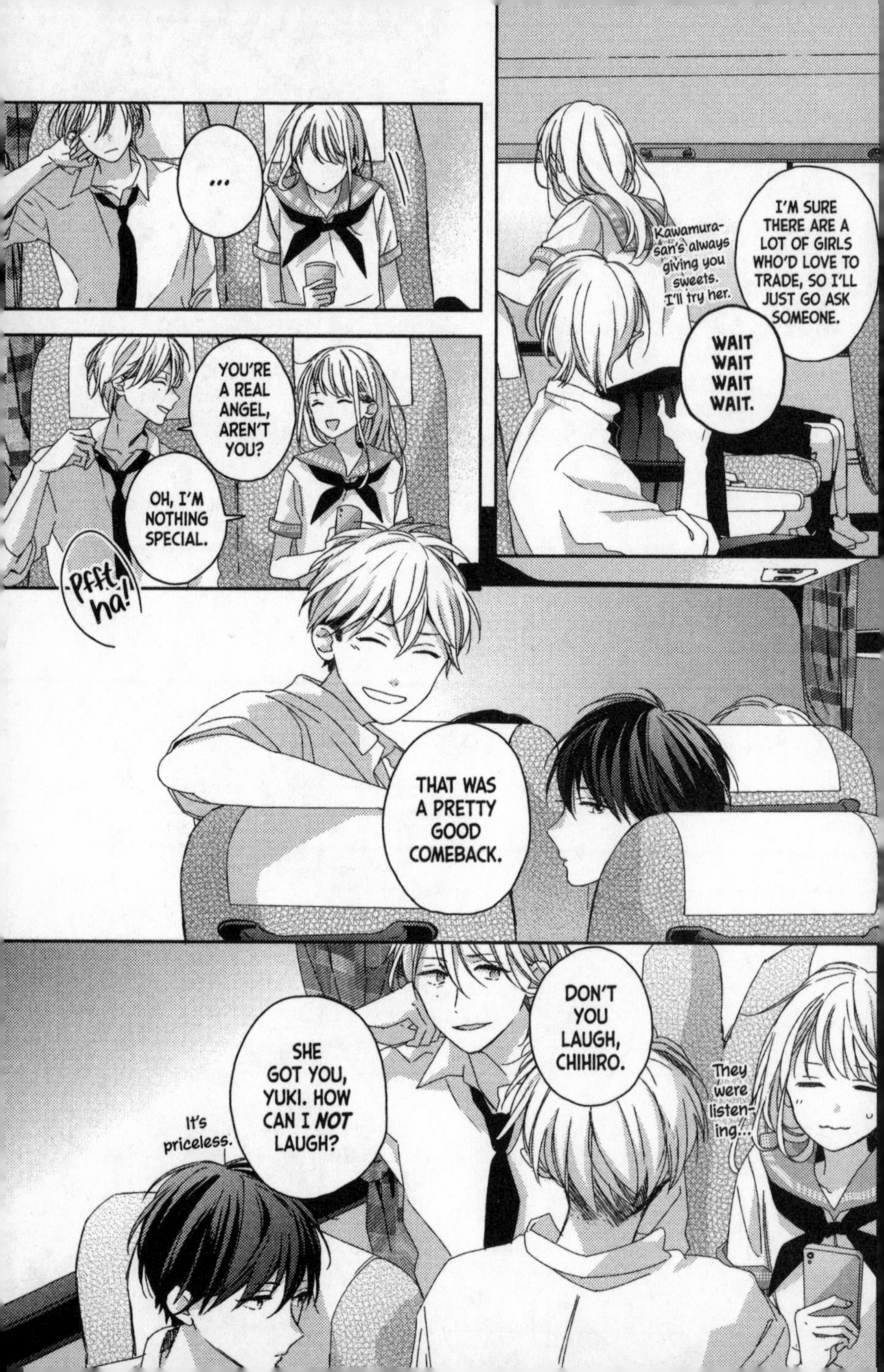
I'M SURE THERE ARE A LOT OF GIRLS WHO'D LOVE TO TRADE, SO I'LL JUST GO ASK SOMEONE.
Kawamura-san's always giving you sweets. I'll try her.
WAIT WAIT WAIT WAIT.
...
YOU'RE A REAL ANGEL, AREN'T YOU?
OH, I'M NOTHING SPECIAL.
Pfft ha!
THAT WAS A PRETTY GOOD COMEBACK.
DON'T YOU LAUGH, CHIHIRO.
They were listening...
SHE GOT YOU, YUKI. HOW CAN I *NOT* LAUGH?
It's priceless.

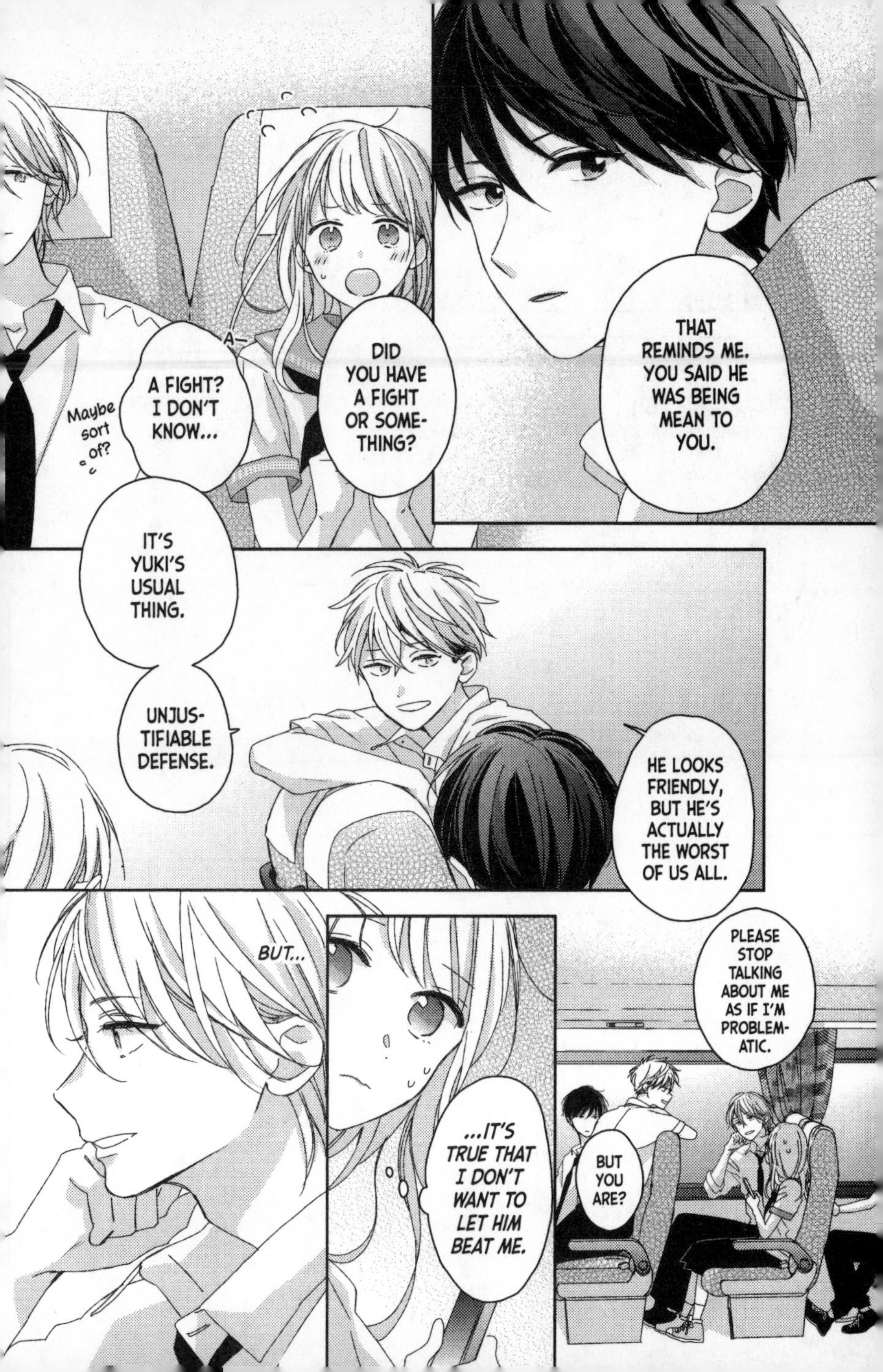
THAT REMINDS ME. YOU SAID HE WAS BEING MEAN TO YOU.
DID YOU HAVE A FIGHT OR SOME-THING?
A—
A FIGHT? I DON'T KNOW...
Maybe sort of?
IT'S YUKI'S USUAL THING.
UNJUS-TIFIABLE DEFENSE.
HE LOOKS FRIENDLY, BUT HE'S ACTUALLY THE WORST OF US ALL.
PLEASE STOP TALKING ABOUT ME AS IF I'M PROBLEM-ATIC.
BUT YOU ARE?
...IT'S TRUE THAT I DON'T WANT TO LET HIM BEAT ME.
BUT...

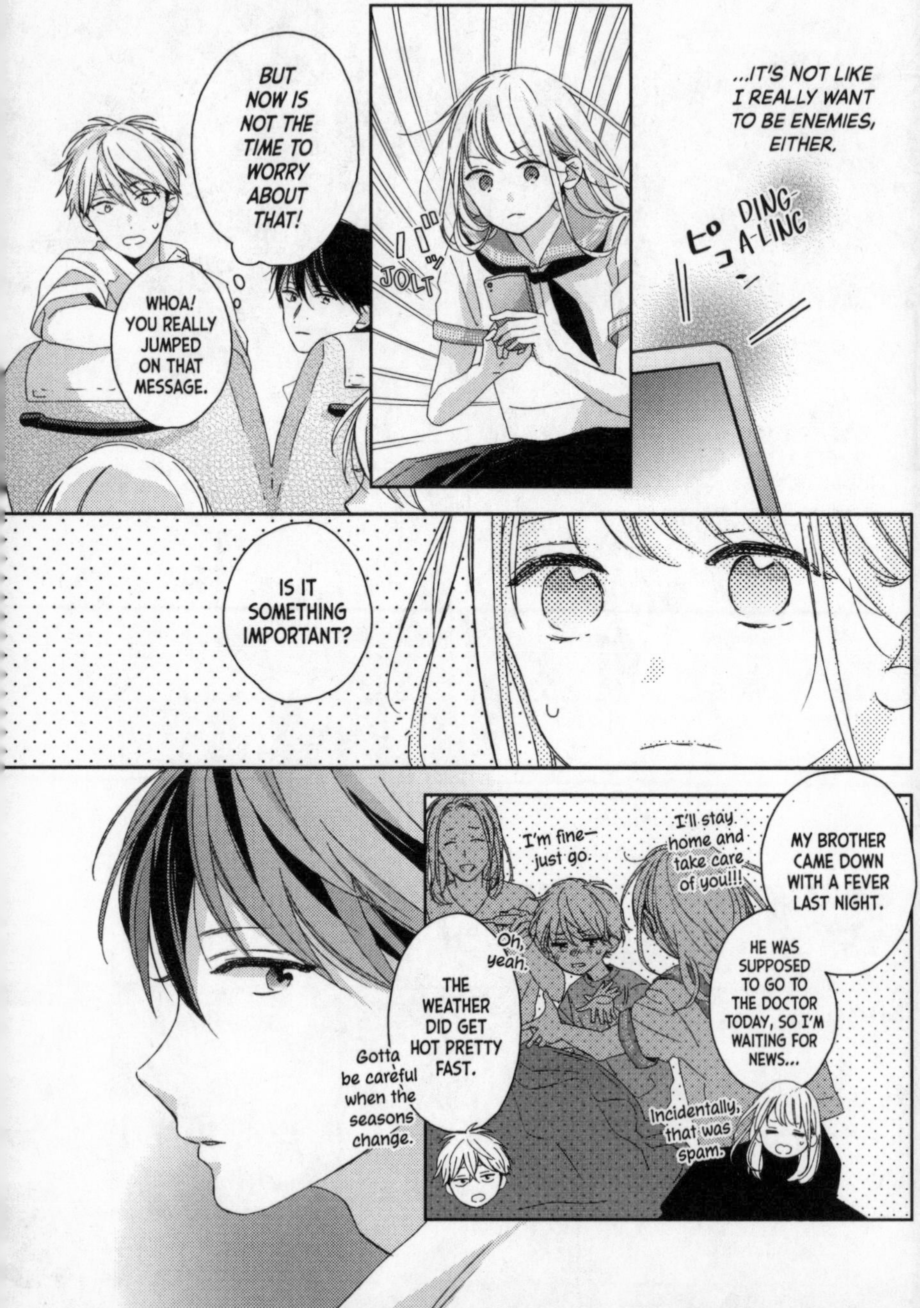
...IT'S NOT LIKE I REALLY WANT TO BE ENEMIES, EITHER.
ピコ
DING-A-LING
JOLT
BUT NOW IS NOT THE TIME TO WORRY ABOUT THAT!
WHOA! YOU REALLY JUMPED ON THAT MESSAGE.
IS IT SOMETHING IMPORTANT?
MY BROTHER CAME DOWN WITH A FEVER LAST NIGHT.
I'll stay home and take care of you!!!
I'm fine—just go.
HE WAS SUPPOSED TO GO TO THE DOCTOR TODAY, SO I'M WAITING FOR NEWS...
Oh, yeah.
THE WEATHER DID GET HOT PRETTY FAST.
Gotta be careful when the seasons change.
Incidentally, that was spam.

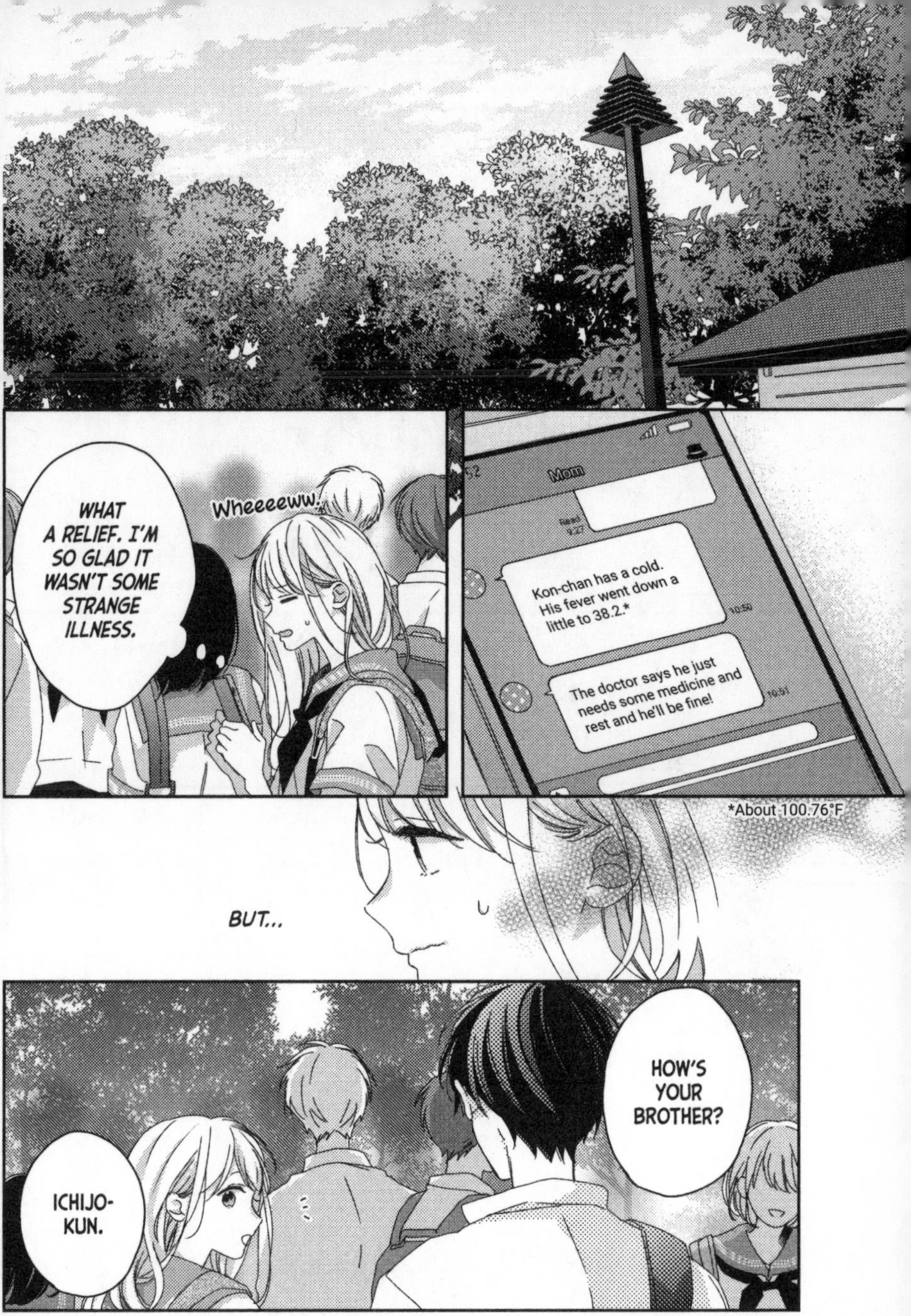
Mom
Read 9:27
Kon-chan has a cold. His fever went down a little to 38.2.*
10:50
The doctor says he just needs some medicine and rest and he'll be fine!
10:51
*About 100.76°F
Wheeeeww.
WHAT A RELIEF. I'M SO GLAD IT WASN'T SOME STRANGE ILLNESS.
BUT...
HOW'S YOUR BROTHER?
ICHIJO-KUN.

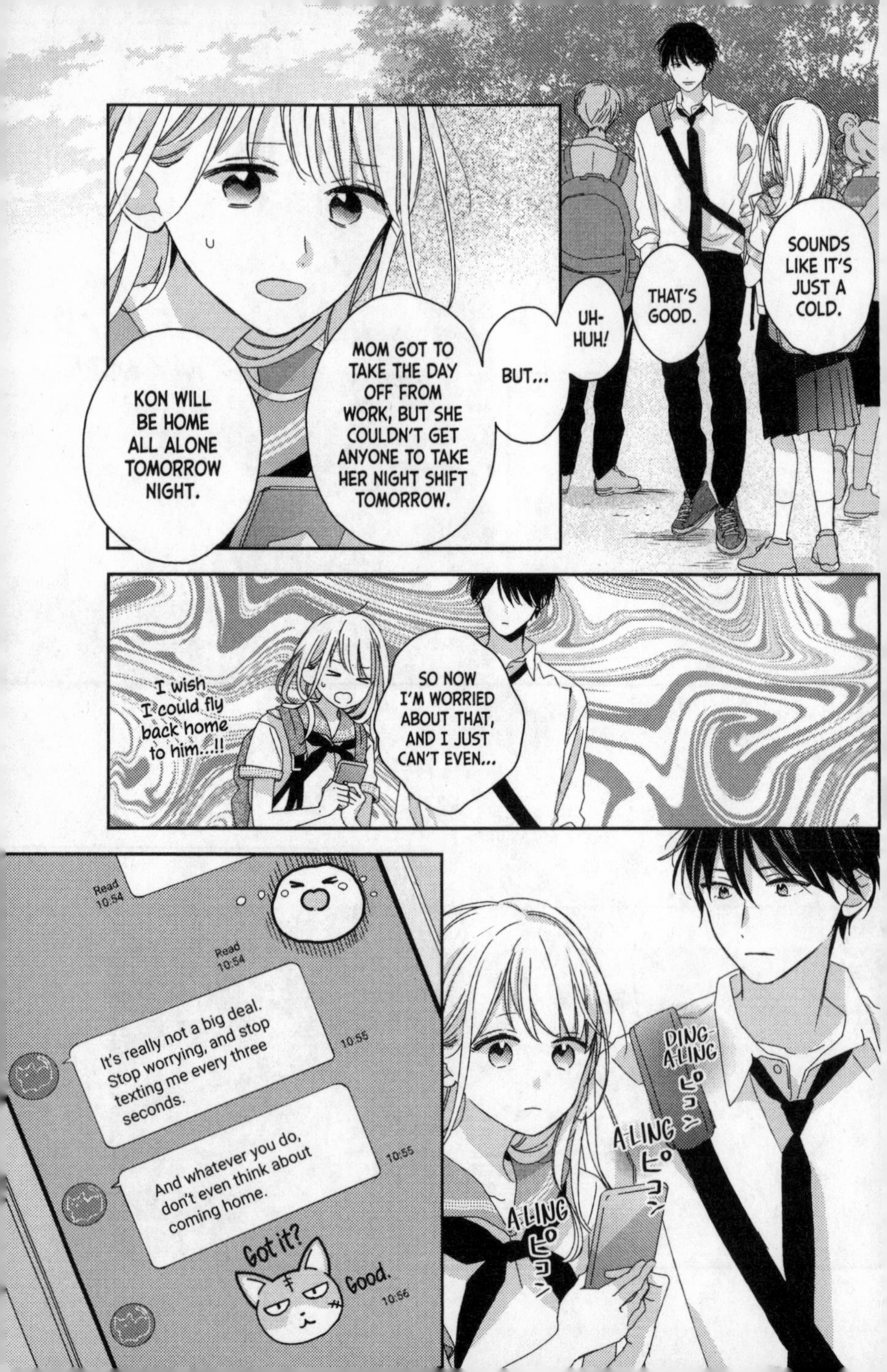
SOUNDS LIKE IT'S JUST A COLD.
THAT'S GOOD.
UH-HUH!
BUT...
MOM GOT TO TAKE THE DAY OFF FROM WORK, BUT SHE COULDN'T GET ANYONE TO TAKE HER NIGHT SHIFT TOMORROW.
KON WILL BE HOME ALL ALONE TOMORROW NIGHT.
SO NOW I'M WORRIED ABOUT THAT, AND I JUST CAN'T EVEN...
I wish I could fly back home to him...!!
DING-A-LING
ピコン
A-LING
ピコン
A-LING
ピコン
Read 10:54
Read 10:54
It's really not a big deal. Stop worrying, and stop texting me every three seconds.
10:55
And whatever you do, don't even think about coming home.
10:55
Got it?
Good.
10:56

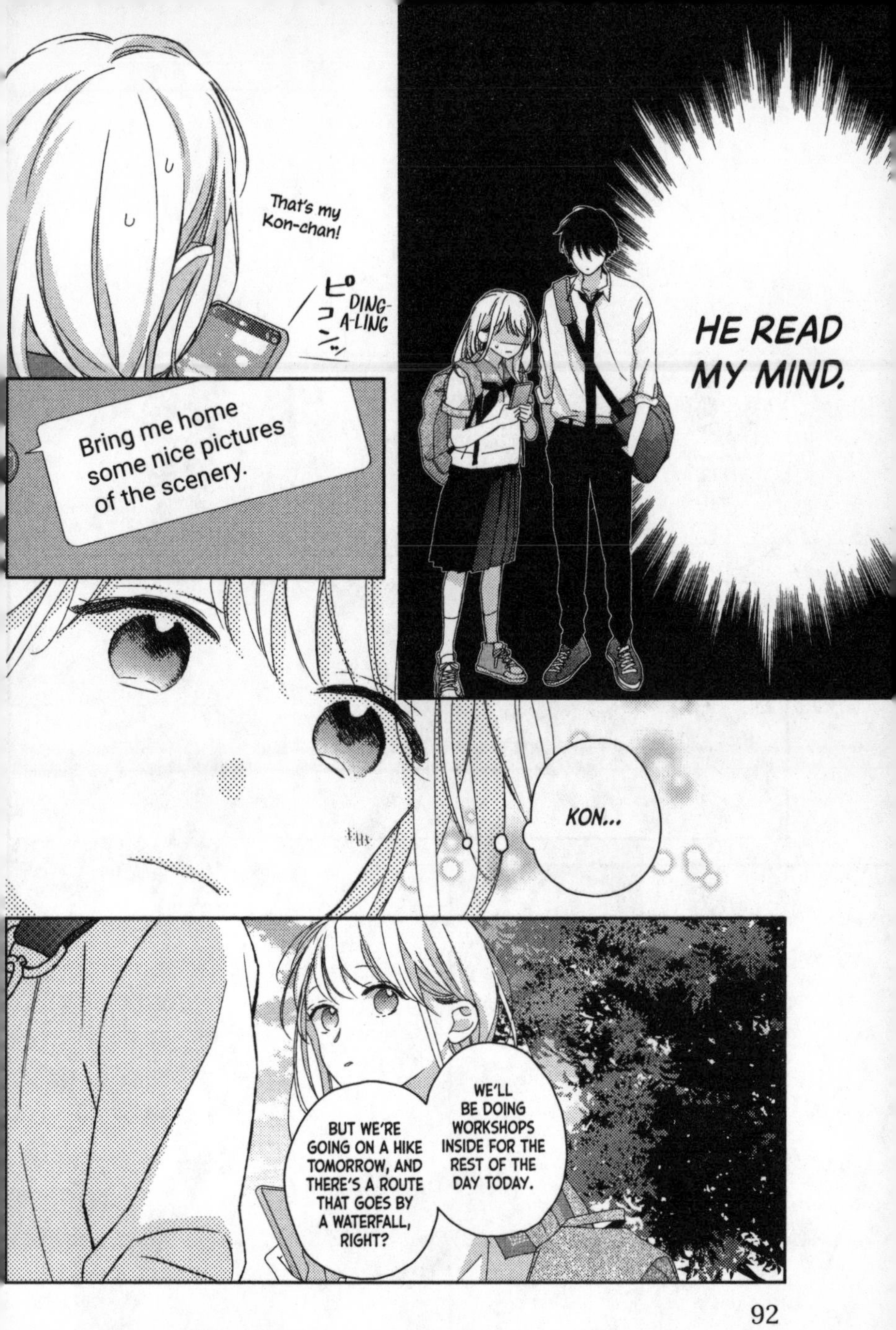
HE READ MY MIND.
That's my Kon-chan!
ピコンッ
DING-A-LING
Bring me home some nice pictures of the scenery.
KON...
WE'LL BE DOING WORKSHOPS INSIDE FOR THE REST OF THE DAY TODAY.
BUT WE'RE GOING ON A HIKE TOMORROW, AND THERE'S A ROUTE THAT GOES BY A WATERFALL, RIGHT?

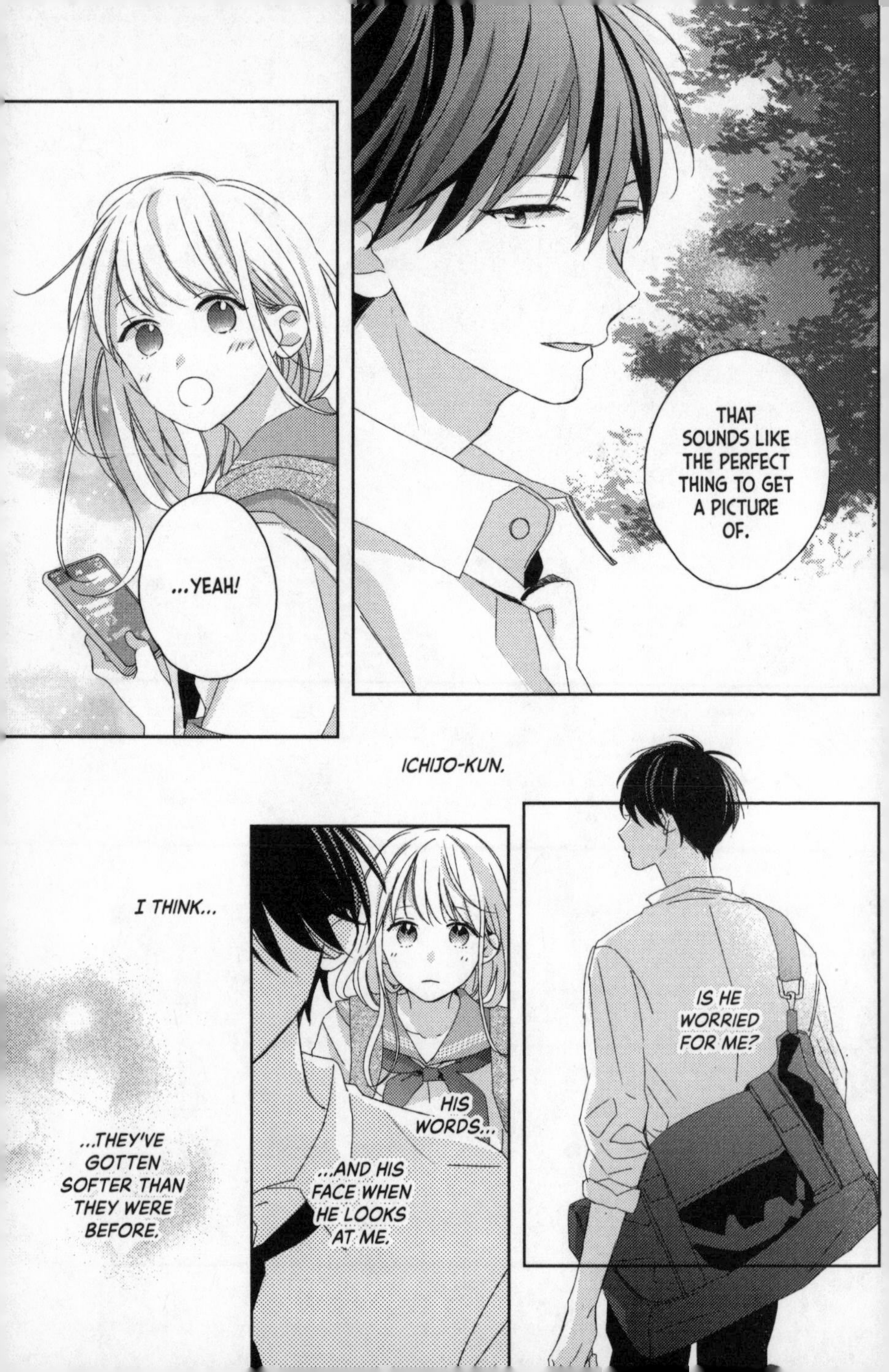
THAT SOUNDS LIKE THE PERFECT THING TO GET A PICTURE OF.
...YEAH!
ICHIJO-KUN.
IS HE WORRIED FOR ME?
HIS WORDS...
...AND HIS FACE WHEN HE LOOKS AT ME.
I THINK...
...THEY'VE GOTTEN SOFTER THAN THEY WERE BEFORE.

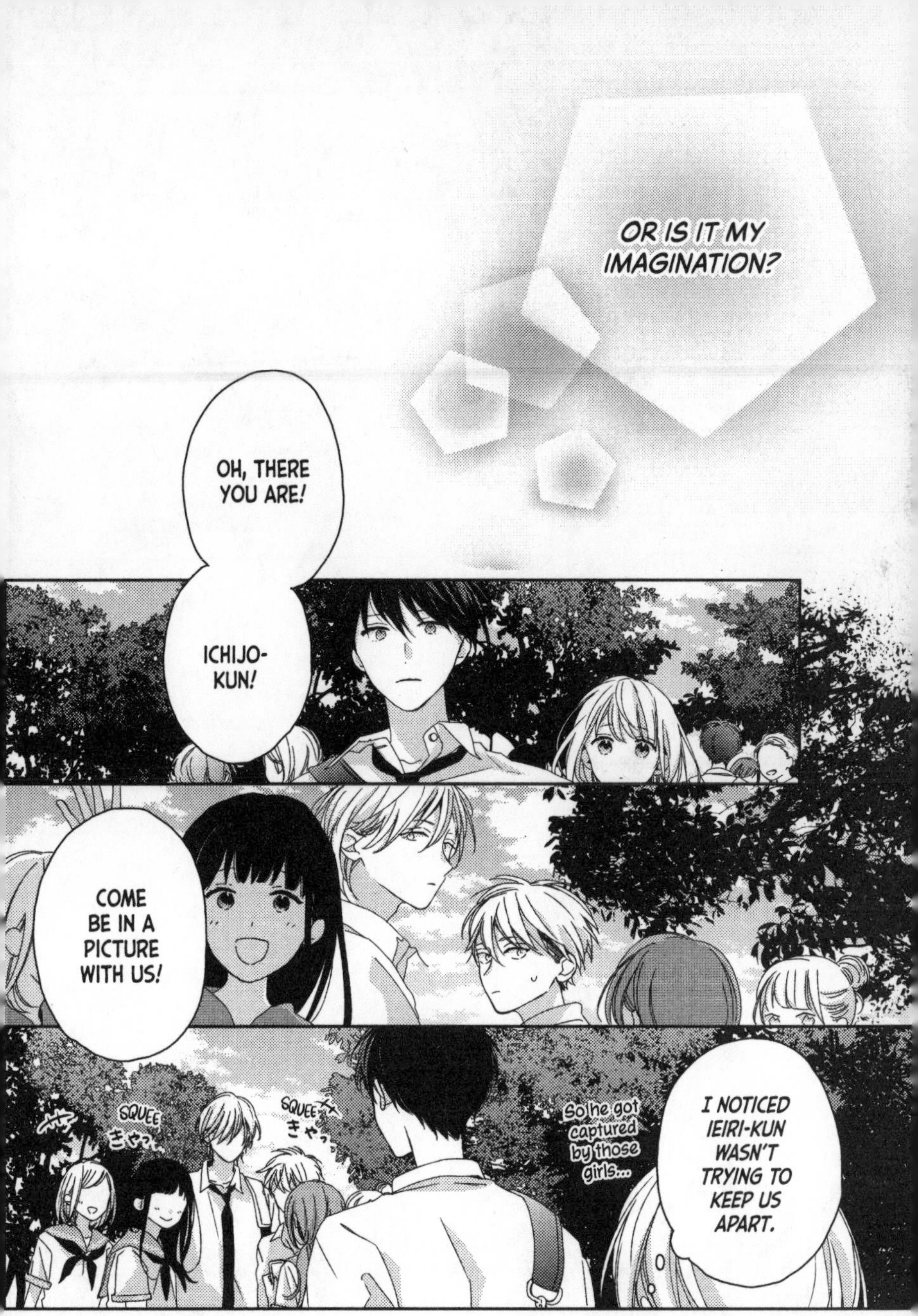
OR IS IT MY IMAGINATION?
OH, THERE YOU ARE!
ICHIJO-KUN!
COME BE IN A PICTURE WITH US!
I NOTICED IEIRI-KUN WASN'T TRYING TO KEEP US APART.
So he got captured by those girls...
SQUEE
きゃっ
SQUEE
きゃっ

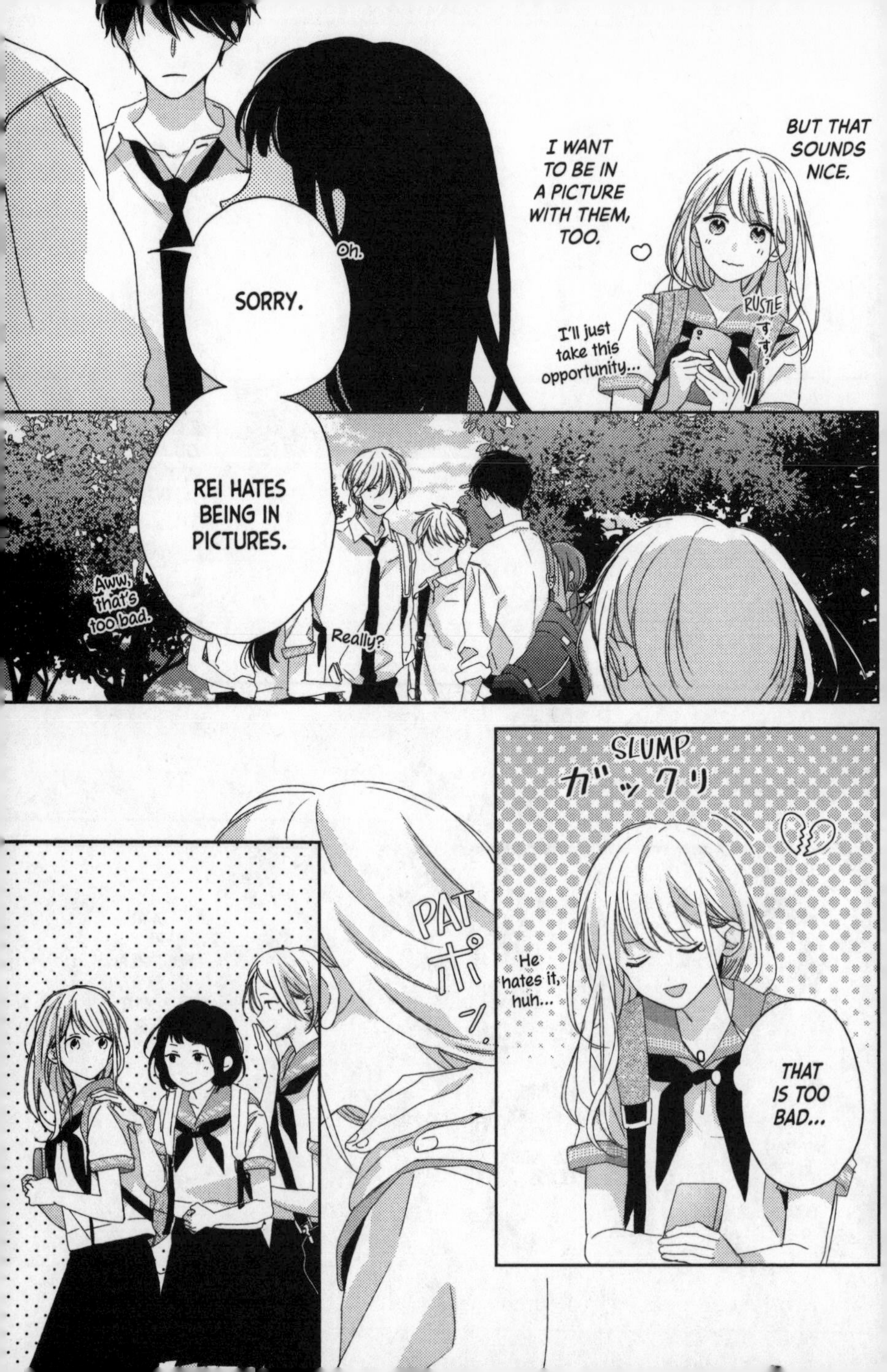
BUT THAT SOUNDS NICE.
I WANT TO BE IN A PICTURE WITH THEM, TOO.
RUSTLE
すす
I'll just take this opportunity...
Oh.
SORRY.
REI HATES BEING IN PICTURES.
Aww, that's too bad.
Really?
SLUMP
ガックリ
He hates it, huh...
THAT IS TOO BAD...
PAT
ポン

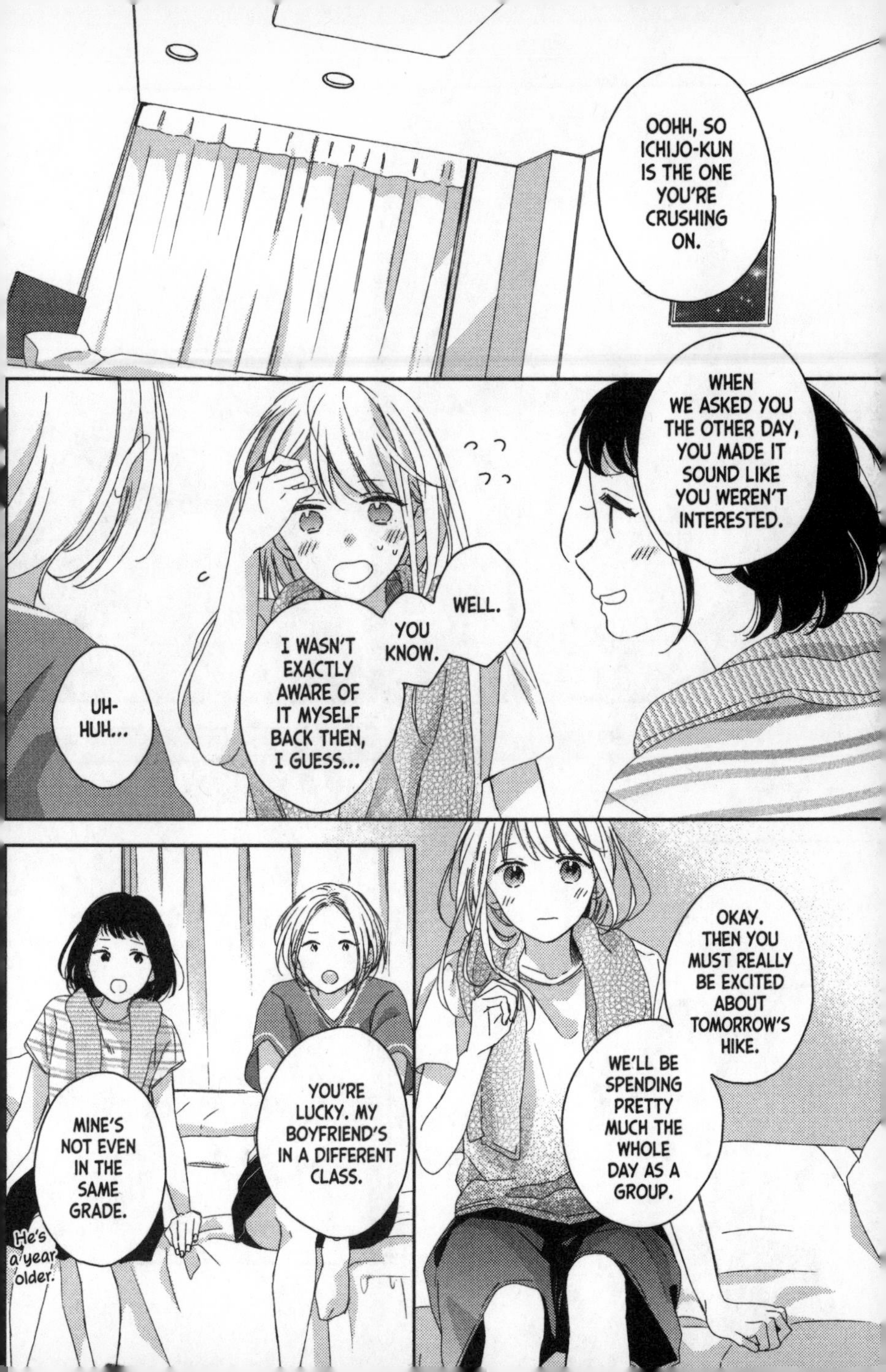
OOHH, SO ICHIJO-KUN IS THE ONE YOU'RE CRUSHING ON.
WHEN WE ASKED YOU THE OTHER DAY, YOU MADE IT SOUND LIKE YOU WEREN'T INTERESTED.
WELL.
YOU KNOW.
I WASN'T EXACTLY AWARE OF IT MYSELF BACK THEN, I GUESS...
UH-HUH...
OKAY. THEN YOU MUST REALLY BE EXCITED ABOUT TOMORROW'S HIKE.
WE'LL BE SPENDING PRETTY MUCH THE WHOLE DAY AS A GROUP.
YOU'RE LUCKY. MY BOYFRIEND'S IN A DIFFERENT CLASS.
MINE'S NOT EVEN IN THE SAME GRADE.
He's a year older.

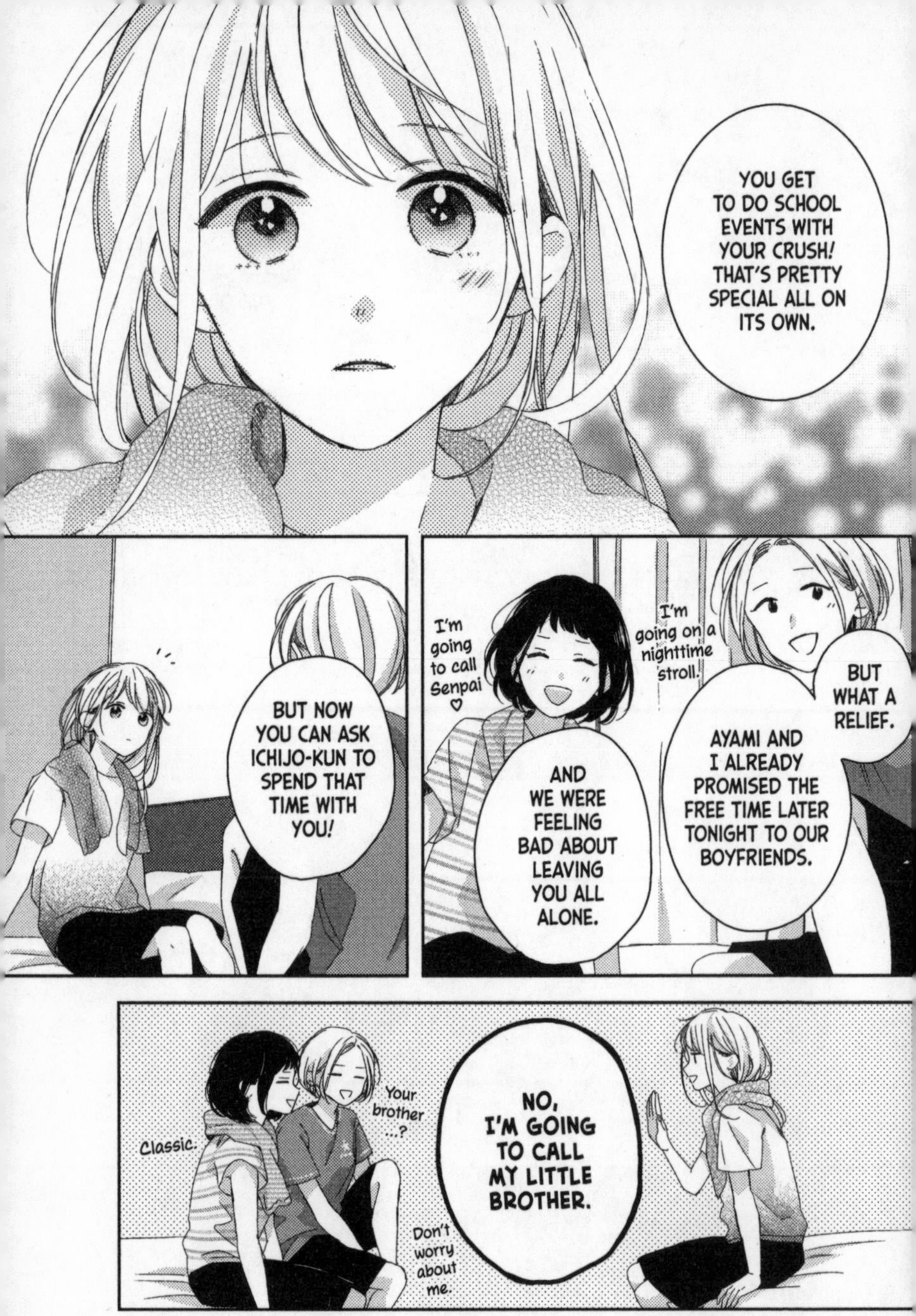
YOU GET TO DO SCHOOL EVENTS WITH YOUR CRUSH! THAT'S PRETTY SPECIAL ALL ON ITS OWN.
BUT WHAT A RELIEF.
AYAMI AND I ALREADY PROMISED THE FREE TIME LATER TONIGHT TO OUR BOYFRIENDS.
I'm going on a nighttime stroll.
AND WE WERE FEELING BAD ABOUT LEAVING YOU ALL ALONE.
I'm going to call Senpai ♡
BUT NOW YOU CAN ASK ICHIJO-KUN TO SPEND THAT TIME WITH YOU!
NO, I'M GOING TO CALL MY LITTLE BROTHER.
Don't worry about me.
Your brother ...?
Classic.

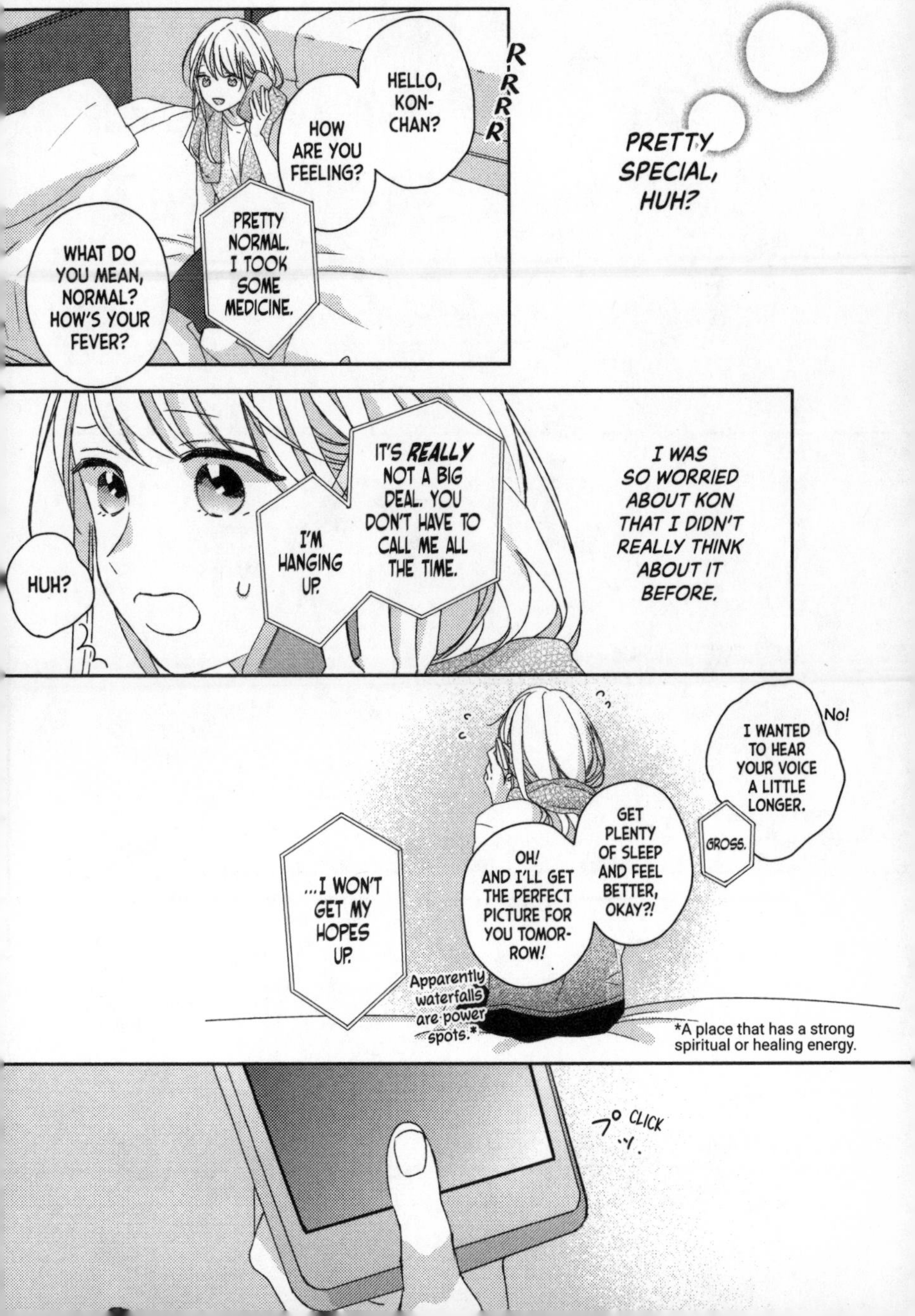
PRETTY SPECIAL, HUH?
RRRR
HELLO, KON-CHAN?
HOW ARE YOU FEELING?
PRETTY NORMAL. I TOOK SOME MEDICINE.
WHAT DO YOU MEAN, NORMAL? HOW'S YOUR FEVER?
I WAS SO WORRIED ABOUT KON THAT I DIDN'T REALLY THINK ABOUT IT BEFORE.
IT'S ***REALLY*** NOT A BIG DEAL. YOU DON'T HAVE TO CALL ME ALL THE TIME.
I'M HANGING UP.
HUH?
No!
I WANTED TO HEAR YOUR VOICE A LITTLE LONGER.
GROSS.
GET PLENTY OF SLEEP AND FEEL BETTER, OKAY?!
OH! AND I'LL GET THE PERFECT PICTURE FOR YOU TOMOR-ROW!
...I WON'T GET MY HOPES UP.
Apparently waterfalls are power spots.*
*A place that has a strong spiritual or healing energy.
CLICK

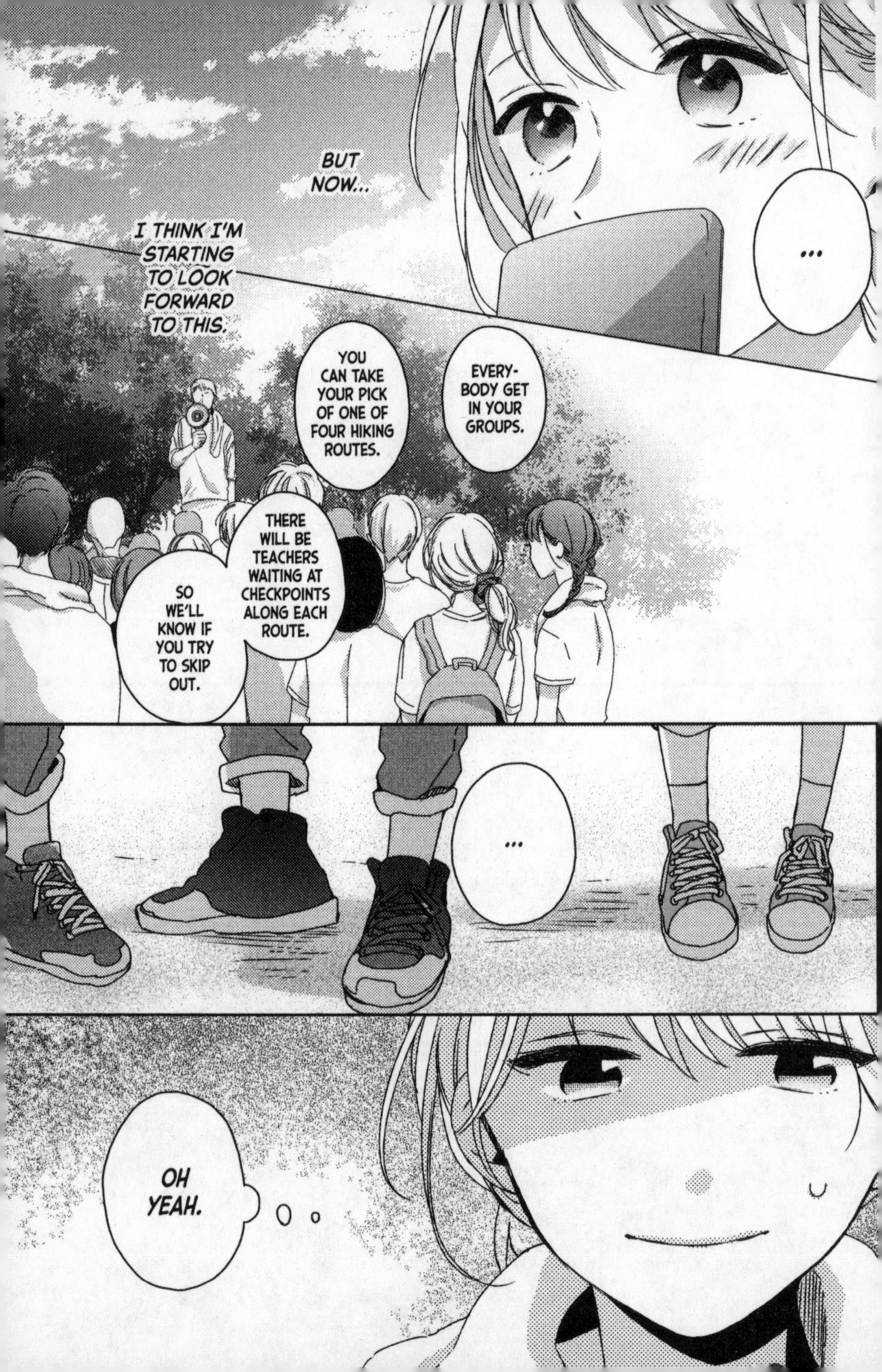
...
BUT NOW...
I THINK I'M STARTING TO LOOK FORWARD TO THIS.
EVERY-BODY GET IN YOUR GROUPS.
YOU CAN TAKE YOUR PICK OF ONE OF FOUR HIKING ROUTES.
THERE WILL BE TEACHERS WAITING AT CHECKPOINTS ALONG EACH ROUTE.
SO WE'LL KNOW IF YOU TRY TO SKIP OUT.
...
OH YEAH.

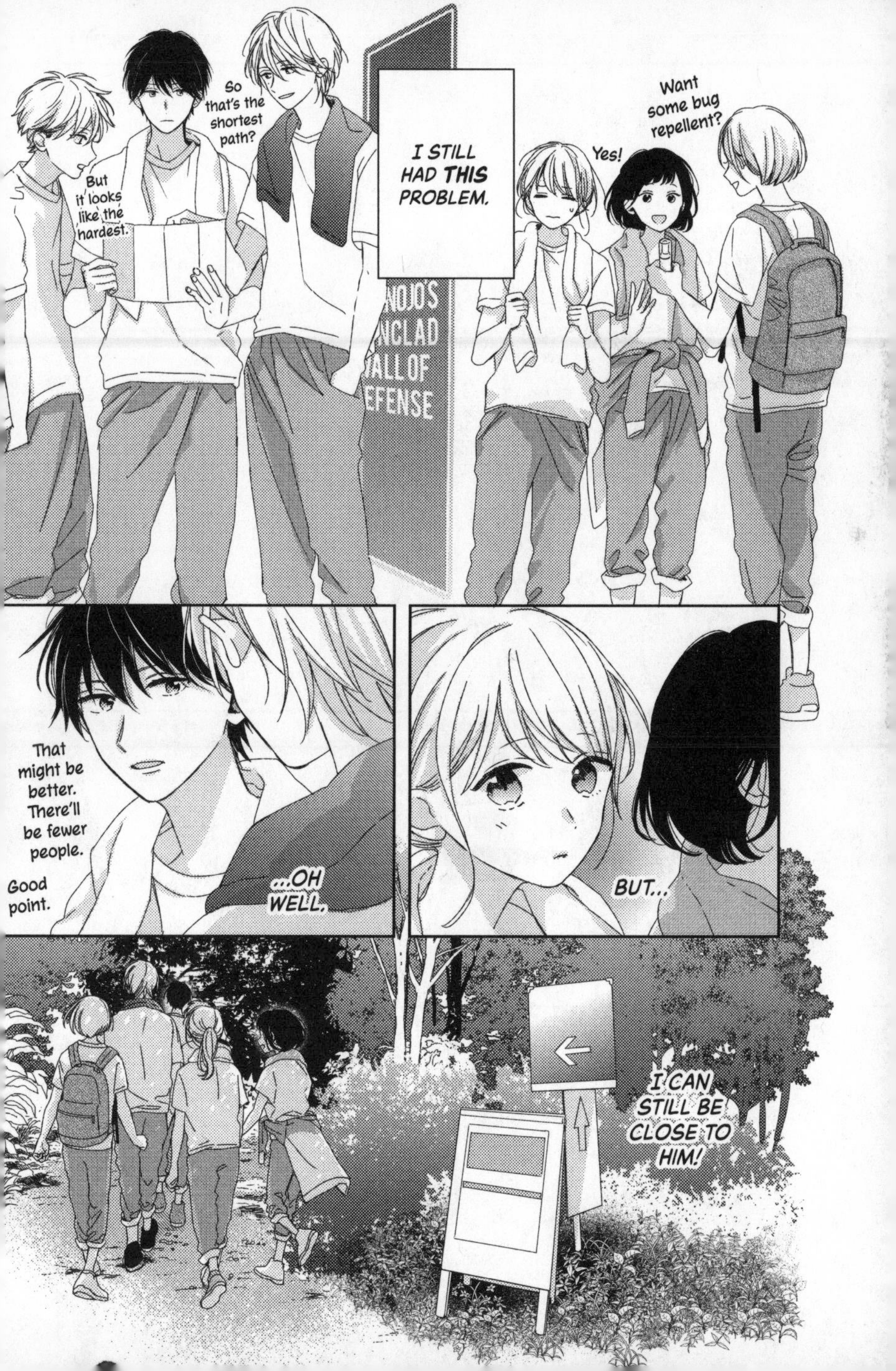
Want some bug repellent?
Yes!
I STILL HAD **THIS** PROBLEM.
So that's the shortest path?
But it looks like the hardest.
BUT...
That might be better. There'll be fewer people.
Good point.
...OH WELL.
I CAN STILL BE CLOSE TO HIM!

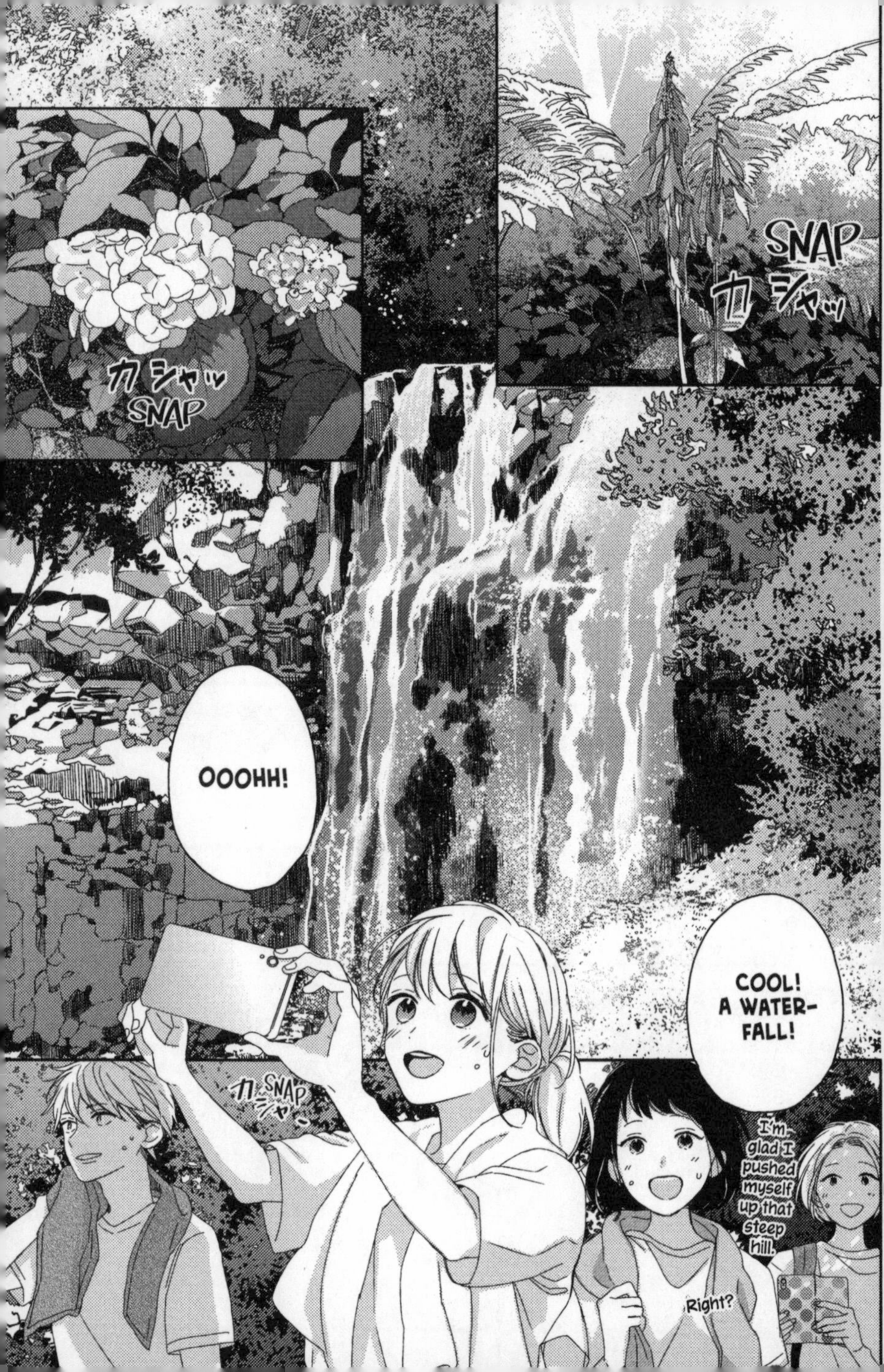
SNAP
カシャッ
カシャッ
SNAP
OOOHH!
COOL! A WATER-FALL!
I'm glad I pushed myself up that steep hill.
Right?
カシャ
SNAP

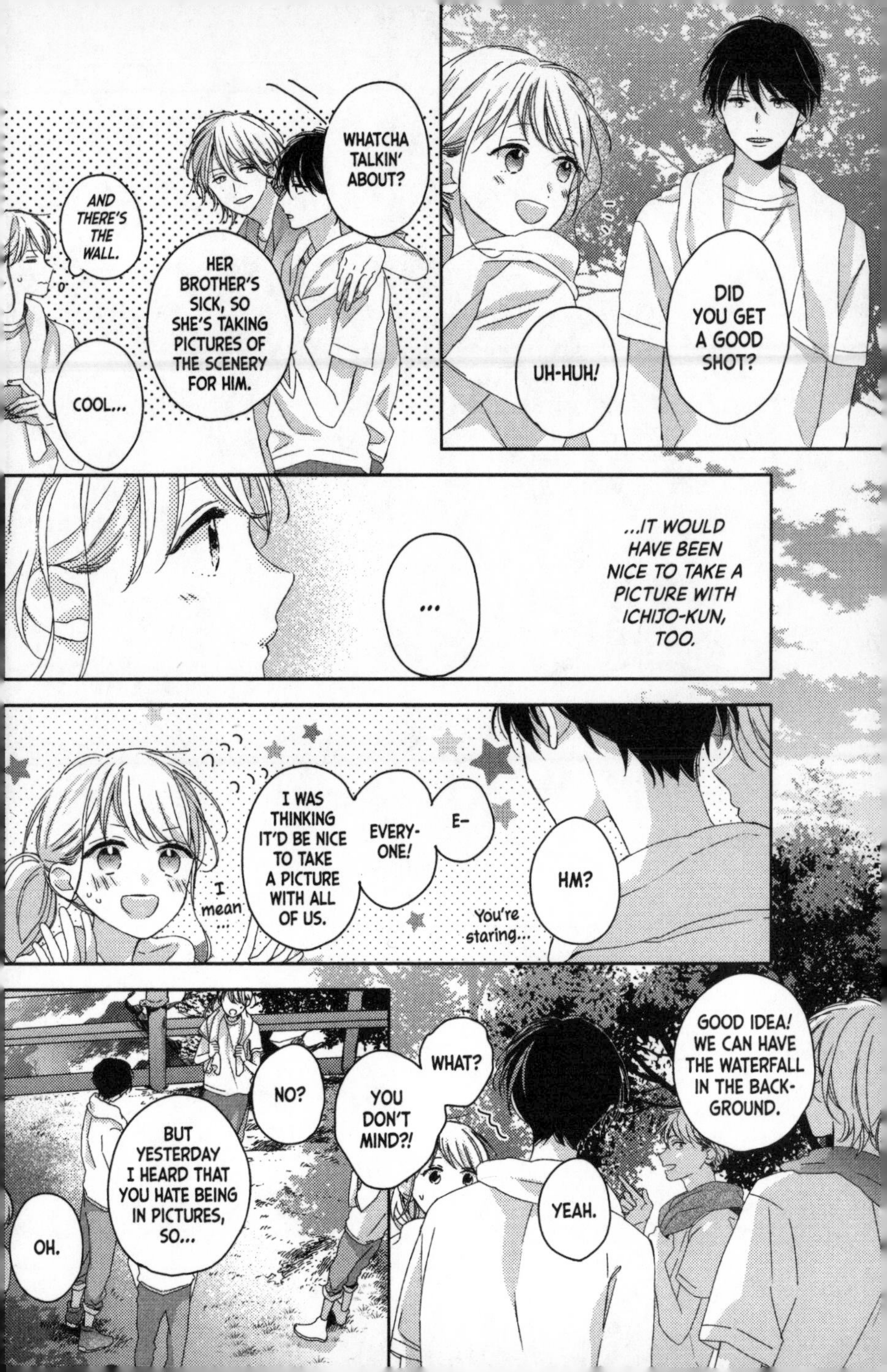
DID YOU GET A GOOD SHOT?
UH-HUH!
WHATCHA TALKIN' ABOUT?
HER BROTHER'S SICK, SO SHE'S TAKING PICTURES OF THE SCENERY FOR HIM.
AND THERE'S THE WALL.
COOL...
...IT WOULD HAVE BEEN NICE TO TAKE A PICTURE WITH ICHIJO-KUN, TOO.
...
HM?
You're staring...
E–
EVERY-ONE!
I WAS THINKING IT'D BE NICE TO TAKE A PICTURE WITH ALL OF US.
I mean...
GOOD IDEA! WE CAN HAVE THE WATERFALL IN THE BACK-GROUND.
YEAH.
WHAT?
YOU DON'T MIND?!
NO?
BUT YESTERDAY I HEARD THAT YOU HATE BEING IN PICTURES, SO...
OH.

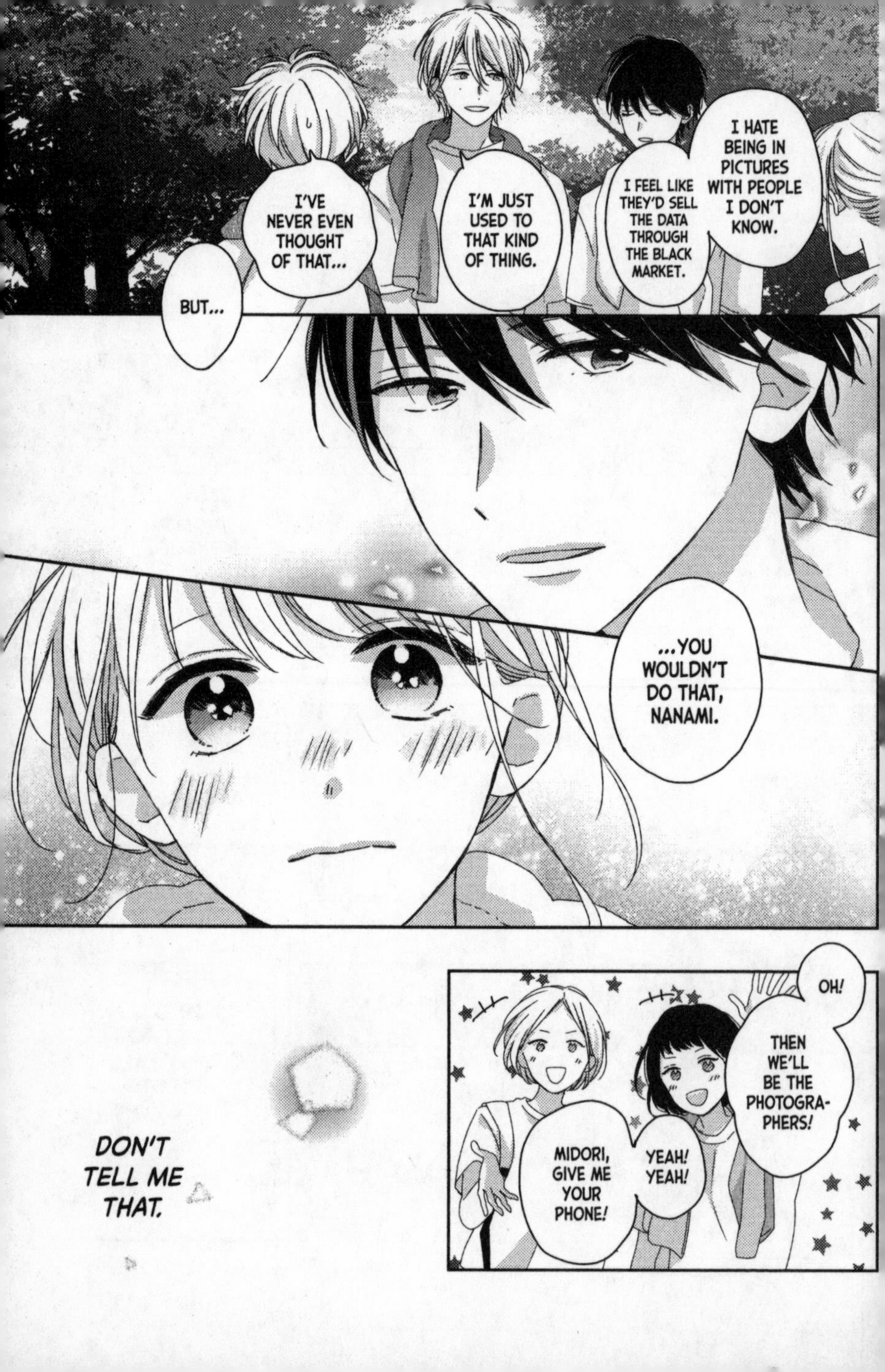
I HATE BEING IN PICTURES WITH PEOPLE I DON'T KNOW.
I FEEL LIKE THEY'D SELL THE DATA THROUGH THE BLACK MARKET.
I'M JUST USED TO THAT KIND OF THING.
I'VE NEVER EVEN THOUGHT OF THAT...
BUT...
...YOU WOULDN'T DO THAT, NANAMI.
OH!
THEN WE'LL BE THE PHOTOGRA-PHERS!
YEAH! YEAH!
MIDORI, GIVE ME YOUR PHONE!
DON'T TELL ME THAT.

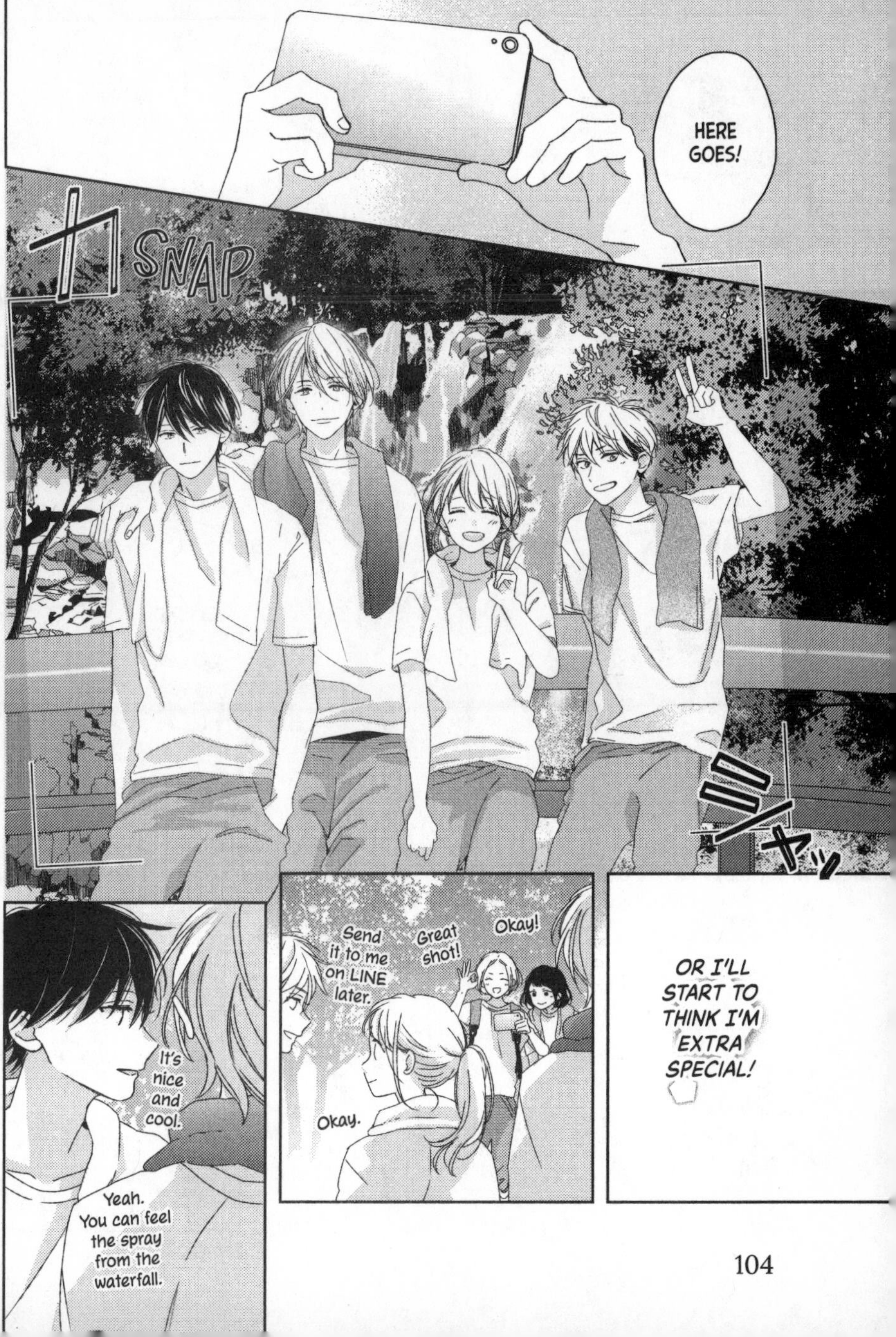
HERE GOES!
SNAP
OR I'LL START TO THINK I'M EXTRA SPECIAL!
Okay!
Great shot!
Send it to me on LINE later.
Okay.
It's nice and cool.
Yeah. You can feel the spray from the waterfall.

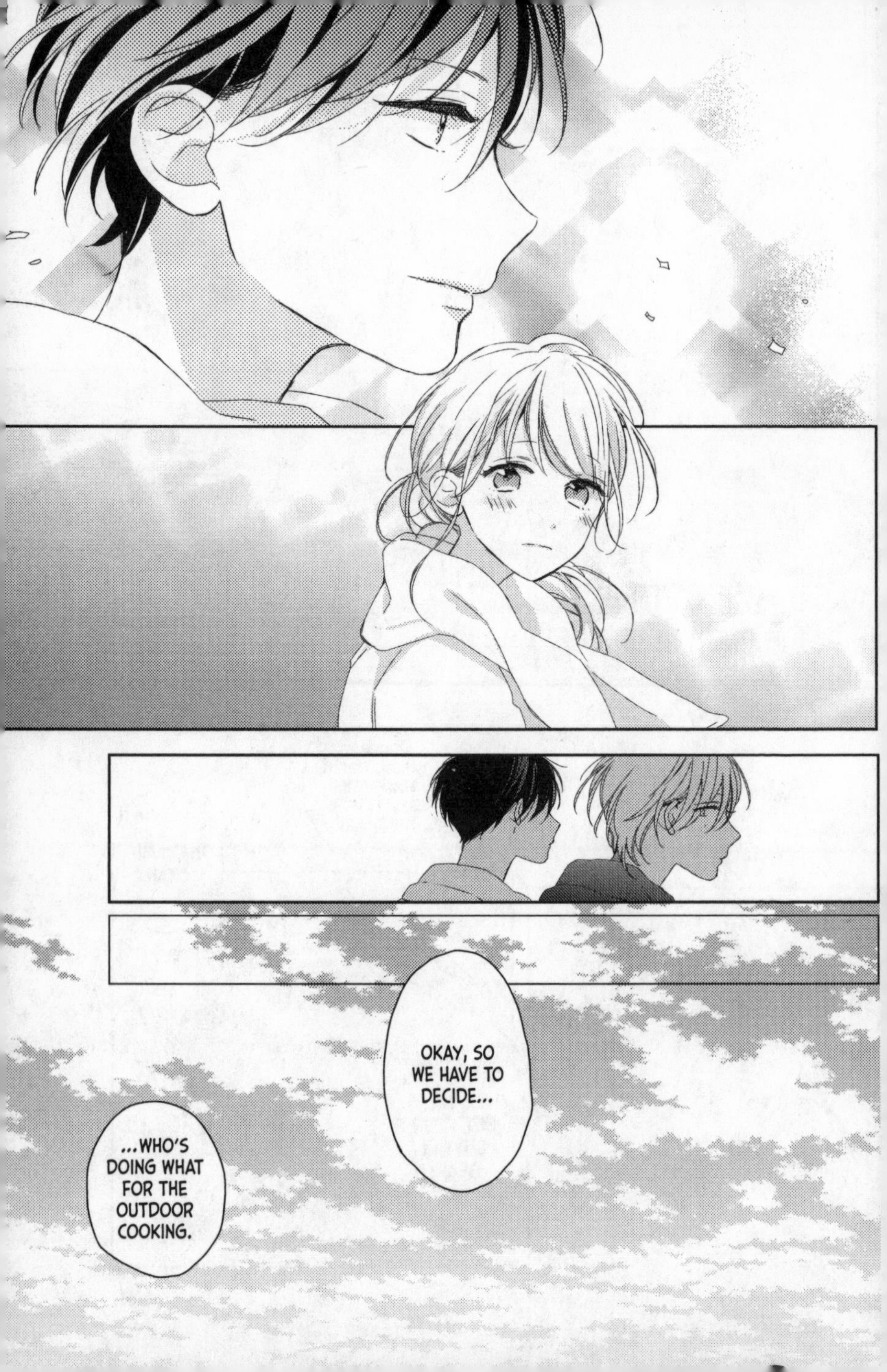
OKAY, SO WE HAVE TO DECIDE...
...WHO'S DOING WHAT FOR THE OUTDOOR COOKING.

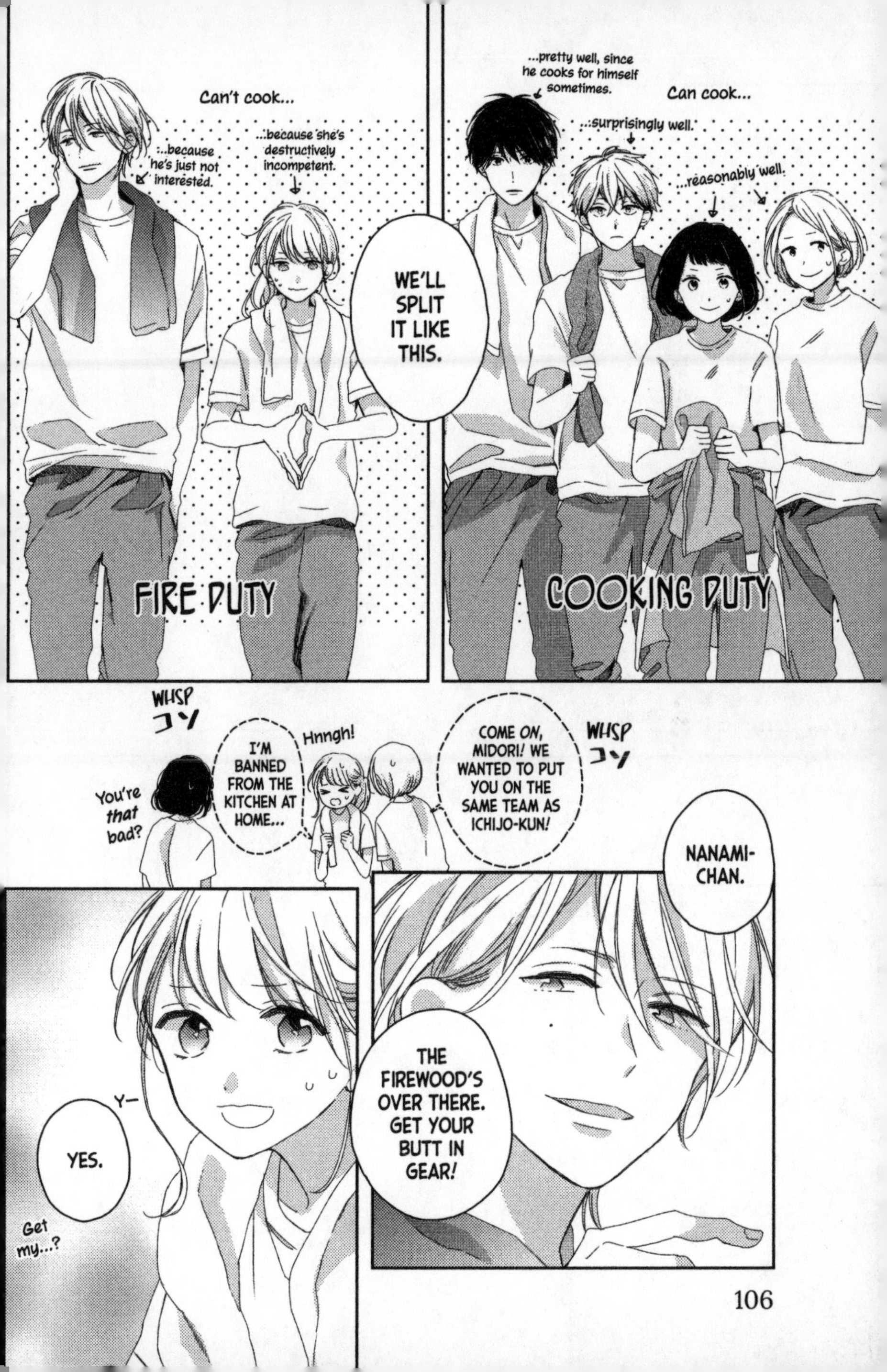
Can cook...
...pretty well, since he cooks for himself sometimes.
...surprisingly well.
...reasonably well.
...reasonably well.
COOKING DUTY
WE'LL SPLIT IT LIKE THIS.
Can't cook...
...because she's destructively incompetent.
...because he's just not interested.
FIRE DUTY
WHSP コソ
COME ON, MIDORI! WE WANTED TO PUT YOU ON THE SAME TEAM AS ICHIJO-KUN!
Hnngh!
I'M BANNED FROM THE KITCHEN AT HOME...
WHSP コソ
You're *that* bad?
NANAMI-CHAN.
THE FIREWOOD'S OVER THERE. GET YOUR BUTT IN GEAR!
Y—
YES.
Get my...?

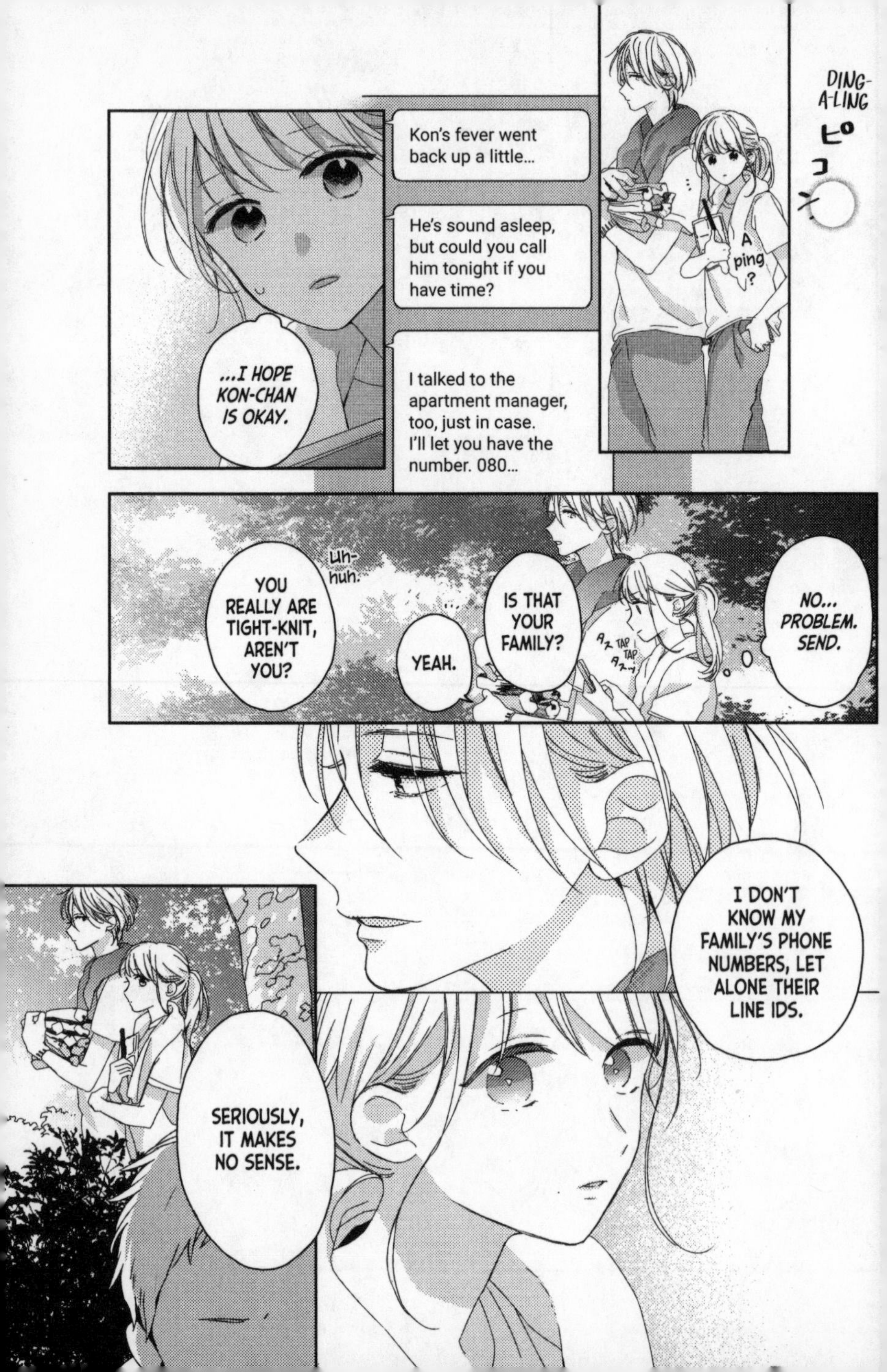
DING-A-LING
ピコン
...
A ping?
Kon's fever went back up a little...
He's sound asleep, but could you call him tonight if you have time?
I talked to the apartment manager, too, just in case. I'll let you have the number. 080...
...I HOPE KON-CHAN IS OKAY.
NO... PROBLEM. SEND.
TAP TAP
IS THAT YOUR FAMILY?
...
YEAH.
Uh-huh.
YOU REALLY ARE TIGHT-KNIT, AREN'T YOU?
I DON'T KNOW MY FAMILY'S PHONE NUMBERS, LET ALONE THEIR LINE IDS.
SERIOUSLY, IT MAKES NO SENSE.

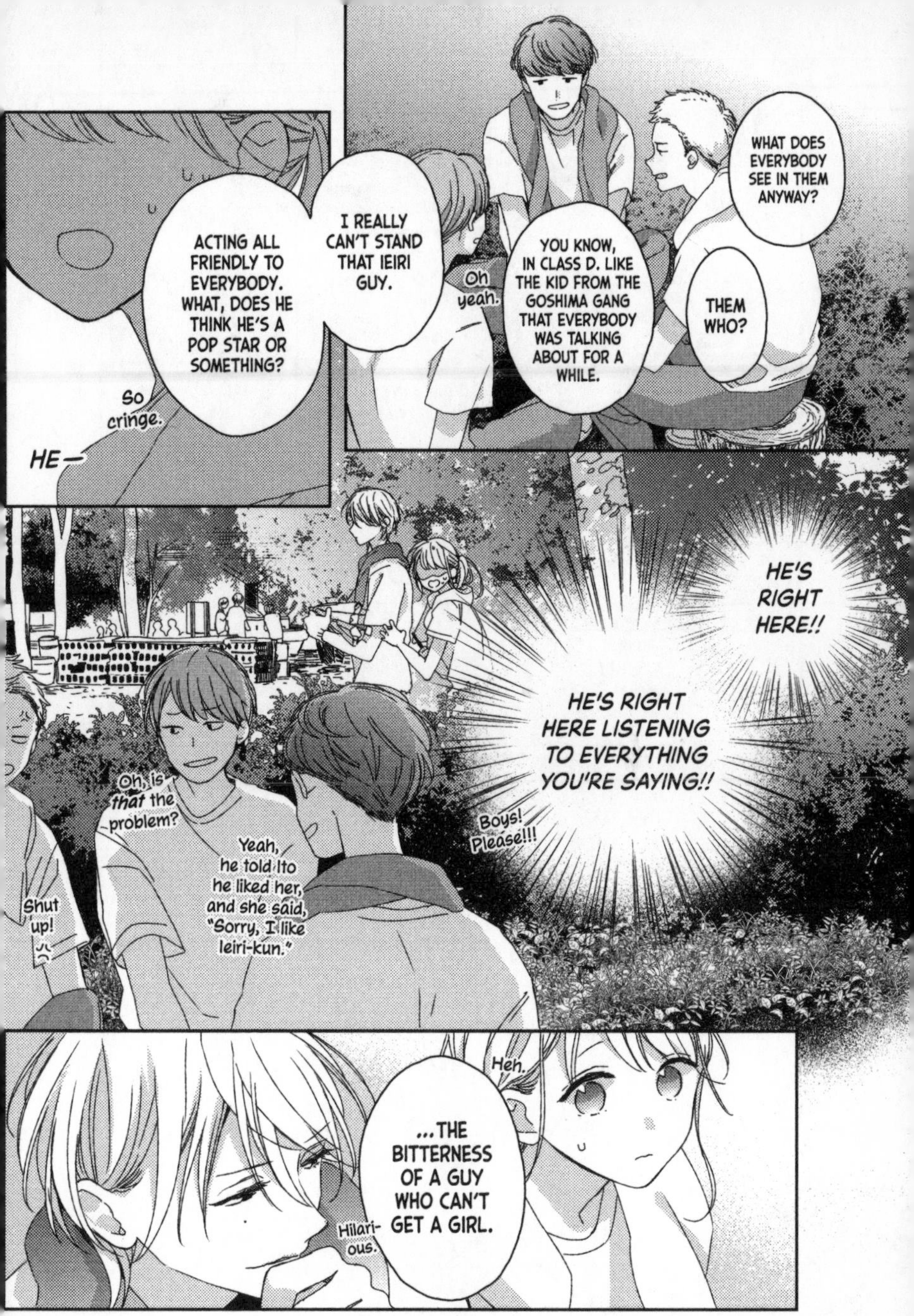
WHAT DOES EVERYBODY SEE IN THEM ANYWAY?
THEM WHO?
YOU KNOW, IN CLASS D. LIKE THE KID FROM THE GOSHIMA GANG THAT EVERYBODY WAS TALKING ABOUT FOR A WHILE.
Oh yeah.
I REALLY CAN'T STAND THAT IEIRI GUY.
ACTING ALL FRIENDLY TO EVERYBODY. WHAT, DOES HE THINK HE'S A POP STAR OR SOMETHING?
So cringe.
HE—
HE'S RIGHT HERE!!
HE'S RIGHT HERE LISTENING TO EVERYTHING YOU'RE SAYING!!
Boys! Please!!!
Oh, is *that* the problem?
Yeah, he told Ito he liked her, and she said, "Sorry, I like Ieiri-kun."
Shut up!
Heh.
...THE BITTERNESS OF A GUY WHO CAN'T GET A GIRL.
Hilari-ous.

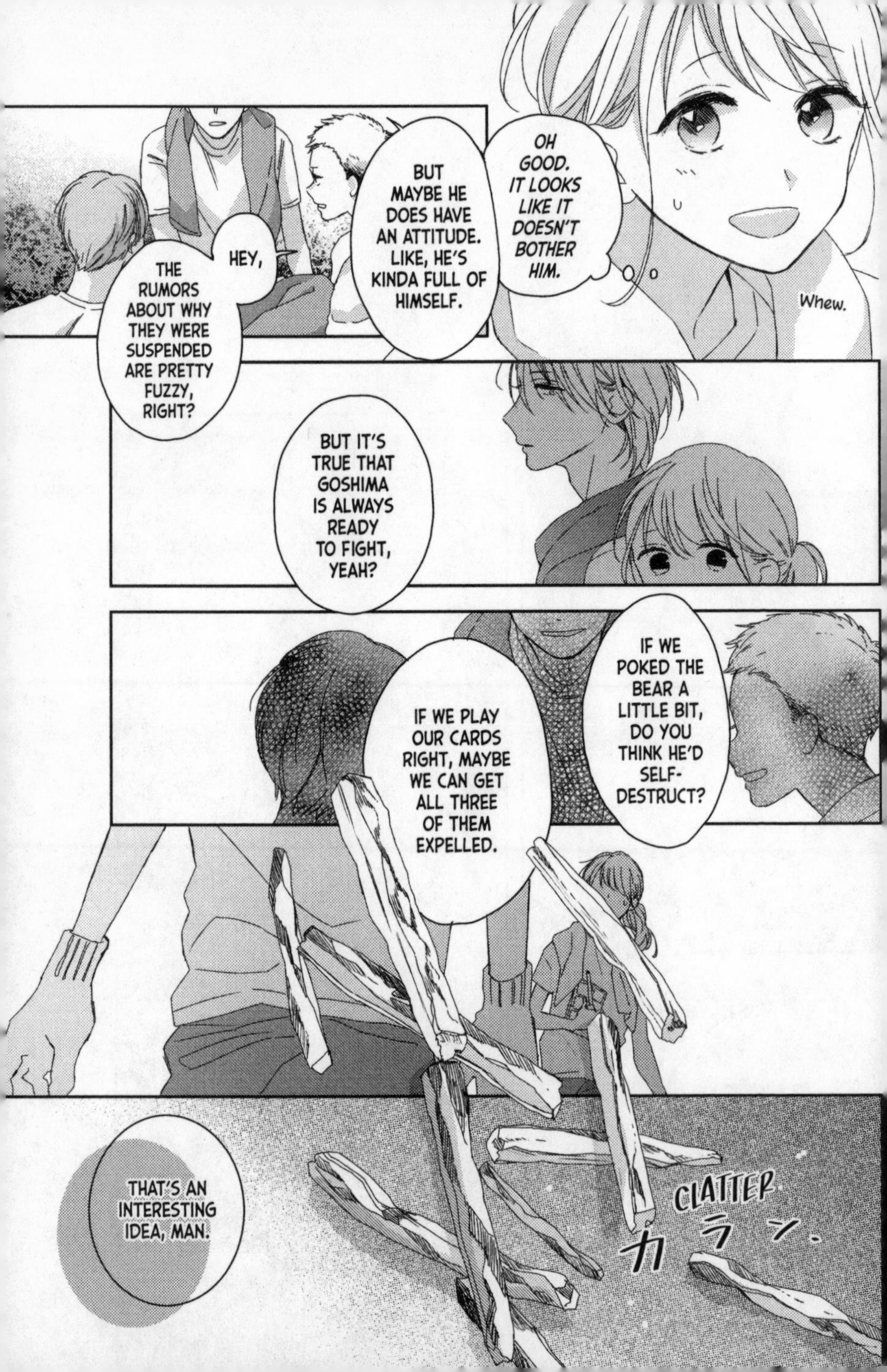
OH GOOD. IT LOOKS LIKE IT DOESN'T BOTHER HIM.
Whew.
BUT MAYBE HE DOES HAVE AN ATTITUDE. LIKE, HE'S KINDA FULL OF HIMSELF.
HEY,
THE RUMORS ABOUT WHY THEY WERE SUSPENDED ARE PRETTY FUZZY, RIGHT?
BUT IT'S TRUE THAT GOSHIMA IS ALWAYS READY TO FIGHT, YEAH?
IF WE POKED THE BEAR A LITTLE BIT, DO YOU THINK HE'D SELF-DESTRUCT?
IF WE PLAY OUR CARDS RIGHT, MAYBE WE CAN GET ALL THREE OF THEM EXPELLED.
CLATTER
カラン.
THAT'S AN INTERESTING IDEA, MAN.

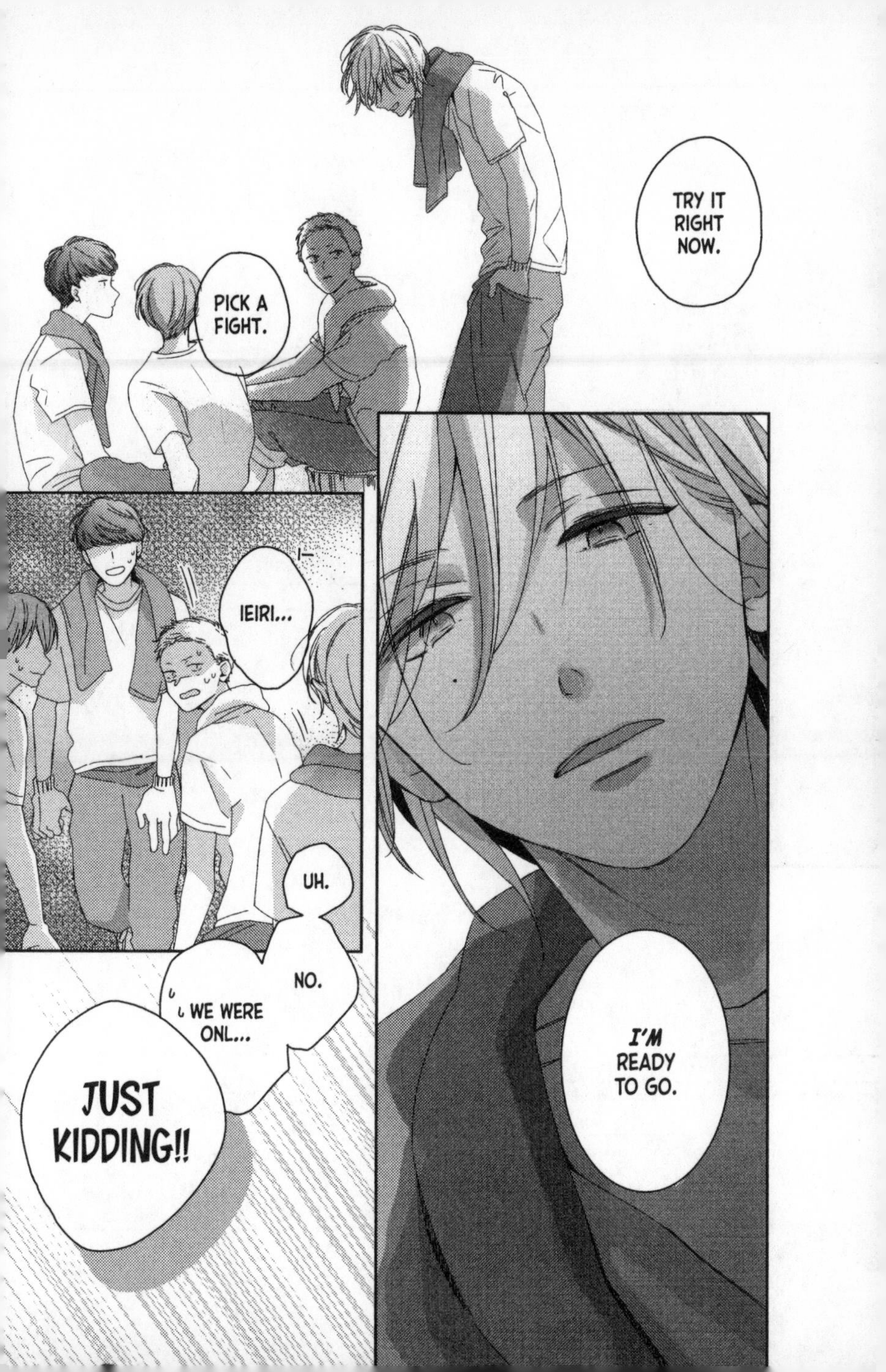
TRY IT RIGHT NOW.
PICK A FIGHT.
I'M READY TO GO.
I—
IEIRI...
UH.
NO.
WE WERE ONL...
JUST KIDDING!!

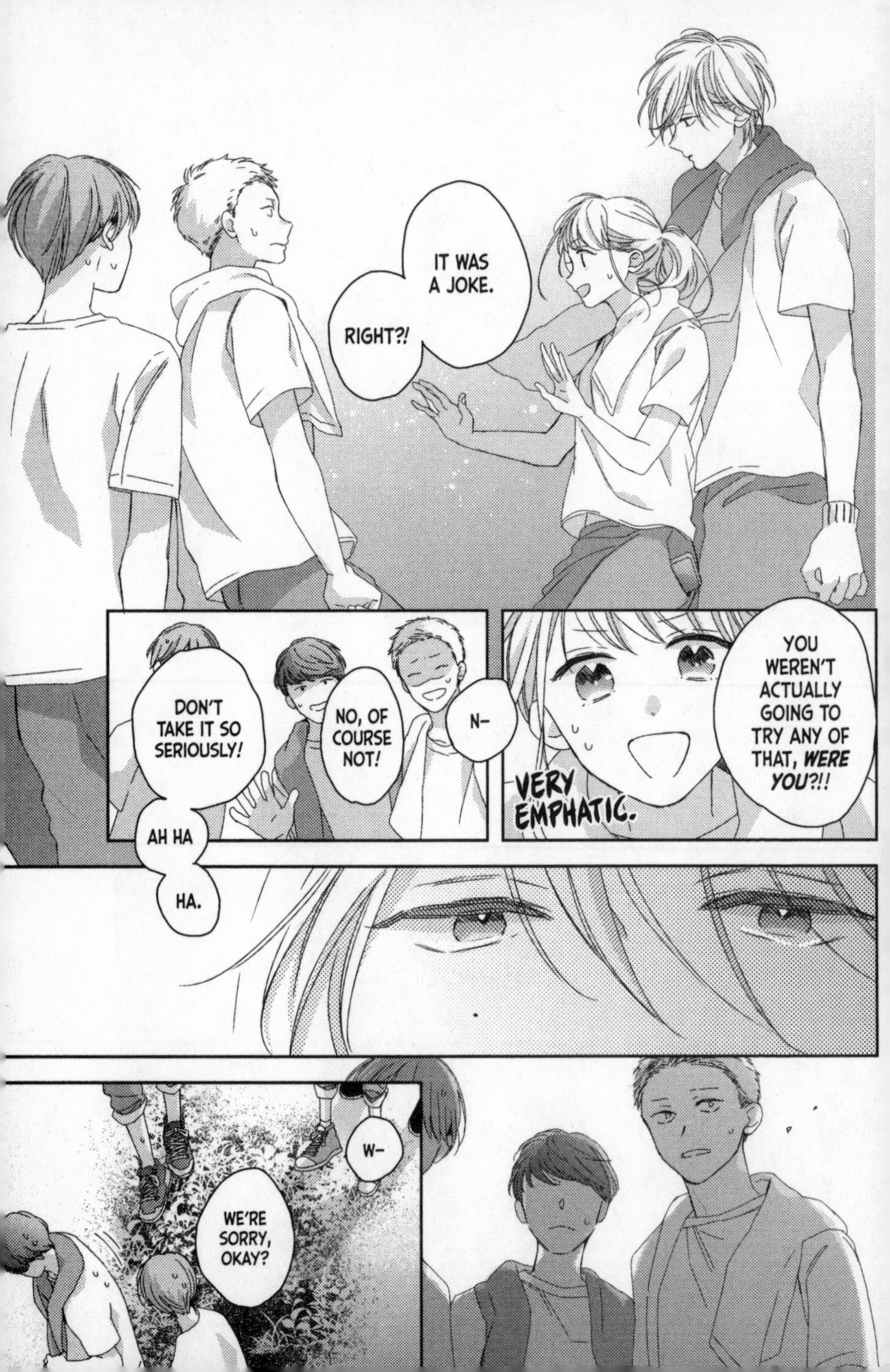
IT WAS A JOKE.
RIGHT?!
YOU WEREN'T ACTUALLY GOING TO TRY ANY OF THAT, *WERE YOU*?!!
VERY EMPHATIC.
N-
NO, OF COURSE NOT!
DON'T TAKE IT SO SERIOUSLY!
AH HA
HA.
W-
WE'RE SORRY, OKAY?

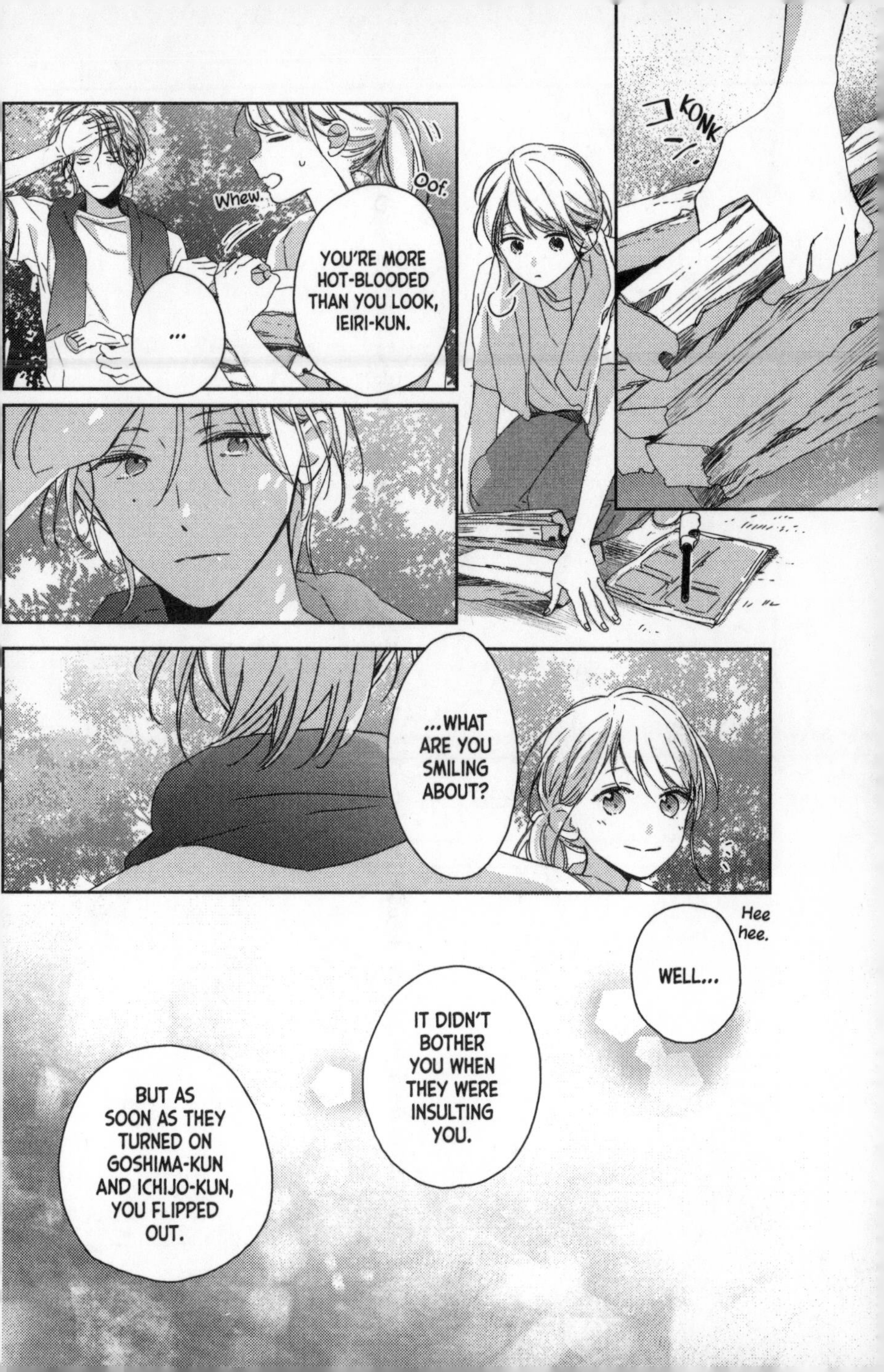
KONK
Oof.
YOU'RE MORE HOT-BLOODED THAN YOU LOOK, IEIRI-KUN.
Whew.
...
...WHAT ARE YOU SMILING ABOUT?
Hee hee.
WELL...
IT DIDN'T BOTHER YOU WHEN THEY WERE INSULTING YOU.
BUT AS SOON AS THEY TURNED ON GOSHIMA-KUN AND ICHIJO-KUN, YOU FLIPPED OUT.

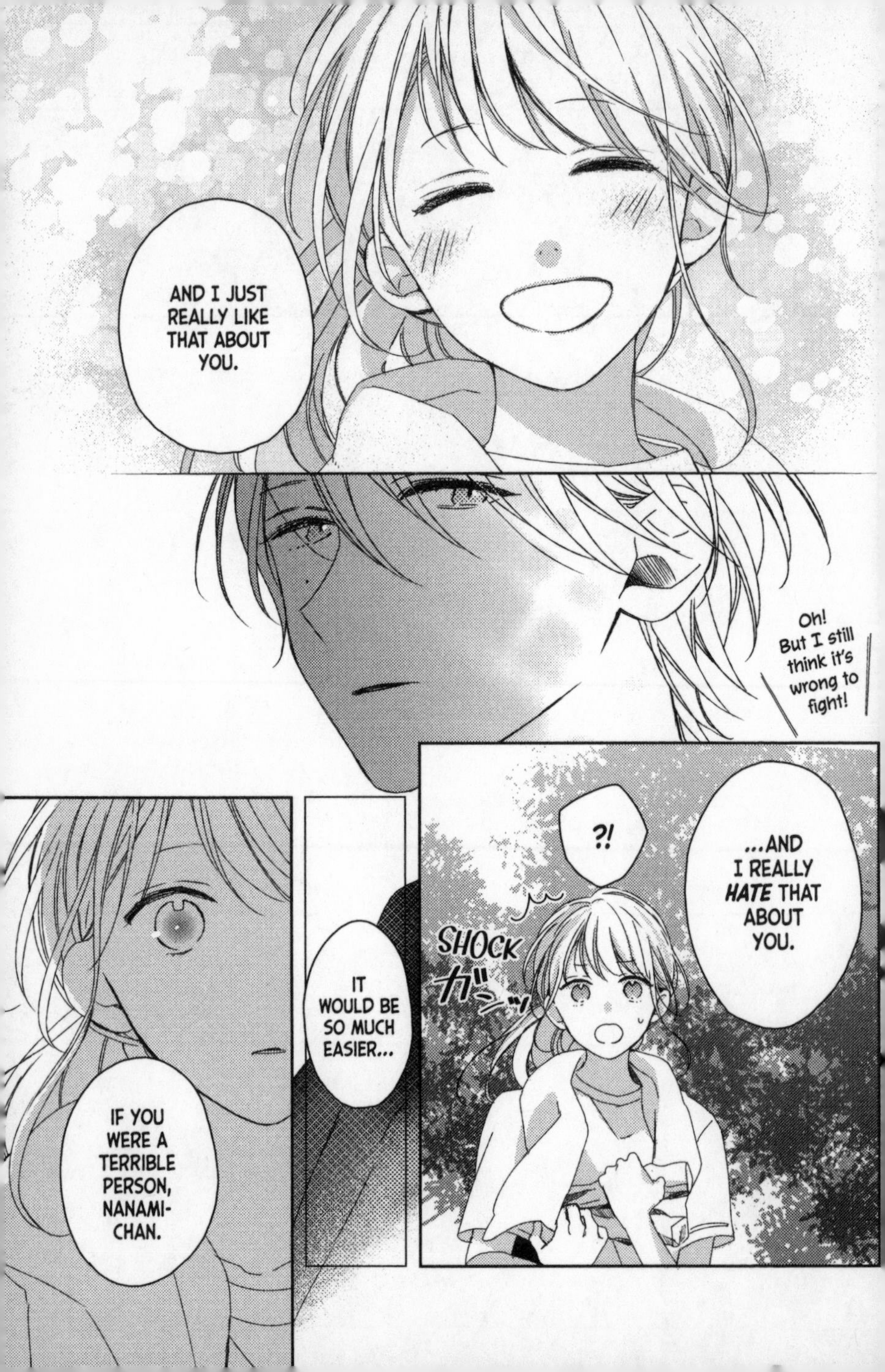
AND I JUST REALLY LIKE THAT ABOUT YOU.
Oh! But I still think it's wrong to fight!
...AND I REALLY HATE THAT ABOUT YOU.
?!
SHOCK
IT WOULD BE SO MUCH EASIER...
IF YOU WERE A TERRIBLE PERSON, NANAMI-CHAN.

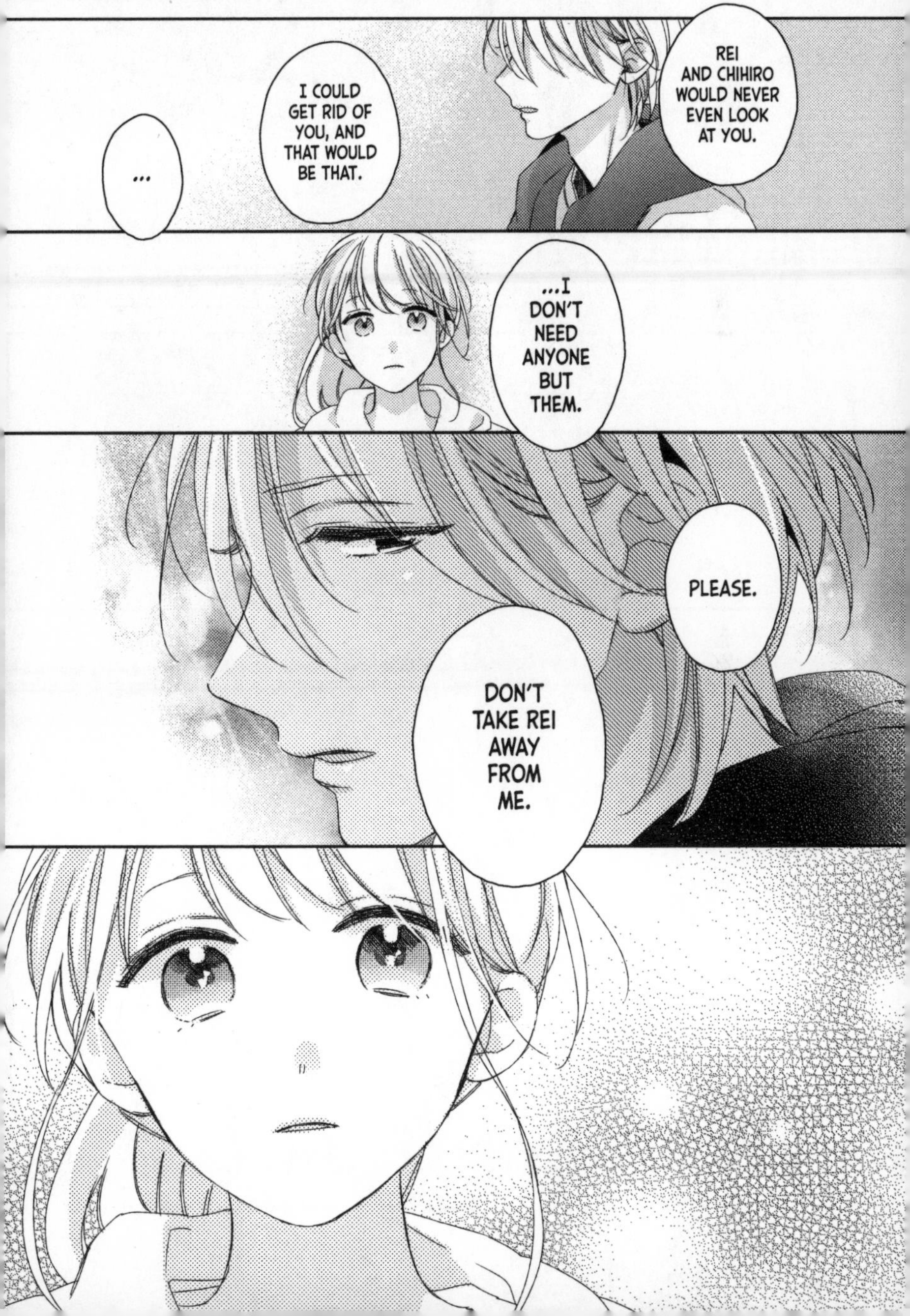
REI AND CHIHIRO WOULD NEVER EVEN LOOK AT YOU.
I COULD GET RID OF YOU, AND THAT WOULD BE THAT.
...
...I DON'T NEED ANYONE BUT THEM.
PLEASE.
DON'T TAKE REI AWAY FROM ME.

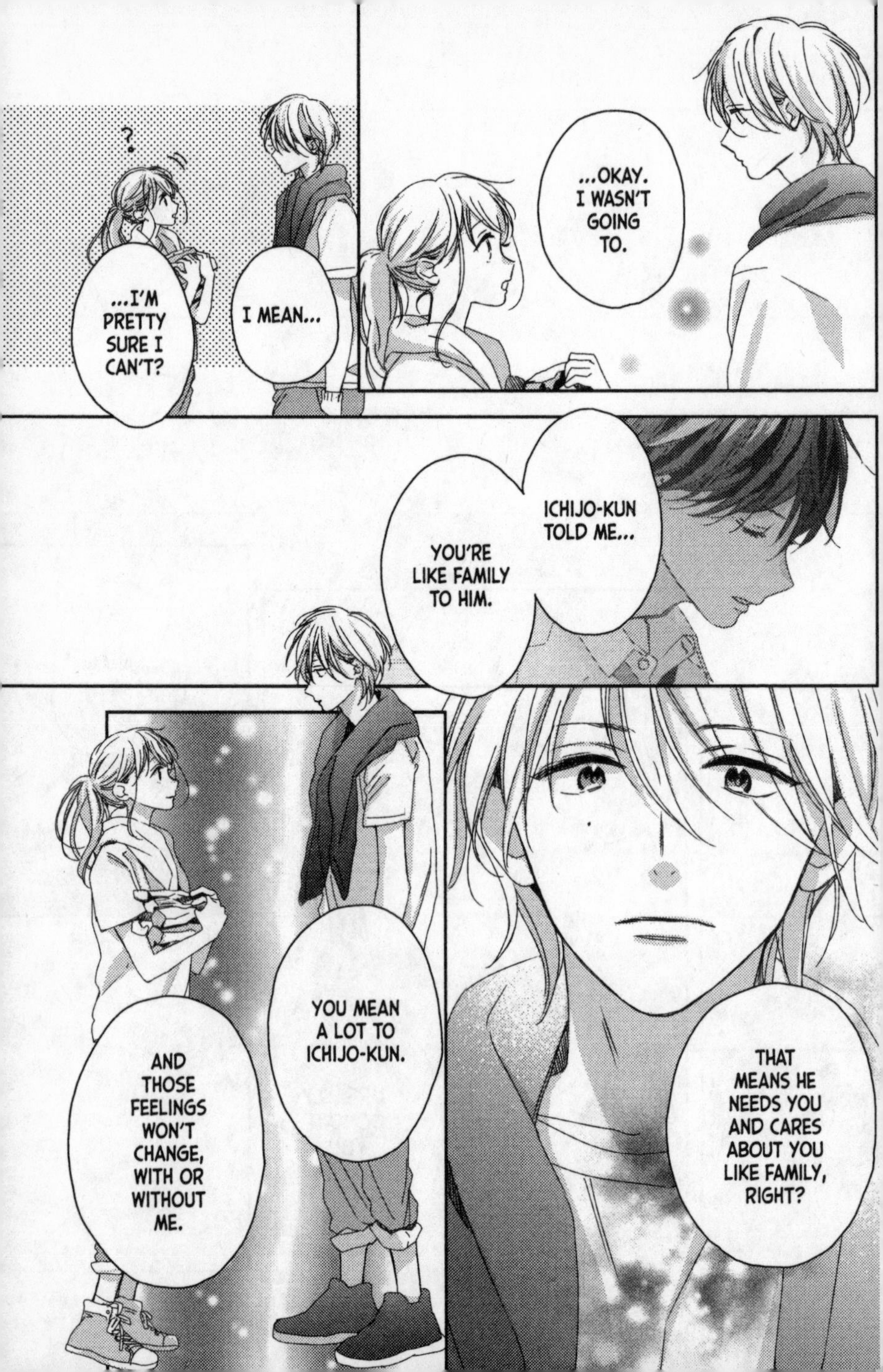
...OKAY. I WASN'T GOING TO.
I MEAN...
...I'M PRETTY SURE I CAN'T?
ICHIJO-KUN TOLD ME...
YOU'RE LIKE FAMILY TO HIM.
THAT MEANS HE NEEDS YOU AND CARES ABOUT YOU LIKE FAMILY, RIGHT?
YOU MEAN A LOT TO ICHIJO-KUN.
AND THOSE FEELINGS WON'T CHANGE, WITH OR WITHOUT ME.

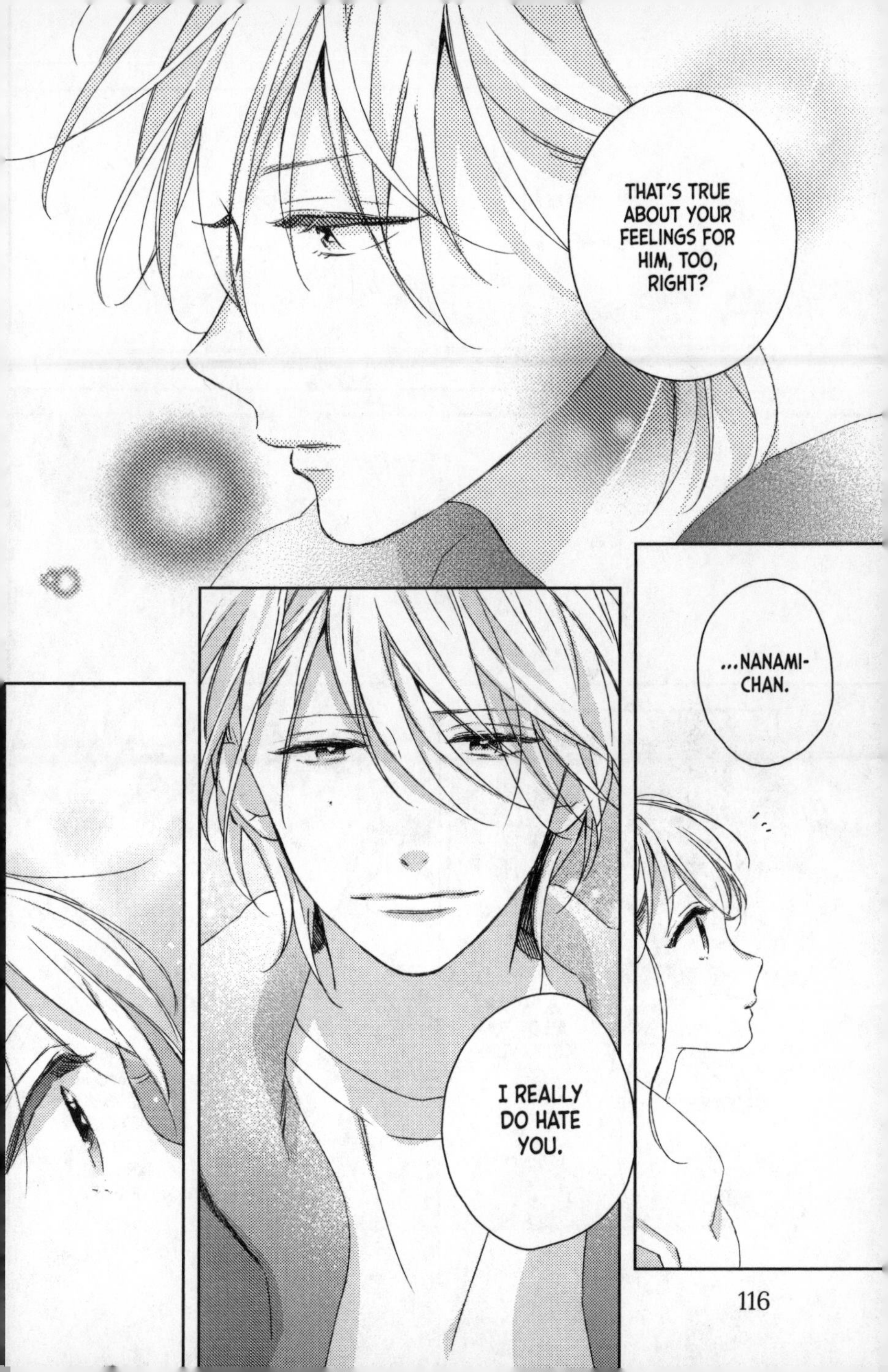
THAT'S TRUE ABOUT YOUR FEELINGS FOR HIM, TOO, RIGHT?
...NANAMI-CHAN.
I REALLY DO HATE YOU.

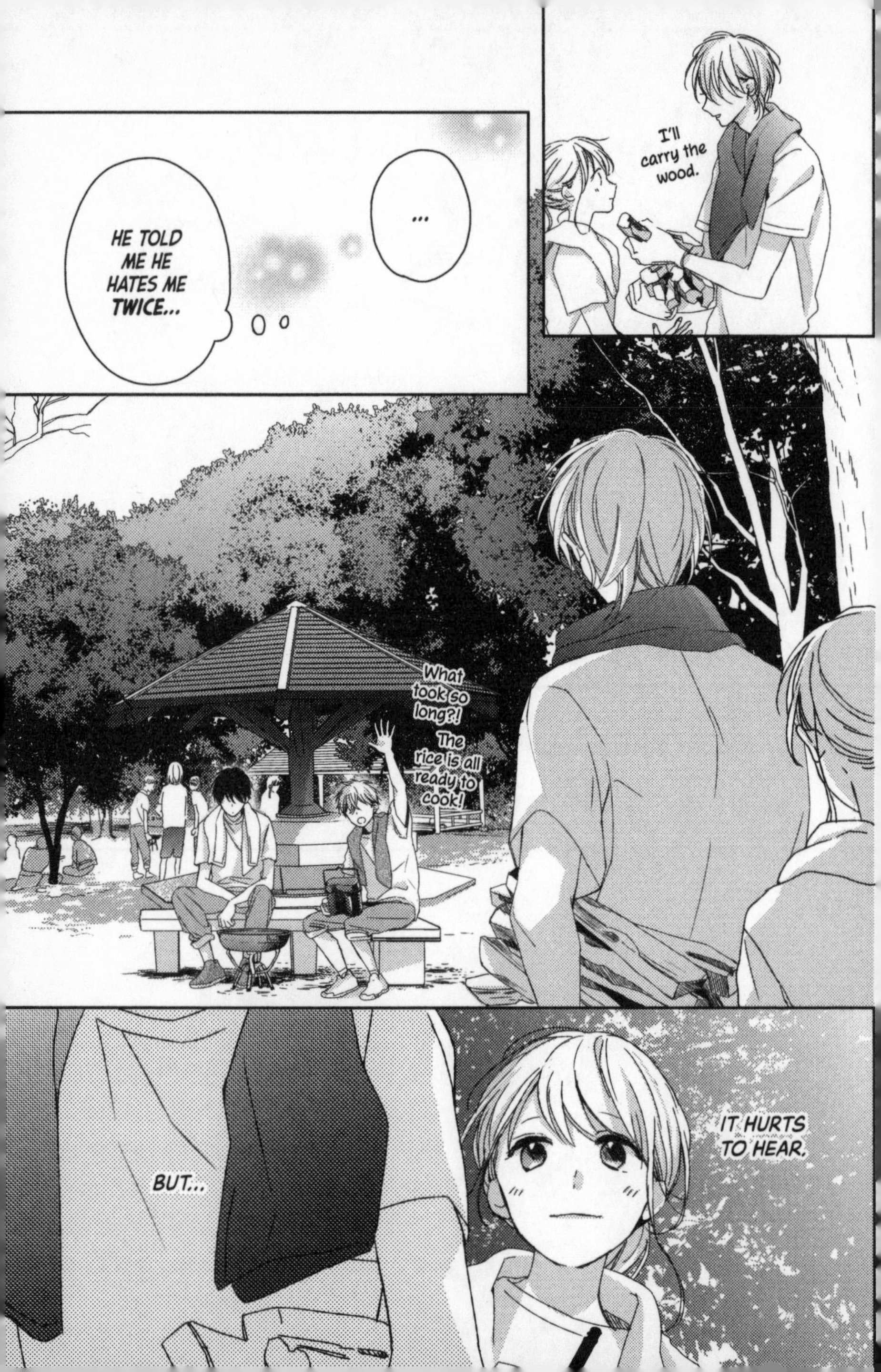
I'll carry the wood.
...
HE TOLD ME HE HATES ME TWICE...
What took so long?!
The rice is all ready to cook!
IT HURTS TO HEAR.
BUT...

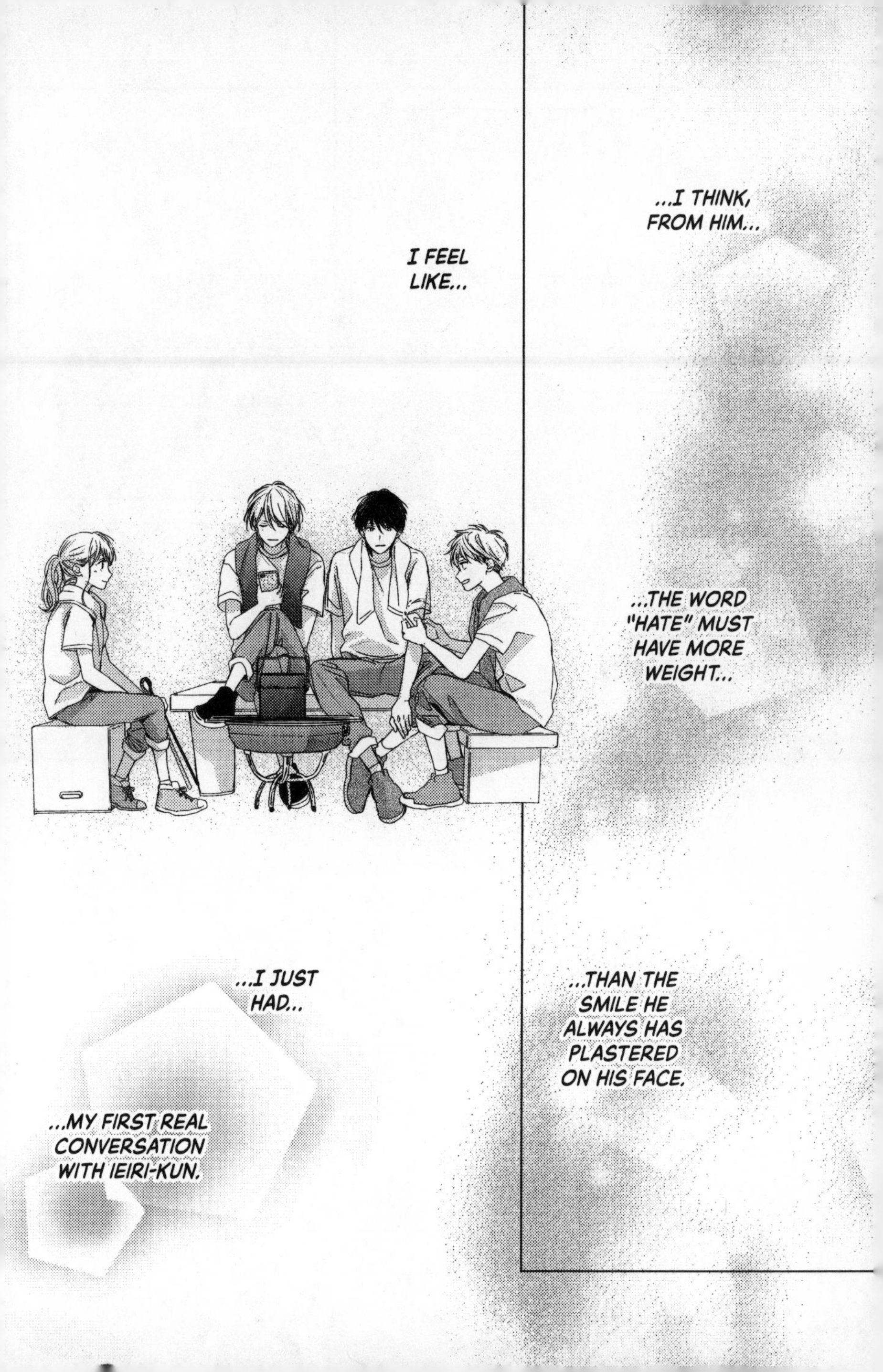
...I THINK, FROM HIM...
...THE WORD "HATE" MUST HAVE MORE WEIGHT...
...THAN THE SMILE HE ALWAYS HAS PLASTERED ON HIS FACE.
I FEEL LIKE...
...I JUST HAD...
...MY FIRST REAL CONVERSATION WITH IEIRI-KUN.

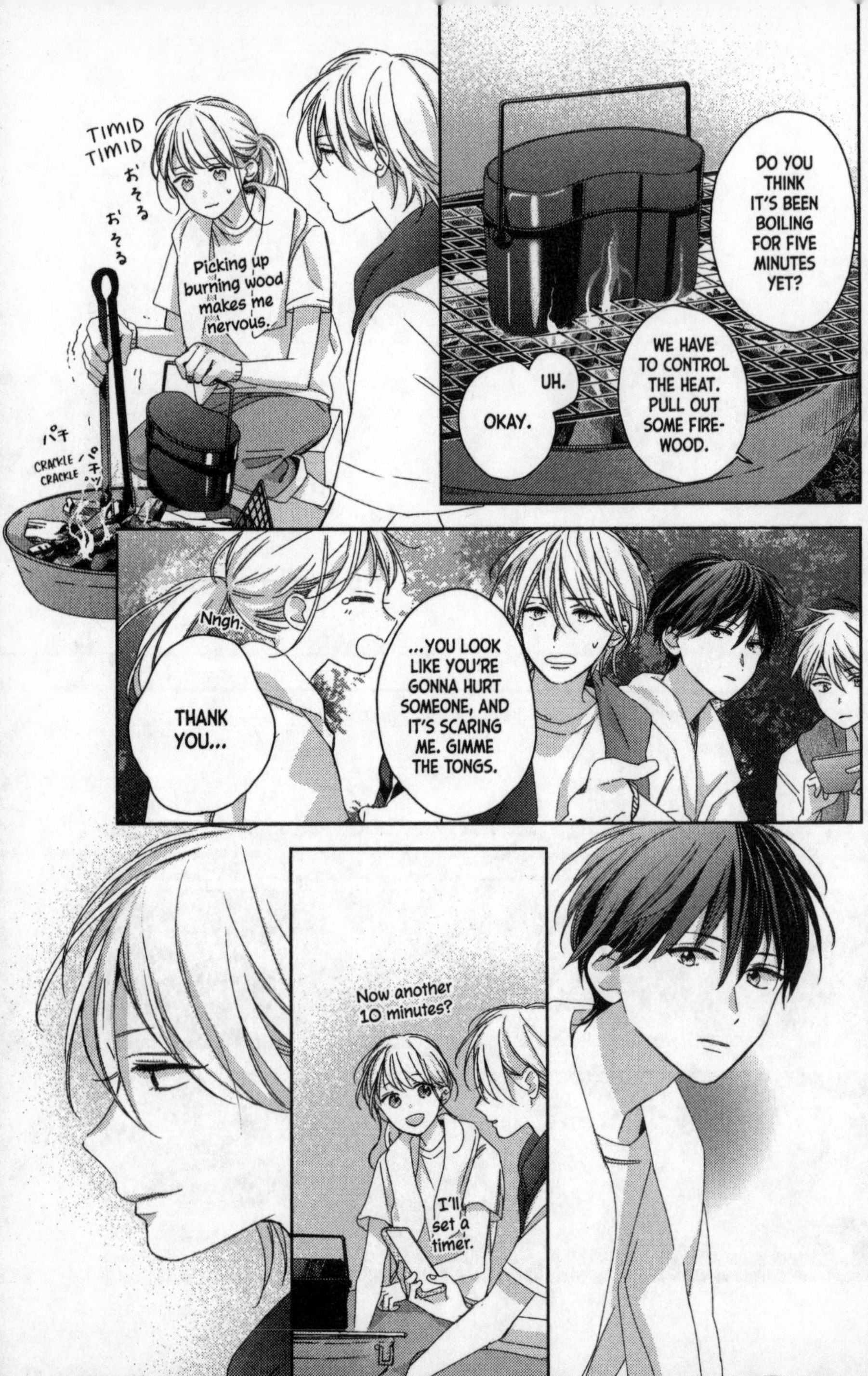
DO YOU THINK IT'S BEEN BOILING FOR FIVE MINUTES YET?
WE HAVE TO CONTROL THE HEAT. PULL OUT SOME FIRE-WOOD.
UH.
OKAY.
TIMID TIMID
おそるおそる
Picking up burning wood makes me nervous.
パチパチッ
CRACKLE CRACKLE
...YOU LOOK LIKE YOU'RE GONNA HURT SOMEONE, AND IT'S SCARING ME. GIMME THE TONGS.
Nngh.
THANK YOU...
Now another 10 minutes?
I'll set a timer.

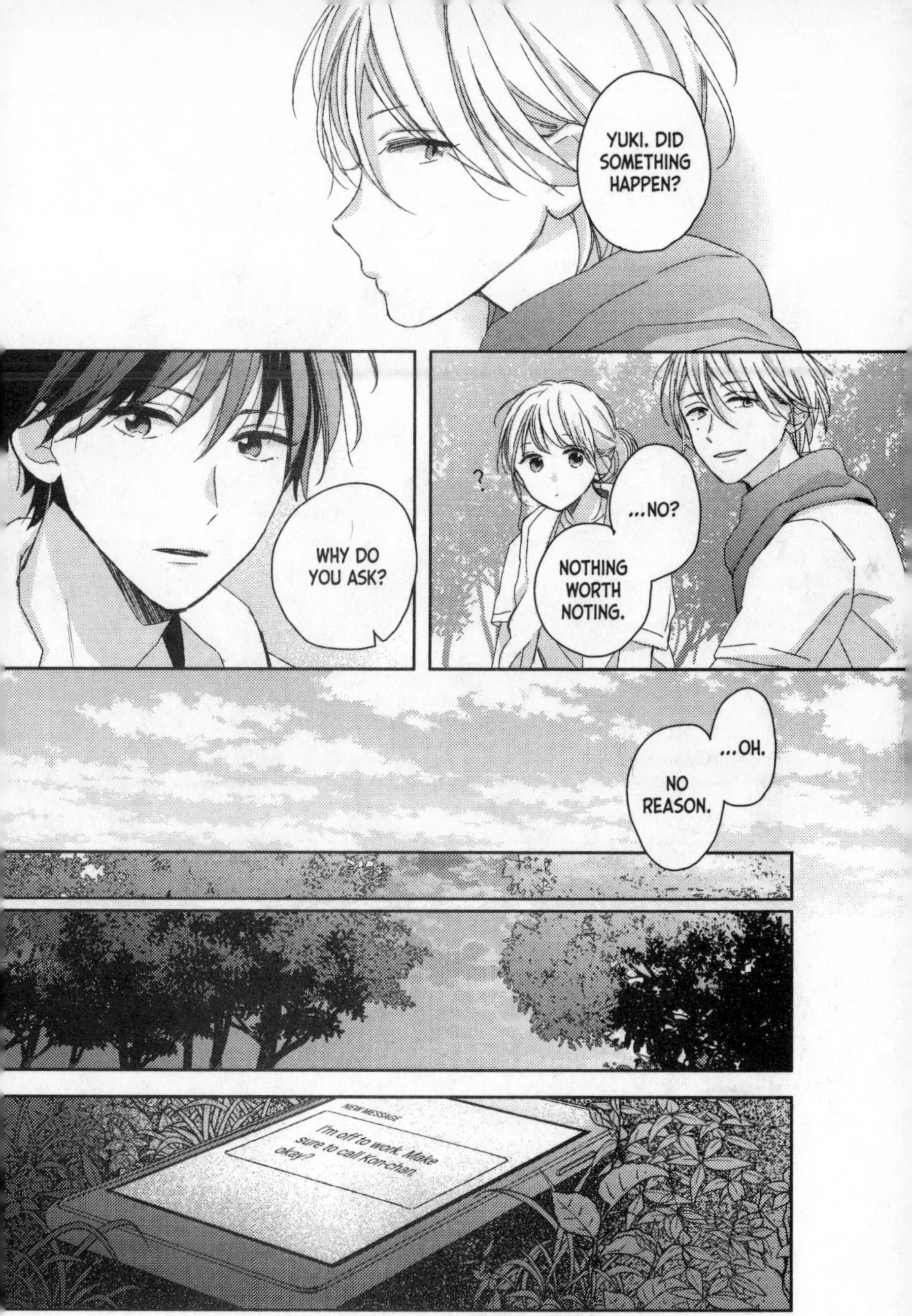
YUKI. DID SOMETHING HAPPEN?
...NO?
NOTHING WORTH NOTING.
WHY DO YOU ASK?
...OH.
NO REASON.
NEW MESSAGE
I'm off to work. Make sure to call Kon-chan, okay?

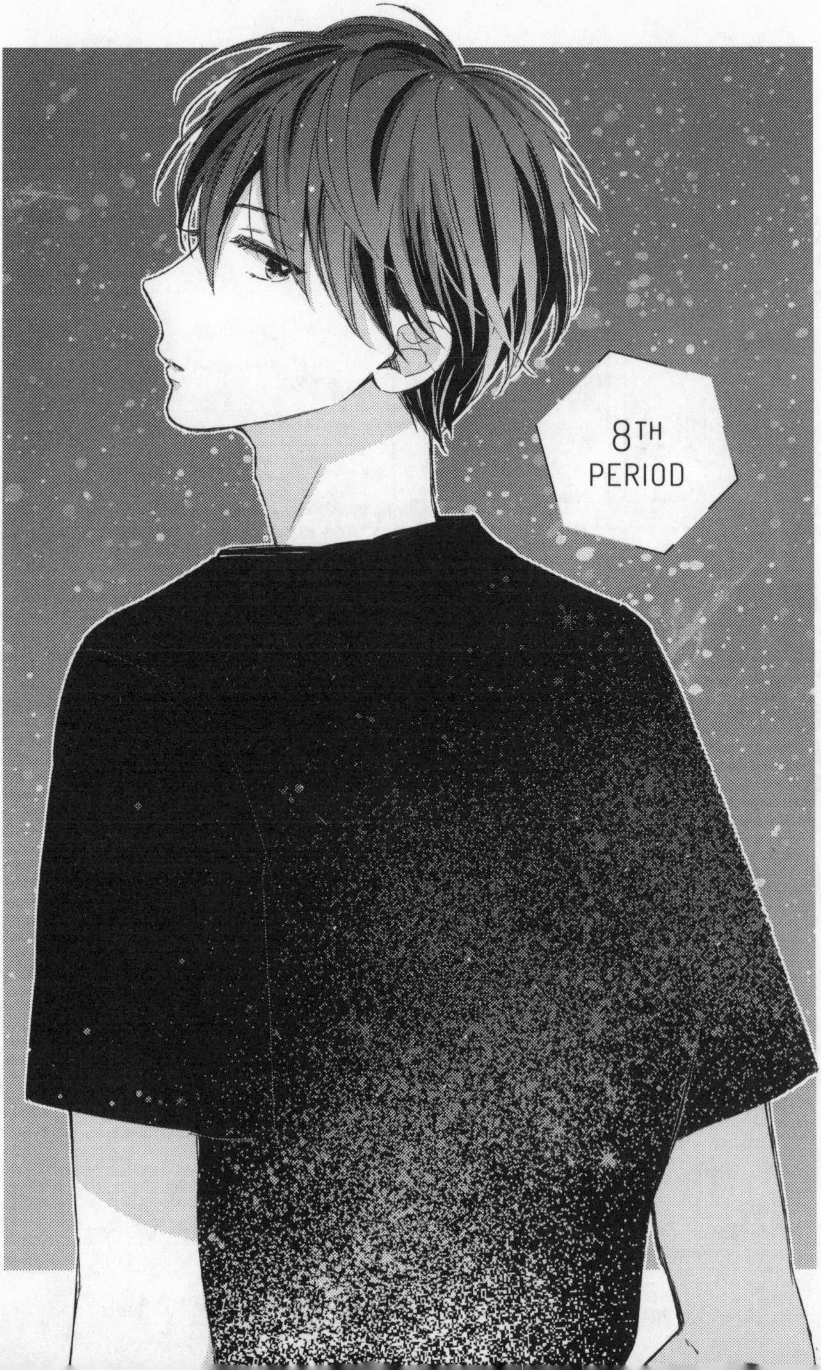
8TH
PERIOD

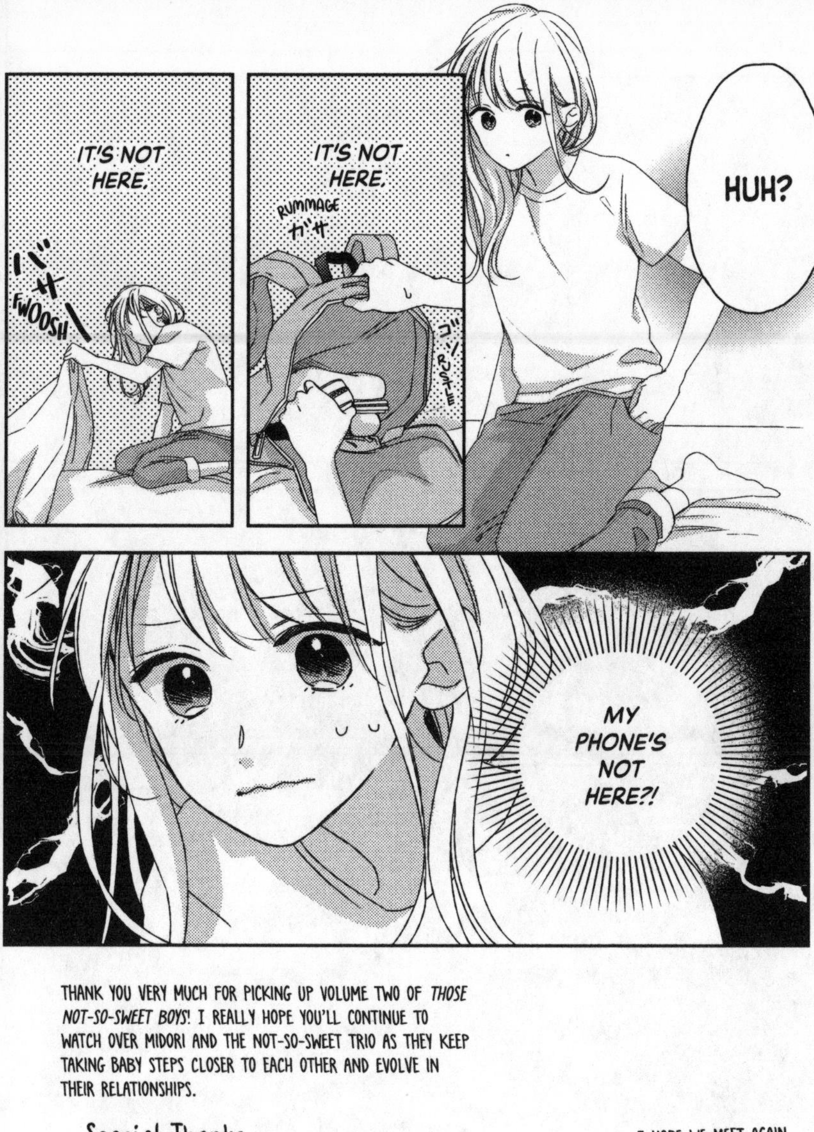
HUH?
IT'S NOT HERE.
RUMMAGE
ガサ
ゴソ
RUSTLE
IT'S NOT HERE.
バサー
FWOOSH
MY PHONE'S NOT HERE?!

THANK YOU VERY MUCH FOR PICKING UP VOLUME TWO OF *THOSE NOT-SO-SWEET BOYS*! I REALLY HOPE YOU'LL CONTINUE TO WATCH OVER MIDORI AND THE NOT-SO-SWEET TRIO AS THEY KEEP TAKING BABY STEPS CLOSER TO EACH OTHER AND EVOLVE IN THEIR RELATIONSHIPS.

Special Thanks

AKI NISHIHIRO-CHAN
FRIENDS, FAMILY

MY EDITOR
KODAMA-SAN
EVERYONE AT THE DESSERT EDITORIAL DEPARTMENT

ARCO INC.
EVERYONE WHO WAS INVOLVED IN THE CREATION AND SELLING OF THIS WORK

I HOPE WE MEET AGAIN IN VOLUME 3...!

野切耀子

YOKO NOGIRI

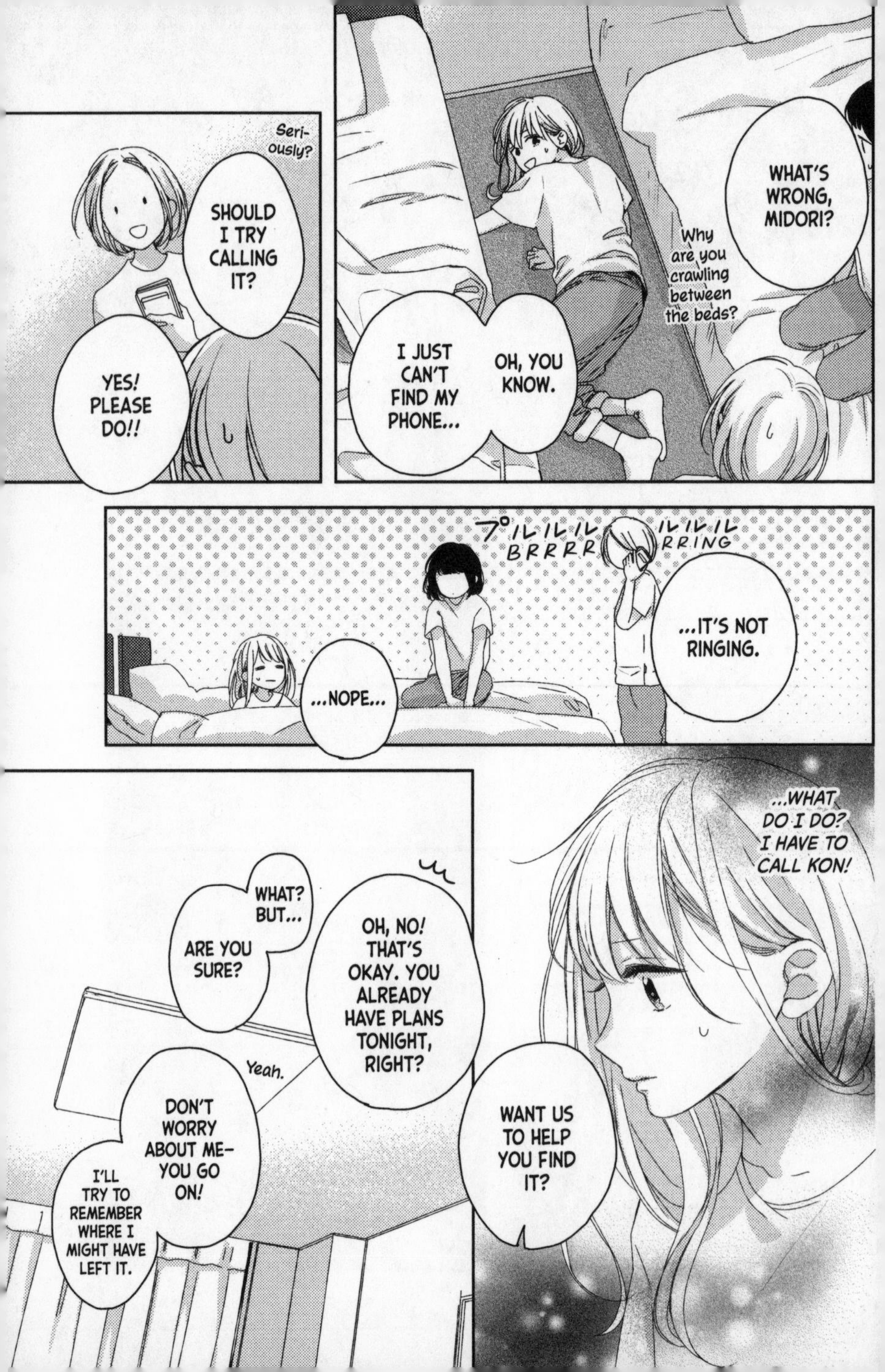
WHAT'S WRONG, MIDORI?
Why are you crawling between the beds?
OH, YOU KNOW.
I JUST CAN'T FIND MY PHONE...
Seri-ously?
SHOULD I TRY CALLING IT?
YES! PLEASE DO!!
プルルル BRRRR
ルルル RRING
...IT'S NOT RINGING.
...NOPE...
...WHAT DO I DO? I HAVE TO CALL KON!
WANT US TO HELP YOU FIND IT?
OH, NO! THAT'S OKAY. YOU ALREADY HAVE PLANS TONIGHT, RIGHT?
WHAT? BUT...
ARE YOU SURE?
Yeah.
DON'T WORRY ABOUT ME—YOU GO ON!
I'LL TRY TO REMEMBER WHERE I MIGHT HAVE LEFT IT.

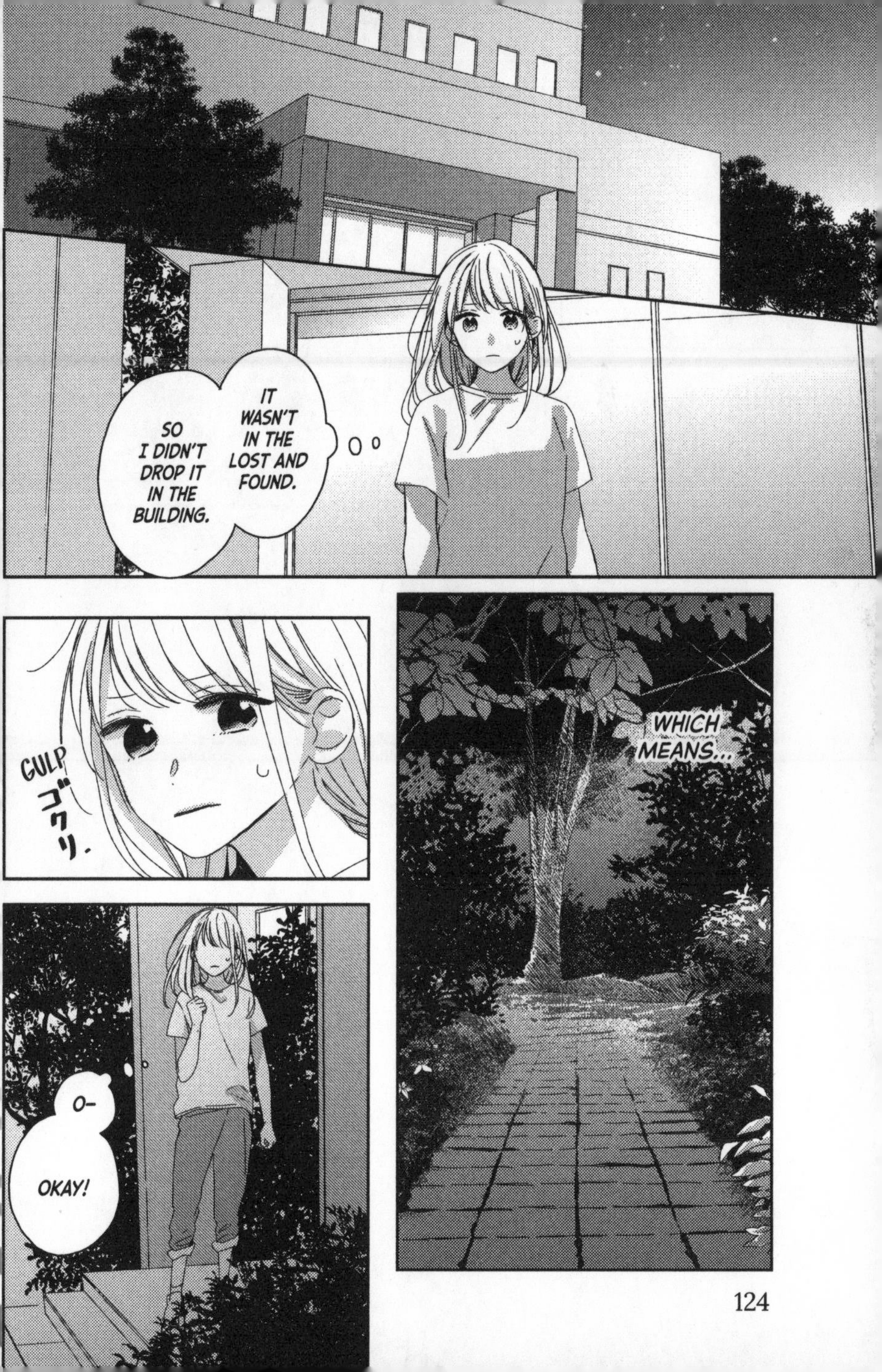
IT WASN'T IN THE LOST AND FOUND.
SO I DIDN'T DROP IT IN THE BUILDING.
WHICH MEANS...
GULP
ゴクリ
O- OKAY!

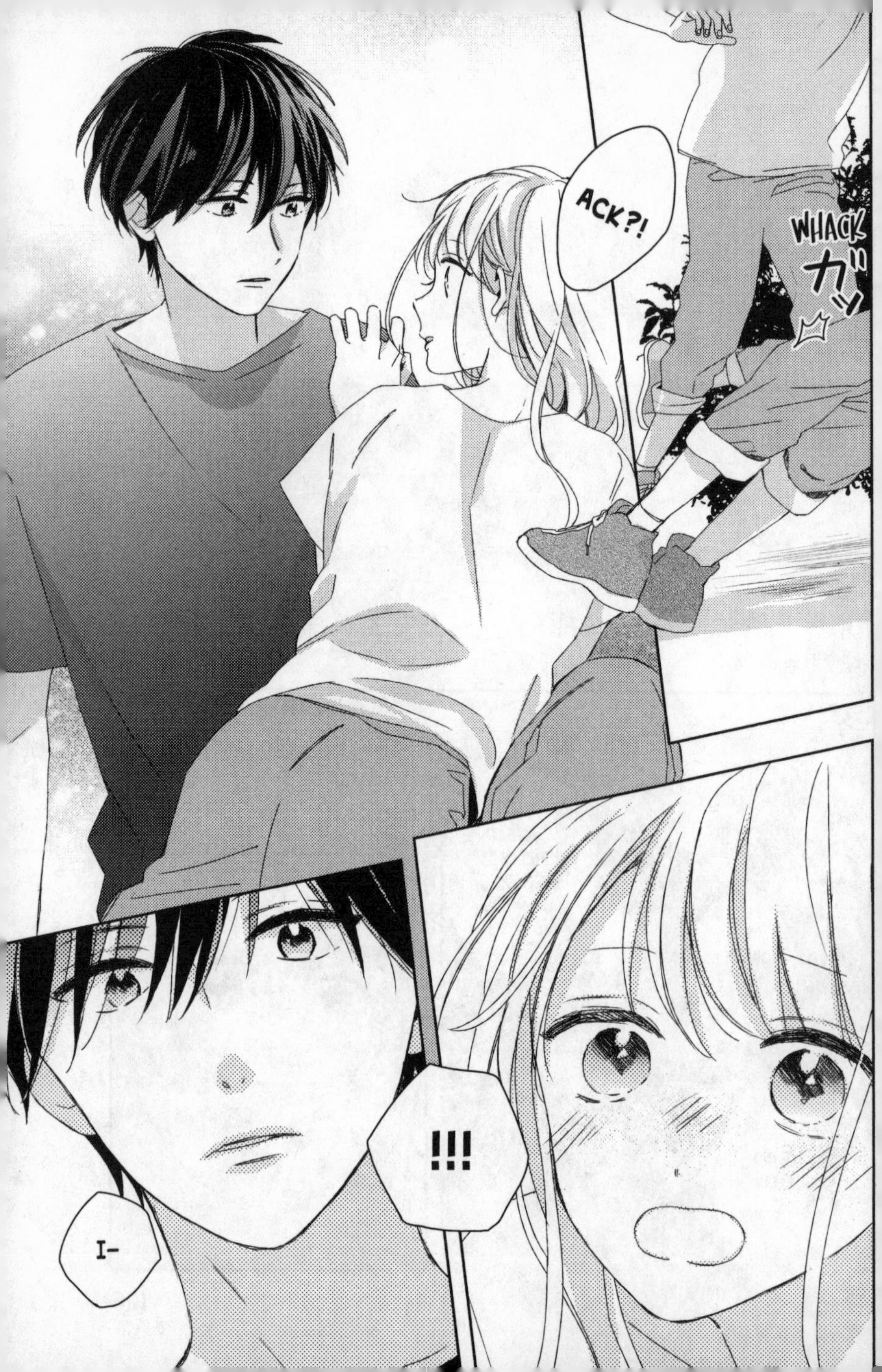
WHACK
ガッ
ACK?!
!!!
I–

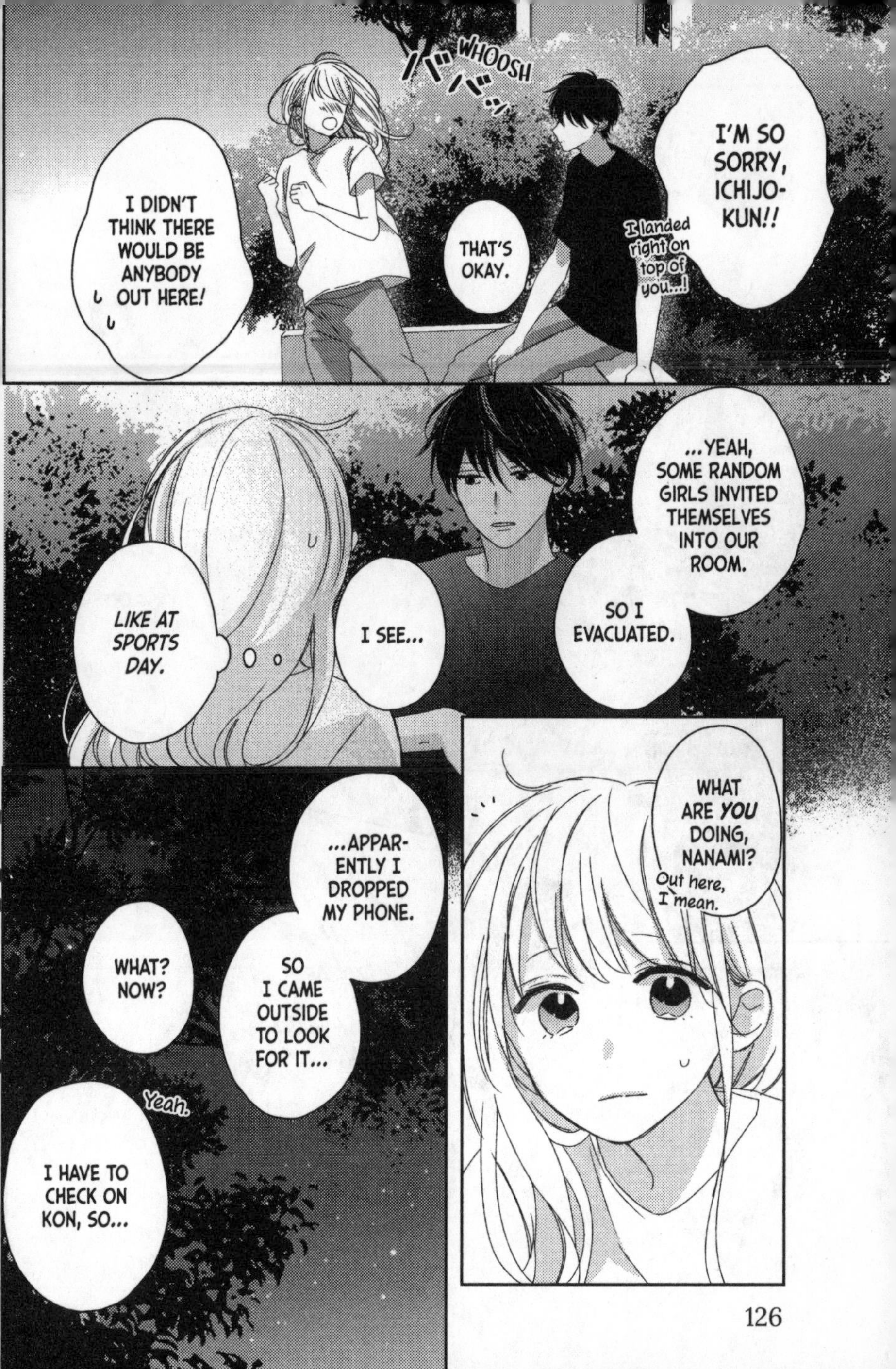
I'M SO SORRY, ICHIJO-KUN!!
I landed right on top of you...!
WHOOSH
バッ
THAT'S OKAY.
I DIDN'T THINK THERE WOULD BE ANYBODY OUT HERE!
...YEAH, SOME RANDOM GIRLS INVITED THEMSELVES INTO OUR ROOM.
SO I EVACUATED.
I SEE...
LIKE AT SPORTS DAY.
WHAT ARE *YOU* DOING, NANAMI?
Out here, I mean.
...APPARENTLY I DROPPED MY PHONE.
SO I CAME OUTSIDE TO LOOK FOR IT...
WHAT? NOW?
Yeah.
I HAVE TO CHECK ON KON, SO...

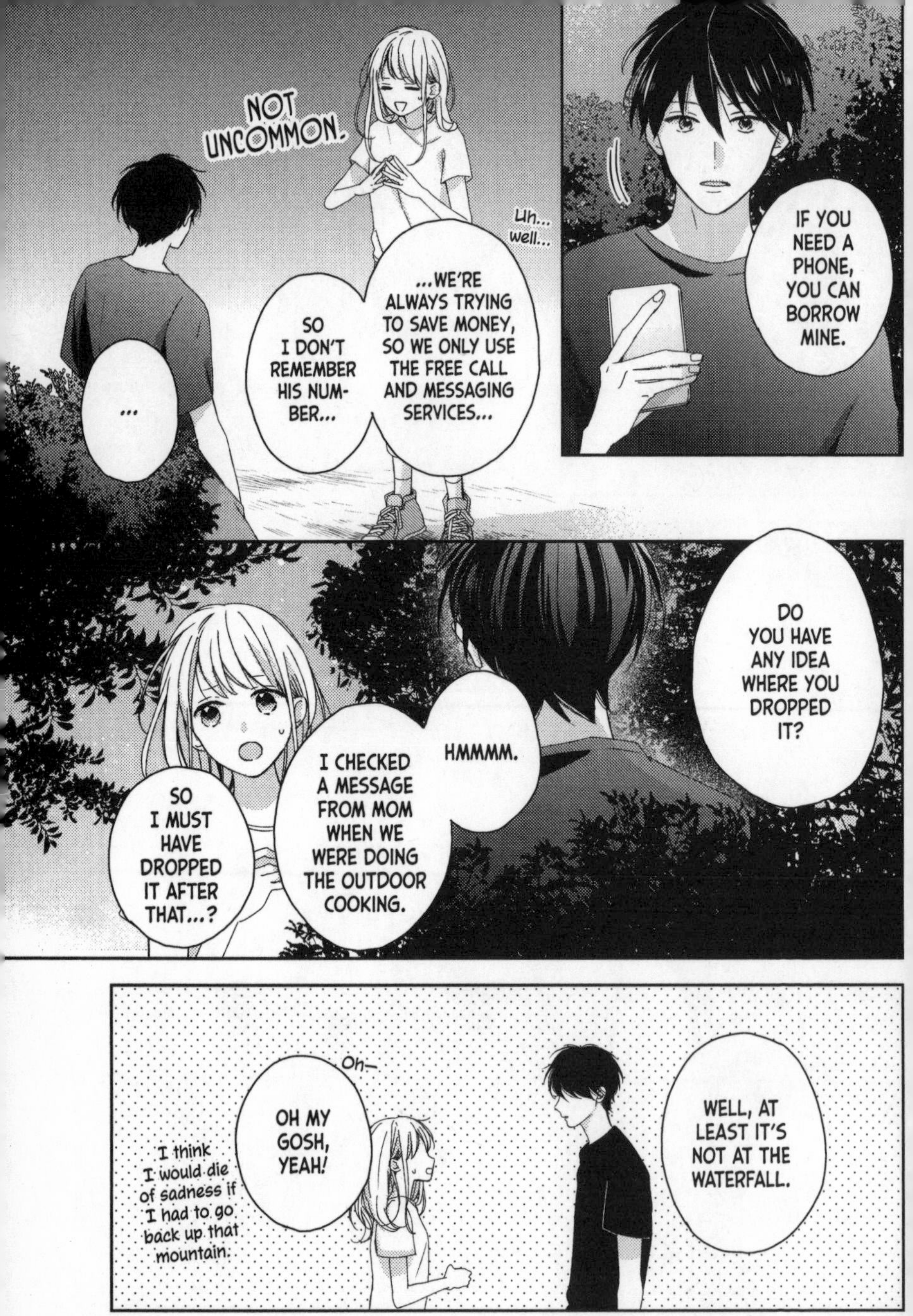
IF YOU NEED A PHONE, YOU CAN BORROW MINE.
...
Uh... well...
...WE'RE ALWAYS TRYING TO SAVE MONEY, SO WE ONLY USE THE FREE CALL AND MESSAGING SERVICES...
SO I DON'T REMEMBER HIS NUMBER...
NOT UNCOMMON.
DO YOU HAVE ANY IDEA WHERE YOU DROPPED IT?
HMMMM.
I CHECKED A MESSAGE FROM MOM WHEN WE WERE DOING THE OUTDOOR COOKING.
SO I MUST HAVE DROPPED IT AFTER THAT...?
WELL, AT LEAST IT'S NOT AT THE WATERFALL.
Oh—
OH MY GOSH, YEAH!
I think I would die of sadness if I had to go back up that mountain.

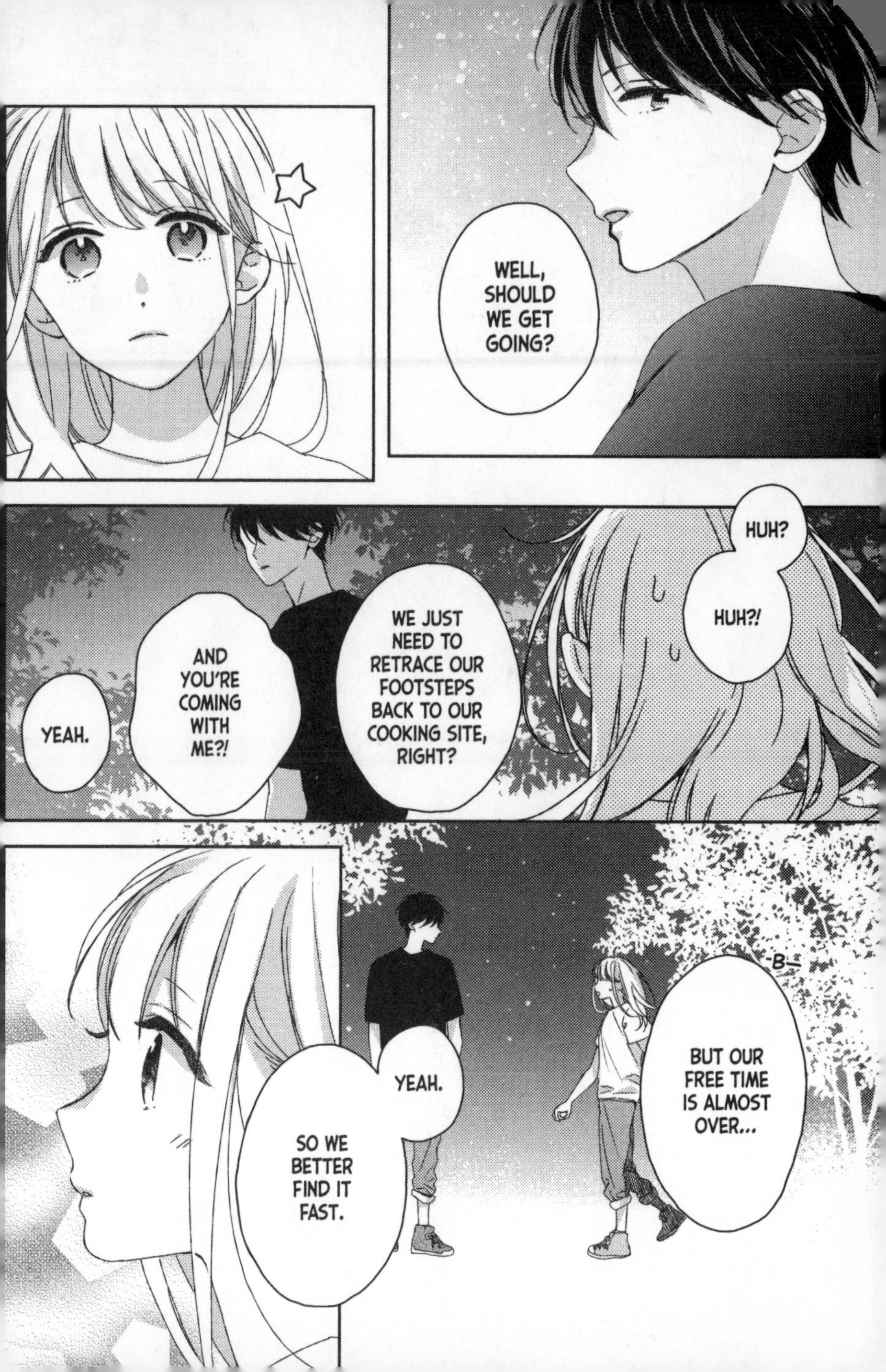
WELL, SHOULD WE GET GOING?
HUH?
HUH?!
WE JUST NEED TO RETRACE OUR FOOTSTEPS BACK TO OUR COOKING SITE, RIGHT?
AND YOU'RE COMING WITH ME?!
YEAH.
-B—
BUT OUR FREE TIME IS ALMOST OVER...
YEAH.
SO WE BETTER FIND IT FAST.

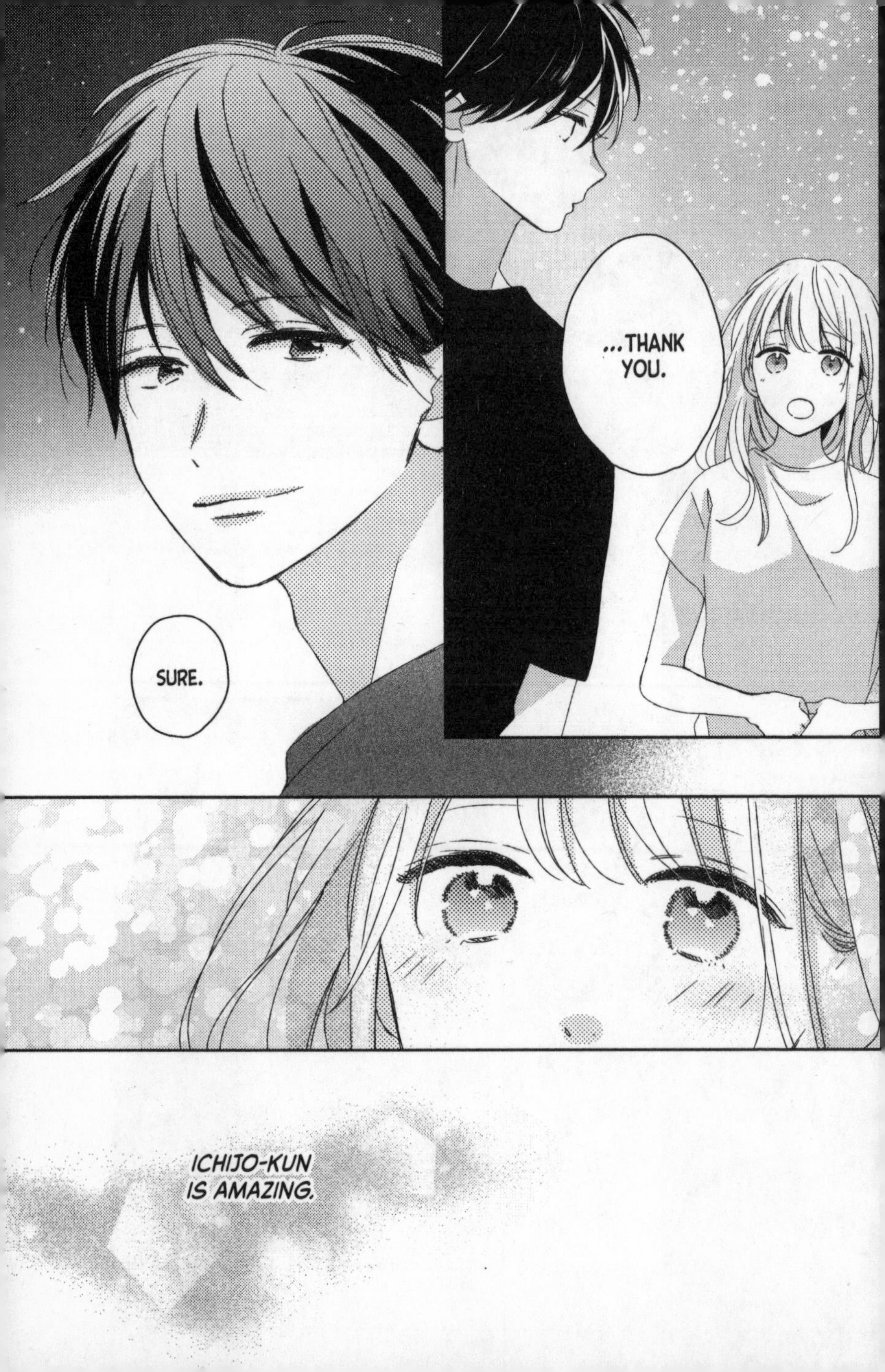
...THANK YOU.
SURE.
ICHIJO-KUN IS AMAZING.

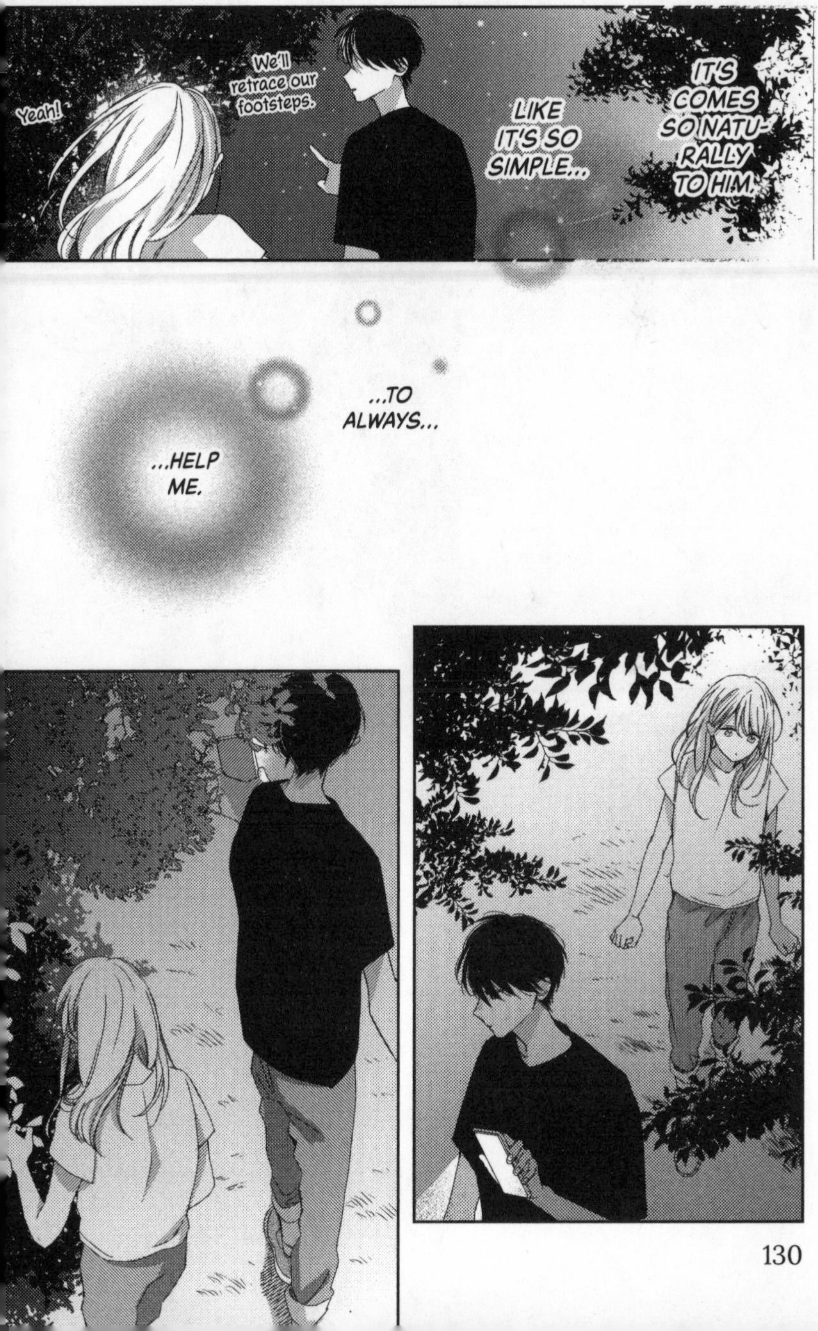
IT'S COMES SO NATU-RALLY TO HIM.
LIKE IT'S SO SIMPLE...
We'll retrace our footsteps.
Yeah!
...TO ALWAYS...
...HELP ME.

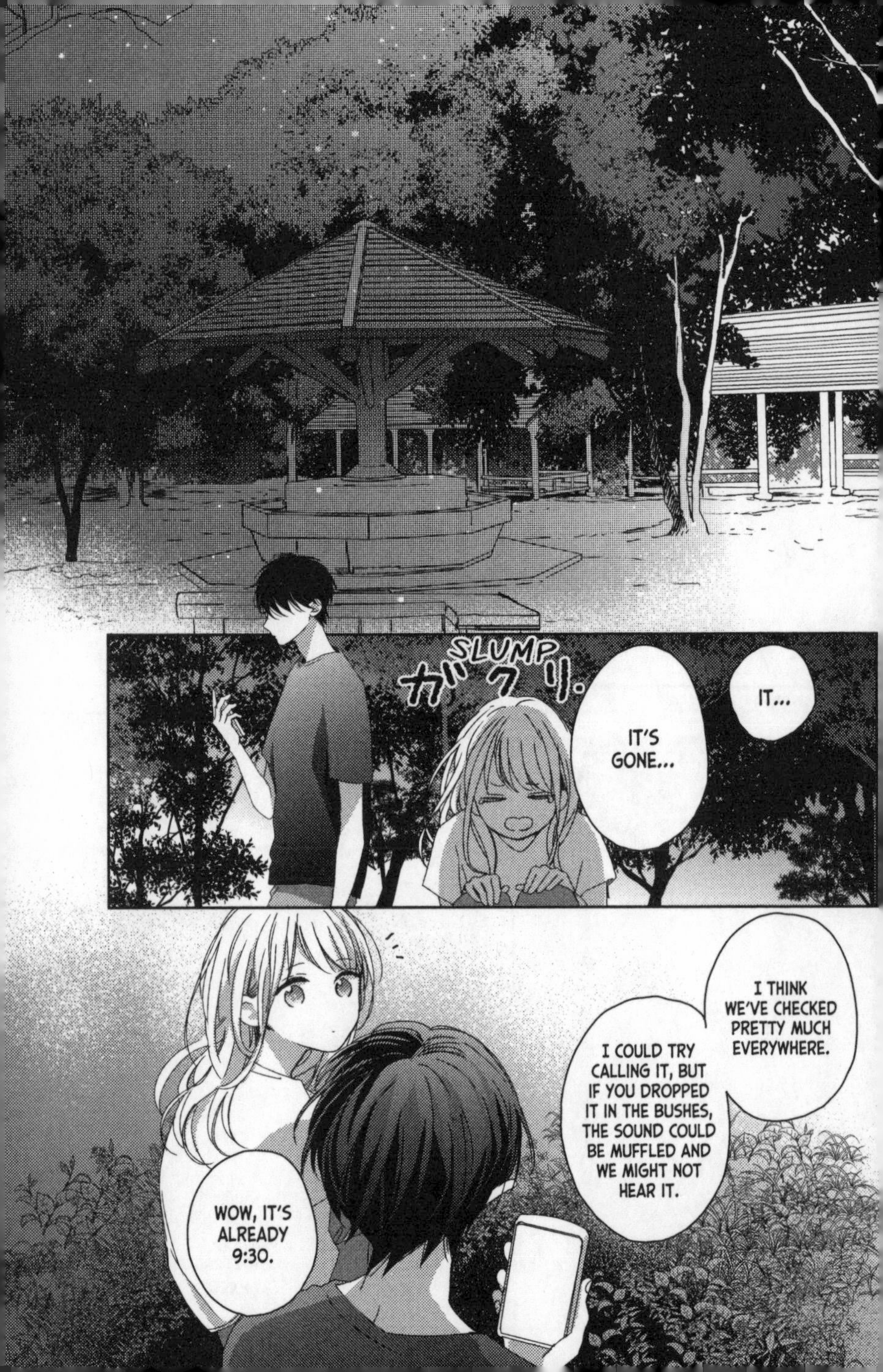
IT...
IT'S GONE...
SLUMP
I THINK WE'VE CHECKED PRETTY MUCH EVERYWHERE.
I COULD TRY CALLING IT, BUT IF YOU DROPPED IT IN THE BUSHES, THE SOUND COULD BE MUFFLED AND WE MIGHT NOT HEAR IT.
WOW, IT'S ALREADY 9:30.

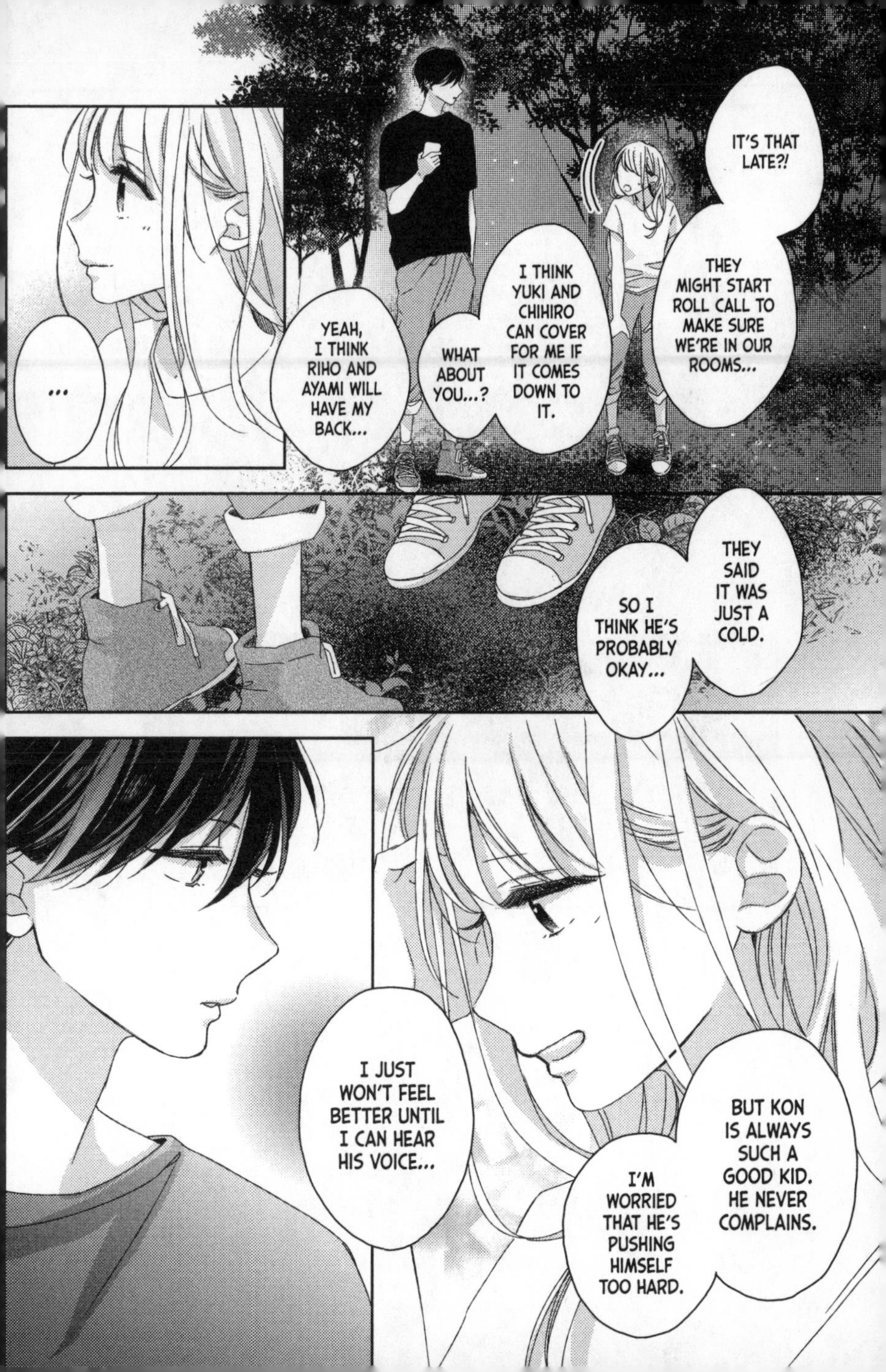
IT'S THAT LATE?!
THEY MIGHT START ROLL CALL TO MAKE SURE WE'RE IN OUR ROOMS...
I THINK YUKI AND CHIHIRO CAN COVER FOR ME IF IT COMES DOWN TO IT.
WHAT ABOUT YOU...?
YEAH, I THINK RIHO AND AYAMI WILL HAVE MY BACK...
...
THEY SAID IT WAS JUST A COLD.
SO I THINK HE'S PROBABLY OKAY...
BUT KON IS ALWAYS SUCH A GOOD KID. HE NEVER COMPLAINS.
I'M WORRIED THAT HE'S PUSHING HIMSELF TOO HARD.
I JUST WON'T FEEL BETTER UNTIL I CAN HEAR HIS VOICE...

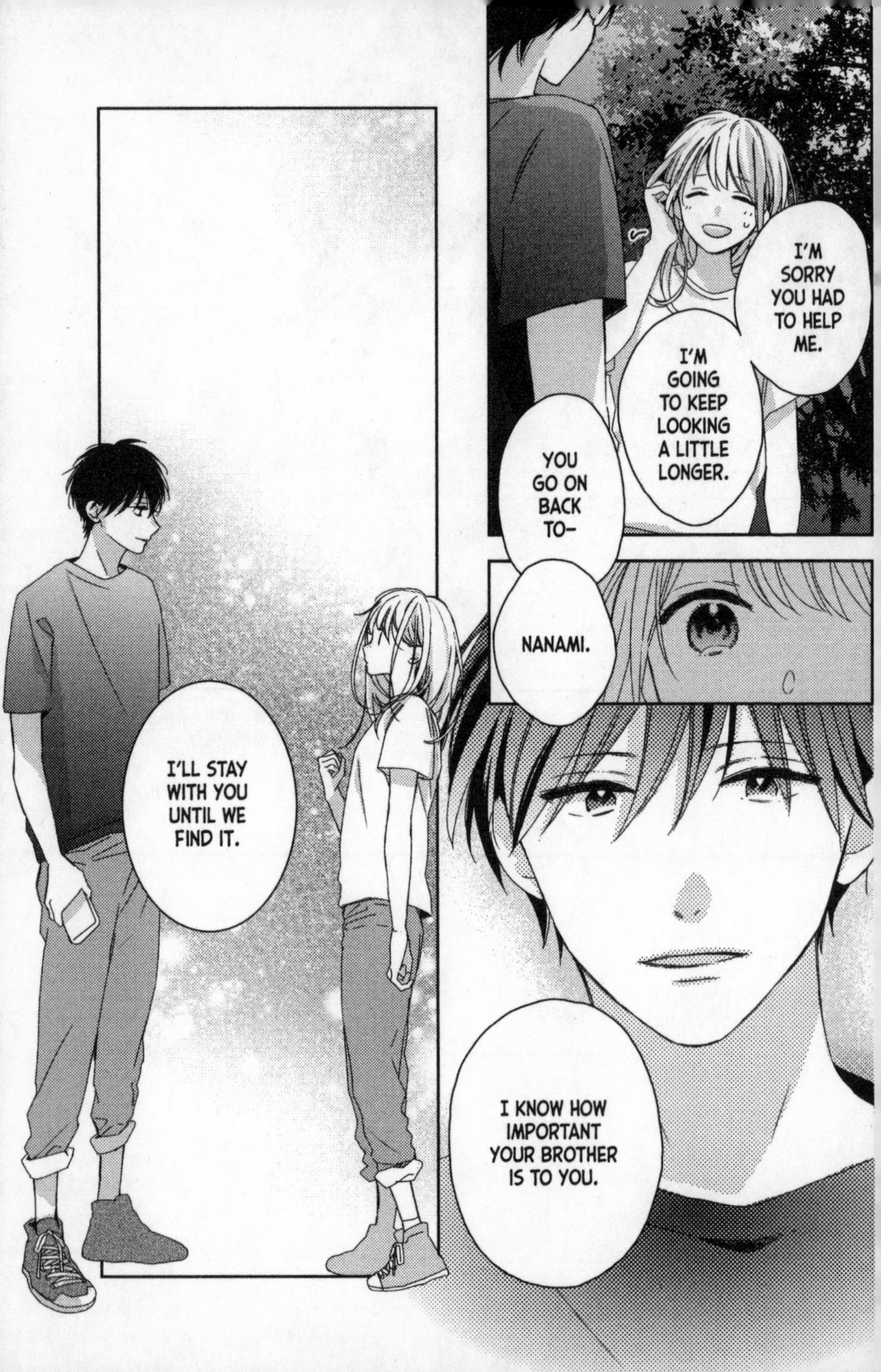
I'M SORRY YOU HAD TO HELP ME.
I'M GOING TO KEEP LOOKING A LITTLE LONGER.
YOU GO ON BACK TO—
NANAMI.
I KNOW HOW IMPORTANT YOUR BROTHER IS TO YOU.
I'LL STAY WITH YOU UNTIL WE FIND IT.

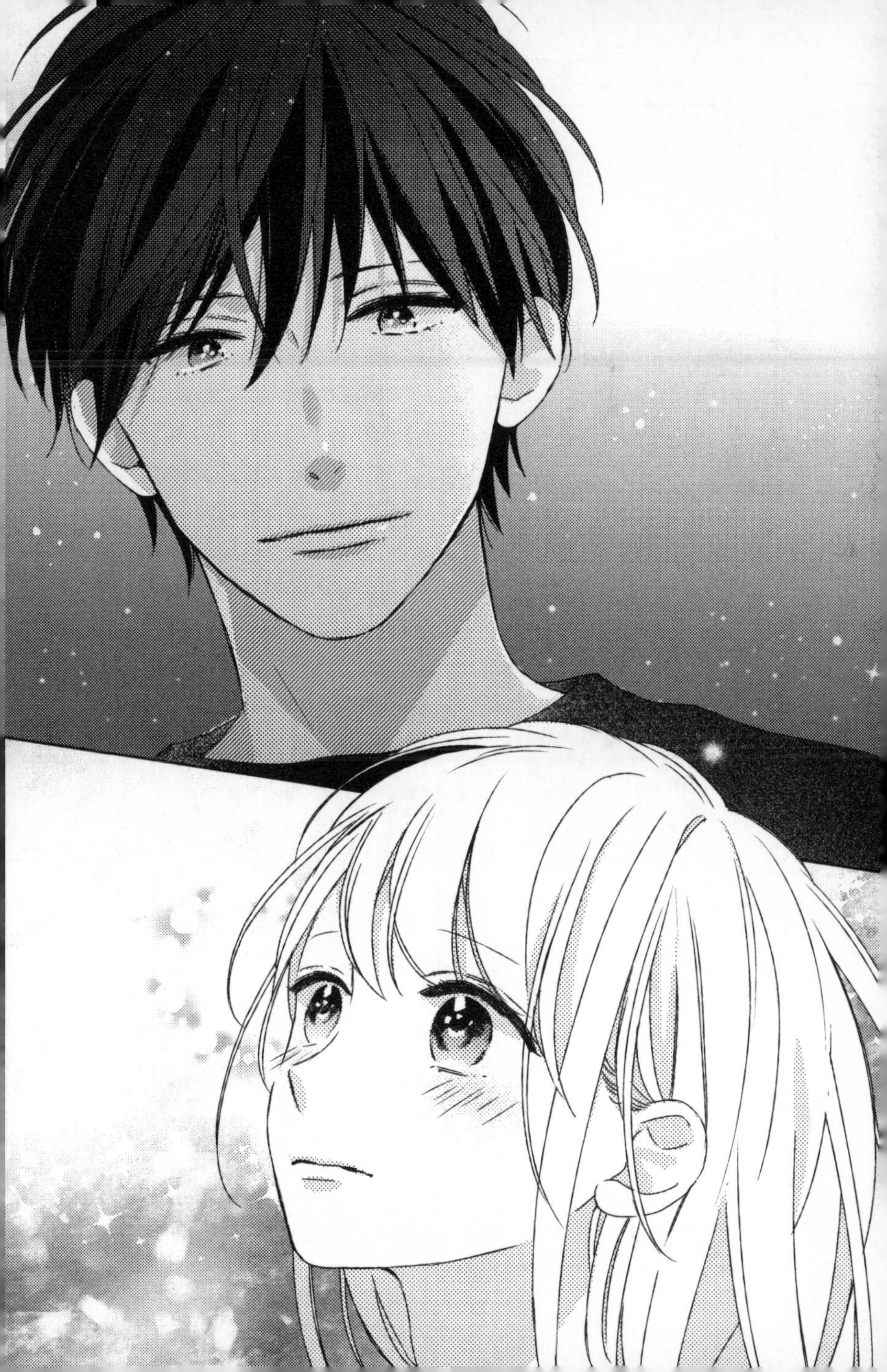

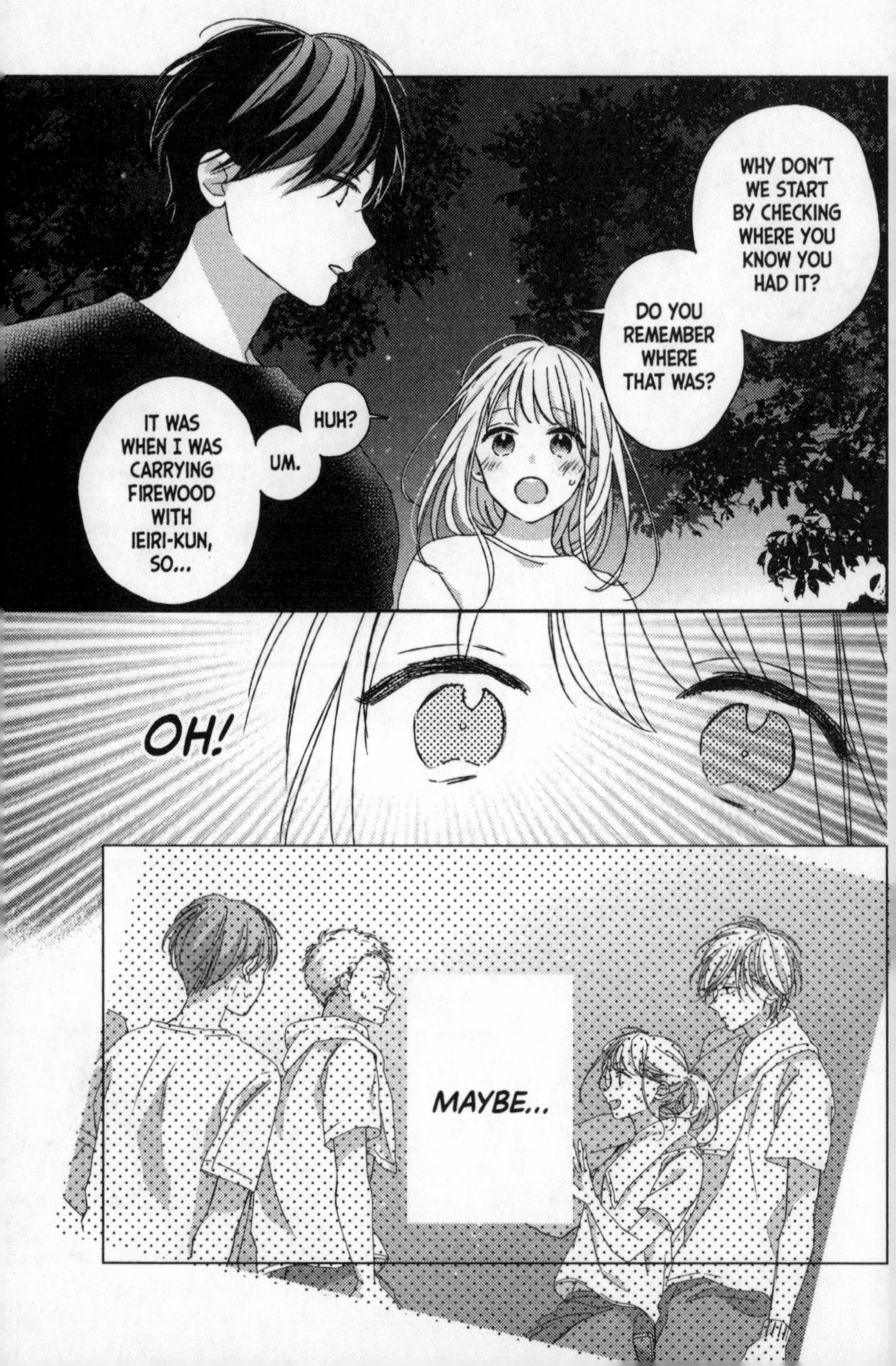
WHY DON'T WE START BY CHECKING WHERE YOU KNOW YOU HAD IT?
DO YOU REMEMBER WHERE THAT WAS?
HUH?
UM.
IT WAS WHEN I WAS CARRYING FIREWOOD WITH IEIRI-KUN, SO...
OH!
MAYBE...

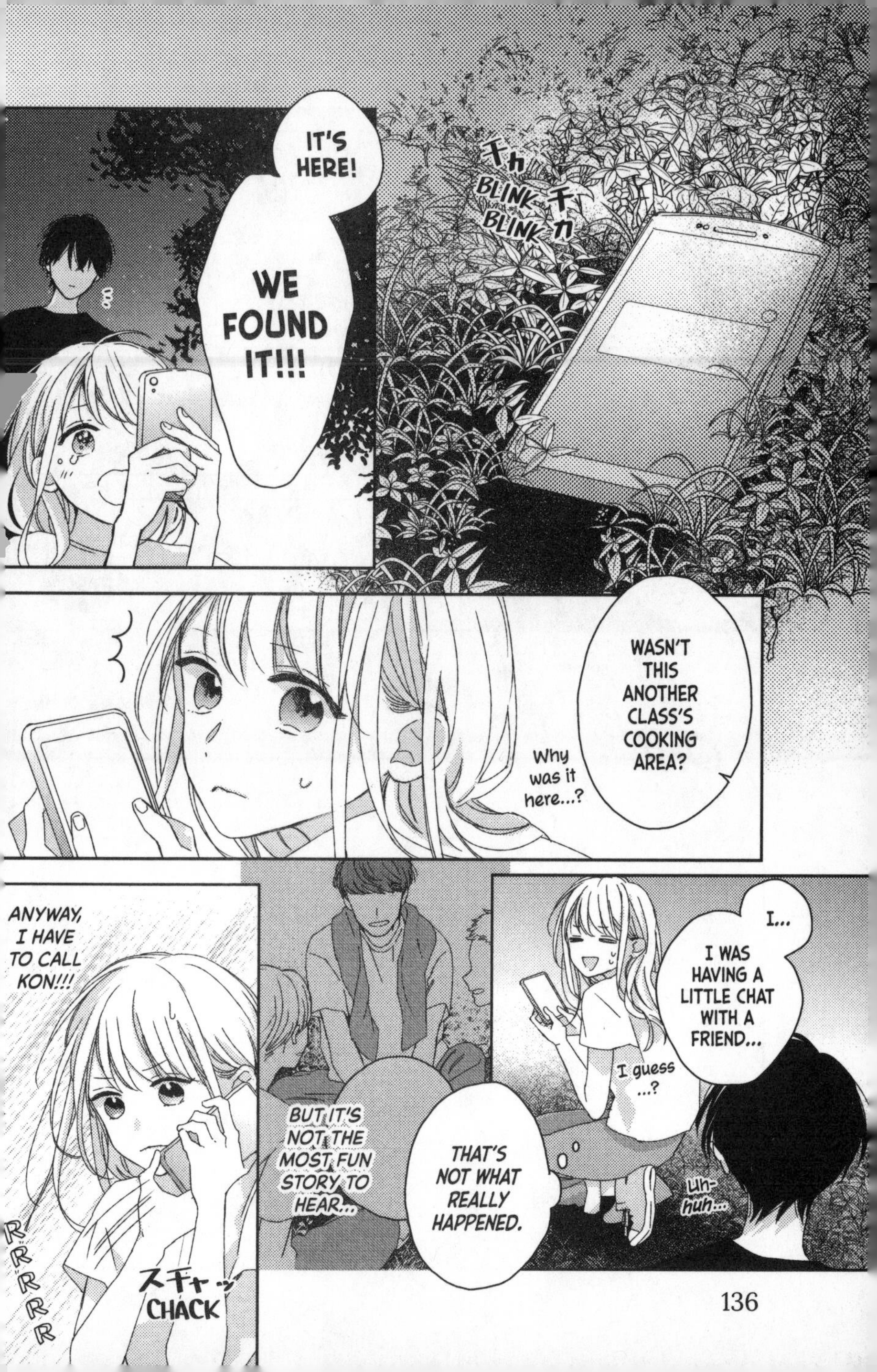

チカ
BLINK
チカ
BLINK
IT'S HERE!
WE FOUND IT!!!
WASN'T THIS ANOTHER CLASS'S COOKING AREA?
Why was it here...?
I...
I WAS HAVING A LITTLE CHAT WITH A FRIEND...
I guess ...?
Uh-huh...
THAT'S NOT WHAT REALLY HAPPENED.
BUT IT'S NOT THE MOST FUN STORY TO HEAR...
ANYWAY, I HAVE TO CALL KON!!!
スチャッ
CHACK
RRRRR

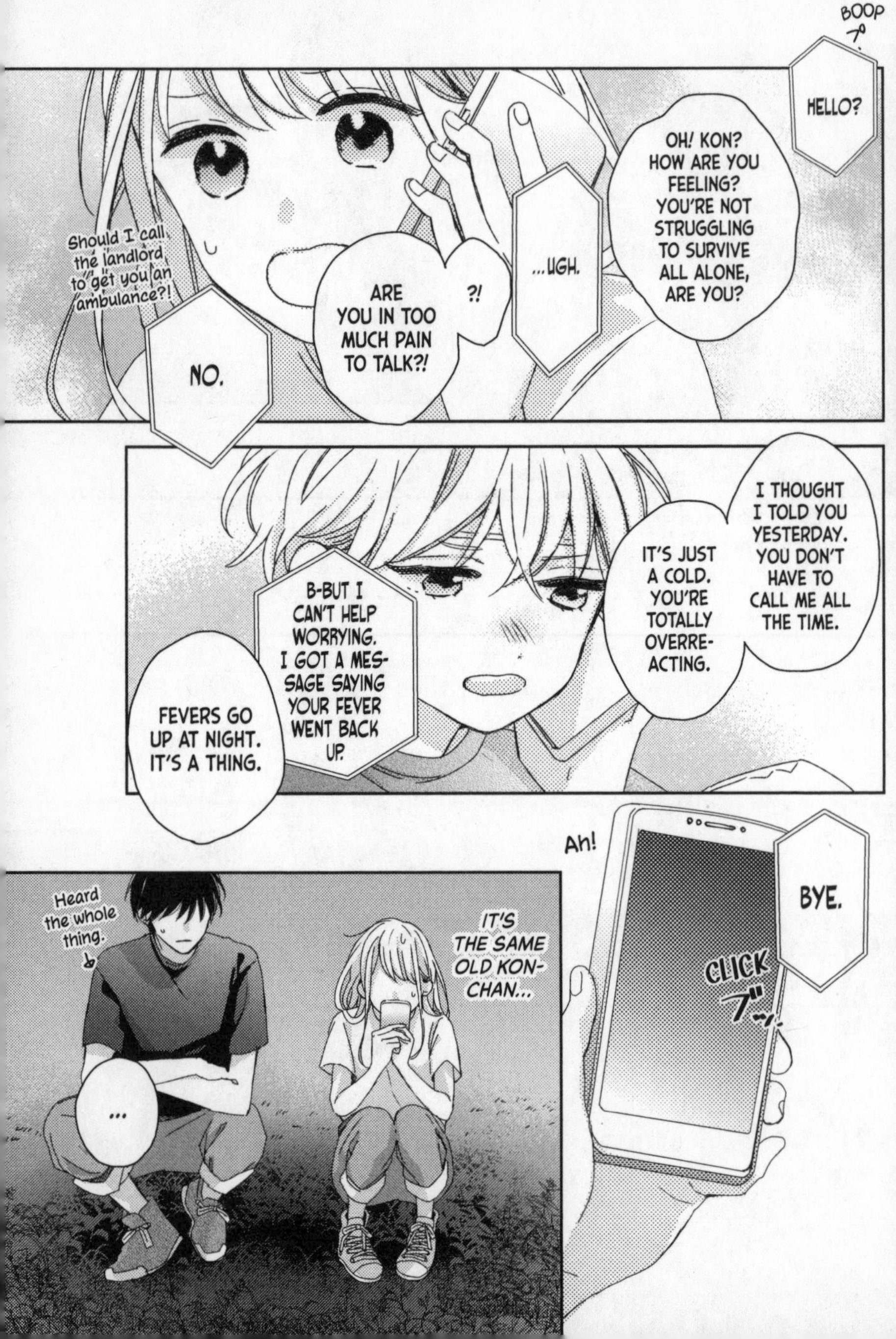
BOOP
HELLO?
OH! KON? HOW ARE YOU FEELING? YOU'RE NOT STRUGGLING TO SURVIVE ALL ALONE, ARE YOU?
...UGH.
?!
ARE YOU IN TOO MUCH PAIN TO TALK?!
Should I call the landlord to get you an ambulance?!
NO.
I THOUGHT I TOLD YOU YESTERDAY. YOU DON'T HAVE TO CALL ME ALL THE TIME.
IT'S JUST A COLD. YOU'RE TOTALLY OVERRE-ACTING.
B-BUT I CAN'T HELP WORRYING. I GOT A MES-SAGE SAYING YOUR FEVER WENT BACK UP.
FEVERS GO UP AT NIGHT. IT'S A THING.
BYE.
CLICK
Ah!
IT'S THE SAME OLD KON-CHAN...
Heard the whole thing.
...

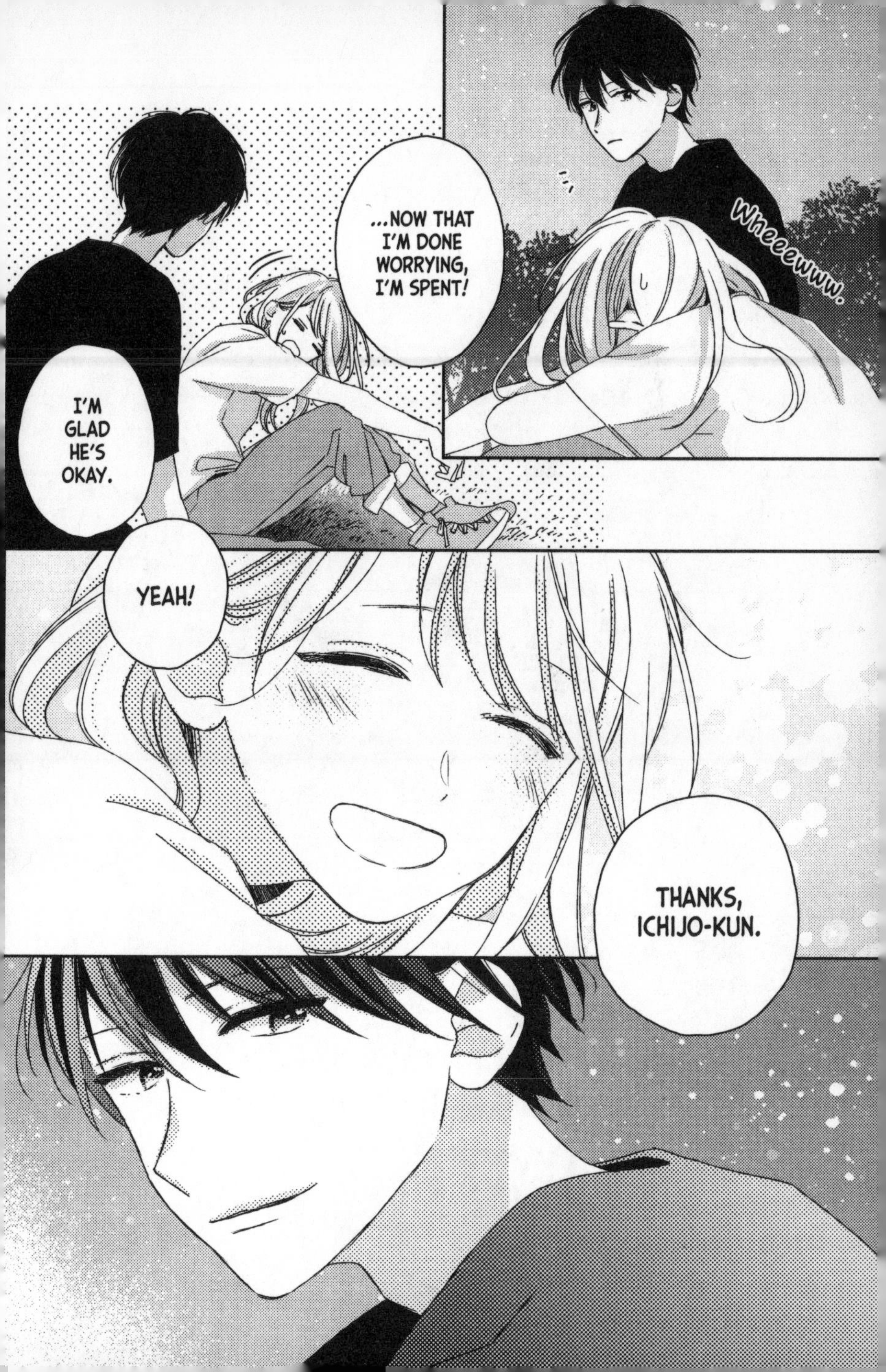
Wheeeewww.
...NOW THAT I'M DONE WORRYING, I'M SPENT!
I'M GLAD HE'S OKAY.
YEAH!
THANKS, ICHIJO-KUN.

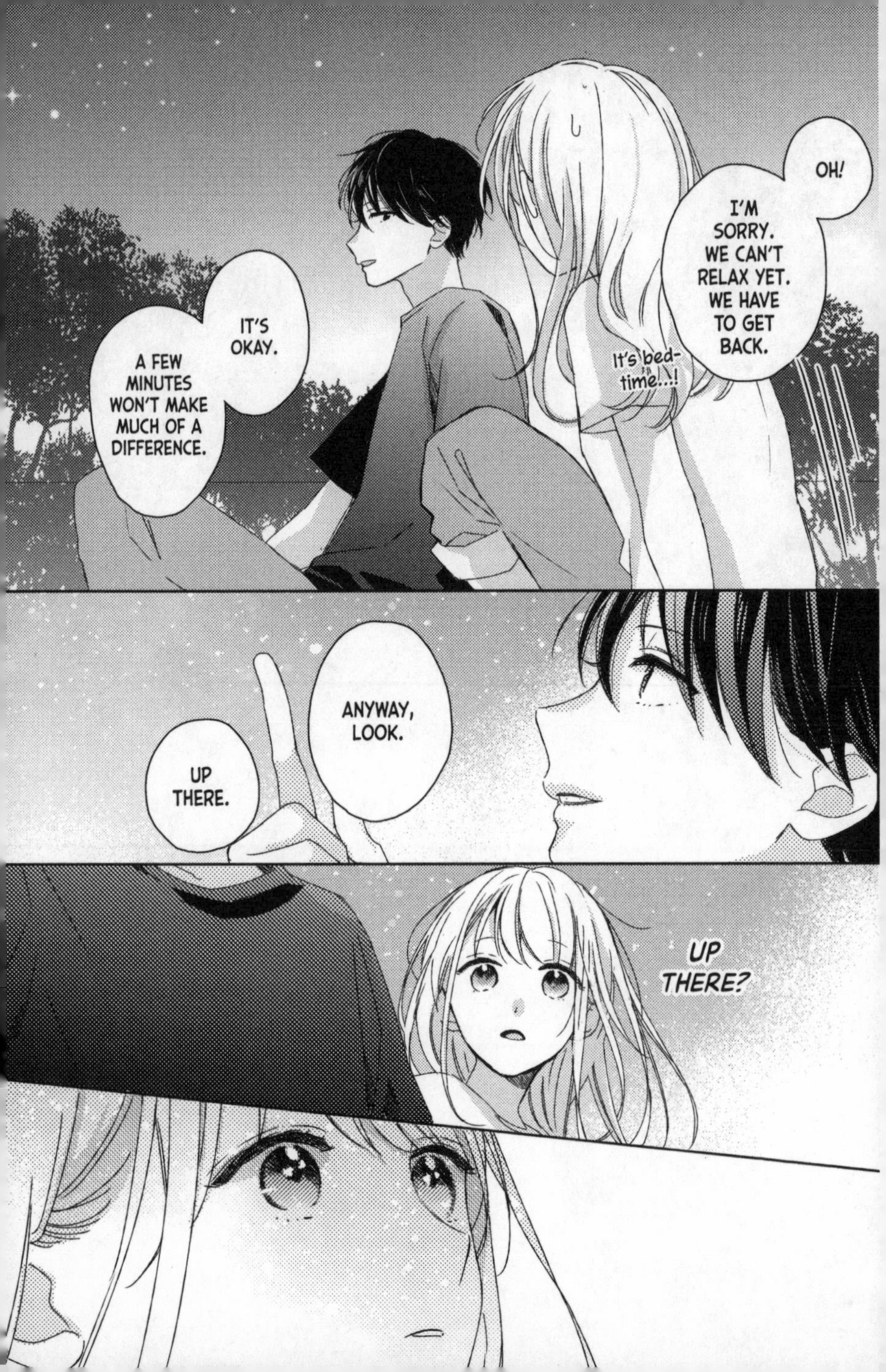
OH!
I'M SORRY. WE CAN'T RELAX YET. WE HAVE TO GET BACK.
It's bed-time...!
IT'S OKAY.
A FEW MINUTES WON'T MAKE MUCH OF A DIFFERENCE.
ANYWAY, LOOK.
UP THERE.
UP THERE?

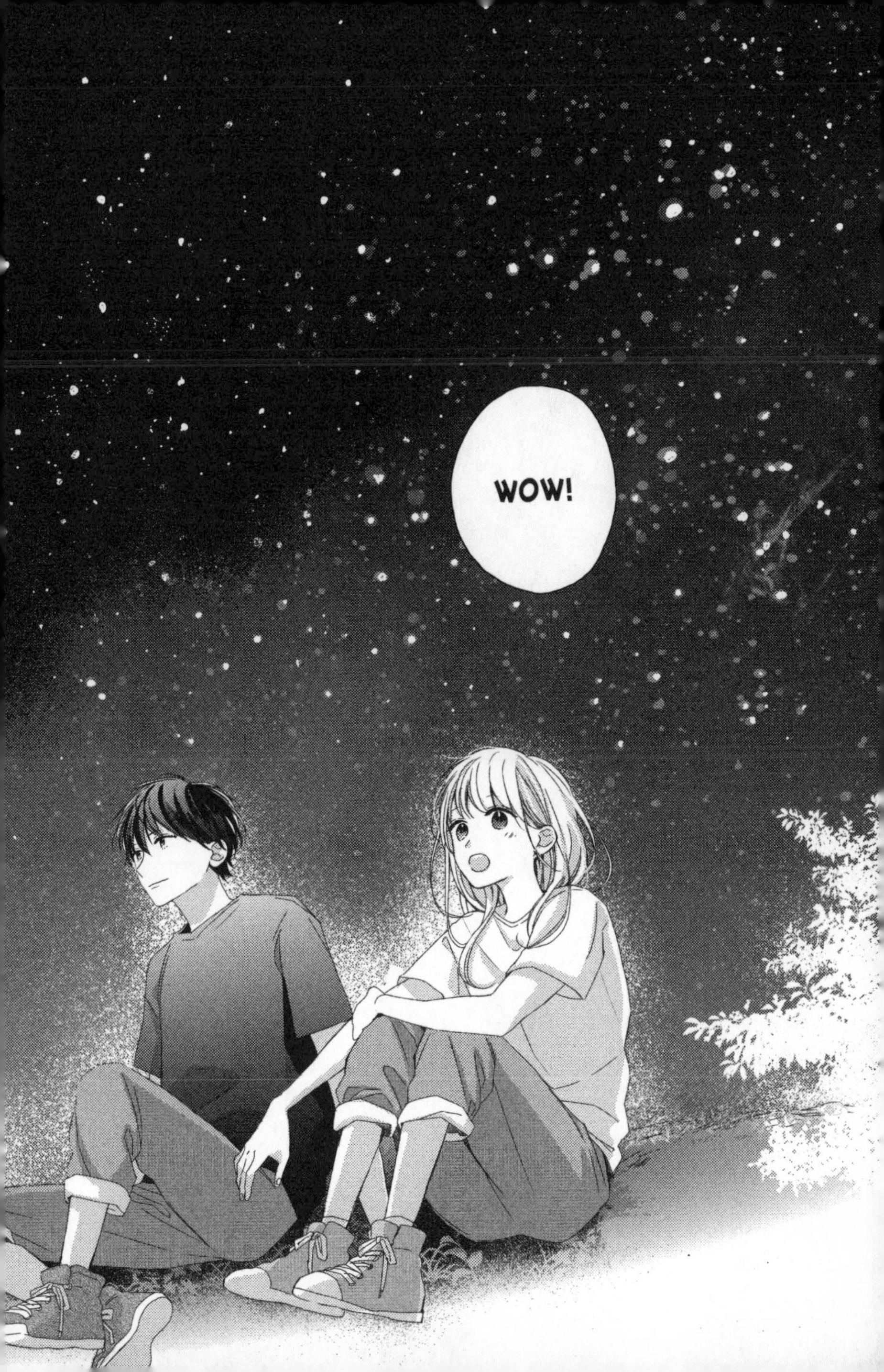
WOW!

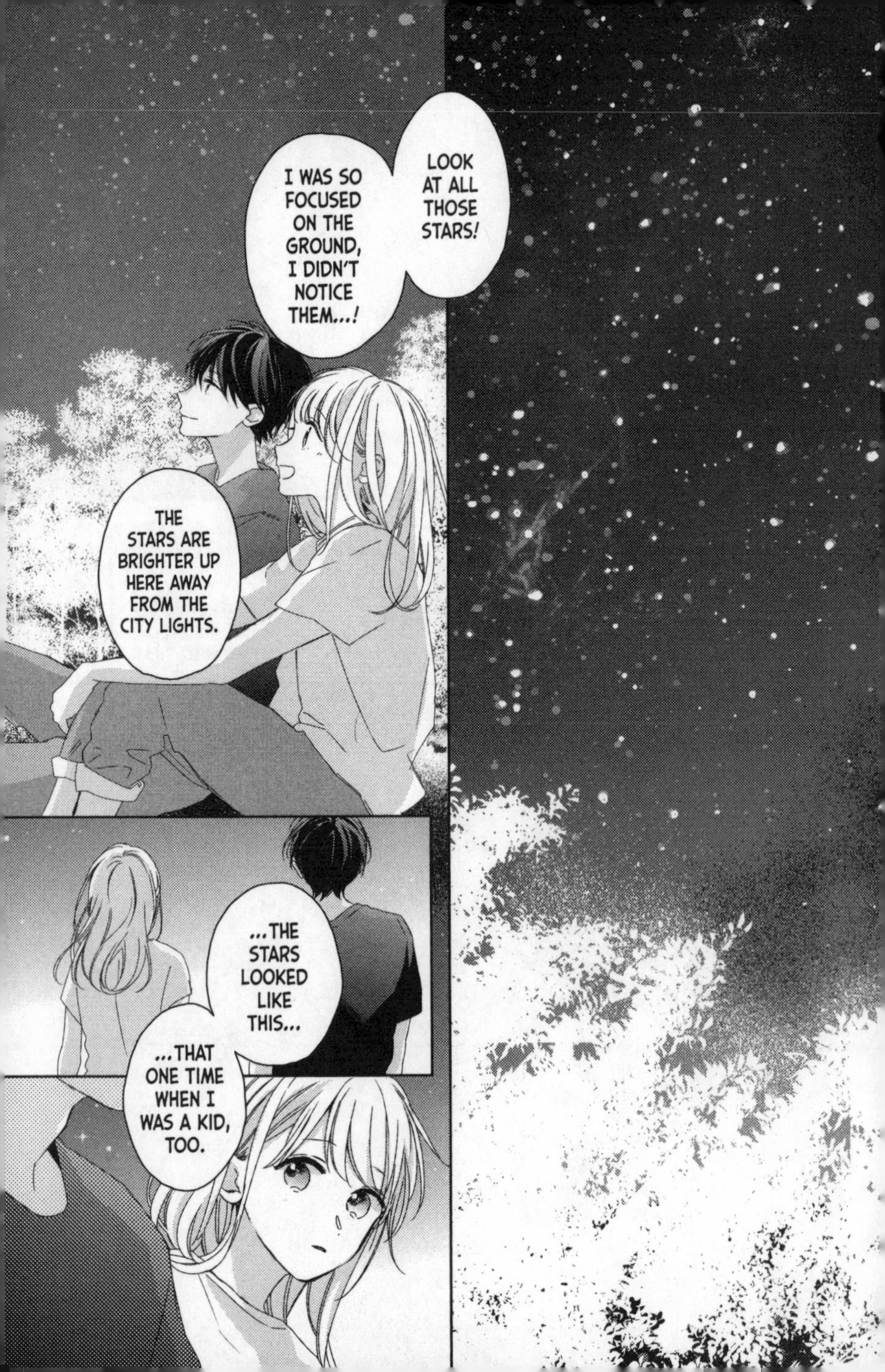
LOOK AT ALL THOSE STARS!
I WAS SO FOCUSED ON THE GROUND, I DIDN'T NOTICE THEM...!
THE STARS ARE BRIGHTER UP HERE AWAY FROM THE CITY LIGHTS.
...THE STARS LOOKED LIKE THIS...
...THAT ONE TIME WHEN I WAS A KID, TOO.

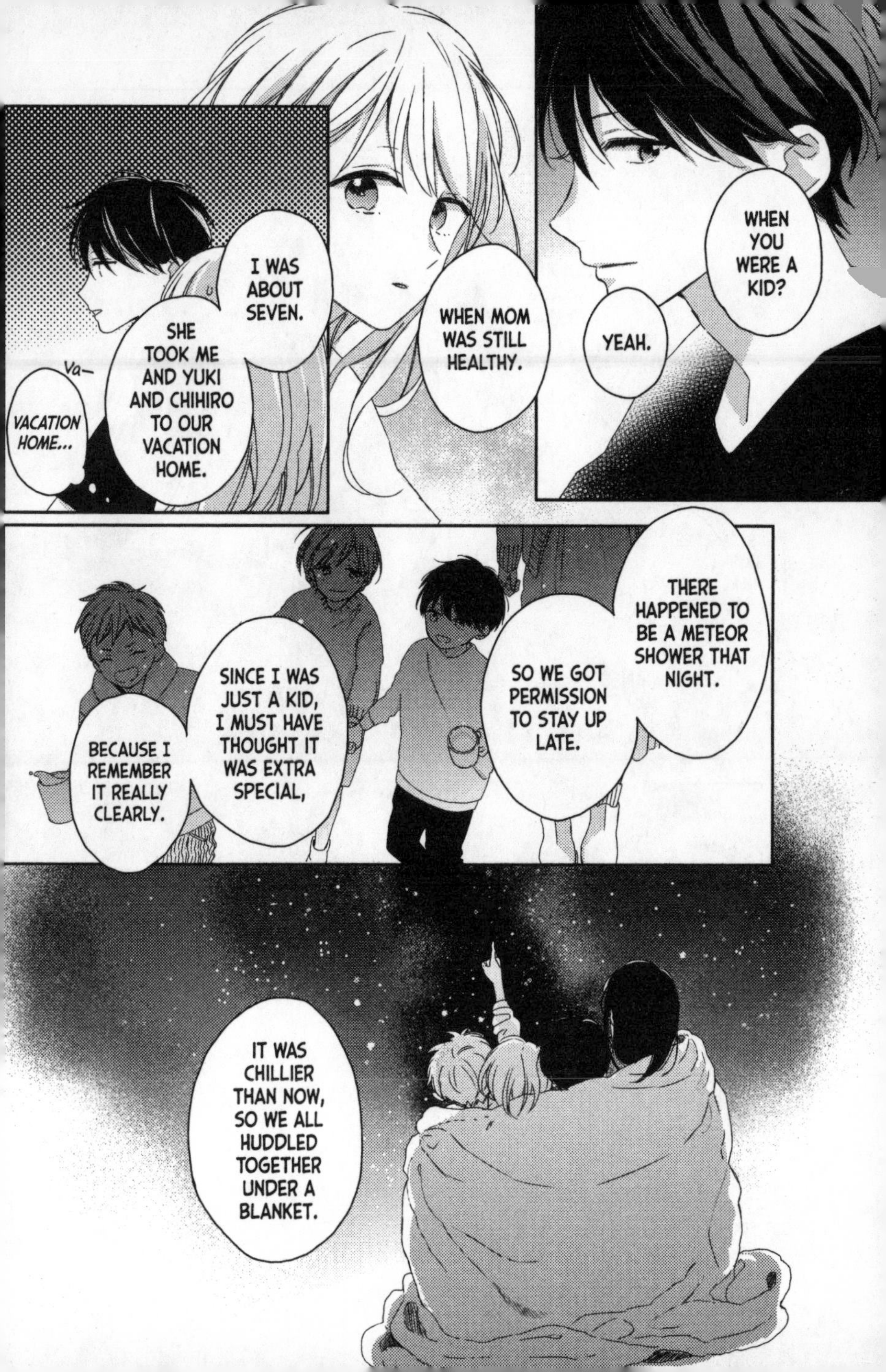
WHEN YOU WERE A KID?
YEAH.
WHEN MOM WAS STILL HEALTHY.
I WAS ABOUT SEVEN.
SHE TOOK ME AND YUKI AND CHIHIRO TO OUR VACATION HOME.
Va—
VACATION HOME...
THERE HAPPENED TO BE A METEOR SHOWER THAT NIGHT.
SO WE GOT PERMISSION TO STAY UP LATE.
SINCE I WAS JUST A KID, I MUST HAVE THOUGHT IT WAS EXTRA SPECIAL,
BECAUSE I REMEMBER IT REALLY CLEARLY.
IT WAS CHILLIER THAN NOW, SO WE ALL HUDDLED TOGETHER UNDER A BLANKET.

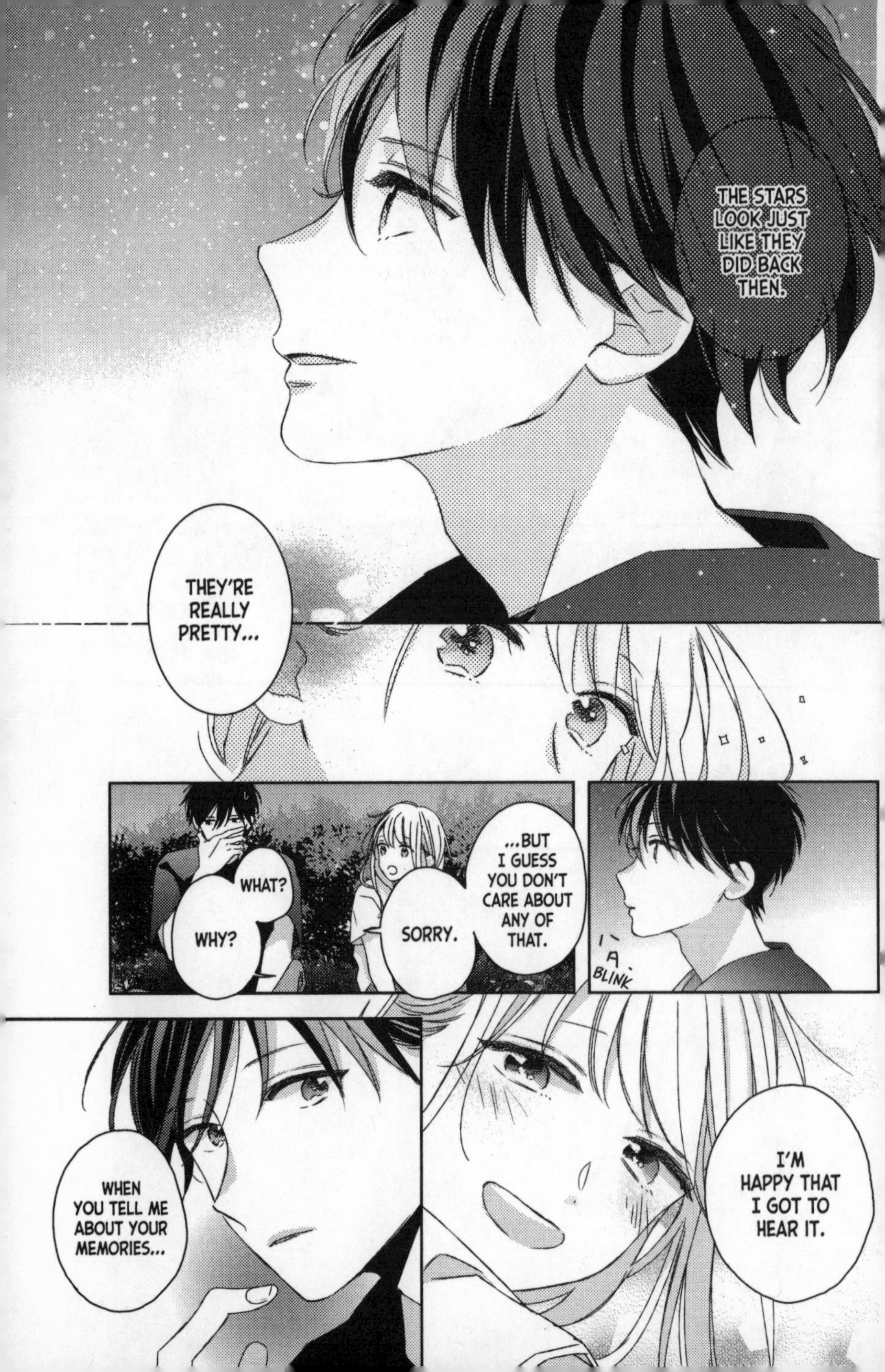
THE STARS LOOK JUST LIKE THEY DID BACK THEN.
THEY'RE REALLY PRETTY...
BLINK
...BUT I GUESS YOU DON'T CARE ABOUT ANY OF THAT.
SORRY.
WHAT?
WHY?
I'M HAPPY THAT I GOT TO HEAR IT.
WHEN YOU TELL ME ABOUT YOUR MEMORIES...

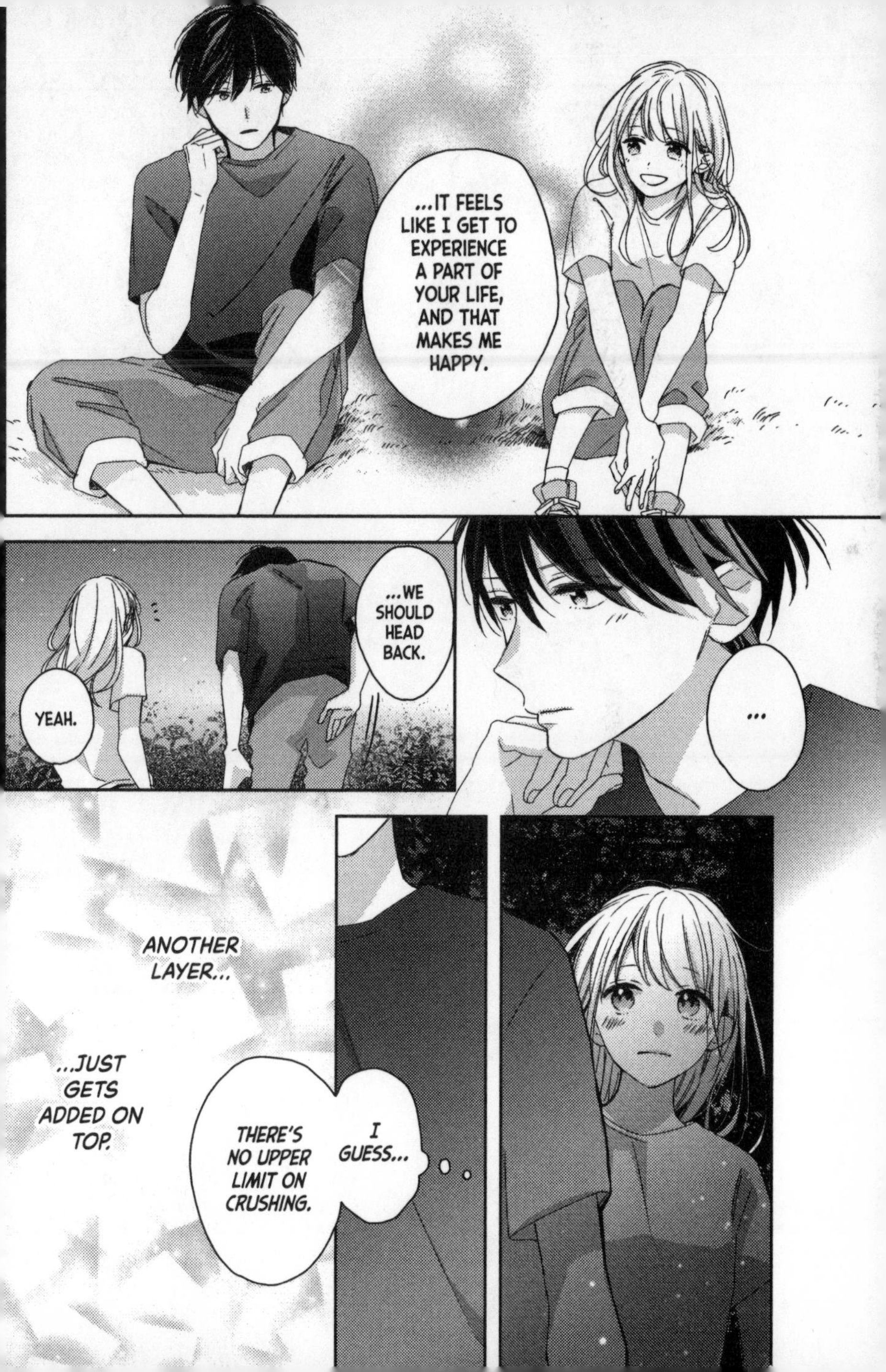
...IT FEELS LIKE I GET TO EXPERIENCE A PART OF YOUR LIFE, AND THAT MAKES ME HAPPY.
...
...WE SHOULD HEAD BACK.
YEAH.
I GUESS...
THERE'S NO UPPER LIMIT ON CRUSHING.
ANOTHER LAYER...
...JUST GETS ADDED ON TOP.

SOMETHING HAPPENED TONIGHT.
AND I WANT TO REMEMBER IT FOREVER.

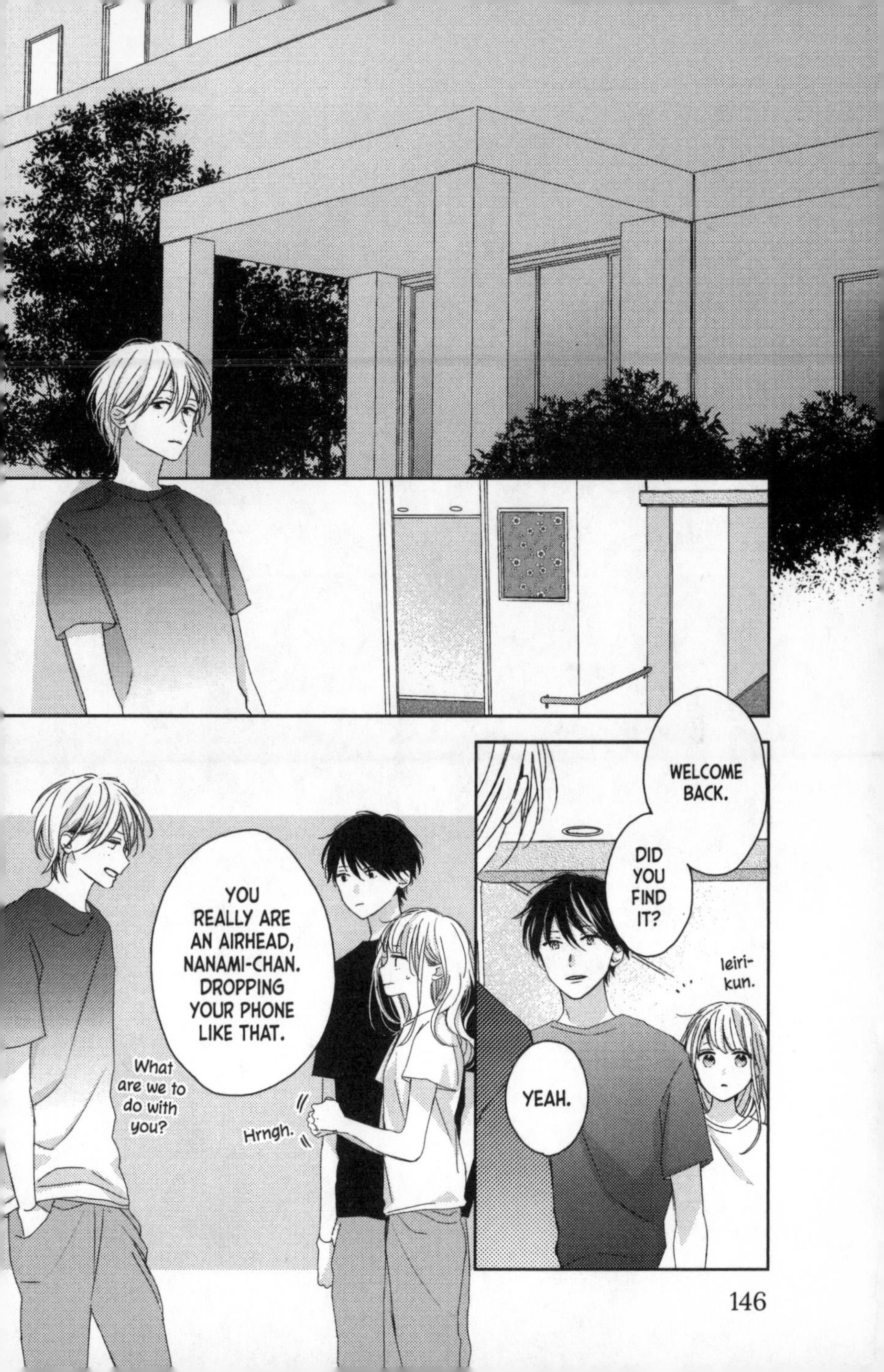
WELCOME BACK.
DID YOU FIND IT?
Ieiri-kun.
YEAH.
YOU REALLY ARE AN AIRHEAD, NANAMI-CHAN. DROPPING YOUR PHONE LIKE THAT.
What are we to do with you?
Hrngh.

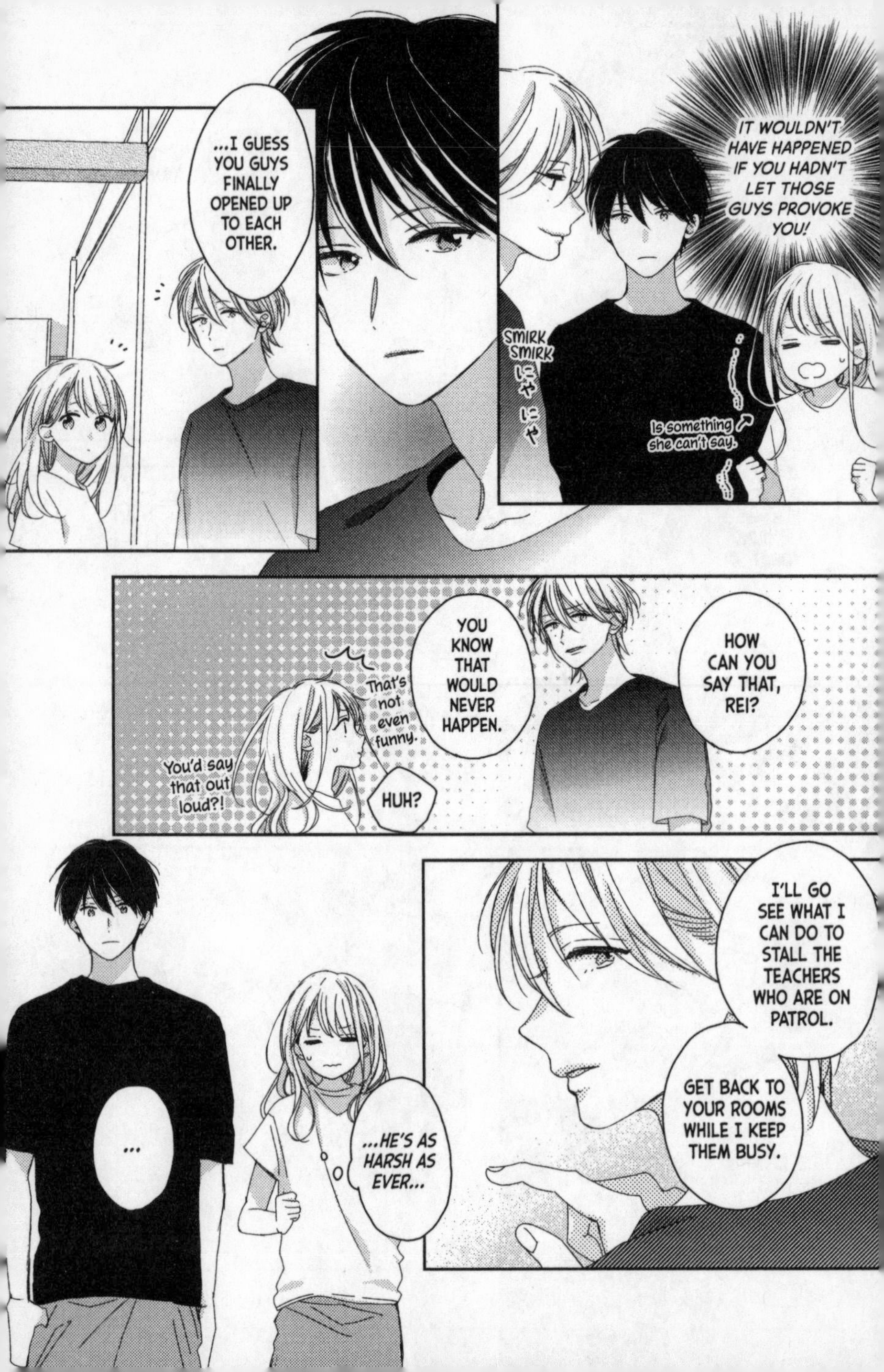
IT WOULDN'T HAVE HAPPENED IF YOU HADN'T LET THOSE GUYS PROVOKE YOU!
SMIRK SMIRK
にや にや
......
Is something she can't say.
...I GUESS YOU GUYS FINALLY OPENED UP TO EACH OTHER.
HOW CAN YOU SAY THAT, REI?
YOU KNOW THAT WOULD NEVER HAPPEN.
That's not even funny.
HUH?
You'd say that out loud?!
I'LL GO SEE WHAT I CAN DO TO STALL THE TEACHERS WHO ARE ON PATROL.
GET BACK TO YOUR ROOMS WHILE I KEEP THEM BUSY.
...HE'S AS HARSH AS EVER...
...

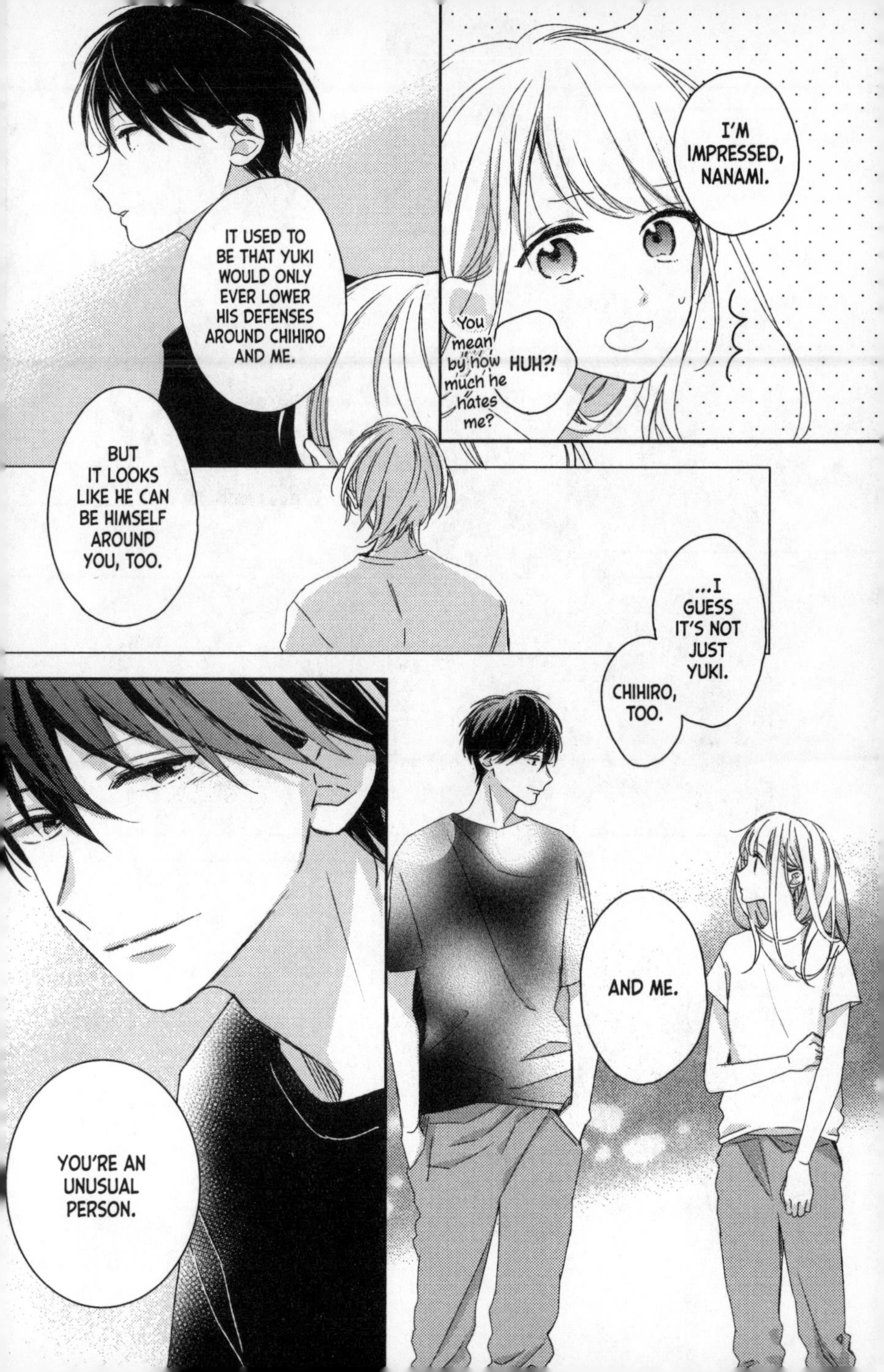
I'M IMPRESSED, NANAMI.
HUH?!
You mean by how much he hates me?
IT USED TO BE THAT YUKI WOULD ONLY EVER LOWER HIS DEFENSES AROUND CHIHIRO AND ME.
BUT IT LOOKS LIKE HE CAN BE HIMSELF AROUND YOU, TOO.
...I GUESS IT'S NOT JUST YUKI.
CHIHIRO, TOO.
AND ME.
YOU'RE AN UNUSUAL PERSON.

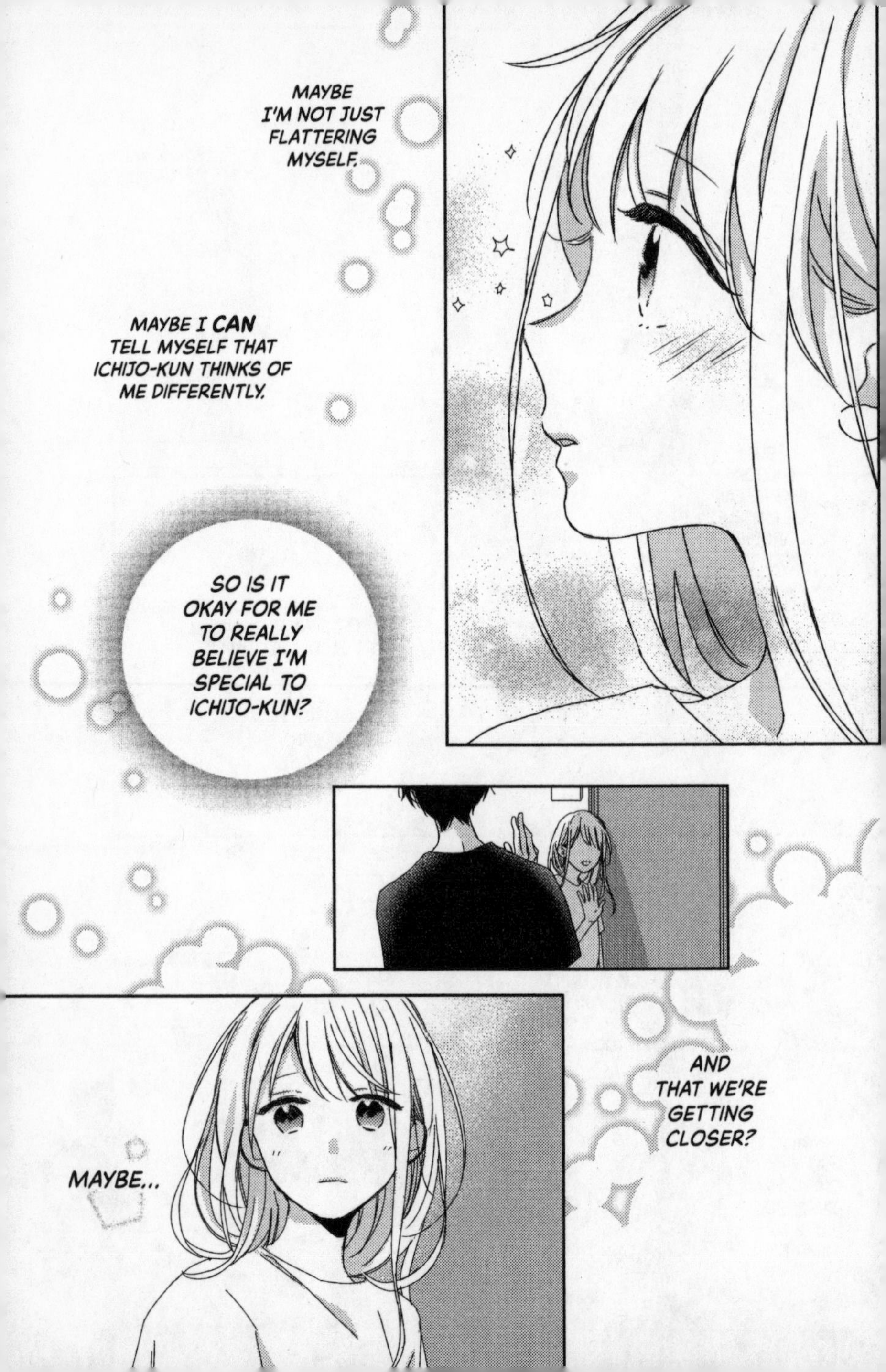
MAYBE I'M NOT JUST FLATTERING MYSELF.
MAYBE I **CAN** TELL MYSELF THAT ICHIJO-KUN THINKS OF ME DIFFERENTLY.
SO IS IT OKAY FOR ME TO REALLY BELIEVE I'M SPECIAL TO ICHIJO-KUN?
AND THAT WE'RE GETTING CLOSER?
MAYBE...

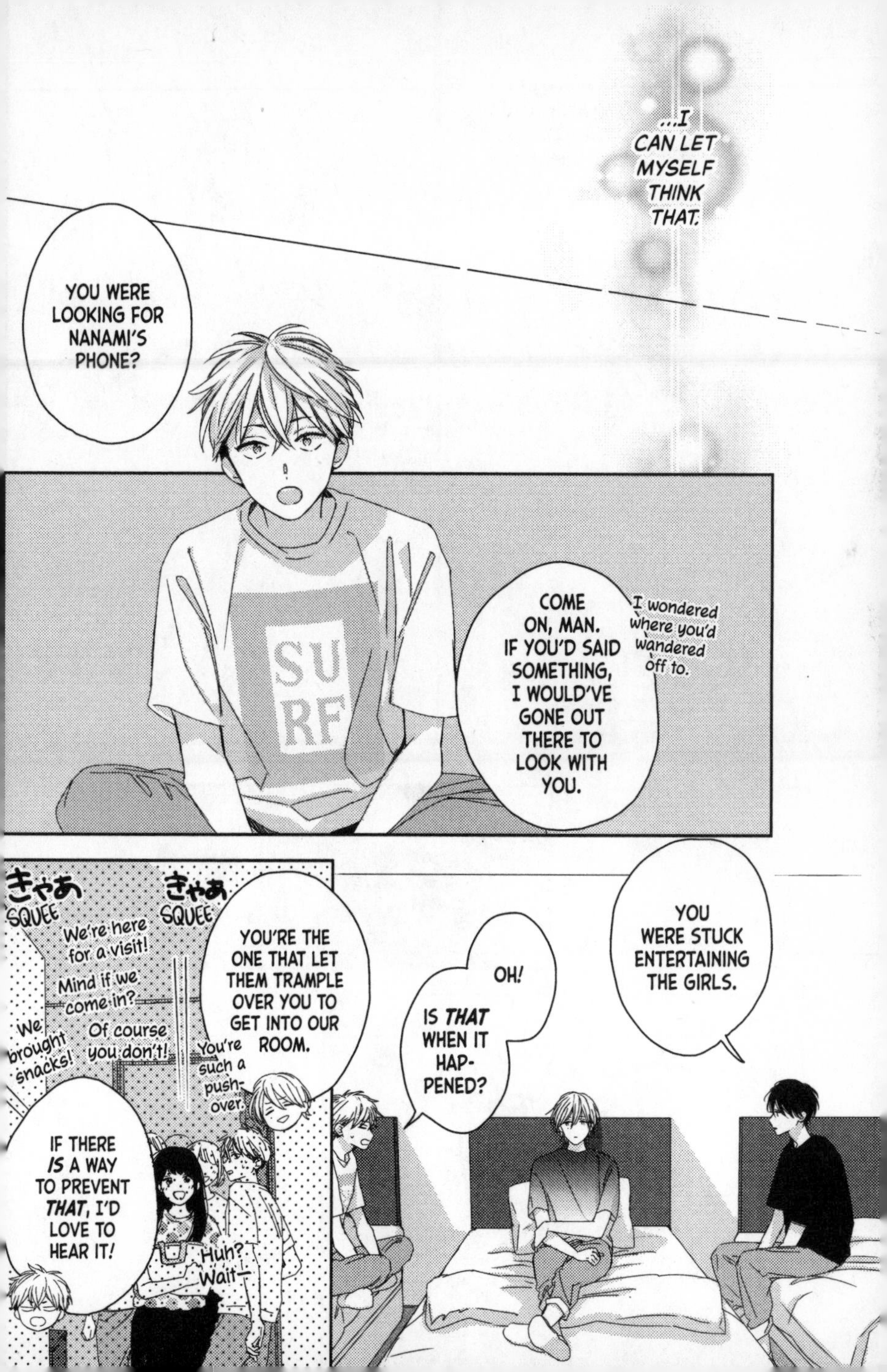
...I CAN LET MYSELF THINK THAT.
YOU WERE LOOKING FOR NANAMI'S PHONE?
I wondered where you'd wandered off to.
COME ON, MAN. IF YOU'D SAID SOMETHING, I WOULD'VE GONE OUT THERE TO LOOK WITH YOU.
YOU WERE STUCK ENTERTAINING THE GIRLS.
OH! IS *THAT* WHEN IT HAP-PENED?
YOU'RE THE ONE THAT LET THEM TRAMPLE OVER YOU TO GET INTO OUR ROOM.
きゃあ SQUEE
きゃあ SQUEE
We're here for a visit!
Mind if we come in?
Of course you don't!
We brought snacks!
You're such a push-over.
Huh? Wait—
IF THERE *IS* A WAY TO PREVENT *THAT*, I'D LOVE TO HEAR IT!

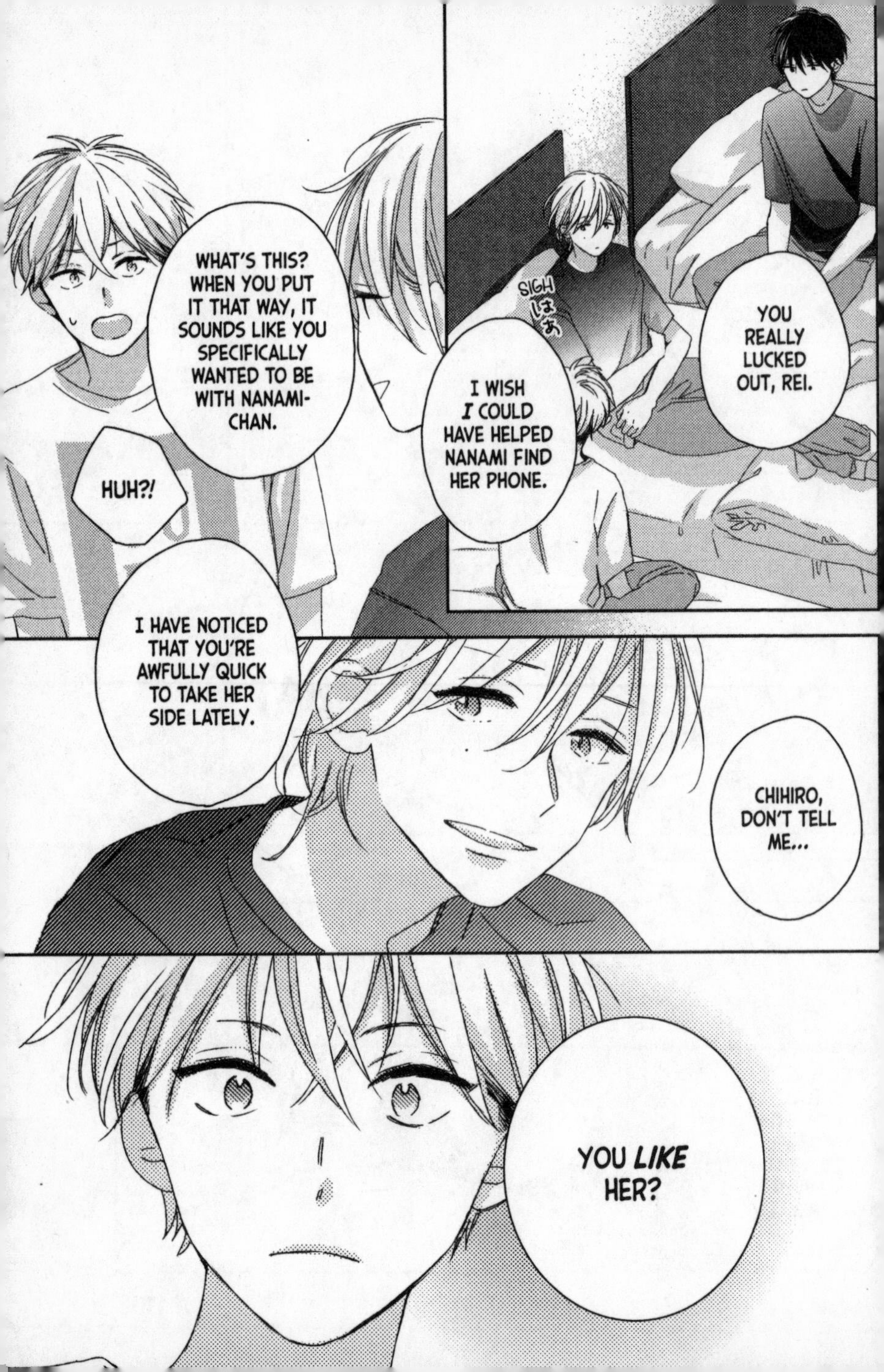
YOU REALLY LUCKED OUT, REI.
SIGH はぁ
I WISH *I* COULD HAVE HELPED NANAMI FIND HER PHONE.
WHAT'S THIS? WHEN YOU PUT IT THAT WAY, IT SOUNDS LIKE YOU SPECIFICALLY WANTED TO BE WITH NANAMI-CHAN.
HUH?!
I HAVE NOTICED THAT YOU'RE AWFULLY QUICK TO TAKE HER SIDE LATELY.
CHIHIRO, DON'T TELL ME...
YOU *LIKE* HER?

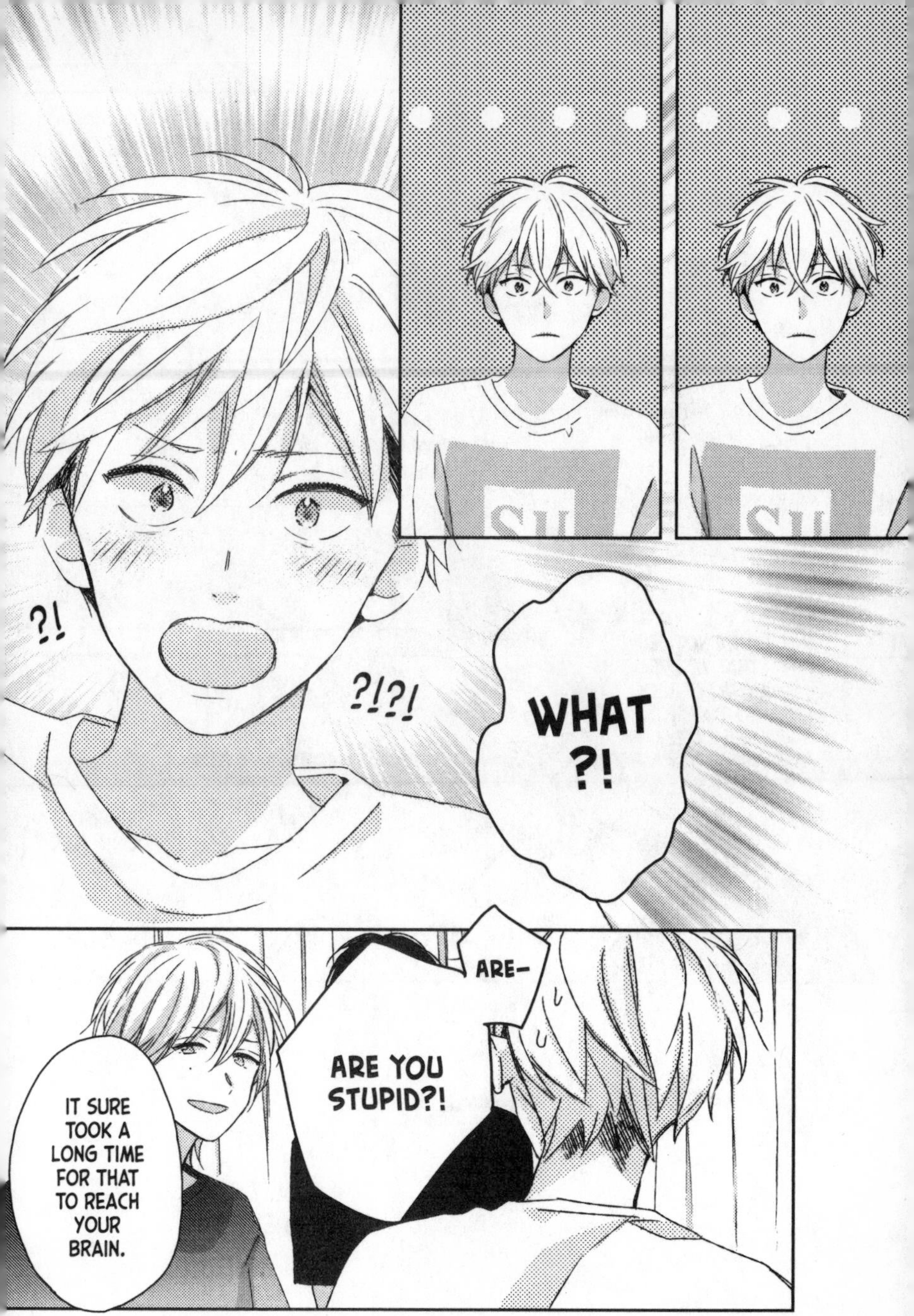

.....
.....
WHAT?!
?!
?!?!
ARE-
ARE YOU STUPID?!
IT SURE TOOK A LONG TIME FOR THAT TO REACH YOUR BRAIN.

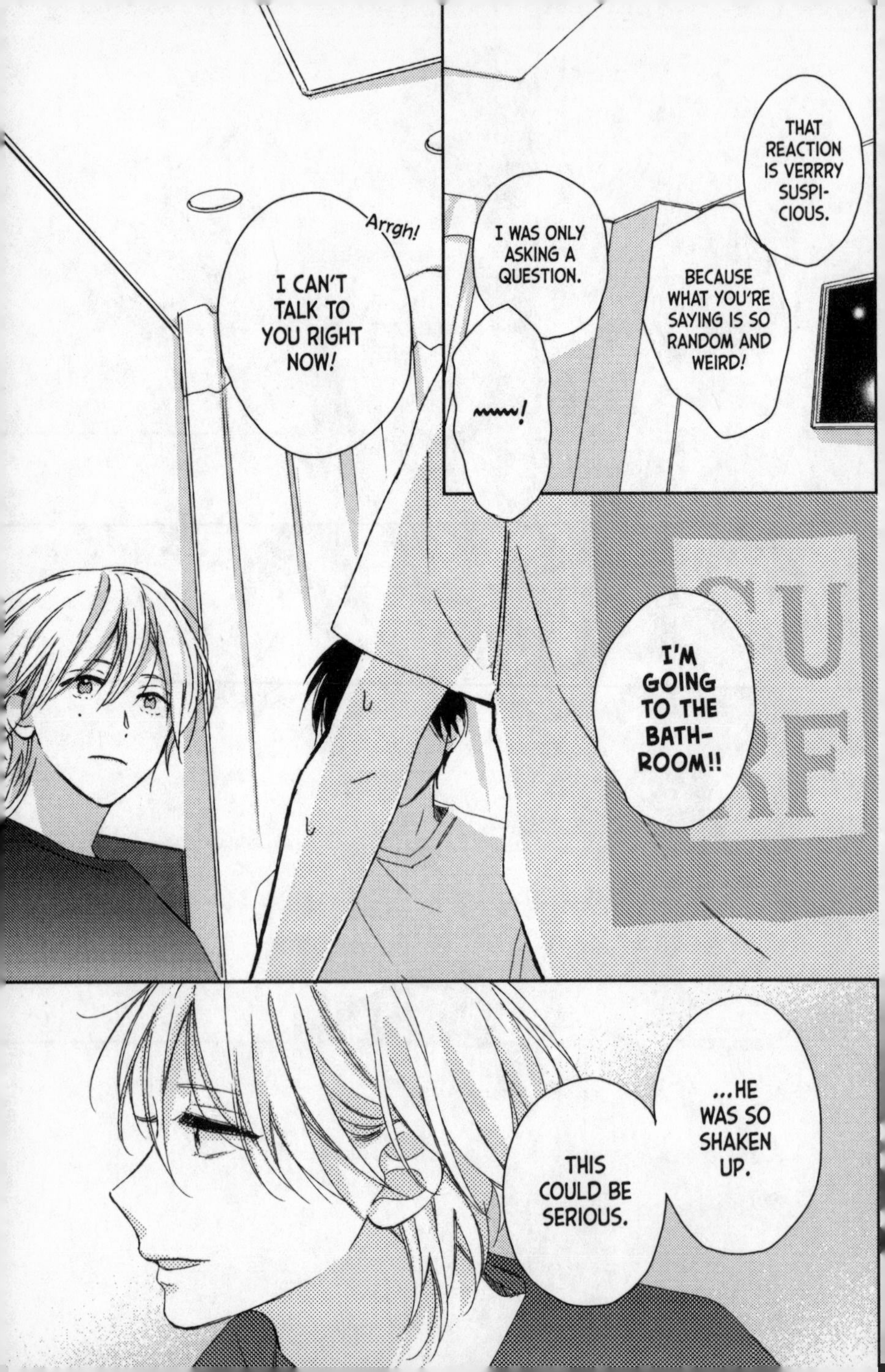
THAT REACTION IS VERRRY SUSPICIOUS.
I WAS ONLY ASKING A QUESTION.
BECAUSE WHAT YOU'RE SAYING IS SO RANDOM AND WEIRD!
Arrgh!
I CAN'T TALK TO YOU RIGHT NOW!
I'M GOING TO THE BATHROOM!!
...HE WAS SO SHAKEN UP.
THIS COULD BE SERIOUS.

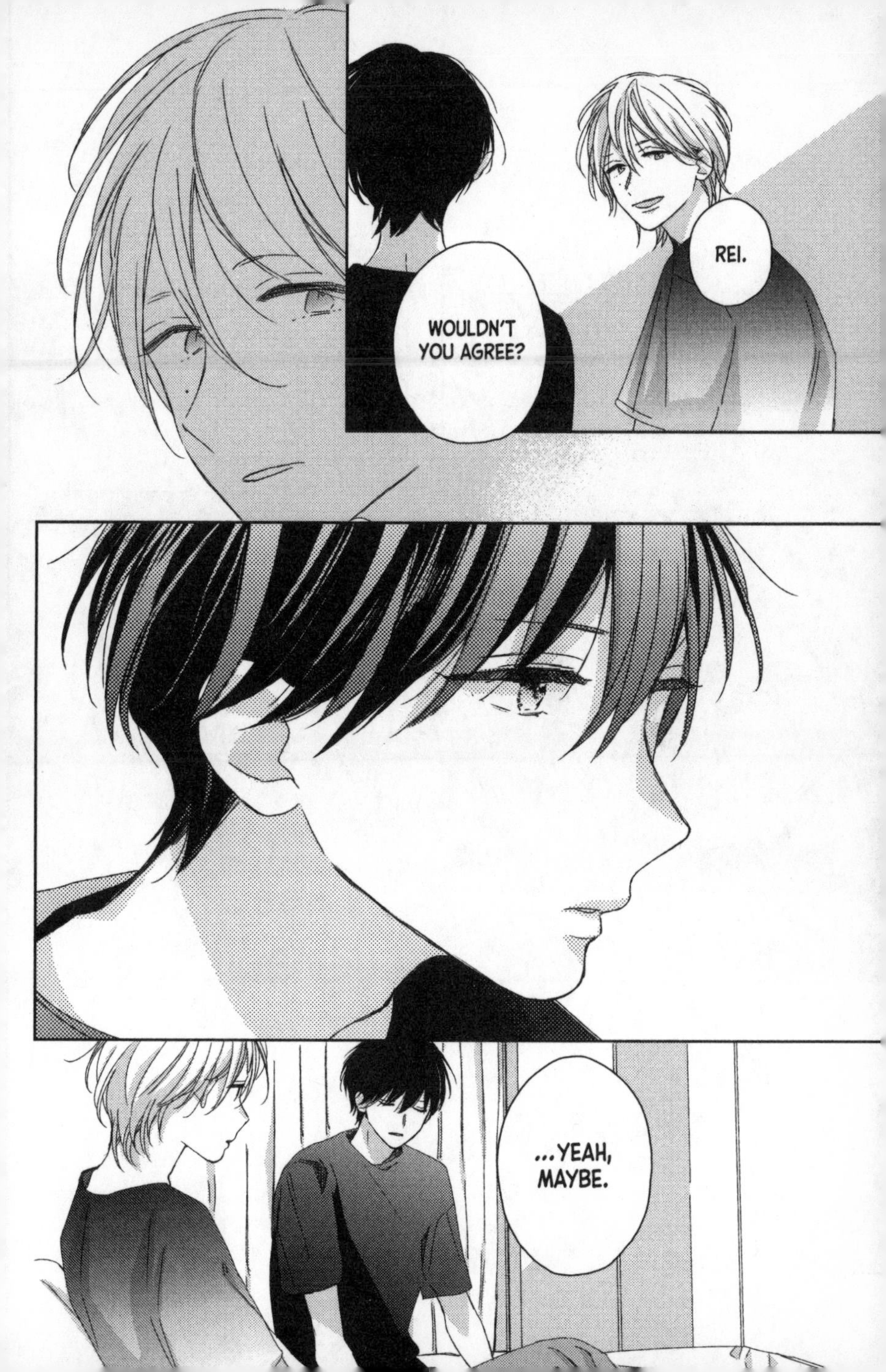
REI.
WOULDN'T YOU AGREE?
...YEAH, MAYBE.

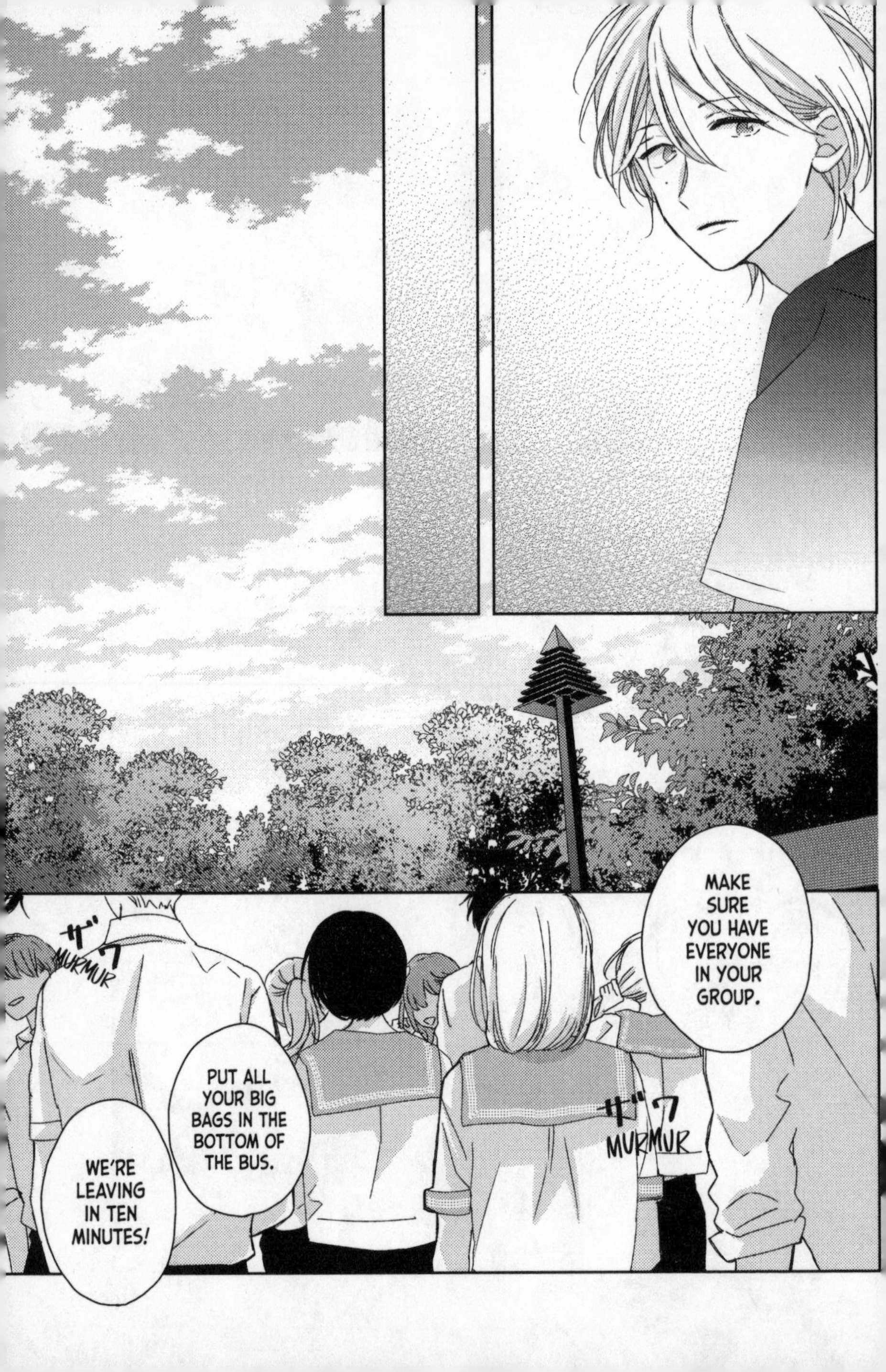
MAKE SURE YOU HAVE EVERYONE IN YOUR GROUP.
ザワ
MURMUR
PUT ALL YOUR BIG BAGS IN THE BOTTOM OF THE BUS.
WE'RE LEAVING IN TEN MINUTES!
ザワ
MURMUR

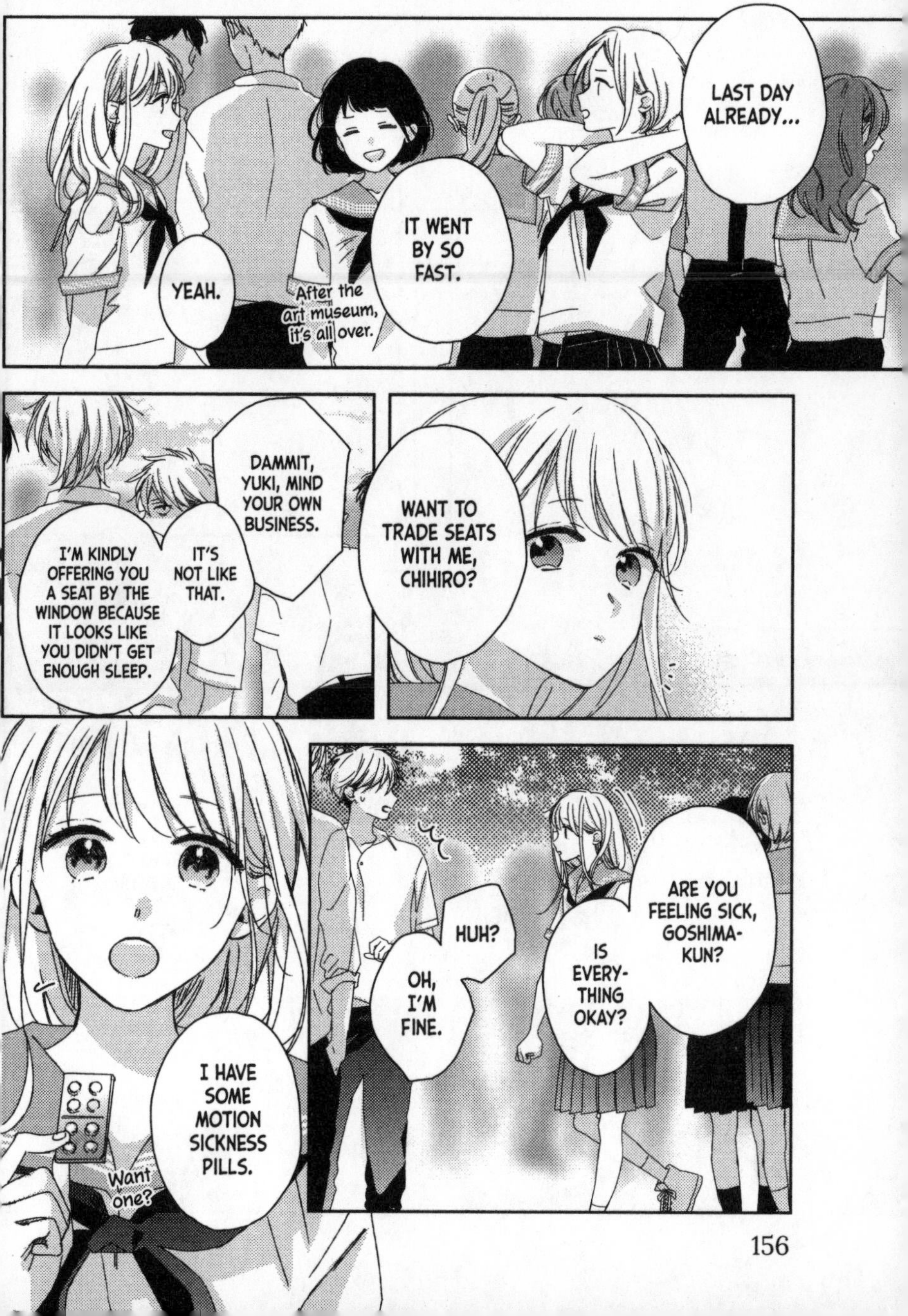
LAST DAY ALREADY...
IT WENT BY SO FAST.
After the art museum, it's all over.
YEAH.
WANT TO TRADE SEATS WITH ME, CHIHIRO?
DAMMIT, YUKI, MIND YOUR OWN BUSINESS.
IT'S NOT LIKE THAT.
I'M KINDLY OFFERING YOU A SEAT BY THE WINDOW BECAUSE IT LOOKS LIKE YOU DIDN'T GET ENOUGH SLEEP.
ARE YOU FEELING SICK, GOSHIMA-KUN?
IS EVERYTHING OKAY?
HUH?
OH, I'M FINE.
I HAVE SOME MOTION SICKNESS PILLS.
Want one?

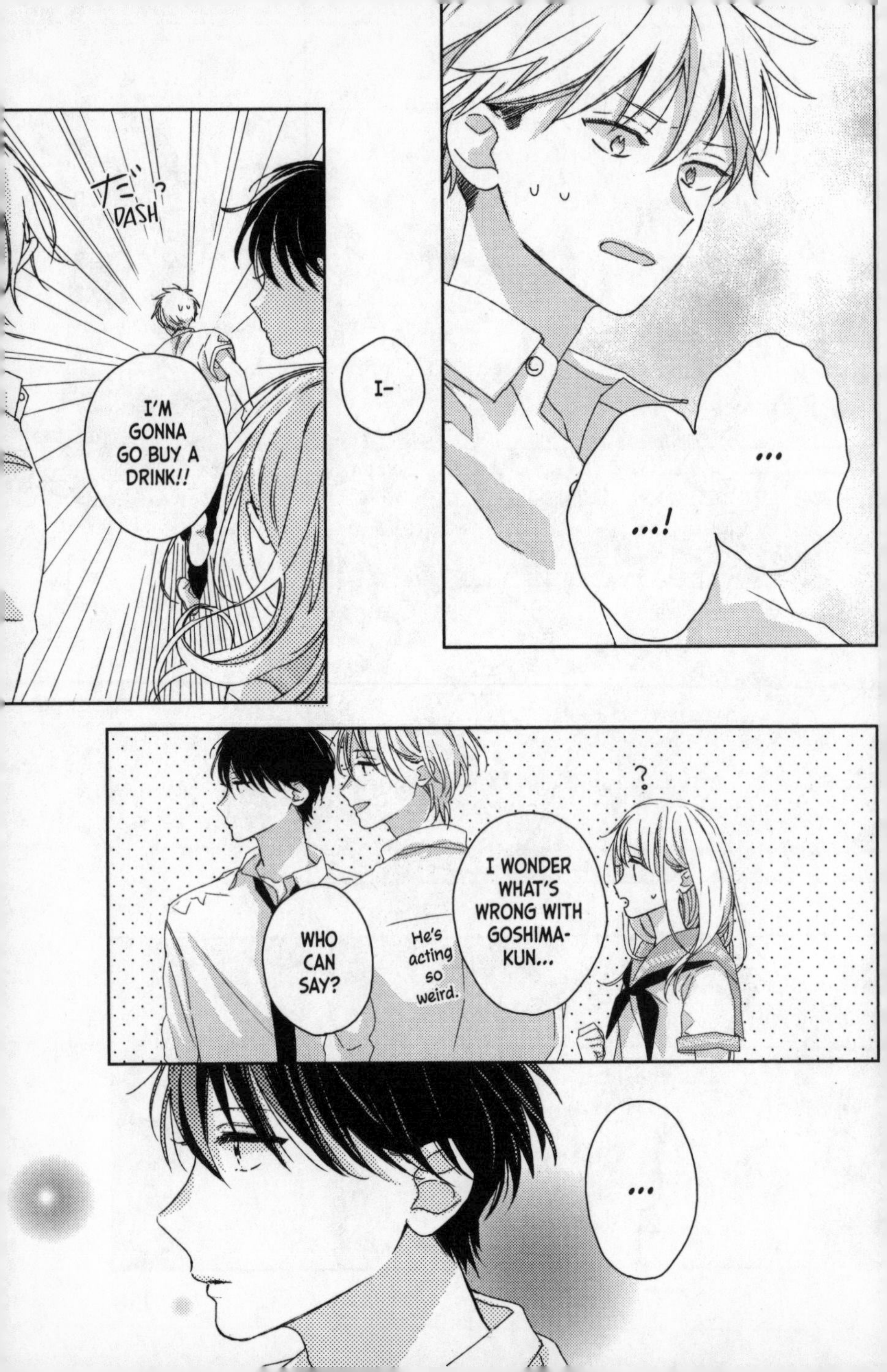
...
...!
I-
DASH
I'M GONNA GO BUY A DRINK!!
?
I WONDER WHAT'S WRONG WITH GOSHIMA-KUN...
He's acting so weird.
WHO CAN SAY?
...

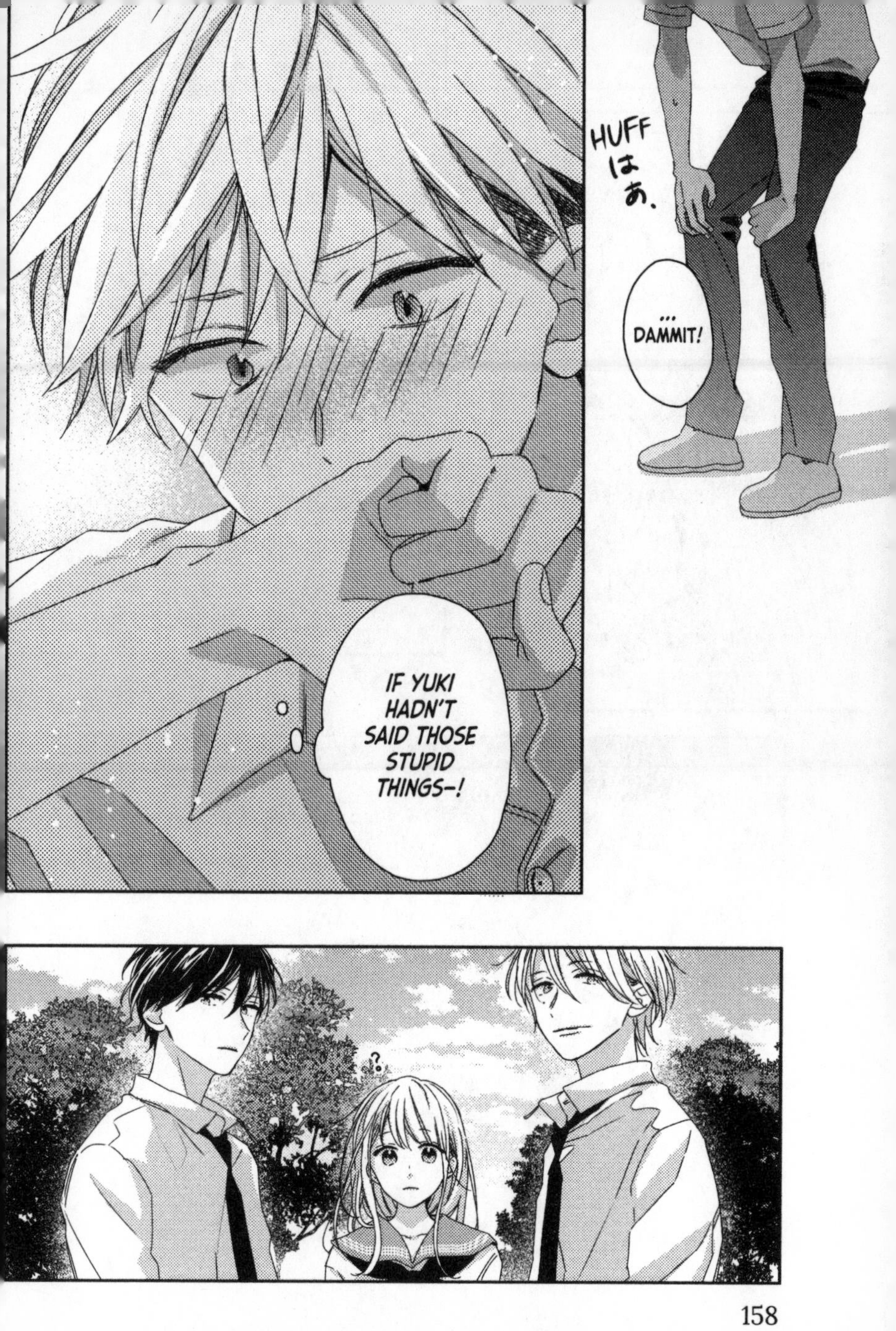
HUFF はあ、
... DAMMIT!
IF YUKI HADN'T SAID THOSE STUPID THINGS-!
?

Those
Not-So-
Sweet
Boys

A Kodansha Comics Trade Paperback Original
Those Not-So-Sweet Boys 2 copyright © 2019 Yoko Nogiri
English translation copyright © 2021 Yoko Nogiri

Published in the United States by Kodansha Comics, an imprint of Kodansha USA Publishing, LLC, New York.

Publication rights for this English edition arranged through Kodansha Ltd., Tokyo.

First published in Japan in 2019 by Kodansha Ltd., Tokyo as *Amakunai Karera no Nichijo wa.*, volume 2.

ISBN 978-1-64651-197-6

Original cover design by Tomohiro Kusume + Sayaka Nagai (arcoinc)

Printed in the United States of America.

www.kodansha.us

9 8 7 6 5 4 3 2
Translation: Alethea Nibley & Athena Nibley
Lettering: Sara Linsley
Editing: Haruko Hashimoto
Kodansha Comics edition cover design by Phil Balsman

Publisher: Kiichiro Sugawara

Director of publishing services: Ben Applegate
Associate director of operations: Stephen Pakula
Publishing services associate managing editor:
Madison Salters, Alanna Ruse, Noelle Webster
Assistant production manager: Emi Lotto, Angela Zurlo
Logo and character art ©Kodansha USA Publishing, LLC

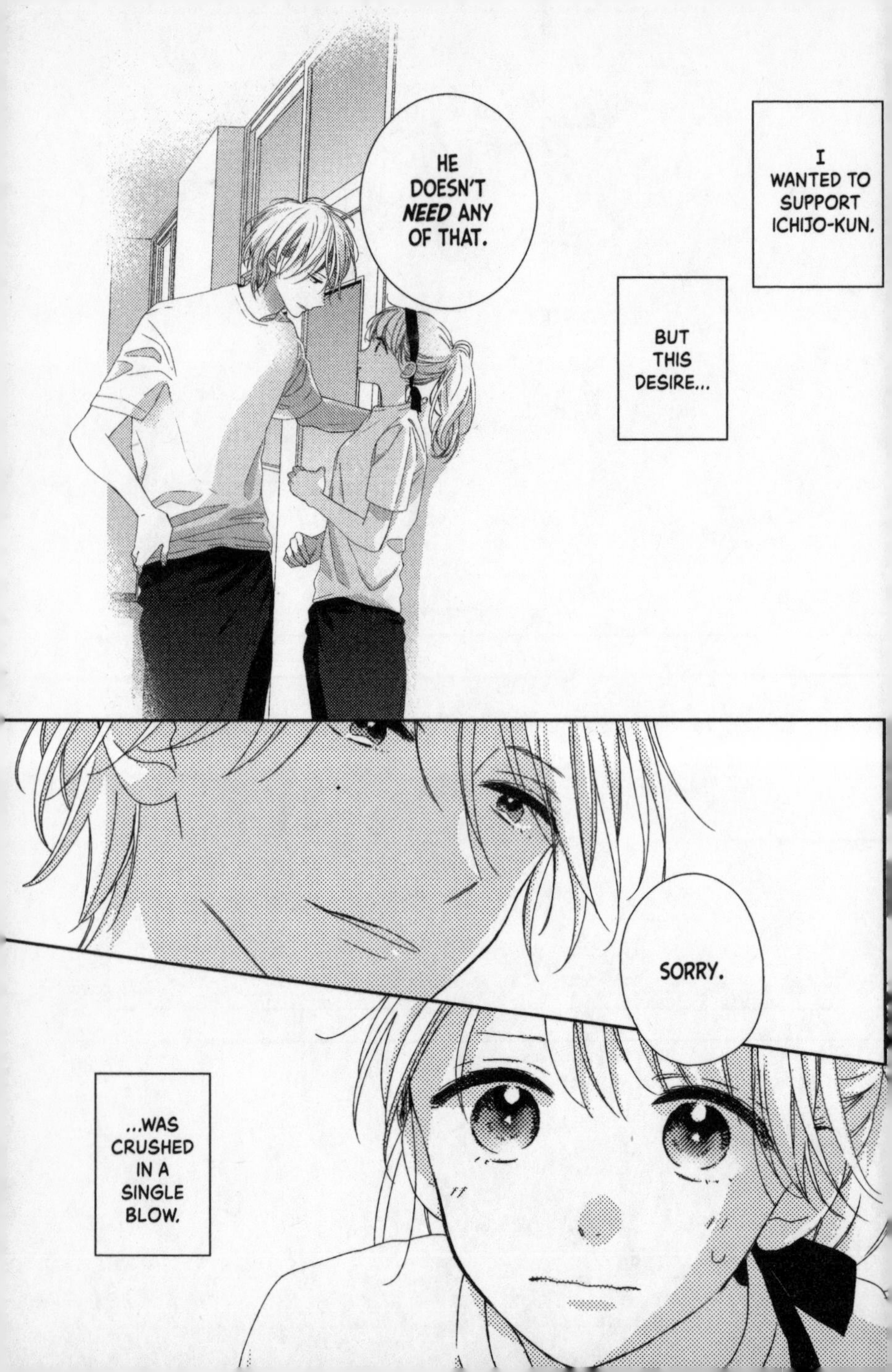
I WANTED TO SUPPORT ICHIJO-KUN.
BUT THIS DESIRE...
HE DOESN'T NEED ANY OF THAT.
SORRY.
...WAS CRUSHED IN A SINGLE BLOW.

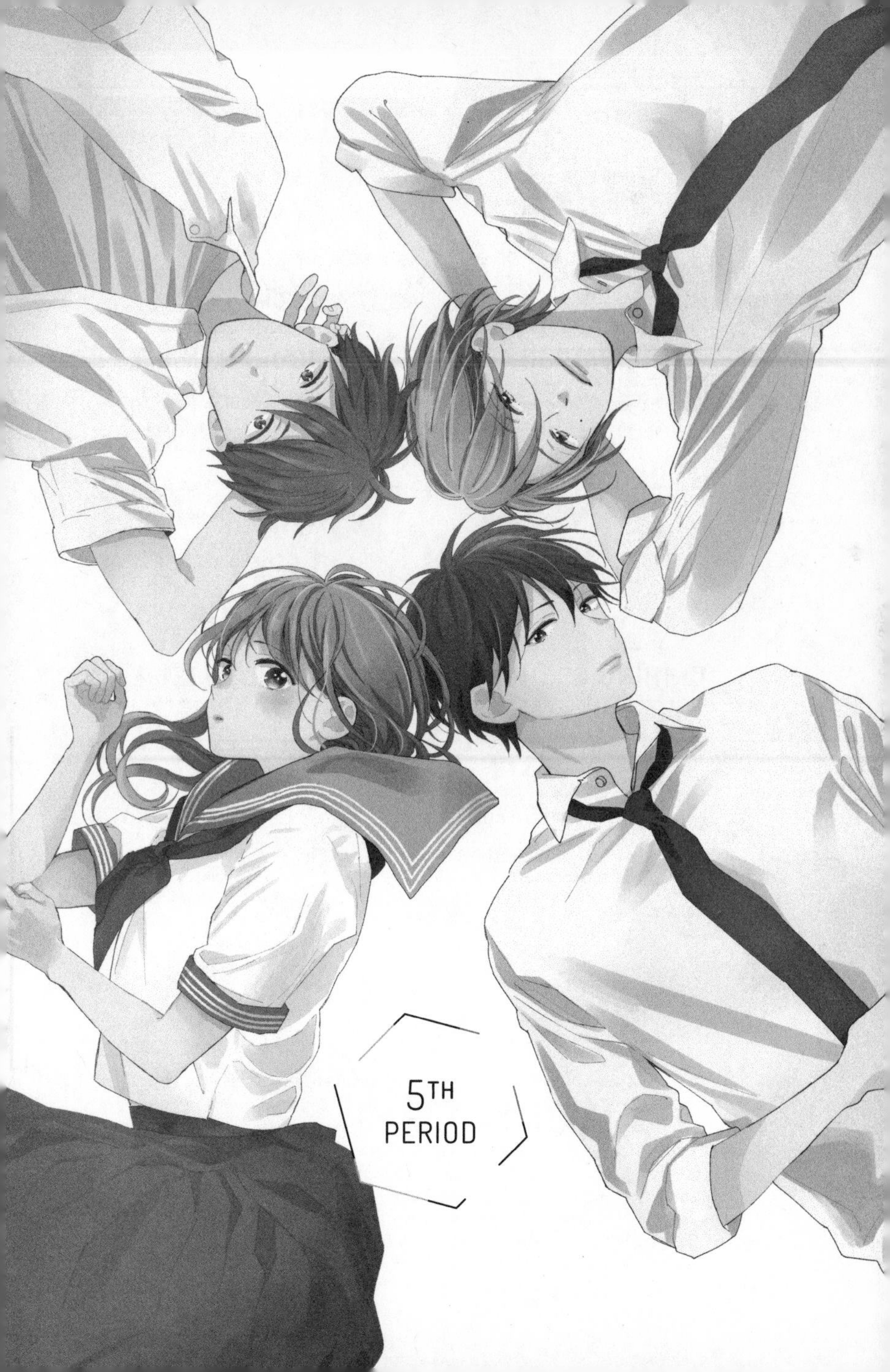
5TH
PERIOD

characters

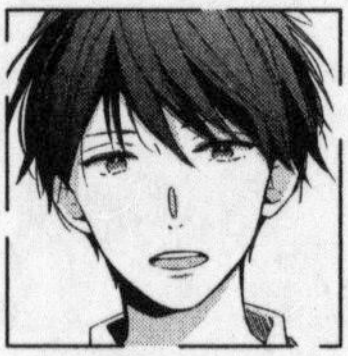

REI ICHIJO

Heir to the Ichijo Conglomerate.
Lives alone in a fancy apartment.

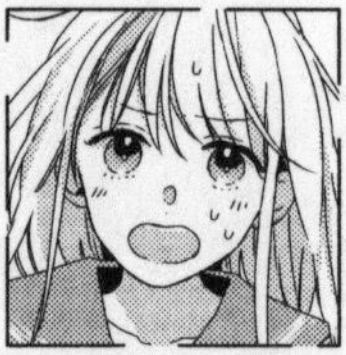

MIDORI NANAMI

Attends high school on a scholarship
to help with her family's finances.
Has Rei on her mind a lot.

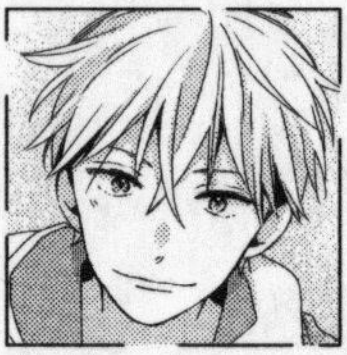

CHIHIRO GOSHIMA

Successor to the Goshima gang.
Is used to the assumptions people
make about him due to his family.

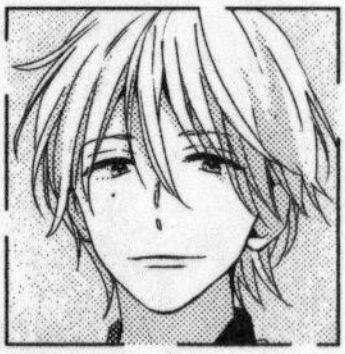

YUKINOJO IEIRI

Son of a doctor. A good friend
to Rei and Chihiro, and an
overall nice person, but...

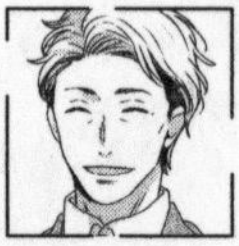

KEIICHI SUZUKI

Chairman of the school
Midori attends. Is concerned
about Rei and his friends.

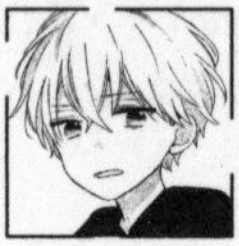

KON NANAMI

Midori's beloved little
brother who's in junior
high school. A great cook,
and super reliable to boot.

story

Midori's school chairman catches her working a part-time job, which is against the school rules!! Instead of revoking her scholarship, the chairman suggests that he could let it go if she brings three truants back to school. At first, the trio won't give Midori the time of day, but when she learns why they stopped coming to class, Midori sets off to prove their innocence. Before long, Chihiro's false charges are overturned and the boys all return to class. They still avoid group activities at school, but Midori's efforts pay off when they become the stars of Sports Day! Now, as she begins to grow closer to Rei, she can't stop thinking about him. Then, out of the blue, Yukinojo informs her that her presence may be unwelcome...

c o n t e n t s

Those Not-So-Sweet Boys

〈2〉

YOKO NOGIRI

Christopher Columbus

by Lola M. Schaefer

Consulting Editor: Gail Saunders-Smith, Ph.D.
Content Consultant: Beverly McMillan,
The Mariners' Museum
Newport News, Virginia

Pebble Books

an imprint of Capstone Press
Mankato, Minnesota

Pebble Books are published by Capstone Press
151 Good Counsel Drive, P.O. Box 669, Mankato, Minnesota 56002
http://www.capstone-press.com

Printed in the United States of America.

1 2 3 4 5 6 07 06 05 04 03 02

Library of Congress Cataloging-in-Publication Data
Schaefer, Lola M., 1950–
Christopher Columbus / by Lola M. Schaefer.
p. cm.—(First biographies)
Includes bibliographical references and index.
Summary: Simple text and photographs introduce the life of the Italian explorer who sailed to America in 1492.
ISBN 0-7368-1173-7
1. Columbus, Christopher—Juvenile literature. 2. Explorers—America—Biography—Juvenile literature. 3. Explorers—Spain—Biography—Juvenile literature. 4. America—Discovery and exploration—Spanish—Juvenile literature. [1. Columbus, Christopher. 2. Explorers. 3. America—Discovery and exploration—Spanish.] I. Title. II. Series: First biographies (Mankato, Minn.)
E111 .S32 2002
970.01'5'092—dc21 2001004832

Note to Parents and Teachers

The First Biographies series supports national history standards for units on people and culture. This book describes and illustrates the life of Christopher Columbus. The photographs support early readers in understanding the text. This book also introduces early readers to subject-specific vocabulary words, which are defined in the Words to Know section. Early readers may need assistance to read some words and to use the Table of Contents, Words to Know, Read More, Internet Sites, and Index/Word List sections of the book.

Table of Contents

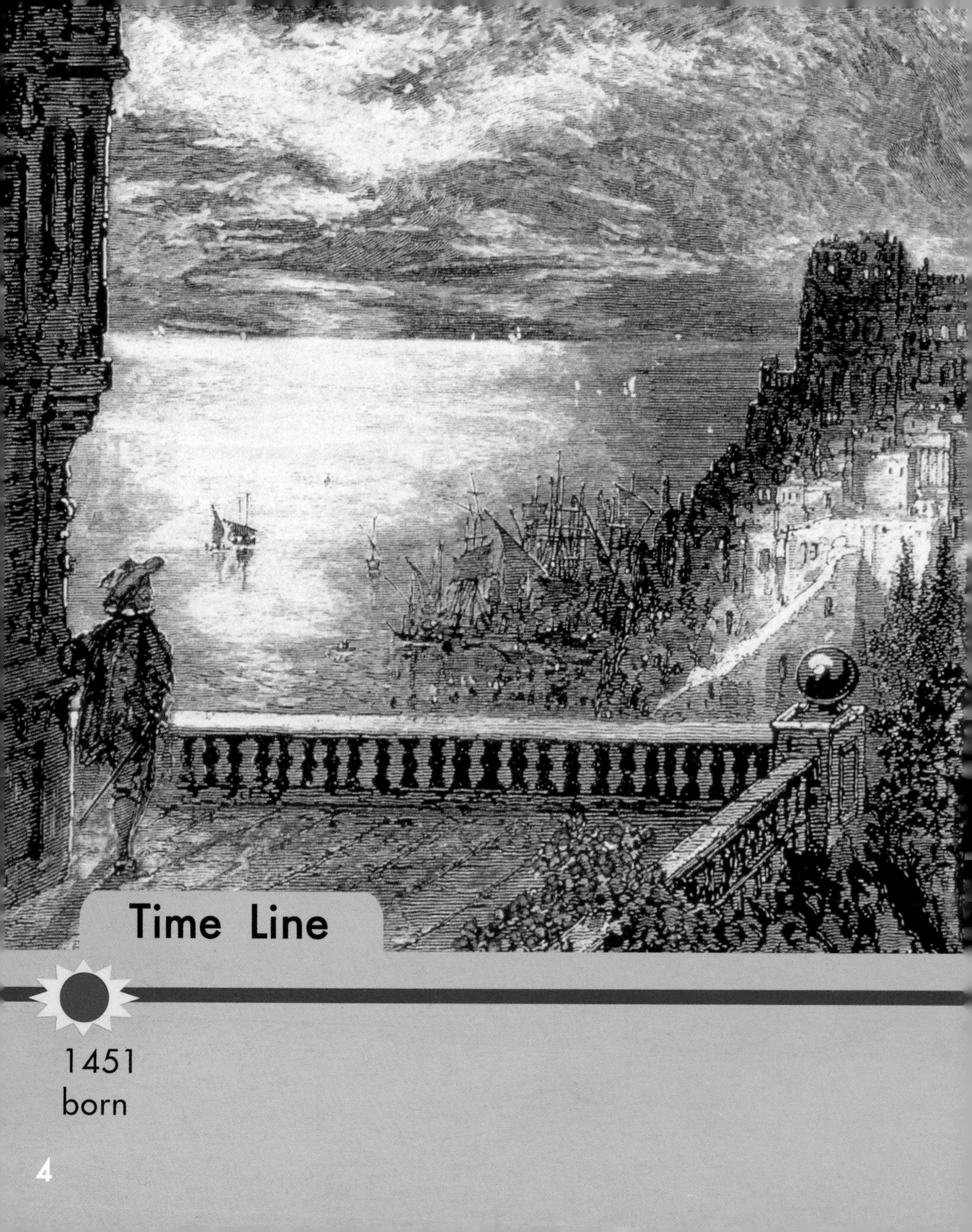

Time Line

1451
born

Christopher Columbus was born in Italy in 1451. His father was a weaver. Christopher made cloth in his father's shop. But he dreamed about sailing on the seas.

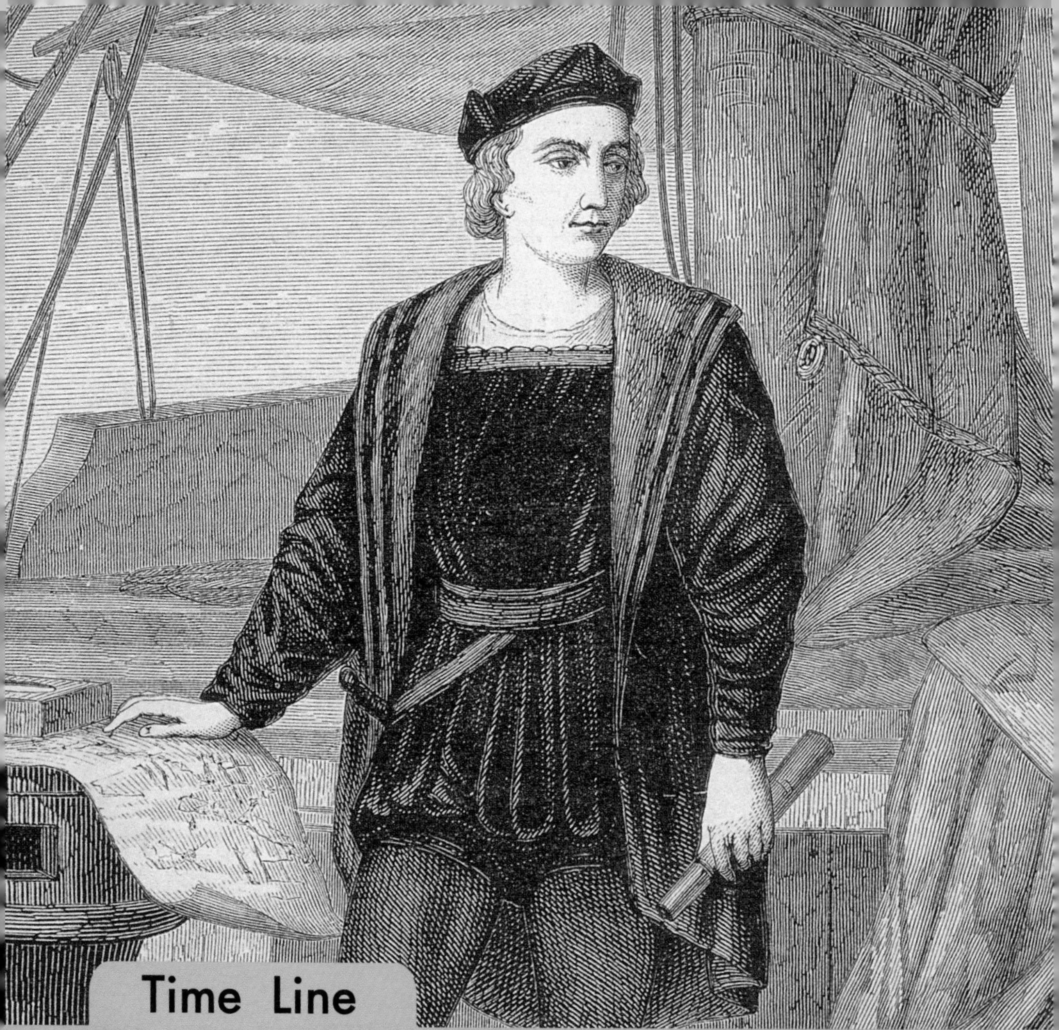

Time Line

1451
born

around 1480
makes voyages
to sell cloth

Christopher's father knew his son loved the sea. He asked Christopher to sell their cloth in faraway places. Christopher learned how to sail large ships.

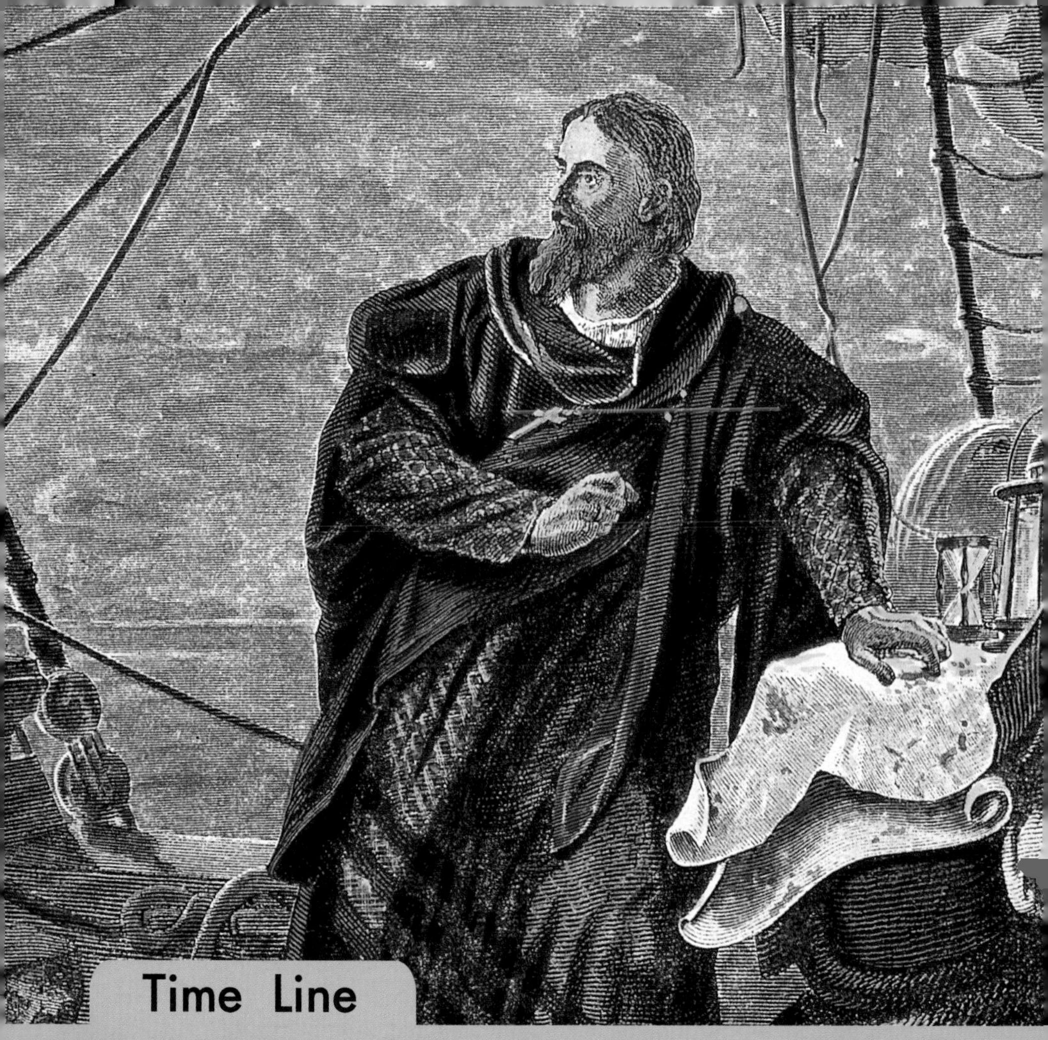

Time Line

1451
born

around 1480
makes voyages
to sell cloth

Christopher became a good sailor. He read charts and maps. He kept the ships on course by following the stars.

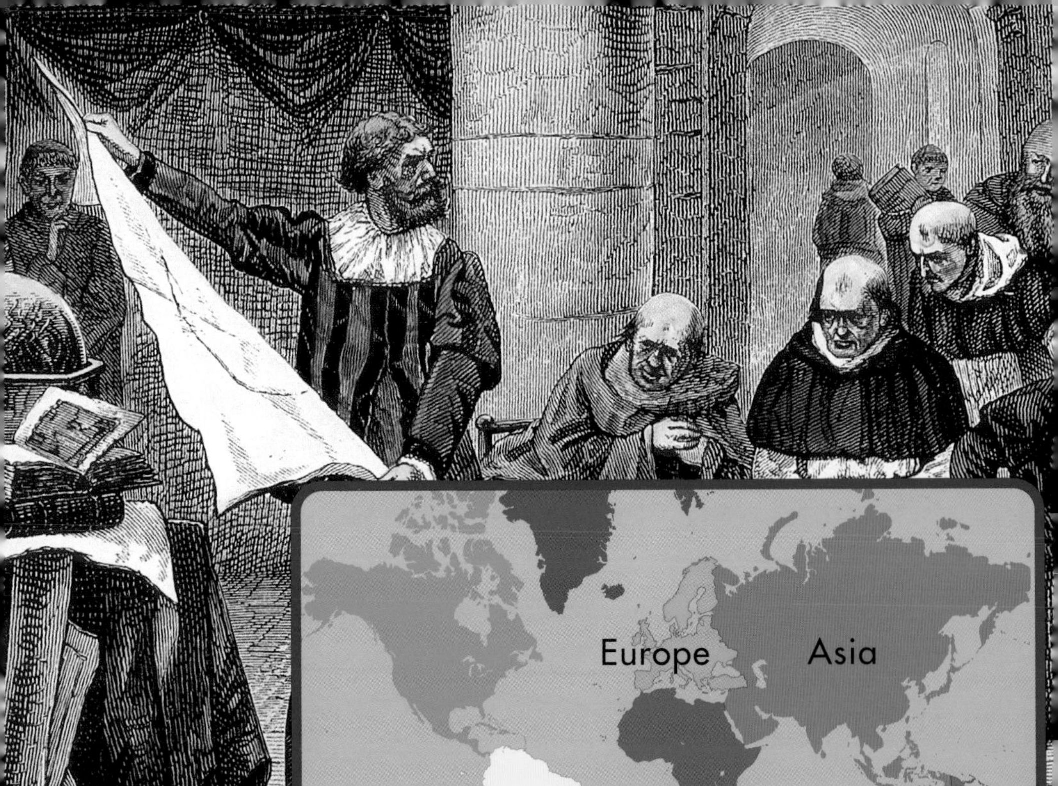

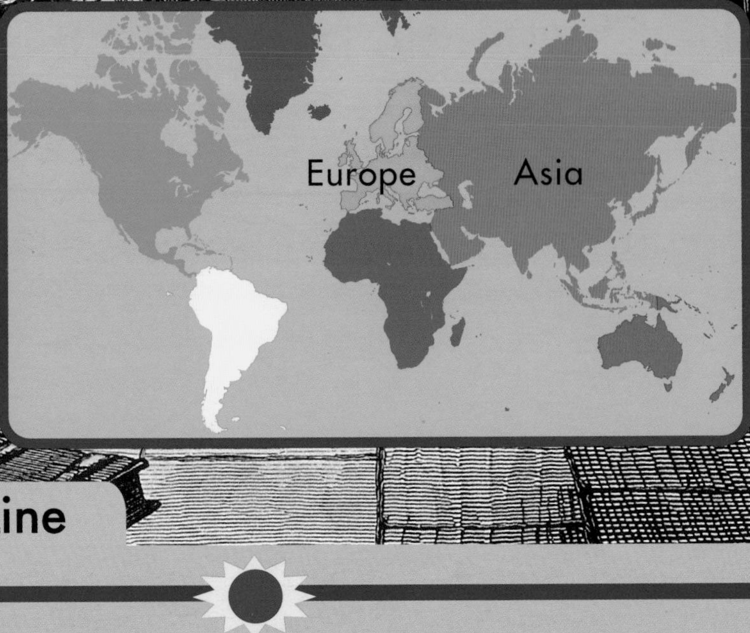
Europe
Asia

Time Line

1451
born

around 1480
makes voyages to sell cloth

1484
first explains his idea to sail west to reach Asia

Sailors had always traveled east from Europe. They sailed to the rich cities of Asia. But Christopher wanted to try sailing west. He talked about finding a new course to Asia.

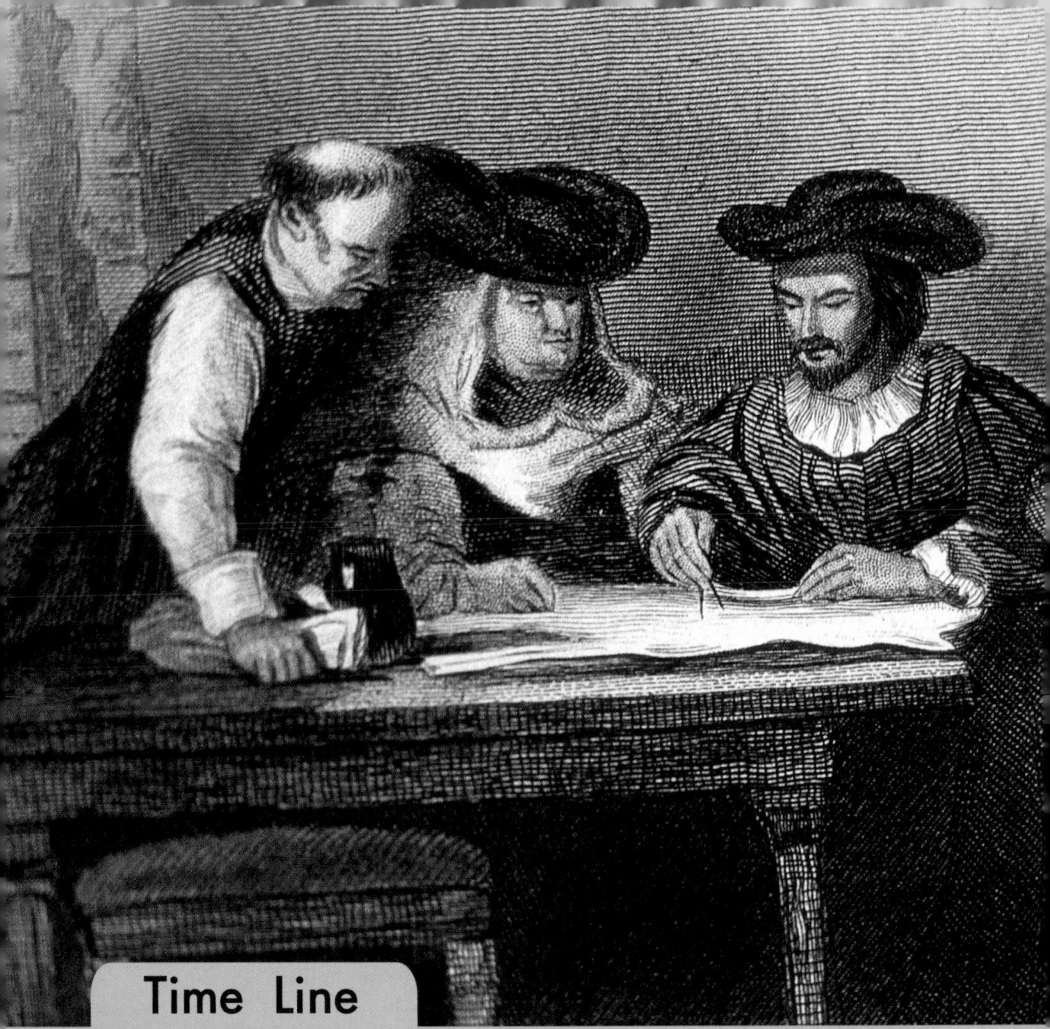

Time Line

1451 born	around 1480 makes voyages to sell cloth	1484 first explains his idea to sail west to reach Asia

Christopher also worked as a mapmaker for his brother. He met great sailors and thinkers. They knew the sea and faraway lands. They thought Christopher's idea could work.

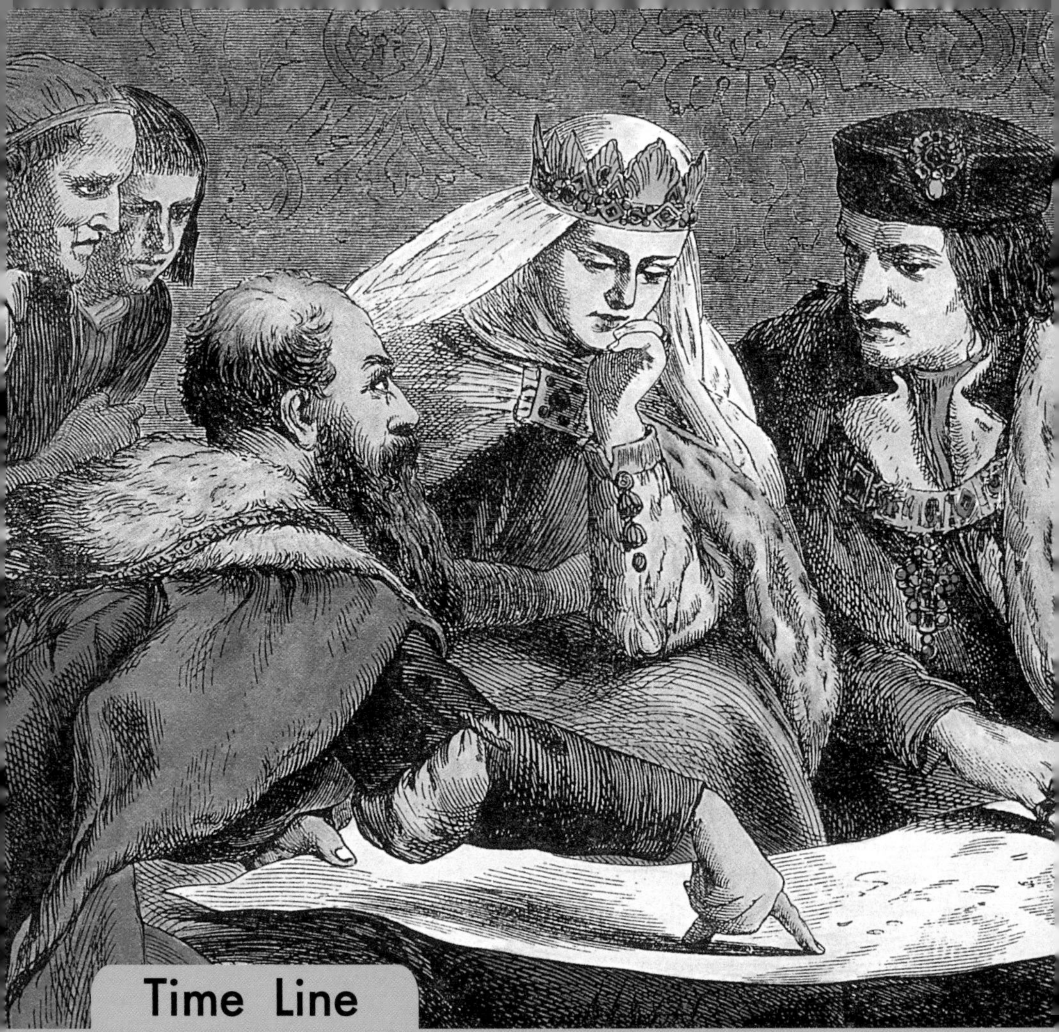

Time Line

1451
born

around 1480
makes voyages
to sell cloth

1484
first explains his
idea to sail west
to reach Asia

1486
asks queen
of Spain
for help

Christopher asked the kings and queens of many countries for money. Some said the trip would cost too much. Others said sailing west to Asia would not work.

◄ Christopher talking to the queen of Spain

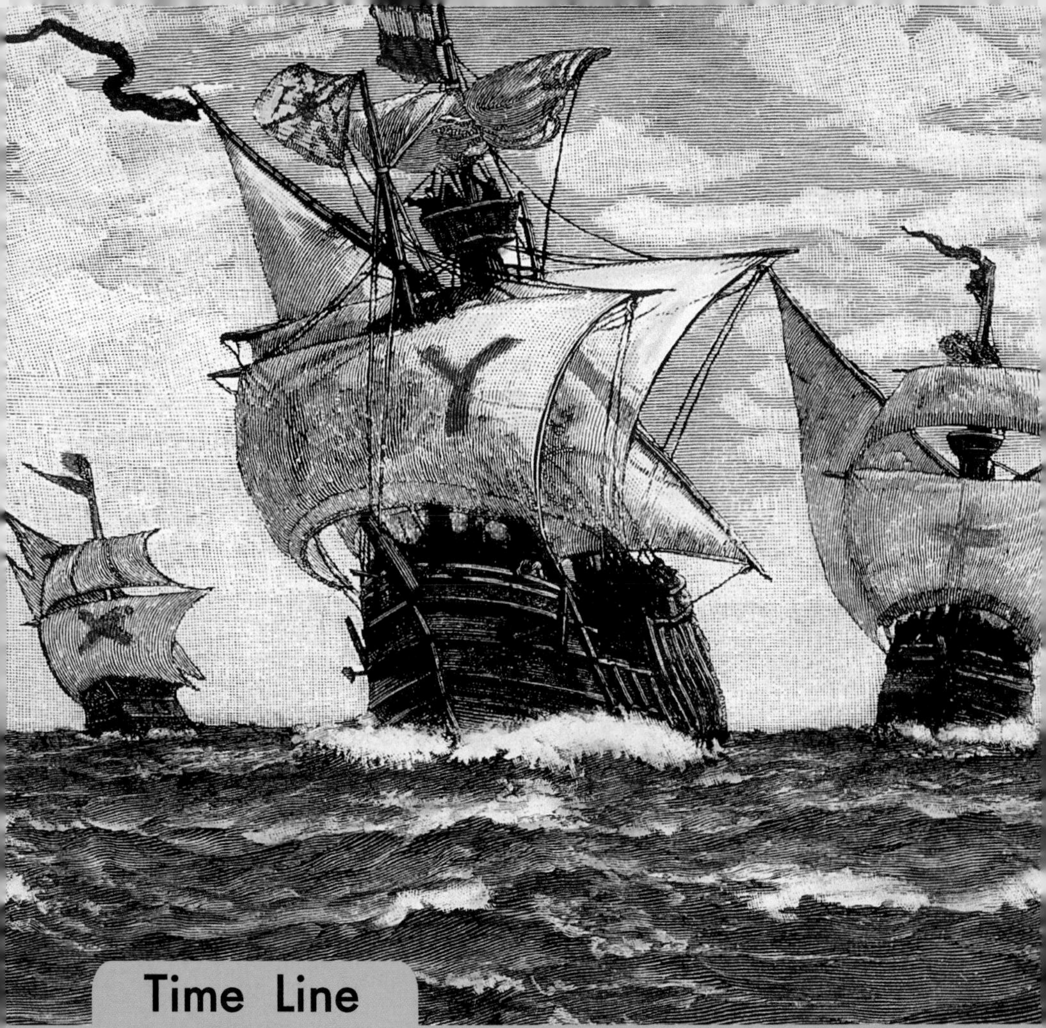

Time Line

1451 born	around 1480 makes voyages to sell cloth	1484 first explains his idea to sail west to reach Asia	1486 asks queen of Spain for help

Finally, the queen of Spain agreed to help Christopher. She gave him a crew, food, money, and three ships. The ships were the *Niña*, the *Pinta*, and the *Santa Maria*.

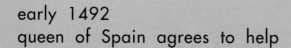

◀ the *Niña*, the *Pinta*, and the *Santa Maria*

early 1492
queen of Spain agrees to help

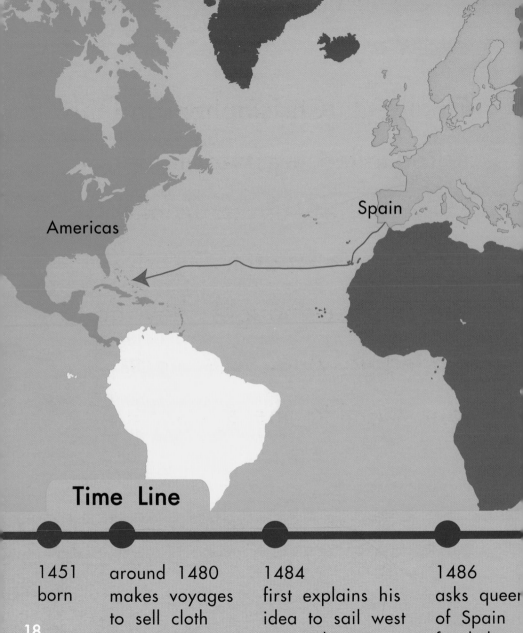

Spain

Americas

Time Line

1451 born	around 1480 makes voyages to sell cloth	1484 first explains his idea to sail west to reach Asia	1486 asks queer of Spain for help

In 1492, Christopher and his crew sailed west from Spain. They landed on an island in the Americas after 71 days. Christopher thought they had landed in Asia. He made four trips to these islands.

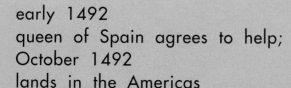

early 1492
queen of Spain agrees to help;
October 1492
lands in the Americas

19

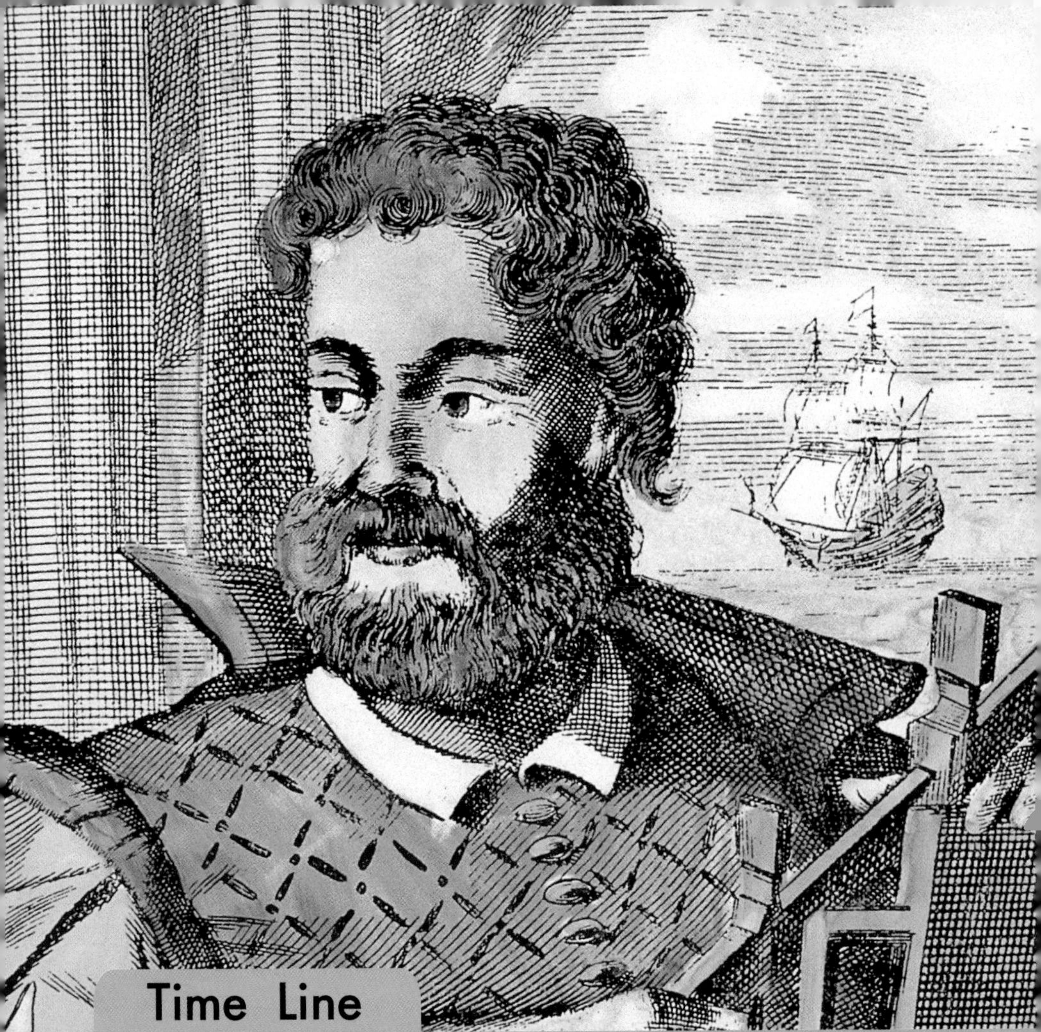

Time Line

1451 born	around 1480 makes voyages to sell cloth	1484 first explains his idea to sail west to reach Asia	1486 asks quee of Spain for help

Christopher never knew he had sailed to the Americas. He thought he had found a new course to Asia. He died in Spain in 1506. Christopher Columbus inspired many other sailors to explore the world.

early 1492
queen of Spain agrees to help;
October 1492
lands in the Americas

1506
dies

Words to Know

Asia—one of the seven continents of the world; countries in Asia include China, Japan, and India.

chart—a type of map; many charts are maps of stars or oceans.

course—a route or a plan for traveling

crew—a team of people who work together on a ship

Europe—one of the seven continents of the world; countries in Europe include England, France, and Spain.

explore—to travel to a new place to study it

inspire—to give someone the idea to do something

queen—a royal woman who rules her country

trip—a long journey; Christopher Columbus traveled more than 3,000 miles (4,800 kilometers) on his first trip to the Americas.

weaver—a person who makes cloth

Read More

Devillier, Christy. *Christopher Columbus.* First Biographies. Edina, Minn.: Abdo, 2001.

Kline, Trish. *Christopher Columbus.* Discover the Life of an Explorer. Vero Beach, Fla.: Rourke, 2001.

Larkin, Tanya. *Christopher Columbus.* Famous Explorers. New York: PowerKids Press, 2001.

Internet Sites

Christopher Columbus: Explorer
http://www.enchantedlearning.com/explorers/page/c/columbus.shtml

Columbus Day: A History
http://wilstar.com/holidays/columbus.htm

The Explorations of Christopher Columbus
http://www.mariner.org/age/columbus.html

The Round Earth and Christopher Columbus
http://www-istp.gsfc.nasa.gov/stargaze/Scolumb.htm

Index/Word List

Americas, 19, 21
Asia, 11, 15, 19, 21
brother, 13
charts, 9
cloth, 5, 7
course, 9, 11, 21
crew, 17, 19
east, 11
Europe, 11
explore, 21
idea, 13

inspired, 21
island, 19
Italy, 5
kings, 15
mapmaker, 13
maps, 9
money, 15, 17
Niña, 17
Pinta, 17
queen, 15, 17
sail, 5, 7, 11, 15, 19, 21
sailor, 9, 11, 13, 21

Santa Maria, 17
sea, 5, 7, 13
ships, 7, 9, 17
shop, 5
Spain, 15, 17, 19, 21
stars, 9
thinkers, 13
trip, 15, 19
west, 11, 15, 19
work, 13, 15
world, 21

Word Count: 260
Early-Intervention Level: 24

Editorial Credits
Martha E. H. Rustad, editor; Heather Kindseth, cover designer and illustrator; Linda Clavel, illustrator; Kimberly Danger and Mary Englar, photo researchers

Photo Credits
North Wind Pictures, 1, 4, 10, 16, 20
Photri-Microstock, cover, 12
Stock Montage, 6, 8, 14